Barbara Kingsolver

Barbara Kingsolver

A Literary Companion

MARY ELLEN SNODGRASS

McFarland Literary Companions, 2

McFarland & Company, Inc., Publishers
Jefferson, North Carolina, and London

LIBRARY OF CONGRESS CATALOGUING-IN-PUBLICATION DATA

Snodgrass, Mary Ellen.
Barbara Kingsolver : a literary companion / Mary Ellen Snodgrass.
p.   cm. — (McFarland literary companions ; 2)
Includes bibliographical references and index.

ISBN 0-7864-1951-2 (softcover : 50# alkaline paper) ∞

1. Kingsolver, Barbara — Criticism and interpretation.
2. Women and literature — United States — History — 20th century.
3. Human rights in literature.   4. Ecology in literature.
I. Title.   II. McFarland literary companion series ; 2.
PS3561.I496Z88   2004   813'.54 — dc22   2004013457

British Library cataloguing data are available

Front cover: Photograph of Barbara Kingsolver by Steven L. Hopp;
background ©2004 PhotoSpin

Manufactured in the United States of America

McFarland & Company, Inc., Publishers
Box 611, Jefferson, North Carolina 28640
www.mcfarlandpub.com

To Madeline

Acknowledgments

I owe thanks to HarperCollins for the photo of Barbara Kingsolver. Also, I acknowledge the advice and research assistance of the following people and institutions:

Avis Gachet, book buyer
Wonderland Books
5008 Hickory Boulevard
Hickory, North Carolina 28601

Wanda Rozzelle, reference librarian
Catawba County Library
Newton, North Carolina

Mark Schumacher, reference librarian
Jackson Library, University of North
    Carolina at Greensboro
Greensboro, North Carolina

Contents

To live is to be marked. To live is to change,
to acquire the words of a story,
and that is the only celebration we mortals really know.

The Poisonwood Bible,
"Exodus," p. 385

Preface

For those who seek a greater knowledge or understanding of Barbara King-solver's varied literary contributions, *Barbara Kingsolver: A Literary Companion* offers an introduction and overview. It provides the reader, ecologist, feminist, student, researcher, teacher, reviewer, and librarian with analysis of characters, events, allusions, literary motifs, and themes from the works of one of America's most prized active writers. The text opens with an annotated chronology of Kingsolver's life, activism, works, and awards, followed by a family tree. The 122 A-to-Z entries combine insights from critics along with generous citations from primary and secondary sources. Each entry concludes with selected bibliography on such subjects as Africa, historical milieu, journey motif, opportunity, pueblos, rescue, survival, television, and wisdom. Charts elucidate the genealogies of the Fourkiller, Greer, Noline, Price, Walker, Widener, and Wolfe families and account for connections between family lines, as with the link by adoption between Taylor Greer and the Stillwaters begun in *The Bean Trees* and concluded in *Pigs in Heaven*, Spanish settlers who prefigured the Nolina family in *Animal Dreams*, a genealogy from *The Poisonwood Bible* that begins with a racist missionary and concludes with Leah Price and Anatole Ngemba's four sons, and the link by marriage of the Wideners and Walkers of Egg Fork in *Prodigal Summer*. Generous cross references point to divergent strands of thought and guide the reader into peripheral territory, e.g., from Congolese Premier Patrice Lumumba to the assassination plot okayed by U.S. President Dwight D. Eisenhower, Cosima "Codi" Noline to discontent, Orleanna Price to self-esteem, Alice Greer to a Cherokee stomp dance, love to motherhood, pollution to nature, and the rituals of All Souls' Day to Latina celebrant Viola Domingos.

Back matter is designed to aid the student, reviewer, and researcher. It orients the beginner with a time line of events in *The Poisonwood Bible*, a political allegory anchored to a revolution that turned the Belgian Congo of 1959 briefly into a republic and then into the dictatorship of Mobutu Sese Seko, who remained in power until his death in 1997. A second appendix provides forty-six topics for group or individual projects, composition, analysis, background material, enactment, and theme development, such as cross-cultural mythology, motifs of matriarchy and marital discord,

1

traits of works winning the Bellwether Prize, character attitudes toward materialism and spirituality, the author's choice of narrative modes, the image of the hovering spirit, realistic elements, and the use of disease as character motivation. Back matter concludes with an exhaustive listing of primary sources and general bibliography, many of which derive from journal and periodical articles and reviews of Kingsolver's documentary, essays, novels, stories, and poems in the newspapers of major cities in the United States, Great Britain, Canada, and Australia. Secondary sources, particularly those by *National Catholic Reporter, Christianity Today, The Mennonite,* and other religious journals, are useful for study of works that have yet to be analyzed thoroughly in collegiate journals. A comprehensive index directs users of the literary companion to major and minor characters, peoples, belief systems, movements, events, place names, landmarks, published works, sources, authors, and issues, e.g., Lou Ann Ruiz, Rachel Carson Rawley, Yaqui, animism, Not in Our Name movement, George Foreman–Muhammad Ali fight, Corregidor, Kinishba, *Last Stand: America's Virgin Lands,* Apocrypha, Doris Lessing, and child abuse.

Introduction

At the peak of her artistry, Barbara Kingsolver is a master writer blessed with moral vision and an innate certainty of place and character. For fiction, documentary, verse, and essay, she undergirds entertaining images and stories with profound themes of ecological responsibility and challenge to the suppression of human rights. As a result of her courageous stands, her works enlarge reader compassion for the earth as well as for the poor and beleaguered.

Kingsolver's first publication, *The Bean Trees*, garnered a huge following for its earnest themes and engagingly paced action. Plucky, down-home-funny Kentuckian Taylor Greer heads a list of admirable characters reflecting just enough insecurity and forgivable faults to balance their virtues. Readers next embraced Codi Noline, protagonist of *Animal Dreams*, for facing no-win family and personal challenges and for turning adversity into a touchstone of self-knowledge. The return of Taylor Greer in *Pigs in Heaven* reprised the author's examination of dedicated motherhood against a backdrop of native American unity and not-so-genteel poverty. After the publication of *The Poisonwood Bible*, Kingsolver rose to a position of authority in feminist writings and ecofiction for her command of political allegory set during the Congo's turbulent emergence from colonialism. She caught the literary world off guard with a fifth novel, *Prodigal Summer*, which restages familiar themes of procreation, parenting, and reverence for nature in a threefold story line filled with exuberant matings and multiple expressions of love.

A key component of Kingsolver's writings is candor. With details culled from a journalistic assignment to cover Arizona's mining strikes, she compiled *Holding the Line: Women in the Great Arizona Mine Strike of 1983*, a documentary of gritty, blue-collar protests and nose-to-nose confrontations with management, media, and police. The text focuses on women who demand workers' rights for their husbands as well as equality for the female laborers who chose underground mining as a career. The same appreciation of pragmatism and persistence enlivens Kingsolver's fictional characters:

- Mattie the tire dealer, a soft-hearted agent for a late twentieth-century under-ground railroad that spirits illegal Central American aliens out of Tucson's hot zones as they begin new lives at less obvious waystations

- Great Mam, a Cherokee matriarch who maintains faith in a dying creed by passing on to her children and grandchildren the value of folkways and respect for the land

- Hallie Noline, an agronomist who risks death on mined roads while taking field knowledge to Nicaraguan cotton farmers and who pays with her life for activating a fierce, unflinching altruism

- Alice Greer, Taylor's salt-of-the-earth mother, a retired domestic worker who supplies her daughter with love and support during the adoption of Tur-tle Greer, Alice's only grandchild

- Leah Price Ngemba, an idealist who learns from her father's failed Baptist mission to Africa and who establishes her own humanistic outreach as teacher, wife, and mother of four Anglo-Congolese sons

- Lusa Maluf Landowski, a "religious mongrel" who turns the feast demands of multiple holy days into a source of income from the sale of prize meat goats.

To even out female-dominated novels and stories, Kingsolver offers male-female match-ups that strike sparks of insight, as with Taylor Greer's unrequited longing for Estevan, a married Mayan refugee; Codi Noline's reigniting of a failed teen fling with Loyd Peregrina while she privately assuages grief for their stillborn child; house-wife Orleanna Price's atonement for remaining loyal to a religious fanatic husband while leaving their four daughters in peril; and forest ranger Deanna Wolfe's willful passion for Eddie Bondo, a bounty hunter who threatens re-establishment of the coyote in the southern Appalachias.

To questions about her published works and opinions, the author is noted for generosity toward interviewers and the media. A penchant for openness leaves her vulnerable to criticism for liberal views on a litany of flash points—crime, bureau-cracy, patriarchy, female autonomy, pacifism, chemical adulteration of food, and the importance of encounters with the world's wilderness as lessons in the sanctity of life. Kingsolver lives by the tenets of her public-spirited fictional characters, whom she sculpts with a keen eye for individuality, e.g. Nannie Land Rawley, a seventy-something orchardist who shocks a fuddy-duddy male neighbor by wearing shorts, and Mama Mwanza, a handicapped Congolese housewife who thrives at delegating authority and overcoming obstacles with a cheery can-do spirit.

A thorough knowledge of Barbara Kingsolver and her deft essays, poems, and fiction reveals the heart of a crusader and the intellect of an alert citizen who scans current affairs for evidence of ethical malfeasance. With her daughter Camille, she withdrew from American society in protest of the Gulf War to live in the Canary Islands. From her homes in the Sonora Desert and in the Appalachians, she continues to rail at the right-wing George W. Bush administration for attacking Iraq, challenging free speech, threatening women's rights, and endangering national forests with reckless dismantling of land protection initiatives. Her willingness to castigate officials for injustice and assaults on humanity provokes the less vocal to follow her example of honor, courage, and right thinking.

Chronology of
Kingsolver's Life and Works

April 8, 1955   A native of Annapolis, Maryland, author Barbara Kingsolver was born April 8, 1955, to family physician Dr. Wendell R. Kingsolver, a navy physician, and Virginia Lee Henry "Ginny" Kingsolver, an avid birdwatcher and true mountaineer in thought and accent. In *I've Always Meant to Tell You: Letters to Our Mothers: An Anthology of Contemporary Women Writers* (1997), Barbara reflects on her mother's unorthodox demand for natural childbirth and insistence on breast-feeding: "You risked the contempt of your peers, went right ahead, and did what you knew was best for your babies" (p. 260). The image of a stubborn, forward-thinking mother is prophetic of the woman that Barbara became.

A shy, intuitive child, Barbara was second after older brother Rob, who specialized in insect pollinators of flowering plants and became department chairman of biology at Kentucky Wesleyan College, and preceded sister Ann, born in 1960, who became an anthropology professor at the University of California, Santa Cruz. Barbara honored both in the introduction to *Prodigal Summer* (2000) by remembering her brother as "mentor and co-conspirator in snake catching and paw-paw hunting" and Ann, who gave wings to Barbara's career (p. xi). The three Kingsolvers grew up in a world of vast disparities between the few rich and the many indigent, between the educated and ignorant, and between the divided races. Because of their parents' altruism and rejection of materialism, Barbara identified with the outsiders and their style of expression. She described her tendencies to side with the underdog in "The Middle Daughter," a poem collected in *Another America: Otra America* (1992), in which she characterizes herself as a history-maker.

Introspective and keenly observant, Kingsolver was a product of the small town of Carlisle in Nicholas County, "a wrinkle on the map that lies between farms and wildness" (*Prodigal Summer*, p. x). The area formed a pocket of eastern Kentucky poverty that relied on tobacco for agricultural wealth. Even before she could write, she sat in the bathtub and entertained her mother with storytelling until the water got cold. From an early awareness of social injustice, she later spoke of life "between the wealth of Lexington and the poverty of Appalachia" and admired Kentuckians for their role in radical labor strikes (Epstein). Memories of small farm yields and cash shortfalls honed her liberal, humanistic conscience, the moral compass of her writing.

Barbara felt fortunate to be the daughter of compassionate medical professionals. Her father set the example of right thinking and actions "regardless of whether or not that's financially or otherwise regarded" (Farrell, p. 29). In an interview for *People* magazine, she recalled the nobility of Wendell Kingsolver, the area's only doctor for thirty-six years. She added wryly, "It's a place where doctors don't play golf and don't get rich" (Neill, p. 110). He honored his patients' pride by accepting vegetables in lieu of payment for medical care, an exchange that lacked financial sense, but respected the dignity of the poor.

From an early age, Barbara knew that her parents foresaw her making a difference in the world. Of their ambitions, she explained, "My parents just expected me to do things like read books—big, good books—and one day go to college. Nobody else I knew had that sort of expectation" (Epstein). At home, the Kingsolvers denied their children television, but allotted instead family read-aloud time that involved young and old in savoring the printed word.

A more prominent teacher in the young Kingsolvers' growing up years was the outdoors. The "equals of Davy Crockett and Pocahontas" in combing the woods, Barbara and her siblings made themselves scarce (*Last Stand*, p. 13). They slipped out to cow pastures, hills and groves of hickory and maple trees, and tobacco fields with their cane fishing poles and bug-collecting jars "as if we intended to make ourselves useful, and [headed] out to spend a Saturday doing nothing of the kind" (*High Tide*, p. 171). The idle days on Horse Lick Creek formed the basis of Barbara's dedication to ecology.

1958 In a memory of childhood, Barbara recalls staying with her grandmother while her parents went to the beach. Barbara missed her mother, the woman who taught her to name the Dianas, monarchs, and swallowtails that court the flowers around their home. On her mother's return, the outburst of shock and rage was typical of three-year-olds: "You're *happy*. Happy without me" (*I've Always*, p. 251). To win back her mother's attention, Barbara climbed the sweet-pea trellis and picked all the blossoms to brighten "our little white clapboard house on East Main" (*Ibid.*, p. 252).

1962 Coming of age during the Cold War left its impact on Kingsolver. She recalled tense days of the Cuban Missile Crisis in *High Tide in Tucson* (1995): "When I was a child in grade school we had 'duck and cover' drills, fully trusting that leaping into a ditch and throwing an Orlon sweater over our heads would save us from nuclear fallout" (p. 213). Parents received homeowners' instructions from the Extension Service on stockpiling canned goods to feed families in the event of a catastrophic war. With the poem "Waiting for the Invasion," anthologized in *Another America*, Kingsolver reflected on "[listening] at night for the Russians," the "death angels" searching out her town, where someone painted the water towers black to conceal them from potential massacre (p. 8). In "The Monster's Belly," she pictures herself as so overwhelmed by Cold War politics that she is unable to absorb the Christian Marxism of Nicaraguan poet Ernesto Cardenal.

1963   Kingsolver, then a second-grader, spent two years in a small village in western Africa during her parents' public health posting in the central Congo after the nation gained independence from Belgium. In the introduction to *The Poisonwood Bible* (1998), she thanked her parents by name for introducing her to Africa and for allowing her to explore "the great, shifting terrain between righteousness and what's right" (p. x). In *High Tide in Tucson*, she commented, "I couldn't begin to imagine the life that was rolling out ahead of me. But I did understand it would pass over me with the force of a river, and that I needed to pin the water to its banks and hold it still, somehow, to give myself time to know it" (p. 119).

While living in a place lacking electricity, running water, and medical services, Kingsolver met missionary families and hobnobbed with African kids who tugged at her long hair, which they doubted was real. Because she was the minority, she looked at people with new understanding: "I came home with an acutely heightened sense of race, of ethnicity" (Kanner). She read Louisa May Alcott, Christina Rossetti, Laura Ingalls Wilder, and children's verse, which became the impetus to her own juvenilia. Of the value of reading to the development of creativity, she explained, "You begin with the words on the page, put there by someone else, but you fill in the scene with pictures that are your own. You do it unconsciously, as you're reading, and the whole thing becomes very familiar and real to you" ("An Address").

Reading triggered plot formation in Kingsolver at an early age. As a result of involvement with the printed word, she personalized readings and extended the action to include her own experience. Along with storytelling, she developed verse and essays. After receiving a red diary with matching pencil and gold lock "easily picked with a bobby pin, it turns out," from age eight, she wrote daily, but didn't consider writing a suitable career goal ("Barbara Kingsolver: Coming").

1966   On return to Kentucky from Africa, Kingsolver flourished within scent of aged burley and later claimed that "the woods were my school and church" (Parsell). In *Last Stand: America's Virgin Lands* (2002), she exults in the fact that her "best memories all contain birdsong and trees" and groves "rich in the pecky music of birds seeking forage" (pp. 11, 12). When classes of farm kids let out in early fall and late spring, she drove the pickup as her family set, cut, stripped, and hung tobacco. The next year, she was strong enough to toss a hay bale onto a truckbed. Of her love of nature, she remarked, "My interest and passion in life science comes from having grown up among farmers, and also from parents who were deeply interested in natural history. They always told me the names of wildflowers and birds. I grew up in the milieu of creating education, entertainment, and pets out of snakes and turtles and every kind of thing we could find" ("A Conversation").

1967   Dr. Wendell Kingsolver practiced medicine at a convent hospital in St. Lucia, a Windward Island of the Caribbean, where he made a temporary home for his family. Barbara reprised the island setting in "Jump-up Day," a piece collected in *Homeland*

and Other Stories (1989). The plot, based on culture clash, depicts Jericha, a good little pupil at a convent school, learning obeah from an island practitioner of voodoo, a West African religion. Daring to violate Catholic teachings, she indulges in animistic ritual blended with Latin from communion liturgy and mention of Anansi, the trickster spider dating to slaves who once worked the cane fields and sugar mills of island plantations.

The author's syncretism of a pagan and a Catholic faith suggests the importance of Jericha's name, a female version of Jericho, the Old Testament city that Joshua defeated by bringing down its walls with the synchronized tramp of his troopers' feet. Similarly, Jericha is a pivotal figure functioning in two spiritual traditions, one carefully walled off from another. The triumph of the obeah man's influence on a pious young Catholic is her release of Maximilian, the sacrificial goat intended for slaughter for the Easter entree. The act is ironic in its violation of Christian expectations of savagery in voodoo worship.

1968 In *I've Always Meant to Tell You*, Kingsolver recalls age thirteen, when she was "a tempest of skinned knees and menarche" (p. 253). She reflected on her parents' Spartan values: "[They] didn't believe in new clothes. They didn't value spending lots of money on superficial things, which of course really irritated me when I was fourteen" (Epstein). The lack of a fashionable wardrobe placed her in the local pecking order among country kids, a caste below the children of store owners, mine bosses, and county bureaucrats. The pain of exclusion recurs in *The Bean Trees* (1988), in which Taylor Greer describes the poor children of her school as the "nutters," the ones who earned extra money by selling shelled walnuts, which stained their hands brown (p. 134).

In this soul-searching adolescent era, Kingsolver developed a political conscience by questioning the Vietnam War. In the essay "And Our Flag Was Still There," published in the *San Francisco Chronicle* September 25, 2001, she criticizes "things my government has done to the world that made me direly ashamed.... When I look at the flag, I see it illuminated by the rocket's red glare," an indelible link between patriotism and militarism. The depth of her pacifism remains unchanged in more recent works, particularly the kidnap and execution of agricultural volunteer Hallie Noline in *Animal Dreams* (1990), a novel that castigates the Reagan administration for bankrolling thugs and murderers during a political upheaval in Nicaragua.

Fall, 1969 Kingsolver entered the ninth grade at Nicholas County High School, where a gender-specific allotment required boys to take shop and girls to study home economics. For intellectual stimulus, the curriculum offered only one math and one science course, both generic. In a rural homeplace in a sea of alfalfa, she had no dates and substituted reading and writing for boyfriends. She once quipped, "I wanted to read Anna Karenina and everybody else wanted to do stuff in the back of cars" (Lyall). Over a decade later, she observed: "I had an excellent education in wallflowerhood. You learn more about people that way, because you are always watching" (Rosenfeld, p. D1).

1970 Kingsolver attended a performance of William Shakespeare's *Measure for*

Measure, her first venture to a play. She tried to discuss the experience with her parents, but shied away from commenting on the comedy's implied sexuality, which she and brother Rob agreed to keep secret. In *Small Wonder,* she divulged, "I felt sick inside, as if by watching this wonderful work, and loving it so much I'd betrayed my parents' trust in me and my own goodness" (p. 148).

As the author describes in *I've Always Meant to Tell You,* her defiance of stereotypical womanhood boiled up in the privacy of her diary: "Why oh why do you want to ruin my life? Why can't you believe I know how to make my own decisions? Why do you treat me like a child?" (p. 253). In misery with the in-betweens of age fifteen, she mourned being tall and gawky, shy, and ignored by her peers.

1971 The essay "How Mr. Dewey Decimal Saved My Life" (1995) characterizes Kingsolver's rescue from a humdrum future. In her junior year, she credits the school librarian, Miss Truman Richey, with "[snatching] me from the jaws of ruin" by selecting Kingsolver to catalogue the kind of books that advanced her horizons—Edgar Allan Poe, Margaret Mitchell, and William Saroyan (*High Tide,* p. 46). Like novelist Gary Paulsen and other childhood readers-turned-writers, Kingsolver was grateful for reprieve from dull, unchallenging school days. Her essay exults, "I'm of a fearsome mind to throw my arms around every living librarian who crosses my path, on behalf of the soul they never knew they saved" (*Ibid.*).

Kingsolver readily attests to her joy in fiction. In "Widows at the Wheel," a 1989 book review for the *Los Angeles Times,* she admits, "Gabriel García Márquez once made me believe that a beautiful child could rise into the sky on a freshly laundered sheet" (p. 1). Intrigued by Doris Lessing's themes, Kingsolver began to study the class strata and racial disparities in eastern Kentucky and incubated a point of view that informs much of her writing. She remarked in an interview on a compassionate class consciousness that directed her works: "I was stunned to discover the world knows almost nothing about 'hillbillies,' and respects them even less. An undercurrent of defensiveness about this has guided my writing and my life, I think, as I've tried to seek out the voices of marginalized people" ("Barbara Kingsolver: Coming"). Those voices became the child care providers, domestics, railroad crews, miners, minimum-wage workers in salsa factories and the night shift at the 7-Eleven, farmers, and grocery store and fast-food counter clerks that form the backbone of her fictional and nonfictional milieus.

1972 In a community devoid of dial telephone service, bookstores, and steady readers, Kingsolver graduated from a high school that, not surprisingly, channeled few teens to higher levels of learning. Girls aimed to marry young and immediately produce babies, a fate the author spares Taylor Greer, her protagonist in *The Bean Trees.* Of the Kentucky youth who nurtured higher aims, Kingsolver asserted, "A lot of us just swore that as soon as we could, we were going to kick the dust of this place from our heels and go away as far as we possibly could" (Barnette). Time and distance softened her urge to separate from the customs of her rural Kentucky homeland, where people tend to be nosy. She later admitted, "After I left, I understood what a rare thing it is to live among people who care that much about your business" (Donahue, p. F3).

Spring, 1972 Instead of dancing at the junior prom, Kingsolver turned to the novels and stories of Flannery O'Connor and rejoiced that she "caught the scent of a world. I started to dream up intoxicating lives for myself that I could not have conceived without the books" (Rubinstein, p. 254). About the time she began composing verse, she discovered Henry David Thoreau's *Walden* (1854) and his intense examination of details from nature, particularly in the posthumous essay "Faith in a Seed." She admits she was "blown away by how carefully this guy paid attention to the details of his immediate surroundings— the seeds, the trees, the behavior of squirrels— and seemed to feel happy and wealthy as a consequence, even though he lived in a tiny house and owned only one chair" ("Barbara Kingsolver: Coming").

Summer, 1972 Leaving behind a loving family and the red cherry four-poster that Grandfather Henry carved on his lathe, Kingsolver entered summer school at the University of Kentucky in Lexington and gained a first boyfriend, a boost to her self-esteem.

1973 In early adulthood, Kingsolver read up on any subject that the Kentucky schools failed to offer. She turned to the strong writers of the South — Carson McCullers, Reynolds Price, and Eudora Welty — as models of local color and craft. She continued her journal and, at the urging of an English teacher, began composing reams of sonnets as a means of disciplining construction, cadence, and diction. She later described this training in versification as "good practice for writing fiction" (Ross, p. 286).

On a music scholarship, Kingsolver entered DePauw University in Greencastle, Indiana, to study composition, theory, and performance. In *I've Always Meant to Tell You*, she composed an untitled reflection on being "driven three hundred miles with our VW bus packed like a tackle box" and shedding tears as her parents departed. Her college days brought the freedom to write, make friends with other intellectuals, test her idealism, and form opinions on war, abortion, and women's rights. By November 20, she exulted over tossing aside Joseph Conrad's *Heart of Darkness* to double-date to the Greencastle Drive-in, where *Cabaret* was showing.

After classes and piano practice, Kingsolver worked as typesetter, housemaid, and artist's model. She read Karl Marx and Friedrich Engels's communist polemics, science fiction by Ursula LeGuin, the Southern novels of William Faulkner, sociological nonfiction by Margaret Mead and Ruth Benedict, and the feminist writings of Gloria Steinem and Betty Friedan. Because other students ridiculed Kingsolver's Kentucky accent and country ways, she distanced herself from the speech of her childhood and took part in campaigns for abortion rights and anti–Vietnam War demonstrations, both attesting to her awareness of the world at large. Gradually, her hill accent weakened like jeans rinsed clean of starch and color, an image she furthers in *High Tide in Tucson*.

As she explained in *I've Always Meant to Tell You*, the mother-daughter camaraderie wore thin as Barbara returned home from college wearing "Army Surplus boots and a five-dollar haircut from a barbershop" (p. 250). She admits that she "[tried] to be shocking" (*Ibid.*). The era inspired her to rip pages from her diary and mail them to her mother. In epistle form, she tried out on Ginny Kingsolver new ideas on "friends, lovers, poetry, freedom, … abortion, Vietnam, the Problem That Has No Name," the feminist term for women's frustrations (p. 249). The contretemps left Barbara feeling "overmothered and motherless" (p. 250). It was not until after college that she "learned the womanly art of turning down the volume" (p. 251).

1974 At age nineteen, Kingsolver was assaulted by a man she met in a bar. Two nights after their introduction, he came to her apartment and, under the guise of a friendly visit, overpowered and raped her. In *I've Always Meant to Tell You*, she recalls retreating into "this knot of nothingness on my bed, this thing I used to call me" (p. 256). Shame at being a bar-room pickup precipitated serious depression and a retreat to bed to sort out her feelings. In retrospect she wrote the poem "This House I Cannot Leave," collected in *Another America*. The imagery depicts her as a victim trapped by corrosive memories in a sullied body. A decade later in *Small Wonder* (2002), she relives the crime: "My head against a wall, suffocation, hard pushing and flat on my back and screaming for air. Fighting an animal twice my size. My job was to stop him, and I failed" (p. 168).

1975 Kingsolver intended to earn a B.F.A. in classical piano, but, for practical reasons, at the end of the sophomore year, she gravitated instead to an unusual hybrid — a B.S. in zoology and an English minor. In science notebooks, she scribbled poems in the margins. In retrospect of her unusual blend of interests, she noted: "It's okay to have hobbies if they are victimless and don't get out of hand, but to confess to disparate passions is generally taken in our society as a sign of attention deficit disorder" (*High Tide*, p. 131).

ca. 1976 Kingsolver discovered Doris Lessing's Children of Violence series and began researching and analyzing global issues, a subject that developed into interest in C.I.A. meddling in Central American politics and the Arizona underground railroad for refugees in *The Bean Trees* and Congolese missions and post-colonial revolution in *The Poisonwood Bible*.

1977 After graduating *magna cum laude* and Phi Beta Kappa, Kingsolver sojourned in European communes. She studied in Athens and Paris for two years, earning her way as a housemaid, archeologist, copy editor, and X-ray technician. Until her visa expired, she also transcribed medical records and compiled data on population biology at a microbiological research lab.

1978 In summer with a dozen other young people, Kingsolver lived in a stone farmhouse in Beaurieux, France, in sight of sugar beet fields dotted with scarlet poppies. A telephone call from home churned up nostalgia. Seeing her country in perspective, she determined to return and live "inside this amazing beast, poking at its belly from the inside with my one little life and the small, pointed sword of my pen" (McMahon).

1979 In a yellow Renault, Kingsolver drove from Carlisle, Kentucky, to Tucson, Arizona, for a short look-see at a land flourishing in chollas, prickly pears, and saguaros. Twelve years later, she recalled: "I came to Tucson as a naive outsider, and I have at bottom a rural outlook on life. That's why I found community in a place that more jaded folks would call bad real estate" (Ross, p. 287). Of her first contact with the Sonoran Desert, she mused, "Living in the Southwest makes you pay attention to color and contrast and hard edges, in terms of both physical landscape and human landscape" (*Ibid.*, p. 286). The heightening of sensibilities undergirds her first three novels, the documentary *Holding the Line: Women in the Great Arizona Mine Strike of 1983* (1989), and many of her poems and essays.

1981   During a conservative backlash against war protesters, Kingsolver chose the Southwestern United States as a comfortable place to settle. She completed an M.S. in animal behavior from the department of ecology and evolutionary biology at the University of Arizona in Tucson with a thesis on termites entitled, "Kin Selection among Heterotermes Aureus." While she studied creative writing, short fiction writer and mentor Francine Prose introduced her to Southern writer Bobbie Ann Mason. Kingsolver pursued post-graduate study in a University of Arizona doctoral program, but grew disillusioned with academia. She fabricated a family emergency that would allow her to withdraw with dignity: "I made up a terrible lie involving a car accident and a permanent disability, and said I needed to take another job to support my unnamed, maimed relative" (Lyall).

1983   For two years, Kingsolver worked as a research assistant in the University of Arizona's physiology department and five years as a technical writer for a desert study at the Arid Lands Institute, covering such agronomic issues as gopher weed as a fuel crop. She turned to free-lance journalism and fiction, publishing travelogues in *Architectural Digest* and *New York Times Magazine* and scientific essays in *Biomass*, *Economic Botany*, and *Phytochemical Adaptations to Stress*. She won a short story contest sponsored by the Phoenix *New Times* and scribbled in her journal her true identity, a writer. To interviewer Michael Neill she confided, "It felt like something dangerous and irrevocable, like cutting down a forest" (Neill, p. 110). To equip her office for wordcraft, she surrounded herself with an array of dictionaries and language books covering modern Romance languages and expanding to Greek, Latin, Cherokee, and Kikongo.

Kingsolver published in *Architectural Digest, Calyx, Cosmopolitan, Denver Post, Heresies, Lexington Herald-Leader, Los Angeles Times Magazine, Mademoiselle, McCall's, Nation, Natural History, New Mexico Humanities Review, Parenting, Progressive, Redbook, Smithsonian, Sojourner, Tucson Weekly,* and *Virginia Quarterly Review* and reviewed for the *Los Angeles Times Book Review* and the *New York Times Book Review*. During a period of crusading journalism, she supported Amnesty International and covered human rights issues in Latin America. She wrote environmental studies, in particular, the exposé of the Palo Verde Nuclear Generating Plant fifty miles from Phoenix for failure to follow specifications for pouring concrete and maintaining quality control.

1985   Kingsolver married University of Arizona chemistry professor Joseph "Joe" Hoffmann, whose specialty is natural products. In "Mormon Memories," a 1989 book review for the *Los Angeles Times*, she remarked, "When I married, ... in a foreign city, the ceremony was conducted hastily in a language I barely understood. The circumstances were admittedly odd but also appropriate, I thought" (p. 13). The couple settled on a Tucson farm "[nestled] into what's called in this region a *bosque*— that is, a narrow riparian woodland stitched like a green ribbon through the pink and tan quilt of the Arizona desert" (*Small Wonder*, p. 34).

Kingsolver's married life reflected the lessons of her childhood. In a home garden, she grew squash, tomatoes, and peppers, figs and grapevines, and wild hibiscus and hollyhocks for color; she later raised rare Bourbon Red turkeys to supply her table at Thanksgiving. In *High Tide in Tucson*, she exults in the beauties of the desert, where a rain ends drought and revives leaves of the ocotillo and the sex life of underground toads. The elements stirred to action by the shower illustrate what she calls basic mortality, the root of passion, the subject of her fifth novel, *Prodigal Summer* (2000).

1986   Dazzled by the contrasts of Arizona's light and color, Kingsolver turned hiking and gardening into pantheism, her avowed religion. Against her mother's advice, she helped rescue Latin American refugees from human rights abuse in Chile, El Salvador, and Guatemala. During a first pregnancy, she freelanced for newspapers. She published her first commercial story, "Why I Am a Danger to the Public," in *New Times* and a co-authored piece on a Kentucky labor strike for the *Progressive*, her first national exposure. She earned an award from the Arizona Press Club for a profile for the *Tucson Weekly* on Harlequin romance writer Regan Forest.

Of her career as a poet, Kingsolver tends to downplay her efforts as though they were a shameful addiction or secret sin, a suggestion of her furtive verses in science notebooks in college. Of versification as an art, she exults in "How Poems Happen" (1998) that poetry is "elementary grace that reassures us of what we know and socks us in the gut with what we don't. It sings us awake. It's irresistible, it's congenital" (p. 37). She divulges that she and other poets have no real understanding of what inspires them to think up images and write poems.

Negative themes influenced Kingsolver as she incubated her response to the death of sister-in-law Jeannie, who was murdered as she slept. The vision of the family losing one member and gaining another through birth recurs in the poem "Family Secrets," published six years later in *Another America*. After the decommissioning of the Titan Intercontinental Ballistic Missiles, the obsolete guardians of the United States during the Cold War, Kingsolver wrote "In the City Ringed with Giants," her impression of one of the eighteen tall weapons displayed in Green Valley, Arizona, as historic museums. Metaphorically, she saw the hostilities as a proliferation of vampires in the forest and described Russian-American detente as the outliving of giants.

During bouts of insomnia before Camille's birth, Kingsolver retreated to a closet, typewriter on knees, and composed fiction by night. She fleshed out *The Bean Trees* with memories, Kentucky colloquialisms, and observations from her journal. Of her writing method, she explained: "I devise a very big question whose answer I believe will be amazing, and maybe shift the world a little bit on its axis. Then I figure out how to create a world in which that question can be asked, and answered" (Rubinstein, p. 254). To humanize the Q & A, she pictures her characters as though they are actors in a movie or house guests at her home. She shoulders the responsibility for rewarding her readers. In a speech to the 1993 American Booksellers Convention, she declared, "I know that if I'm going to make you sit down and listen to me for ten and a half hours, I owe you, big. I need to entertain you" ("An Address").

Winter, 1987 "Rose-Johnny" appeared in the *Virginia Quarterly* and was later collected in *New Stories from the South* (1988) and *Homeland and Other Stories*. The plot features one of Kingsolver's tomboys, a ten-year-old who serves as the unreliable or naive narrator trying to piece together the reason that a local lesbian is an outcast. Similar in anti-female haircut and dress to the butch girls in Carson McCullers's *The Heart Is a Lonely Hunter* (1940) and *The Member of the Wedding* (1946) and to Taylor Greer in *The Bean Trees* and Leah in *The Poisonwood Bible* (1998), Rose is an anomaly, a hillbilly androgyne. Rumors label her "half man and half woman, something akin to the pagan creatures whose naked torsos are inserted in various shocking ways into parts of animal bodies" (p. 204). The truth of Rose's past is more terrible — her father was lynched, her baby brother Johnny drowned in the creek, and Rose converted into Rose-Johnny to comfort her grieving mother.

April 1, 1987 A week before her thirty-third birthday, Kingsolver returned home from the hospital with a daughter, Camille Hoffmann. The new mother marveled at her child's femininity and saved the umbilical cord to bury under a tree in the style of the Tohono O'odham. The cord tethers their children to Mother Earth and returns their spirits to the land after death. Of the fun of motherhood, Kingsolver observed: "At the end of the day, when Camille and I are reunited after our daily cares, I'm ready for joyful mayhem" (*High Tide*, p. 93).

1988 Voicing "everything I believe in," Kingsolver's first novel, *The Bean Trees,* certified her selection of writer as a profession (McMahon). No less accurate a form of reportage than Kingsolver's nonfiction, the text demonstrates a command of fictional dialogue in her intermingling of zany, down-home word play and sensitivity to rural life with concern for destitute people, particularly single mothers, loners, and refugees. The contrasting female protagonists — Taylor Greer and Lou Ann Ruiz — represent activism and nurturing, outgrowths of the warring poles of the author's personality. After a mugger assaults three-year-old Turtle Greer in Chapter 12, activism threatens to subsume nurturing. Taylor mourns, "Nobody feels sorry for anybody anymore, nobody even pretends they do. Not even the President," a direct slap at Ronald Reagan (p. 171).

The book did so well that Kingsolver later marveled, "This strikes me as a miracle on the order of the loaves and fishes" (*Small Wonder*, p. 218). The novel garnered an Enoch Pratt Library Youth-to-Youth Books Award, American Library Association Notable Book, and *New York Times* Notable Book. The text was translated into some fifteen languages. Her resonant blend of realism and fiction found favor with Meg Ryan, who optioned the novel for film; Paramount renewed the option in 1989 and offered the author a role as consultant.

November, 1988 Kingsolver's interest in the peculiarities and strengths of the ordinary endeared her to devoted fans for her novels, stories, verse, and nonfiction. For want of a book store, residents of Carlisle, Kentucky, sponsored a celebration of King-solver's first novel at the railway depot. Of the community's embrace of her stardom, she responded: "I love my hometown as I love the elemental stuff of my own teeth and bones" (*High Tide*, p. 44).

1989 Kingsolver's venture into nonfiction, *Holding the Line: Women in the Great Arizona Mine Strike of 1983*, documents company civil rights infractions against work-ers during an eighteen-month mining strike on the Phelps Dodge Copper Corpora-tion. She walked into a situation that made her feel like Rumpelstiltskin spinning straw into gold. With a mania for the truth, she verified the role of women — many of them Hispanic and native American single parents from four largely Catholic towns in southern Arizona. For material, she stayed on the scene at the Morenci cop-per pit, recording statements and analyzing aims, sources of tension, and commit-ment to ideals. Her interviews uncovered "truth [that] was generally shocking enough without embroidery" (p. xii).

The face-off erupted after the company tried to cheat workers of cost-of-living raises by freezing wages of men and women who performed heavy lifting and worked unrelieved seven-day-a-week schedules for a month. Although management won, the firm lost business and face. People like Berta Chavez, Flossie Navarro, and Anna O'Leary of the Morenci Mine Women's Auxiliary gained self-confidence for defend-ing their communities and homes during the trials of SWAT teams, tear gas, capri-cious arrests, even a flood of the San Francisco River. The *Arizona Daily Star* featured mothers, sisters, wives, and daughters as dedicated to union principles.

Although Kingsolver was a beginning reporter, she came from the appropriate background to understand working-class issues and the strength of local people fac-ing armed goon squads and government officials who sided with management. For data, she and partner Jill Barrett Fein collared police, National Guardsmen, mining supervisors, and some of the twenty-three hundred striking workers and their sup-porters. Of Kingsolver's interest in collective bargaining, she explained, "I grew up in eastern Kentucky, so honestly union membership has always been profoundly associated with things like honor, integrity, responsibility towards community, and basically survival, security" (Kjos, p. 13).

Kingsolver made use of her eighteen-month trial by fire. In the story "Why I Am a Danger to the Public" collected in *Homeland and Other Stories*, she reprised the misery of female miners toiling for a bigoted outfit that "don't like cunts or col-oreds" (p. 235). Influencing tone and mood are the words of Vicki Morales, a fictional Chicana single mother and crane operator who declares, "I was not going to support my kids in no little short skirt down at the Frosty King" (p. 227).

These life lessons made their way into the author's classroom lectures, as she reports in "Widows at the Wheel," a 1989 book review for the *Los Angeles Times*: "I recently asked a roomful of writing students, as I waved an article about a man who piloted a plane 2,000 miles while unconscious, then crashed into the sea, then swam to safety — what could be more implausible than a true story?" (p. 1). Her advice led students through exercises that paralleled her on-the-job training at the mine strike: "The trick is to construct a story readers will want to believe, with all their hearts, and to play it out in a world so detailed and appealing that they're prepared to pack their bags and move in" (*Ibid.*). For literary achievement, Kingsolver earned a Citation of Accomplishment from the United Nations National Council of Women of the United States.

Kingsolver's experience at turning real events into short fiction gave her the confidence to review other writers' efforts. The next year, she reported in a second book review for the *Los Angeles Times*, "Where Love Is Nurtured and Confined," the pitfalls of short fiction: "Getting a short story off the ground and safely landed again in its few allotted pages is a risk. In a collection of stories, the risk is multiplied, like an airplane flight that includes many stops: There are just that many more chances for failure" (p. 2). With understanding of the difficulties of maintaining quality in an anthology, she added, "It's a rare collection that delivers its passenger smoothly from first page to last without a few hard landings" (*Ibid.*).

September 1, 1989   In President Ronald Reagan's last year in office, the author found it difficult to restrain outrage over American warmongering in Central America, a major theme in *The Bean Trees*. In an interview with Jean Ross for *Contemporary Authors*, Kingsolver vented her distress over "what some of my tax dollars are doing in El Salvador right now, today. And yes, I'd like to scream" (Ross, p. 286). To avoid preaching to readers, she trusted her craft to express personal passion for human rights and justice.

September, 1990   Channeling her despair over the duplicity of the Reagan administration in conducting a covert war in Central America, Kingsolver published a second Southwestern novel, *Animal Dreams*, which also taps her experience with the Phelps Dodge mine strike of 1983. The carefully plotted text incorporates her favorite themes—female autonomy, cross-cultural understanding, parenting, native Americans, violence, human freedoms, and ecology. The author characterized the themes as "responsibility to our future, the political choices we make, how to begin paying back the debt to rivers and air and oceans and soil we've been borrowing on, cheating on, for decades" (Ross, p. 289). In the opinion of critic Meredith Sue Willis, *Animal Dreams* is the most fully realized effort of the author's early works. A popular and critical success, the novel won an American Library Association Notable Book and Best Book for Young Adults, Pen/USA West Fiction Award, Edward Abbey Award for Ecofiction, Arizona Library Association Book of the Year, and *New York Times* Notable Book.

Christmas, 1990   During a visit home to Carlisle for the holidays, Kingsolver looked out on the spare Kentucky town and wondered how she ever lived there. A memory recorded in *I've Always Meant to Tell You* reports that she feels contentment in her choice of career and lifestyle: "Competent and slightly rushed, as usual. A woman of my age" (p. 259).

1991   Kingsolver began research in earnest on Congo history in preparation for writing *The Poisonwood Bible*, her most demanding project. Over a ten-year incubation, her siftings grew into a huge file awaiting a literary maturity that could comprehend the fall of the Congo during the Cold War and turn it into the basis for fiction. Of her pacing, she explained to *San Francisco Chronicle* interviewer Sylvia Rubin, "I knew this couldn't be my first book, or my last. I think many writers have 'The Big One' they keep in a separate place" (Rubin, p. C1).

January 15, 1991   As described in the poem "Deadline," later anthologized in *Another America*, Kingsolver took part in a candlelight vigil for peace on the night before the United States precipitated the Gulf War. Accompanied by three-year-old Camille, bundled in a nylon parka, the author pondered parental responsibility to protect children. The poem acknowledges the impossibility of saving Middle Eastern children from "a holocaust of heaven" comprised of liquid gasoline that ignites in the air before falling on the innocent below (p. 3).

August, 1991   When the United States bombed Baghdad during the Gulf War, Kingsolver questioned political expediency in her essay "And Our Flag Was Still There": "We rushed to the aid of Kuwait, a monarchy in which women enjoyed approximately the same rights as a nineteenth-century American slave" (p. 242). She blamed the appeasement of American oil companies as the main reason for a conflict that devastated Iraqi civilians. Her candid response is moving: "I search my soul and find I cannot rejoice over killing" (p. 241). The wording ventures near the perimeter of the author's steely control of emotion, revealing a seething anger that empowers her pen.

Distressed, Kingsolver and Camille, like the character Hallie Noline in *Animal Dreams* (1990), abandoned their country's war, left Tucson, and took a flat in Santa Cruz, capital of Tenerife in the Canary Islands off Morocco's west coast. The rain of bombs on Baghdad filled the author with a pacifist's anguish. Describing her retreat from home, she observed, "Five hundred years after colonialism arrived in the New World, I booked a return passage" (*High Tide*, p. 109). In reference to the Gulf War, she composed "Escape" (1992), a poem that pictures her in flight from the United states like a lizard molting from its outgrown skin. Regretfully, she concludes that nothing has changed at home, where sin stains the national altar. In "Bridges," she states outright that war settles nothing.

The sojourn among Spaniards nourished Kingsolver's regard for socialized medicine and the absence of child malnutrition. She told interviewer David Gergen: "I loved the personal freedom of being able to walk around at night.... I loved living in a place where there wasn't an immense disparity between rich and poor, where you don't have a lot of poverty, you don't have a lot of violent crime" (Gergen). After hours of writing, she tended pots of basil and tomatoes on the balcony, enjoyed relaxed dining on the Avenida de Anaga, watched the play of dolphins in the ocean, and weekended at San Sebastián, port city of the isle of La Gomera.

Another bromide for Kingsolver's frazzled state of mind was the islanders' love of children: "People in Spain look at children as the meringues and éclairs of their culture" (*High Tide*, p. 100). In the essay "Everybody's Somebody's Baby" (1992), she concluded that Spanish children "[grow] up the way leavened dough rises surely to the kindness of bread" (p. 106). The essay warns child-haters, "Be careful what you give children, or don't, for sooner or later you will always get it back" (p. 107).

1992   In a difficult year, Kingsolver traveled to Kyoto, Japan, and visited Hiroshima's Ground Zero. She won the first of eight consecutive Best Local Author annual citations from the *Tucson Weekly* and a Woodrow Wilson Foundation/Lila Wallace Fellowship. Kingsolver published her first poetry anthology, *Another America: Otra America*, a dual text of poems in English and Spanish issued by Seal Press of Seattle, a venue for feminist writings. The pairing of verse replicates the survival of the American underclass in a society dominated by wealthy and privileged whites.

February, 1992   Kingsolver moved back to the United States at a difficult pass in her life and relationship with Joe Hoffmann. In addition to loneliness, she battled community property mediation that threatened the ownership of her own works. After Kathi Kamen Goldmark formed a band of authors, Kingsolver joined to sing and play keyboard and percussion at the 1992 American Booksellers Association convention, a vast meeting in Anaheim, California, of members of the book publishing and vending trades. The combo, called the Rock Bottom Remainders, consisted of Al Kooper directing, Roy Blount in Hawaiian shirt keeping order, lead guitarist Dave Barry, rhythm guitarist Stephen King, Ridley Pearson on bass, and Ted Bartimus, Amy Tan, and Goldmark doing vocals. Kingsolver reported in the essay "Confessions of a Reluctant Rock Goddess" (1995): "We did our crossover talent show, and made a big hit with the tipsy booksellers and publishers of North America" (*High Tide*, p. 124). The proceeds of their amateurish, but earnest musicales supported literacy campaigns and First Amendment rights.

May, 1992   Kingsolver traveled from Boston with the Rock Bottom Remainders on a two-week tour. Although nervous and diffident, she stated, "I wanted to belong to this gang, and I wasn't going to do it by being the class clown or the silver tongue" (*Ibid.*, p. 127). They performed "These Boots Are Made for Walkin'," "Chain of Fools," "Money," "Nadine," "Leader of the Pack," "Teen Angel," "Louie Louie," and "Gloria"; Kingsolver practiced but did not star in "Dock of the Bay." In her one moment of glory, she bounded onstage in black lace stockings and mitts to blow kisses to the audience.

Christmas, 1992   In "Mormon Memories," a book review for the *Los Angeles Times* in November 1989, the author observed, "Contrary to all the romantic literature on the subject, marriage seems finally to be an almost absurd act of faith; we have no idea what we are promising." Three years later, her words proved prophetic to her own life. During a visit home to Kentucky for the holidays, she had difficulty announcing a failing marriage to her mother.

1993   After divorcing Hoffmann, Kingsolver was so shaken that she reneged on fourteen years of abstinence from smoking. She confided to Sarah Lyall, interviewer for the *New York Times*: "I don't much enjoy being single. I hear it's supposed to be fun, but what it means is that you fix dinner and you do the dishes and you bring in the groceries and you balance the checkbook, and you do it all while you're on a book tour" (Lyall).

Kingsolver was able to summarize her thoughts on going-nowhere marriages in the essay "Stone Soup": "A nonfunctioning marriage is a slow asphyxiation. It is waking up despised each morning, listening to the pulse of your own loneliness before the radio begins to blare its raucous gospel that you're nothing if you aren't loved" (*High Tide*, p. 138). To depict pain, Kingsolver described parting in medical terms: "[It's] as much *fun* as amputating your own gangrenous leg. You do it, if you can, to save a life — or two, or more" (*Ibid.*).

February, 1993   After the bleak sales of *Another America*, Kingsolver admitted to coveting the wider readership of fiction. As she explains her view of the prose writer's use of imagery in "Poetic Fiction with a Tex-Mex Tilt," a 1991 book review for the *Los Angeles Times:* "From poetry to fiction and back doesn't seem too long a stretch for some writers" (p. 3). She adds with an insider's wry knowledge, "It's a practical thing for poets in the United States to turn to fiction" (*Ibid.*). Most troubling to her is the American devaluation of poets: "Elsewhere, poets have the cultural status of our rock stars and the income of our romance novelists.... Even the most acclaimed [U.S. poets] could scarcely dine out twice a year, let alone make a living, on the sales of their poetry collections" (*Ibid.*).

For *The Poisonwood Bible*, the author set out to probe life on a distant continent. Because of the strictures of Mobutu's regime, she could not return to the Congo of her childhood. Instead, she spent a month in Benin to gather background material in anticipation of writing a novel about the area. She justified her interest in Africa: "The point [of portraying other cultures] is not to emulate other lives, or usurp their wardrobes. The point is to find sense" (Van Boven, p. 76). To incorporate the Congo's history into fiction, she set up a problem to solve concerning the wrongs that colonialism did to the Congolese: "All right, given our country did these things in our name, what do we make of it? Where do we go from here? How do we take that awful piece of our own history and reconcile it with who we believe we are as people?" (Krasny).

June, 1993   In Miami in a speech at the American Booksellers convention, Kingsolver declared the life of a writer to be a privilege rather than a curse. She valued the opportunity to speak important principles by creating empathy for fictional characters: "It's my opinion that the world is a wonderful and an awful place, and for all the quiet desperation out there, there is also a whole lot of joyful noise. I want to write about that" ("An Address"). She added earnestly, "Somehow we have to find a way of getting across those truths that are too huge and maybe too terrible to say in simple language" (*Ibid.*). To people who try to read autobiography into her scenarios, she replies in disgust: "I set my novels in geographic and psychic territory that I know.... People don't give writers enough credit for the power of the lie" (Karbo, p. 9).

Kingsolver's *Pigs in Heaven*, the non-sequel to *The Bean Trees*, was published with a considerable budget and promotion from HarperCollins. In an interview with Michael Grant of KAET-TV at Arizona State University, she summarized the premise of the book as "two really completely different ideas of what a family is, what constitutes a family" (Grant). According to interviewer Sarah Lyall: "Some men seem puzzled by her appeal, pigeonholing her as a touchy-feely women's author even as their sisters, mothers, girlfriends, and wives read, reread, borrow, lend and discuss her books" (Lyall). The novel, which pushed her book sales mark above one million, won acclaim from the National Cowboy Hall of Fame and Western Heritage Museum in Oklahoma City, Oklahoma, which recognizes the pioneering spirit of the West in fiction. Her award took the form of a Wrangler statue sculpted by John D. Free, an Oklahoma artist of Cherokee-Osage heritage. *Pigs in Heaven* also garnered a *Los Angeles Times* Fiction Prize, Mountains and Plains Booksellers Award, American Booksellers Book of the Year nomination, Publishers Weekly Audio Best of Year, and *New York Times* Bestseller and Notable Book. Actor Jane Fonda contracted to produce the novel on film for Turner Pictures.

Kingsolver began leading workshops in creative writing and downplayed her role as bestselling fiction writer. She explained, "I don't fool myself that I have written the eighth best book in the country; it's the publicity machine that does that, and someone else achieved that. At the same time I know without that I'd be permanently mid-listed, and have to teach in a college or waitress or something to support my writing habit" (Rosenfeld, D. 1). She was a visiting writer at Emory & Henry College when she met future husband Steven L. Hopp of southwestern Virginia, an environmentalist and specialist in bioacoustics or bird calls, particularly the vireo.

1994   Still shaken by a failed first marriage, Kingsolver wed Steve Hopp "in the sight of pine-browed mountains, a forget-me-not sky, and nearly all the people I love most" (*High Tide*, p. 268). The couple teamed to write essays and articles on natural history. After three years of marriage, she confesses in *I've Always Meant to Tell You*, "I love him inordinately" (p. 261).

To keep herself centered, annually, Kingsolver and family made the drive from the Southwest to Virginia near the Kentucky line to take up summer residence in "a log cabin in a deep, wooded hollow at the end of Walker Mountain" (*Small Wonder*, p. 31). During the long trek, she read aloud to her child. The varying climates allowed her to plant a Southern garden in Kentucky and winter crops in southern Arizona. She also kept hens and cows and shared recipes for fresh goods with *Mother Earth News*.

1995   From her four-acre home outside Tucson at the base of the Tucson Mountains, Kingsolver polished twenty-five essays for inclusion in *High Tide in Tucson: Essays from Now and Never*, which won an American Library Association Best Book of the Year citation. Her alma mater, De Pauw University, awarded her an honorary doctorate. To preserve authenticity and narrative flow, she chose to narrate the taped version as well as an audio of *Homeland and Other Stories*. That same year, Perennial issued *The Complete Fiction: The Bean Trees, Homeland, Animal Dreams, Pigs in Heaven*.

1996   Kingsolver was pleased that Camille had Tohono O'odham and Yaqui playmates in the Southwest, a camaraderie that increased the child's awareness of native Americans. In *I've Always Meant to Tell You*, the author pictures her beautiful, opinionated older daughter as "a Raphael cherub" (p. 260).

July, 1996   Kingsolver's protracted second pregnancy dragged into its eleventh month. She moaned, "I am a beached whale, a house full of water, a universe with ankles" (*Ibid.*). The family's offspring doubled after she gave birth to Lily. In delight at her family, the author rejoiced, "I could not bear to be anyone but the mother of my two daughters" (*Ibid.*, p. 261).

1997   Kingsolver dickered with HarperCollins over placement of her next book. At odds with the company for publishing *To Renew America* (1995) by right-wing politician Newt Gingrich, she had the clout to protest representation by a firm that distributes extreme conservative views. She and Harper came to an agreement for issuance of *The Poisonwood Bible*. With the million-dollar advance, Kingsolver, in conjunction with Gerald Freund, Rona Jaffe, and Lila Wallace, established the biennial Bellwether Prize, the nation's largest literary prize, to honor American writers engaged in writing a novel of social change. Judges value authors who could "[create] empathy in a reader's heart for the theoretical stranger" ("Bellwether"). The awards include $25,000 cash plus a book contract for serious fiction addressing issues of social justice.

May, 1997   Kingsolver, along with editors Constance Warloe and Hilma Wolitzer, issued *I've Always Meant to Tell You: Letters to Our Mothers: An Anthology of Contemporary Women Writers*, a tribute to parenting containing essays by Rita Mae Brown, Rita Dove, Ellen Gilchrist, Joy Harjo, Carolyn Kizer, Maxine Kumin, Joyce Carol Oates, Marge Piercy, and Ntozake Shange.

November, 1997   Cornell University Press re-released *Holding the Line: Women in the Great Arizona Mine Strike of 1983*. In a new introduction, Kingsolver answered charges from critics who missed or ignored her intent to concentrate on the actions of female protesters. Of the valor of striking workers, she expressed her sympathy and admiration for the underclass, who profited from "the survival value of collective action" (p. xix).

Late in the month, Kingsolver joined Gary Paul Nabhan, Richard Nelson, and Ofelia Zepeda in a benefit public reading in Tucson to support Native Seeds/SEARCH, a non-profit effort to conserve the traditional seeds, farming methods, and crops of native peoples in the greater Southwest.

1998   With the publication of the author's fourth and most critically acclaimed novel, Paul Gray of *Time* magazine stated, "Barbara Kingsolver's reputation achieved something like critical (and commercial) mass with *The Poisonwood Bible* (1998)" (Gray, p. 90). For the complex, ambitious research project, she coordinated daily readings in the King James bible with the diaries of missionaries, political handbooks, the Kikongo-French dictionary, and stacks of *Life*, *Look*, and *Saturday Evening Post* magazines dating from 1958 to 1961. Fact-finding included visits to the American Museum of Natural History and the Reptile House of the San Diego Zoo and treks into Western and Central Africa to live with natives, shop in local markets, and ask questions about history, religion, and African families. The choice of political allegory as a literary mode gave her a forum for condemning colonialism in third-world countries. The writing was difficult and, at times, repugnant, causing her to observe, "I've known for years and years I wanted to tell the story of what the U.S. did to the Congo. It's not a pretty story" (Rubin, p. C1).

The Poisonwood Bible had a remarkable impact on readers. Lee Siegel, a columnist for *New Republic*, proclaimed that "this easy, humorous, competent, syrupy writer has been elevated to the ranks of the greatest political novelists of our time" (Siegel, p. 36). Reviewer Julian Markels called the novel "Dickensian" for its energized language, scope, and humanitarian appeal. He declared: "Kingsolver was propelled exponentially to gender/class/race as her holistic point of entry by the explosive political energy bottled up in her earlier novels" (Markels). The novel earned Kingsolver the National Book Prize of South Africa, American Booksellers Book of the Year, *Los Angeles Times* Best Book, *New York Times* "Ten Best Books of 1998," Canada's North Forty-Nine Books Most Valuable Picks, Village Voice Best Book, New York Public Library "25 Books to Remember," Britain's Orange Prize of £30,000, nomination for the PEN/Faulkner award, and an Oprah Book Club selection. With the publication of her fourth novel, she became the first author to be nominated four times in succession for the Sierra Club's Edward Abbey Award for Ecofiction. As her fame grew, HarperCollins honored her first novel with a tenth anniversary reissue of *The Bean Trees* and a new edition of *Another America: Otra America*.

June, 1998   Kingsolver, Joseph Barbato, Lisa Weinerman Horak, Lisa Weinerman, and the Nature Conservancy issued stories about nature preserves in *Off the Beaten Path: Stories of Place*. The focus suits Kingsolver's interest in human interaction with physical locale, particularly in *The Poisonwood Bible* and her fifth novel, *Prodigal Summer*, which she set in a forest preserve. In a fall interview with Bill Goldstein of the *New York Times*, she explained her method of making characters come alive: "I invest in them emotionally, I light them up like Christmas trees, with details of personality and psyche and motivation" (Goldstein).

1999   To complaints from critics of heavy-handed didacticism, Kingsolver retorted on post–McCarthy Era prejudices: "There is a nervousness in this country about art that addresses issues of social change and social justice. It's a very provincial and backward attitude that is pretty much absent in the rest of the world" (McMahon). Despite snide comments from conservative reviewers, she won the Patterson Fiction Prize, a *Writer's Digest* 100 Best Writers of the Twentieth Century honorarium, and a nomination for a Pulitzer Prize. She shared her expertise at the Natural History Writing Workshop for the North Cascades Institute, a Creative Writing Workshop for the University of Arizona, and Journalists Workshop, sponsored by the *Arizona Daily Star*.

May, 1999   After the shooting of students at Columbine High School in Littleton, Colorado, Kingsolver composed "Life Is Precious—or It's Not," a stinging editorial in the *Los Angeles Times*. She placed the blame for the murders on America's pro-war faction for celebrating destructive means of settling international crises: "In, oh let's say, Yugoslavia, Iraq, the Sudan, Waco—anywhere we get fed up with mean-spirited tormentors—why do we believe guns and bombs are the answer?" (p. 5). Speaking from a mother's point of view, she questioned media mayhem and a nation that exonerates armed aggression as the only protection of its unique way of life. Her remedy was strong medicine for the average American parent: "Start by removing from your household and your life every television program, video game, film, book, toy and CD that presents the killing of humans (however symbolic) as an entertainment option" (*Ibid.*).

2000 As guest editor of Houghton-Mifflin's *Best American Short Stories of 2001*, Kingsolver met the needs of a demanding public with savvy choices. In the introduction, she commented, "For a story to make the cut, I asked a lot from it—asked of it, in fact, what I ask of myself when I sit down to write" (p. xiii). Her criteria required the writer to choose a serious topic and move directly to the core of the issue. She envisioned the result as "a small enough amulet to fit inside a reader's most sacred psychic pocket" (*Ibid.*).

Kingsolver published *Prodigal Summer*, a delightful hymn to the wilderness, and narrated the unabridged audio version, winner of an *AudioFile* Earphones Award. She commented, "I wanted to do it myself—I didn't trust a hired actor to get those accents right, and I can't abide a fakey, condescending hillbilly accent" ("Barbara Kingsolver: Coming"). For background, her husband, Steve Hopp, an adjunct associate professor in the Department of Ecology and Evolutionary Biology at the University of Arizona, recorded birdsongs from southwestern Virginia. Her citations for the novel include a Best American Science and Nature Writing honorarium and a Kentucky Governor's Award in the Arts.

February, 2000 Harper hosted a million-book party for *The Poisonwood Bible*, which the company published in Catalan, Japanese, and Polish. A reviewer from the *Los Angeles Times* exulted at Kingsolver's success: "She has with infinitely steady hands worked the prickly threads of religion, politics, race, sin, and redemption into a thing of terrible beauty" (Barnette).

June 2, 2000 *The Poisonwood Bible* won the Book Sense Book of the Year Award, voted by independent dealers of the American Booksellers Association and announced at BookExpo. The honorarium included five thousand dollars and an engraved Steuben crystal prism. Of her stack of awards, this one thrilled Kingsolver. She remarked, "For them to say that Poisonwood was the book they most treasured putting into people's hands, it did mean a lot. I told them I don't need any more awards, ever" (Barnette).

September, 2000 Kingsolver and husband Steve Hopp published "Seeing Scarlet," a travel essay about their trek to Corcovado National Park in the Talamanca Highlands of Costa Rica's Osa Peninsula two days south of San Jose. Rich diversity included one hundred forty mammals, four hundred bird species, and twice the number of tree species found in North America.

November, 2000 To advertise *Prodigal Summer*, Kingsolver coped with multi-city publicity hops and scads of interviews. Of the unfamiliar terrain, she quipped, "All TV studios look exactly alike; all bookstore *bathrooms* look alike; all NPR stations are in the basement" (*High Tide*, p. 159). During the book tour, she used the podium as an opportunity to collect $30,000 for such worthy causes as the San Dieguito River Project in California, the Huron River Watershed Council in Michigan, and the Washington State Environmental Learning Center.

December 20, 2000   At Constitution Hall, President Bill Clinton and First Lady Hillary Rodham Clinton presented Kingsolver the National Humanities Medal for activism and welcomed her to dinner with the First Family. The author shared the evening with a select company of winners—writer Maya Angelou, country singer Eddy Arnold, dancer Mikhail Baryshnikov, playwright Horton Foote, novelists Ernest Gaines and Toni Morrison, violinist Itzhak Perlman, sculptor Claes Oldenburg, and singer Barbra Streisand.

Spring, 2001   To promote literacy, Virginia G. Fox, CEO of Kentucky Educational Television, and one hundred KET affiliates launched a statewide reading campaign that introduced ninety-seven hundred participants to *The Bean Trees.* The outreach coordinated discussions and activities among eighteen hundred and fifty students at thirty-eight high schools, the eight hundred seventy students at thirty-nine adult education and family literacy centers, eight hundred members of forty-four book groups, and thousands of patrons of thirteen libraries. In addition to a one-hour biography and a live call-in program with Kingsolver, she and the publisher offered some four thousand copies of the novel free to worthy institutions. KET's book project earned a Blue Pencil Award from the National Association of Government Communicators.

May, 2001   An English teacher at an Ohio high school noted similarities between Kingsolver's *The Bean Trees* and Melany Neilson's *The Persia Cafe* (2001), a homey novel reflecting Southern lifestyles in a small Mississippi town. A court charged first-time novelist Neilson with lifting eight passages. Speaking through agent Frances Goldin, Kingsolver expressed outrage and demanded that both author and publisher apologize for plagiarism. St. Martin's Press refused to withdraw the novel's first run from book stores, but did issue a new edition that deleted the stolen passages.

June, 2001   In the June/July issue of *Ms.*, R. Erica Doyle cited Kingsolver's writings as tools to change the world. The author justified her altruistic purpose by citing events of the past: "Throughout history, every movement toward a more peaceful and humane world has begun with those who imagined the possibilities" (Doyle, p. 89). She named the biennial Bellwether Prize as one effort to encourage activist literature and stressed the need for political issues in art that "reinforces pieces of our lives that we know to be true or that are unpleasant or challenging" (*Ibid.*). In her opinion, readers are hungry for novels of substance rather than the "empty calories" of the fripperies offered by mass market publishing (*Ibid.*).

September 12, 2001   In response to the destruction of the World Trade Center, the author issued "A Pure, High Note of Anguish" in the *Los Angeles Times.* Concerning the loss of life, she honored "Americans who read and think" as first-class patriots and asserted, "It is desperately painful to see people die without having done anything to deserve it." To uplift readers and promote citizenship, she remarked, "You bear this world and everything that's wrong with it by holding life still precious, each time, and starting over." As a contribution to world reaction, she began writing *Small Wonder*, a study of the grieving process. She donated profits to Environmental

Defense, Habitat for Humanity, Heifer International, and Physicians for Social Responsibility.

⌐Kingsolver's liberal bent angered some readers for her assertion that "Some people believe our country needed to learn how to hurt in this new way." In the opinion of Ross Douthat, reviewer for *National Review*, the author is too eager to view the nation as dark, savage, and edging toward authoritarianism. He sneered, "However healthy and wealthy and successful she may become, she can never truly enjoy it — because the jackboots are always sounding on the street, and the Gestapo is always at the door" (Douthat).

September 27, 2001   Maintaining her stance as writer-as-activist, Kingsolver became more vocal in her criticism of President George W. Bush and his "petroleocracy" (Doyle, p. 89). Under the burden of the conservative backlash promoted by the Bush administration, she joined other activists in warning that fanatic patriotism squelches free speech. Her rededication to activism included continued support for affirmative action, the environment, and women's rights. She urged others to devote part of every week to transforming the way people think about the world.

October 14, 2001   In "No Glory in Unjust War on the Weak," an essay for the *Los Angeles Times*, Kingsolver pressed a pacifist agenda. While American bombers struck Afghanistan, she flinched at the thought of human misery from "explosives raining from the sky on a place already ruled by terror, by all accounts as poor and war-scarred a populace as has ever crept to a doorway and looked out" (p. M1). Against the national juggernaut pouring death on the disadvantaged, she declared, "I fight that, I fight it as if I'm drowning" (*Ibid.*). She softened the hard-edged tone with a self-effacing quip: "Some people are praying for my immortal soul, and some have offered to buy me a one-way ticket out of the country, to anywhere" (*Ibid.*).

November, 2001   Kingsolver received the National Award, which recognizes a Kentucky native who has achieved national acclaim. Previous recipients include singer Rosemary Clooney and playwright Marsha Norman.

November 22, 2001   Pursuing a crusade against retaliatory war, Kingsolver published "Reflections on 'Wartime'" in the *Washington Post*. Her distrust of President George W. Bush's philosophy derives from a love of First Amendment rights. She blamed the backlash against anti-war activism on "our president's statement: 'Either you're with us, or you are with the terrorists.' He was addressing nations of the world, but that 'us' keeps getting narrower" (p. A43). Taking a parent's point of view, she mourned the endangerment of the world's children as fiercely as she warded off threats to her own two girls.

2002   In a busy year, Kingsolver published twenty-three essays in *Small Wonder* and narrated the audio version for HarperAudio. The book won the annual Nautilus Award honoring a book that contributes significantly to conscious living and positive social change. With the aid of photographer Annie Griffiths Belt, the author also compiled *Last Stand: America's Virgin Lands* for the National Geographic Society. The text contains the writings of five landmark naturalists and conservationists:

Edward Abbey, William Bartram, Aldo Leopold, John Muir, and Henry David Thoreau. In an interview with *National Geographic*, Kingsolver noted the impetus of Belt's photos of fragile habitats: "I was overwhelmed with a sense of both time-lessness and urgency" (Parsell). She concluded that the United States is a selfish, profit-centered society and charged: "We've behaved for two hundred years as if the resource base is unlimited" (*Ibid.*). That same year, Kingsolver added to her honors a board membership in PEN/USA, a John P. McGovern Award for the Family, a Physicians for Social Responsibility National Award, a Frank Waters Award, and nomination for the International Impac Dublin Literary Award.

March 1, 2002   Kingsolver joined Bruce Babbitt, Jimmy Carter, John Travolta, Ted Turner, Stewart Udall, and other activists in issuing a full page ad in the *Arizona Republic* supporting the work of Americans for Alaska. The consortium called for protection of the Arctic National Wildlife Refuge from oil drilling, an energy option supported by the Bush administration.

May 24, 2002   In her writings and activism, Kingsolver maintained the fine distinction between humanist and polemicist. In a PBS interview with Bill Moyers, Kingsolver rejected the role of policymaker, but accepted the task of "[re-engaging] people with their own humanity" (Moyers).

Winter, 2002   In an article for the *Los Angeles Times*, Kingsolver stated her outrage at protracted American involvement in the post–Taliban conflict in Afghanistan. She likened her anguish to an adult's irritation at little boys throwing rocks on the playground and blaming each other for starting the melee. To denigrate George W. Bush's jingoistic speeches, she noted wryly: "I keep looking for somebody's mother to come on the scene saying, 'Boys! Boys!' Who started it cannot possibly be the issue here" (Stolba).

January 27, 2003   Kingsolver joined the controversial antiwar group Not In Our Name, which published a two-page statement of conscience in the *New York Times* attacking the Bush administration and calling on citizens to resist the policies and overall political drift toward right-wing extremism. The statement called for due process, a public forum on retaliation, defiance of the Patriot Act, and adherence to a global common cause. In addition to Kingsolver and writers Allan Gurganous, Toni Morrison, Grace Paley, William Styron, Studs Terkel, Gore Vidal, Kurt Vonnegut, and Alice Walker, signers included some five hundred people — musicians Odetta and Pete Seeger, singer Bonnie Raitt, black leaders Jesse Jackson and Al Sharpton, radio star Casey Kasem, linguist Noam Chomsky, the Maryknoll sisters, former *Ms.* editor Robin Morgan, scholar Edward Said, physician Patch Adams, philosopher Deepak Chopra, feminist Gloria Steinem, activists Angela Davis and Martin Luther King III, poets Adrienne Rich and Lawrence Ferlinghetti, and actors Murray Abraham, Ed Asner, Kevin Bacon, Jill Clayburgh, George Clooney, John Cusack, Ossie Davis, Ruby Dee, Roma Downey, Sandy Duncan, Danny Glover, Susan Sarandon, Martin Sheen, and Marisa Tomei.

February 14, 2003   Kingsolver supported the Women's International League for Peace and Freedom by signing the Women to Women Peace Letter Project. Within three weeks, the initiative collected 1,700 signatures from Australia, Belgium, Brazil, Canada, China, Denmark, Ecuador, Germany, Ireland, Italy, Mexico, Norway, Peru, Poland, Romania, Russia, Sweden, Switzerland, Tanzania, the United Kingdom, and the United States.

April 14, 2003   For writing about timely environmental issues, Kingsolver won an Earth Day Award from the Kentucky Environmental Quality Commission, which Dr. Wendell and Virginia Kingsolver accepted for their daughter.

• *Further Reading*

Banks, Russell. "Distant as a Cherokee Childhood." *New York Times Book Review*, July 11, 1989, p. 16.
"Barbara Kingsolver: Coming Home to a Prodigal Summer." http://www.ivillage.com/books/intervu/fict/articles.
Barkley, Tona. "KET Reading Program Takes First Place in National Competition." *Commonwealth Communique*, April 2003.
Barnette, Martha. "Back to the Blue Ridge: A Kentucky Writer Rediscovers Her Roots." *Louisville Courier-Journal*, June 24, 2000.
"The Bellwether Prize." http://www.bellwetherprize.org/default.htm.
Cincotti, Joseph. "Intimate Revelations." *New York Times*, September 2, 1990.
"A Conversation with Barbara Kingsolver." http://www.readinggroupguides.com/guides/animal_dreams-author.asp.
Donahue, Deirdre. "Interview." *USA Today*, July 15, 1993, p. F3.
Douthat, Ross. "Kumbaya Watch: Barbara Kingsolver's America." *National Review*, September 26, 2001.
Doyle, R. Erica. "Barbara Kingsolver: The Bellwether Prize." *Ms.* June/July 2001, p. 89.
Epstein, Robin. "Barbara Kingsolver." *Progressive*, Vol. 60, No. 2, February 1996, pp. 33–37.
Farrell, Michael J. "In Life, Art, Writer Plumbs Politics of Hope." *National Catholic Reporter*, May 22, 1992, pp. 21, 29–30.
Gergen, David. "Interview: Barbara Kingsolver." *U.S. News and World Report*, November 24, 1995.
Goldstein, Bill. "An Author Chat with Barbara Kingsolver." *New York Times*, October 30, 1998.
Grant, Michael. "Interview." *Books & Co.*, KAET-TV, April 4, 2002.
Gray, Paul. "On Familiar Ground." *Time*, Vol. 156, No. 18, October 30, 2000, p. 90.
"Homegrown Talent." *Tucson Weekly*. November 20, 1997.
Kanner, Ellen. "Barbara Kingsolver Turns to Her Past to Understand the Present." *Book Page*, 1998.
Karbo, Karen. "And Baby Makes Two." *New York Times Book Review*, June 27, 1993, p. 9.
Kjos, Tiffany. "Kingsolver Touts National Writers' Union." *Inside Tucson Business*, Vol. 9, No. 49, February 28, 2000, p. 13.
Koza, Kimberly. "The Africa of Two Western Women Writers: Barbara Kingsolver and Margaret Laurence." *Critique*, Vol. 44, No. 3, Spring 2003, pp. 284–294.
Krasny, Michael. "Interview: Barbara Kingsolver, Author, Discusses Her New Book." *Talk of the Nation* (NPR), December 13, 1999.
Labuik, Karen. "President's Message." *PNLA Quarterly*, Vol. 64, No. 3, Spring 2000, p. 1.

Lyall, Sarah. "Termites Are Interesting But Books Sell Better." *New York Times*, September 1, 1993.

Markels, Julian. "Coda: Imagining History in *The Poisonwood Bible*." *Monthly Review Press*, September 2003.

McGee, Celia. "'Bible' Offers Two Good Books in One." *USA Today*, October 22, 1998, p. 6D.

McMahon, Regan. "Barbara Kingsolver: An Army of One." *San Francisco Chronicle*, April 28, 2002.

Moyers, Bill. "Interview with Barbara Walters." *PBS*, May 24, 2002.

"Ms. Kingsolver: Well, that's really a very large...." *Talk of the Nation, National Public Radio*, December 13, 1999.

Neill, Michael. "La Pasionaria." *People*, Vol. 40, No. 15, October 11, 1993, pp. 109–110.

Parsell, D. L. "New Photo Book an Homage to Last U.S. Wildlands." *National Geographic News*, October 29, 2002.

Quinn, Judy. "HarperCollins Gets to Keep Kingsolver." *Publishers Weekly*, Vol. 244, No. 6, February 10, 1997, p. 19.

Reid, Calvin. "SMP Author Copies Kingsolver Text." *Publishers Weekly*, April 30, 2001.

"Review: *Prodigal Summer*." *AudioFile*, June/July 2001.

Rosen, Judith. "Kingsolver Tour Helps Indies Clean Up." *Publishers Weekly*, Vol. 247, No. 48, November 27, 2000, pp. 26–27.

Rosenfeld, Megan. "Novelist in Hog Heaven; 'Pigs' Brings Home the Bacon While Its Author Writers Her Heart Out." *Washington Post*, July 14, 1993, p. D1.

Ross, Jean W. "Interview." *Contemporary Authors*, Vol. 134. Detroit: Gale Research, 1992, pp. 284–290.

Rubin, Sylvia. "Africa Kept Its Hold on Kingsolver." *San Francisco Chronicle*, October 30, 1998, p. C1.

Rubinstein, Roberta. "The Mark of Africa." *World & I*, Vol. 14, No. 4, April 1999, p. 254.

Siegel, Lee. "Sweet and Low." *New Republic*, Vol. 220, No. 12, March 22, 1999, pp. 30–37.

Stolba, Christine. "Feminists Go to War." *Women's Quarterly*, Winter 2002.

Van Boven, Sarah. "Review." *Newsweek*, Vol. 132, No. 19, November 9, 1998, p. 76.

Vilbig, Pete. "Meet the Author." *Literary Cavalcade*, Vol. 52, No. 1, September 1999, p. 13.

"We Won't Deny Our Consciences: Prominent Americans Have Issued This Statement on the War on Terror." *Guardian Unlimited*, June 14, 2002.

Weaver, Teresa K. "Stranger Than Fiction: Writers Turn Rockers—Musical Talent Optional." *Atlanta Journal-Constitution*, May 18, 2003, p. M1.

Willis, Meredith Sue. "Barbara Kingsolver, Moving On." *Appalachian Journal*, Vol. 22, No. 1, 1994, pp. 78–86.

York, Byron. "At War, Follow the Money." *National Review*, February 24, 2003.

Kingsolver's Genealogy

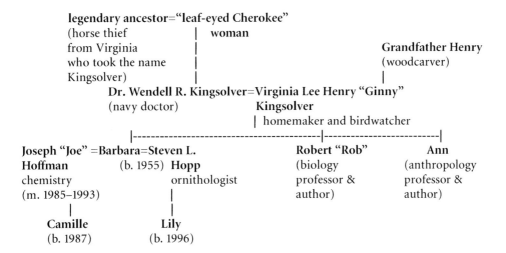

legendary ancestor="leaf-eyed Cherokee"
(horse thief | woman
from Virginia | **Grandfather Henry**
who took the name | (woodcarver)
Kingsolver) | |
         Dr. Wendell R. Kingsolver=**Virginia Lee Henry "Ginny"**
          (navy doctor)   **Kingsolver**
                                 | homemaker and birdwatcher
         |---|------------------------|
Joseph "Joe" =**Barbara**=**Steven L.**   **Robert "Rob"**   **Ann**
Hoffman   (b. 1955) **Hopp**   (biology   (anthropology
chemistry   ornithologist   professor &   professor &
(m. 1985–1993)   author)   author)
     | |
    Camille   **Lily**
    (b. 1987)   (b. 1996)

Barbara Kingsolver:
A Literary Companion

activism

Writer Barbara Kingsolver's life falls neatly into two segments—the day-to-day ecofeminist who battles right-wing militarists and polluters and the quicksilver literary mind that produces fiction, nonfiction, and verse armed with unsubtle barbs directed at the same enemies. She explained her purpose in a speech to the 1993 American Booksellers Convention: "I believe that writing about people who believe in a better world—creating at least the possibility of that—is the next best thing to living in one" ("An Address"). Critical gibes don't bother her. She openly rejoices in ruffling the opposition: "The people who have panned my work as being political are people who are not on my side, so I feel kind of proud of that" (Epstein). Her success with the reading public attests to a skill at uniting powerful fiction with timely opinions.

Contributing to Kingsolver's pride are the gung-ho humanistic scenarios in her fiction. In *The Bean Trees* (1988), Mattie, operator of the Jesus Is Lord tire store, aids Father William, a blue-jeans priest, in shuttling Guatemalan and Salvadoran refugees in and out of her over-the-shop residence. For backup, she consults with Terry, a doctor on a bike who treats torture wounds without reporting them to authorities. On television she speaks toward the camera the trio's simple credo: "We have a legal obligation to take in people whose lives are in danger" (p. 103). The declaration directs the actions of Mattie's friend Taylor Greer, who decides that a child thrust into her car deserves the best mothering that an inexperienced single mom can provide. The strength of that decision forms the warp and woof of the novel and its non-sequel, *Pigs in Heaven* (1993).

In her third novel, *Animal Dreams* (1990), Kingsolver pursues grassroots issues by attacking willful poisoning of a river by the Black Mountain Mining Company. The text describes slow strangulation of Grace, Arizona, from the acid leachate of copper tailings that taint the river. Adding to the citizens' desperation are threats that the mining firm will interrupt the water supply entirely by damming the river, a dodge intended to stave off charges from the Environmental Protection Agency. The nation's strongest environmental watchdog, the EPA began monitoring air, soil, water, and animals and plants in 1970 by maintaining strict standards and prosecuting flouters of the law. One possible counter action against mining authorities is the curtailing of operations, which would settle the issue of the poisoned river and give it a chance to self-clean and reduce its toxicity.

The answer to Grace's pollution problem comes from within. A biology teacher, Codi Noline, gains insight into community activism by supporting Hispanic women who craft piñatas with peacock tail feathers supplied by Doña Althea. On December 10, 1986, the women peddle their wares in front of Tucson's Café Gertrude Stein with the rapport of old hands at street commerce. By January, slick magazines cheer the community effort, making the women's handiwork "a hot decorator item in gentrified adobe neighborhoods" (p. 263). Of their success, critic Meredith Sue Willis described the community of Grace as "a world in which folk art and *esprit de corps* can save the environment" (Willis, p. 83).

As a proponent of human rights, Kingsolver reserves her most potent accusations for *The Poisonwood Bible* (1998), a masterwork that depicts the post-colonial turmoil of central Africa. A missionary's wife, Orleanna Price, speaking the author's point of view about blame, notes that the modern world thinks of exploitation as an act of the first profiteers of treasure from the dark continent. She remarks, "It's easy to point at other men, conveniently dead, starting with the ones who first scooped up mud from the riverbanks to catch the scent of a source" (p. 9). She batters herself for the cost of a "snow-white conscience," which she sullies by taking literally the command of the book of Genesis, which urges Adam to "have dominion over every creature that moved upon the earth" (*Ibid.*).

Orleanna's activism is chiefly motherhood. From her womb come four girls, who give themselves to black Africa, the site of their father's misguided mission. The first donation is five-year-old Ruth May, who plays cheerfully with Kilangan village children, teaches them "Mother, May I?," then dies at age six from the bite of a green mamba. In grief and self-blame, her twin sisters bear the pain of loss and turn their adult lives to a selfless activism that suits each. In Atlanta, Georgia, Adah becomes Dr. Price, a specialist and researcher in contagious disease indigenous to the Congo. Leah, under the married name Madame Ngemba, returns to America only for training on agronomics and carries information on nutrition and sanitation to the refugees who flee Zaire to shelter at a communal farm in Angola. Like her mother, she offers womanly gifts of acceptance and compassion and shares the life of the Congolese as though she were a native.

Kingsolver's fifth novel, *Prodigal Summer* (2000), perpetuates her interest in the environment by blending the voices of three outspoken female altruists. Deanna Wolfe, a hermetic forest ranger on Zebulon Mountain, voices the conservationist's call to protect natural habitats and foster the return of the coyote to the wild. In the valley below, Nannie Land Rawley, Deanna's foster mother, fights a neighbor's insecticides in order to maintain an organic apple orchard. Both Nannie and Lusa Maluf Landowski, a nearby goatherd, symbolize community activists who are willing to appear eccentric by rebelling against accepted agricultural practice. The small triumphs of the female trio express Kingsolver's belief that world betterment is accomplished one increment at a time.

See also **altruism, bureaucracy, ecofeminism, Ben Linder, Adolph Murie, nature, Anatole Ngemba, pollution, Nannie Rawley, recycling, women**

• *Further Reading*

Doyle, R. Erica. "Barbara Kingsolver: The Bellwether Prize." *Ms.* June/July 2001, p. 89.
Epstein, Robin. "Barbara Kingsolver." *Progressive*, Vol. 60, No. 2, February 1996, pp. 33–37.
Willis, Meredith Sue. "Barbara Kingsolver, Moving On." *Appalachian Journal*, Vol. 22, No. 1, 1994, pp. 78–86.

Africa

Over a decade, Kingsolver debated about writing a book on Africa and seesawed on the most appealing form. In the essay "Why I Am a Danger to the Public" (1986), she states her choices: "If I were to write a nonfiction book about the brief blossoming and destruction of the independence of the Congo, and what the CIA had to do with it, then probably all eighty-five people who are interested in the subject would read it." She chooses to cloak the global issue under less volatile themes of family, ethnicity, and life in the jungle. Her instincts were right — *The Poisonwood Bible* (1998) succeeds because it entertains while it enlightens. In response to so broad an undertaking, a *Washington Post* reviewer, novelist Jane Smiley, saw greatness. She observed, "Kingsolver's novel is ambitious in that it calls into question the whole history of the European and American exploitation of Africa" (Smiley).

Kingsolver's fictional re-creation of the Congo bustles with the elements of life and commerce that she gained from visits to places she saw during a family sojourn in Africa at age six. The task of reshaping life in a foreign continent, she declared, "was a challenge on a whole new order of magnitude," referring to her previous fictional scenarios set in the American Southwest, literally her own backyard (Hoback, p. 1e). Her fictional Congolese microcosm reflects what reviewer Sally Gabb calls "a world of violence and violation, a people of endurance and energy," whom characters view through the framework of American experience (Gabb). Challenging survival for hygiene-minded Georgians are the buzzard-decked meat market in Kilanga village and the daily struggle for sanitation and sustenance. Within enchanting beauties of vine and flower, Orleanna Price, a missionary's wife and mother of four girls, marvels at "hours of labor spent procuring the simplest elements: water, heat, anything that might pass for disinfectant" (p. 92). More fearful are epidemic *kakakaka* (enteritis), seasonal malaria, marauding ants, and serpents that "could knock a child dead by spitting in her eyes" (p. 96).

The author pictures arrival at Kilanga on the Kwilu River in June 1959 through the introduction of an Episcopalian missionary couple, Frank and Janna Underdown, who are leaving their mission outpost after "it had gone into a slump" (p. 17). The comment suggests that the Underdowns failed to proselytize villagers to Episcopalianism, but choose not to accept blame. The Reverend Nathan Price rapidly compounds the theological lapse with his failure to acknowledge the humanity of Kilangans, a leap of faith that his wife and three of his children eventually make. On familiarizing herself with local customs, Orleanna understands such folkways as the pacing of days in hands rather than weeks. By denoting market day on the fifth finger, the Congolese hold in their digits the span of days that regularly returns, like the seasons, to markets for their produce and the barter of food for their tables. In contrast, Nathan is too stiff-necked to acknowledge that Africa demands that its people adapt to a unique, sometimes life-threatening environment.

The novel, which presents from the peasant point of view an explosive revolutionary era, is what reviewer John Leonard describes as a two-edged tool — "a magnificent fiction and a ferocious bill of indictment" (Leonard, p. 28). Leah realizes that the continual begging of village children for food and money is a cultural element: "They were accustomed to the distribution of excess, and couldn't fathom why we held ourselves apart" (p. 453). Even Rachel Price, the teen queen complainer, perceives that "you can't just sashay into the jungle aiming to change it all over to the Christian style, without expecting the jungle to change you right back" (p. 515). After three and a half decades in Africa, she realizes the faulty logic in investors and exploiters who expect an easy time in the Congo: "If it was as easy as they thought it was going to be, why, they'd be done by now, and Africa would look just like America with more palm trees" (p. 515).

Orleanna views the colonial Congo in feminist terms as the "barefoot bride of men who took her jewels and promised the Kingdom," a dual diatribe against profiteers and missionaries (p. 201). She sees its ultimate fate as being "left in the hands of soulless, empty men," the metaphoric chess players she envisions in the introduction to Book Four (p. 323). But ultimately, "Africa swallowed the conqueror's music and sang a new song of her own," Orleanna's praise for a nation that is able to reclaim, recycle, and get on with life (p. 385). Critics laud this celebration of the stalwart Congolese and elevated Kingsolver to a new height for commending local survivors of the post-colonial backlash. One naysayer, Brad S. Born, contested praise for Kingsolver's post-colonial sensitivity with an opposing view: "Instead of Africa in the hands of bad American man, we have Africa in the heart of good American woman. And Africa is still being had" (Born).

Kingsolver introduces the wave of Lumumba popularity in the late 1950s through the Price children's point of view, an immature grasp of a global issue. In a riposte to a pro–Lumumba Belgian doctor who sets Ruth May's arm, she hears Nathan roar, "American aid will be the Congo's salvation. You'll see!," a pathetic, yet ominous opinion based on his ignorance of African history and American do-gooderism (p. 121). Rachel's curiosity about a newspaper from December 1959 reveals the plan of Soviet Premier Nikita Khrushchev to seize the Belgian Congo. The article, an erroneous overview composed by a New York reporter, pictures the Belgians as heroes for battling native cannibalism. With her usual narcissism and lobbying to return to Georgia, she responds, "Jeez Louise, if Khrushchev wants the Congo he can have it, if you ask me," a Western dismissal of the country ironically shared by many (p. 161).

The Congolese earn a brief independence, a small compensation for decades of woe. The Prices learn from Frank and Janna Underdown that, under the aegis of King Baudouin I of Belgium, the Congo will hold elections in May 1960 and declare independence the following June thirtieth. After the province of Katanga secedes under Moise Tshombe, chief of the Lunda tribe, turmoil in Léopoldville and Stanleyville results in rioting, looting, and murder. The swirl of violence forces Nathan to side with other whites, including Eeben Axelroot, a brigand who roughs up and threatens Ruth May for spying on his diamond-smuggling. To Rachel, he indicates that changes in the Congo's government require him to make more trips south to Elisabethville, a repeated round trip for nefarious purposes to undermine the people's cry for liberation from foreign meddlers.

In the Congo's metamorphosis under strongman Mobutu Sese Seko, after the dictator slaughters Premier Patrice Lumumba and quells the people's idealism, punishment exacted on peasants is brutal and protracted. Mobutu sets the region in a perilous direction under the new name of Zaire, a churning crucible heated with foreign funds and stirred by the military. At an oddly upbeat turning point in world opinion, the 1974 Muhammad Ali–George Foreman championship prizefight, called the "Rumble in the Jungle," draws the wrong kind of attention to the tottering nation. By staging the fight in Africa, Mobutu acquires global respectability for a regime later internationally denounced as savage. Kingsolver retreats from the historic era with a brief glimpse of neighboring Angola, the kind of country that the Congo might have become under an egalitarian like Lumumba.

To *New York Times* interviewer Bill Goldstein, in 1998, Kingsolver expressed continued interest in Africa's miseries. In particular, she stated a hope for self-determination for the Congolese: "I believe that the legacy of U.S. intervention in Africa is so ghastly, it would be an enormous relief to see it end altogether. In the Congo specifically, thirty-five years under the dictator Mobutu, who was installed and continuously supported by the U.S., has resulted in complete devastation" (Goldstein).

See also **Tata Kuvudundu, Patrice Lumumba, Mobutu Sese Seko, Mama Mwanza, Tata Ndu, Anatole Ngemba,** *The Poisonwood Bible*, **poverty, Mama Tataba**

• *Further Reading*

Arten, Isaac. "Review: *The Poisonwood Bible*." *Midwest Book Review*, December 2001.

Born, Brad S. "Kingsolver's Gospel for Africa: (Western White Female) Heart of Goodness." *Mennonite Life*, Vol. 56, No. 1, March 2001.

Bromberg, Judith. "A Complex Novel About Faith, Family and Dysfunction." *National Catholic Reporter*, Vol. 35, No. 20, March 19, 1999, p. 13.

Fletcher, Yael Simpson. "History Will One Day Have Its Say: New Perspectives on Colonial and Postcolonial Congo." *Radical History Review*, Vol. 84, 2002, pp. 195–207.

Gabb, Sally. "Into Africa: A Review of *The Poisonwood Bible*." *Field Notes*, Vol. 11, No. 1, Summer 2001.

Goldstein, Bill. "An Author Chat with Barbara Kingsolver." *New York Times*, October 30, 1998.

Hoback, Jane. "Kingsolver's Holy Grail Mythic in Tone." *Denver Rocky Mountain News*, October 18, 1998, p. 1e.

Leonard, John. "Kingsolver in the Jungle, Catullus & Wolfe at the Door." *Nation*, Vol. 268, No. 2, January 11–18, 1999, pp. 28–33.

Markels, Julian. "Coda: Imagining History in *The Poisonwood Bible*." *Monthly Review Press*, September 2003.

Smiley, Jane. "In the Fields of the Lord." *Washington Post*, October 11, 1998.

All Souls' Day

In *Animal Dreams* (1990), Kingsolver opens the text on November 2, 1986, *El Dia del Muerte* (The Day of the Dead) or All Souls' Day, a Roman Catholic feast day on which families commemorate the deceased and celebrate their part in the life cycle. The purpose of intercessory prayers and ritual is to purify departed souls of earthly sin to free them of purgatory and ready them for heaven. Celebration of the day began in the mid-eleventh century from the activism of Abbot Odilo of Cluny, the archangel of monks, as a complement to All Saints' Day, November 1, a commemoration of the lives of the blessed. In Kingsolver's novel, children celebrate the occasion by adorning the graves of their forebears with marigolds. The graves become an indelible landscape drenched in love and respect. The hillside setting is replete with the family history necessary to reconnect Codi Noline with her homeland and what critic Vicky Newman calls the "bricolage of her memory" that her father concealed with lies and posturing (Newman, p. 110).

The "bittersweet Mexican holiday" returns in mid-text as families go about the business of cleaning, decorating, and honoring burial sites (p. 159). Codi is enjoying the trimming of graves with stones, bottles, and marigold petals and the gilding of children with flower pollen when she stumbles across the interment site of the Nolinas, a coming-to-knowledge that her family has more connection with Grace than she ever knew. In token of the love bestowed on community children, she notes, "I have never seen a town that gave so much — so much of what *counts*— to its children" (p. 165). The action and thought reveal Codie's longing for strong familial love, an element missing in her upbringing, and for release from grief over her dead child.

By novel's end, All Soul's Day has grown into a powerful motif of reclamation. In the company of Viola Domingos, one of the fifty mothers who foster Codi, the two return to the graveyard on November 2, 1989, to decorate family plots two years after Hallie Noline's murder in Nicaragua and Doc Homer's death from Alzheimer's disease. Of her own participation in the feast day, Codi murmurs, "I don't know why," a suggestion of the subconscious forces that impel her toward local ritual and family gatherings (p. 339). No longer demanding restitution for her wretchedness in childhood, Codi uses her hands to smooth the stones on Doc's resting place, bringing a final "order to his cosmos," a kinetic forgiveness echoed in her peaceful heart (p. 340).

See also **Viola Domingos, love, survival**

• *Further Reading*

Gonzalez-Crussi, Frank. *The Day of the Dead and Other Mortal Reflections.* New York: Harcourt-Brace, 1993.

Newman, Vicky. "Compelling Ties: Landscape, Community, and Sense of Place." *Peabody Journal of Education*, Vol. 70, No. 4, Summer 1995, pp. 105–118.

altruism

Altruism is the force in Kingsolver's novels that elevates them from entertainment to didactic humanism. She explained to *New York Times* interviewer Bill Goldstein:

> I would like to write literature that invites readers to examine their society, their prejudices, their relationships, and the balances or imbalances of power contained within our culture. If this illuminates a life, that's wonderful. If it motivates progress towards a more humane society, even better [Goldstein].

Her writings have energized a cadre of Kingsolver readers who absorb and practice the idealism of her themes and deck her with honors.

Kingsolver's ability to amuse and simultaneously elucidate serious problems is a rare gift. As reviewer Karen Karbo explains in the *New York Times Book Review*, "Her medicine is meant for the head, the heart, and the soul — and it goes down dangerously, blissfully, easily" (Karbo, p. 9). The microcosm of neighborhood and female networking in *The Bean Trees* (1988), for example, enhances Taylor Greer's job repairing wheels at the Jesus Is Lord tire store and her relationship with an activist employer modeling everyday applications of "Love thy neighbor." In time, Taylor unravels the mysterious comings and goings from Mattie's apartment and finds herself involved in a late twentieth-century underground railroad.

To set up opposing arguments for aiding Central American refugees, Kingsolver creates a loving safety net comprised of Father William, Mattie the tire dealer, Terry the doctor, and Taylor, the amateur courier. On the anti side, the author proposes a stiff, overdressed matron named Virgie Mae Valentine Parsons, who does little more than sniff at the influx of Central American refugees. Mouthing the conservative line mainly out of ignorance, she predicts, "Before you know it the whole world will be here jibbering and jabbering till we won't know it's America" (p. 106). She charges with a tedious truism: "They ought to stay put in their own dirt, not come here taking up jobs" (p. 107). Kingsolver positions Parsons's ethnocentric comments as a lone island in the stream, leaving to the reader the task of deciding the ethics of civil disobedience when lives are in danger.

As a testimonial to women's mutual powers to rescue, heal, and uplift, Kingsolver admires individual females for their coping skills and their insistence on a safe, decent place in which to work, live, and rear their young, a theme that also empowers the documentary *Holding the Line: Women in the Great Arizona Mine Strike of 1983* (1989) and the novels *Animal Dreams* (1990) and *The Poisonwood Bible* (1998). To avoid demeaning all males, the author assures a spot of heroism in *The Bean Trees* to bold, generous-hearted men like the priest and doctor, magistrate Jonas Wilford Armistead, Dr. Pelinowsky, and Estevan, a low-key hero torn by devotion to profession and family. Working together, the altruists alleviate a depth of heartache that wracks all concerned. The text reduces the war against domestic abuse, pedophilia, poverty, discrimination, and political brutality to a one-on-one resolve to improve the world one victim at a time. As Taylor Greer explains to Lou Ann Ruiz about pornography's discounting of women, the individual must take action: "You can't just sit there, you got to get pissed off" (p. 150). After the non-sequel, *Pigs in Heaven* (1993), reached the bestseller list, Kingsolver accounted for her altruism: "I was trained to believe that you must, as an individual, do something about the wrong things you see" (Rosenfeld, p. D1).

See also **activism, bureaucracy, Brother Fowles, humanism, Patrice Lumumba, Mama Mwanza, Anatole Ngemba, rescue, survival**

• *Further Reading*

Epstein, Robin. "Barbara Kingsolver." *Progressive*, Vol. 60, No. 2, February 1996, pp. 33–37.

Goldstein, Bill. "An Author Chat with Barbara Kingsolver." *New York Times*, October 30, 1998.

Karbo, Karen. "And Baby Makes Two." *New York Times Book Review*, June 27, 1993, p. 9.

Rosenfeld, Megan. "Novelist in Hog Heaven; 'Pigs' Brings Home the Bacon While Its Author Writes Her Heart Out." *Washington Post*, July 14, 1993, p. D1.

ambition

Characters in Kingsolver's writings seesaw on the issues of individual drive and accomplishment. While investigating an Arizona mine strike, she compiled interviews and impressions for a documentary, *Holding the Line: Women in the Great Arizona Mine Strike of 1983* (1989). At the core of the text is an authorial admiration for women who intend to better their homes and families by challenging the niggardliness of the mining industry. In Kingsolver's view, "the women who walked to work every morning in their coveralls, hairnets, and hard hats, telling jokes and swinging their lunch buckets, were tugging at the moorings of the status quo" (p. 1). Their ambition kept them at the forefront of a grassroots demand for steady work, on-the-job fairness, racial and gender equality, and worker benefits for all who kept the Phelps Dodge mining corporation in business.

Kingsolver's fiction models a similar regard for ambition, especially among females, non-whites, the working class, and other marginalized people. In *Pigs in Heaven* (1993), the prick of ambition impels Cherokee scholar Annawake Fourkiller to enter law school to serve her people as an efficient ambassador. Cash Stillwater, a Cherokee beadworker, resettles in Jackson Hole, Wyoming, to make jewelry for rich tourists. Both characters return to the tribal womb to shelter in an extended family that respects them for moral judgment more than for fame or wealth.

In the novel's resolution, the author employs the coming-to-knowledge in both Annawake and Cash as a means of settling the dilemma of how to assure Turtle Greer's ethnicity without violating the bond she shares with Taylor Greer, her non-native adoptive mother. Annawake conducts the hearing that lays before the community the rights of both claimants. Cash, who has romanced Taylor's mother Alice, provides the touch of grace — an unexpected marriage proposal that links all parties in a widening framework of kinship. Thus, ambition serves both Annawake and Cash as they expand their focus beyond self to the Cherokee people.

Kingsolver examines more thoroughly the career aims of biology teacher Codi Noline, protagonist of *Animal Dreams* (1990). In a no-win argument with Doc Homer about following his profession up to the point of licensing, she admits to being a drop-out medical student, a "bag lady with an education" (p. 259). She ponders the ebb and flow of her career drive: "I know that a woman's ambitions aren't supposed to fall and rise and veer off course this way, like some poor bird caught in a storm" (p. 107). While delivering a baby feet first on a slope of Mount Ida on the island of Crete, she discovered that she required nerve and empathy to become a full-fledged physician. Lacking the fierce drive of her younger sister Hallie, Codi excuses flight from the birthing scene on the basis of the strangeness of living among the poor in a far-off place. Her return to Grace, Arizona, allows her to apply medical skills in the high school classroom, a setting in which she feels secure and valued for her knowledge. In the end, Codi's success comes through a form of educational recycling, a teaching job that improves local teens' understanding of biology and human reproduction.

Late in the twentieth century, Kingsolver moved farther afield to study ambition. In *The Poisonwood Bible* (1998), the strictures of life in equatorial Africa force characters to rethink their aims. The Reverend Nathan Price, a self-ennobling missionary, eclipses his family's individual hopes by volunteering them for a post in the Congo. There they find uneducated children like the houseboy Nelson with obvious skills. Because of their birth in a third world country, they stand zero chance of going to college.

In contrast to the yearnings of Congolese children, the author presents the mundane longings of Nathan's teenage girls. Leah Price, in her more introspective moments, cultivates self-loathing for skipping two grades and becoming a flat-chested seventh-grader in the ninth grade. Because of the maturity lag, she disdains male-female camaraderie and declares, "Kissing looks like too much of somebody else's dental hygiene if you ask me" (p. 149). Choosing among missionary or teacher or farmer, she opts for an unconfining outdoor career where she can "wear pants if at all possible" (p. 149). Surprisingly, Kingsolver is able to salvage Leah through a romance with Anatole Ngemba, an African idealist.

Kingsolver uses layers of the Price genealogy as evidence of unfulfilled hopes from one generation reaching fruition in the next. To stimulate dreams of the future, Orleanna Price sets her girls to learning needlework to fill their hope chests. Leah, whose horizons remain occluded, remarks: "Rachel hoped too much and ran out of material, while the rest of us hoped too little and ran out of steam" (p. 152). Ironically, it is Leah who undergoes a transformation that revamps her father's selfish ambitions into her own pragmatic aid to the Congolese. She fulfills her mother's dreams by rearing four biracial sons, Pascal, Patrice, Martin-Lothaire, and Nataniel, who establish worthy ambitions of their own. In the end, Leah Price Ngemba is the book's crowning success story, followed by the medical research career of Leah's twin, Dr. Adah Price.

The struggle for attainment in *Prodigal Summer* (2000), Kingsolver's fifth novel, aligns the lives of disparate citizens of Zebulon Valley, a farming community overlooked by a national forest preserve. The text depicts no-nonsense wildlife biologist

Deanna Wolfe as an idealistic naturalist who adopts her job as a holy calling. Down in the lowlands, Garnett S. Walker III, a former adviser to a 4-H club, professes the same sanctity in agriculture, his chosen field. He states an unyielding set of principles regarding the supervision of property and the control of weeds and insects. After a rainy summer, the collapse of a fifty-year-old oak requires immediate attention. In his view, "Any farmer worth his salt walked his property lines after every storm to look for damage like this," a dictum he apparently takes seriously (p. 269). Kingsolver implies that, unlike Deanna, the stiff-necked farmer is more concerned with local opinions of his husbandry than with nature itself. She redeems Garnett by expressing his late-in-life intent to hybridize a strain of chestnut trees resilient to disease. The return of the grand chestnut to American forests is a worthy endeavor that would reap no monetary profits in his lifetime, but would ally Garnett's name with a noble conservation effort.

See also **autonomy, Barbie, Brother Fowles, Tata Nganga Kuvudunda, Nathan Price**

• *Further Reading*

MacEoin, Gary. "Prodigal Summer: A Novel." *National Catholic Reporter*, Vol. 38, No. 3, November 9, 2001, p. 19.
Pritchard, Melissa. "Review." *Chicago Tribune Books*, May 18, 1988.

Animal Dreams

Typified as ecofeminism disguised as romance, Kingsolver's *Animal Dreams* (1990) builds a multi-layered series of conflicts into a satisfying conclusion. After the Noline family experiences a fourteen-year separation, Codi Noline rebonds with her ailing father while absorbing the native American values of family, community, education, and love of land. At her arrival in Grace, Arizona, in August 1986, the Black Mountain Mining Company has been closed for a decade. Upon learning that a human-generated poison from the mine's copper tailings strangles the river and threatens to flood Gracela Canyon, she aids a women's collective in fighting big business with an unusual money-raising scheme. Her reasoning is idealistic: "People can forget, and forget, and forget, but the land has a memory. The lakes and the rivers are still hanging on to the DDT and every other insult we ever gave them" (p. 255). The words spring from the author's own dedication to earth and its survival.

Critic Meredith Sue Willis categorizes the novel as a fiction of community for its realliance of Codi with fostering women, a disgruntled father, and a former love, the father of her stillborn child. Willis characterizes the residents of Grace as "Earthy, humorous, intensely interested in one another's business, and deeply, gratifyingly good," a trait they hold in common with picketers in Kingsolver's feminist documentary *Holding the Line: Women in the Great Arizona Mine Strike of 1983* (1989), Mattie and Estevan in *The Bean Trees* (1988), Alice Greer and Cash Stillwater in *Pigs in Heaven* (1993), Kilangan village women in *The Poisonwood Bible* (1998), and Nannie Land Rawley and the five loving Widener sisters in *Prodigal Summer* (2000)

(Willis, p. 83). Contributing to Kingsolver's perception of self-effacing village women morphing into protesters was her experience in covering the Phelps Dodge Company mine strike and writing *Holding the Line*, a tribute to female spirit and innovation.

The town's name becomes a convenient image for building metaphors. Grace, the gift that doesn't have to be deserved, accrues to Codi as she allows other people to love and nurture her. With lover Loyd Peregrina, she ventures into Santa Rosalia Pueblo and finds family members eager to incorporate her in seasonal ritual. Among members of the Stitch and Bitch Club, Codi receives acknowledgement of her scientific expertise. With Uda Odell, Codi clarifies murky memories of the day her dying mother was loaded into the helicopter and of the loving females who tried to replace Alice in the Noline children's lives. Eventually, the flow of grace within Codi trickles out to Doc Homer, the demanding single parent who was unable to embrace his girls in a father-to-daughter relationship or to bid farewell to the small bundle that might have developed into a grandchild.

Near the novel's end, Codi can look back on her pilgrimage home as a personal struggle for self. Of the geographic and emotional terrain, she declares, "No route out of Grace was an easy climb" (p. 340). Troubling her spirit is the helplessness she feels against the news of her sister Hallie's kidnap by Contras and the long wait for the final word that Hallie was shot through the head along a Nicaraguan roadside in the company of seven other volunteer teachers. Codi rules out contacting the president of the United States and charges that the enemy is "fully supported by the richest sugar daddy in the modern world" (p. 258). The gracelessness of the sociopolitical message freights the novel with despair until Kingsolver restores hope in Codi's reinterment of her stillborn child on family property, her reunion with the spot where Alice Noline died, and the anticipation of another child fathered by Loyd. Kingsolver uses the children as elements of blessing that unite characters and give them hope.

See also **All Soul's Day, Emelina Domingos, Viola Domingos, journey motif, motherhood, Cosima "Codi" Noline, Halimeda "Hallie" Noline, Homer Noline, Noline genealogy, Loyd Peregrina**

* *Further Reading*

Gray, Paul. "Call of the Eco-Feminist." *Time*, Vol. 136, No. 13, September 24, 1990, p. 87.

Murrey, Loretta Martin. "The Loner and the Matriarchal Community in Barbara Kingsolver's *The Bean Trees* and *Pigs in Heaven*." *Southern Studies*, Vol. 5, No. 1–2, Spring & Summer 1994, pp. 155–164.

Rubinstein, Roberta. "The Mark of Africa." *World & I*, Vol. 14, No. 4, April 1999, p. 254.

Willis, Meredith Sue. "Barbara Kingsolver, Moving On." *Appalachian Journal*, Vol. 22, No. 1, 1994, pp. 78–86.

Another America: Otra America

Midway in her career, Kingsolver's composition of *Another America: Otra America* (1992) freed her from prose restraints with a venture into verse. The thirty-two entries appear in a harmonious arrangement on facing pages in English and in Spanish, translated by Chilean writer Rebeca Cartes. Kingsolver opens with six poems grouped under the heading "The House Divided." She took the phrase from Abraham Lincoln's 1858 speech warning that "A house divided against itself cannot stand," an image he drew from Mark 3:25 and Mark 37:20 to express his belief that the United States could not survive if some states allowed slavery and some didn't. In similar fashion, Kingsolver uses the metaphor to picture the classism, racism, sexism, violence, militarism, and other issues that separate and isolate people.

The first poem, "Deadline," dated January 15, 1991, refers to the onset of the Gulf War. Protesters holding candles bear "old hearts in your pockets," a metaphor for the longstanding tradition of pacifists who have consistently rejected aggression as a solution to world problems (p. 3). In "What the Janitor Heard in the Elevator," the author captures the materialism and thoughtlessness of a woman who casually fires a maid for breaking a vase. To simplify relations in their homes, the speaker and her wealthy friend reject domestic help who can't speak English. The last of the section, "Justicia," describes the wolf that threatens McAllen, Texas, and alludes to fleeing Central Americans who deserve hospitality rather than annihilation. The motif reflects Kingsolver's persistent placement of human beings in the animal kingdom and her belief that the laws of nature impinge on all dwellers on planet earth.

The second division describes newcomers to America as "The Visitors," a term that implies a situation requiring welcome and courtesy toward outsiders. The first poem, "Refuge," depicts a Chicana named Juana whom immigration agents raped before deporting. Kingsolver empathizes with the woman, who is determined enough to "use the last of [her] hunger" in an illegal crossing of the border (p. 19). In writing "For Sacco and Vanzetti," the poet honors another bureaucratic scenario in which two immigrant pacifists are unjustly executed for murder. She singles out for recognition Ethel Rosenberg, the first woman put to death for treason. The poem connects Kingsolver with the *cause célèbre* of the 1920s, when leftists openly revolted against the repression of immigrants to America. Overall, the stirring, eloquent volume speaks Kingsolver's humanism and compassion for the underdog.

See also **Ernesto Cardenal**

• *Further Reading*

DeMarr, Mary Jean. *Barbara Kingsolver: A Critical Companion.* Westport, Conn.: Greenwood, 1999.
Kuhn, Deanna. "Review: *Another America: Otra America.*" *School Library Journal,* August 1992.
Ratner, Rochelle. "Poetry: Barbara Kingsolver." *Library Journal,* February 15, 1992.

autonomy

The emergence of the individual is a forceful action in Kingsolver's writings. Her female seekers— Taylor Greer and Lou Ann Ruiz in *The Bean Trees* (1988), miners in the documentary *Holding the Line: Women in the Great Arizona Mine Strike of 1983* (1989), Codi Noline in *Animal Dreams* (1990), Alice Greer and Annawake Fourkiller in *Pigs in Heaven* (1993), Orleanna, Leah, and Adah Price in *The Poisonwood*

Bible (1998), and widowed farmer Lusa Maluf Landowski and single parents Deanna Wolfe and Nannie Land Rawley in *Prodigal Summer* (2000)—travel circuitous, punishing routes to physical and emotional growth. Out of self-respect and a generous amount of cussedness, they attempt to build their own nests and line them with consolation to insulate the spirit from external battery. Ultimately, Taylor, Lou Ann, Codi, and the striking miners discover the synergy of autonomy amid a loving community while Orleanna, Leah, Adah, Lusa, Deanna, and Nannie gain from woman-to-woman networking and a reliance on nature. As a result, the reward of self-definition chimes harmoniously with the support of others who want to see the striver succeed.

More self-directed than Taylor Greer's two-novel fight to retain custody of her child and Lou Ann's acceptance of divorce and single motherhood, Codi's battle returns her to unfinished business in her hometown of Grace, Arizona, where she never felt accepted. By flourishing as a teacher in a high school biology classroom and rekindling love for her first beau, Loyd Peregrina, she summons the courage to grieve for her dead mother and stillborn child and to survive a subsequent loss, both sister and father, all that is left of the nuclear family. According to reviewer Carolyn Cooke, Codi "discovers the comforts of tradition and obligation and migrates from the shapeless melancholia of youth to a deeper humanity" (Cooke). By embracing the fifty mothers of the Stitch and Bitch Club and allowing herself to claim membership in the town, she drops the animosities that corrode her heart and inhibit the ripening of her personality, two deterrents mirrored in the local copper mine's pollution of the river and stunting of orchards.

In Kingsolver's African odyssey, *The Poisonwood Bible* (1998), the wife and teen daughters forced to follow the Reverend Nathan Price to a mission in the Congo obtain their independence only through tragedy. After snakebite kills Ruth May, the youngest child, Orleanna Price strikes out with daughters Rachel and twins Leah and Adah toward relief from starvation and from Nathan Price's persistent sabotage of home and community harmony. During a national revolution that promises the Congo's autonomy, Rachel, the self-seeking oldest girl, moves directly toward civilization with the aid of an unlikely rescuer, Eeben Axelroot, a bush pilot who shackles her in a mercenary sexual relationship, an insidious form of debasement. To achieve autonomy, she falls back on money, land, sexual manipulation of her lovers, and control of the Equatorial Hotel, a fiefdom that grants her a medieval form of power and self-esteem.

After Orleanna and Adah make their way home to Georgia, Leah remains behind and takes the most difficult path toward self-actualization by marrying Anatole Ngemba, an idealistic Congolese revolutionary. Thoroughly acclimated to life among poor peasants, she manages to embrace autonomy as a Congolese wife who still harbors American chutzpah. Her evolving motherhood in a Kinshasa slum survives Anatole's imprisonment and sources of kwashiorkor and parasites in her children. After brief sojourns in Georgia with Orleanna and Adah and training at Emory University in agronomics, Leah returns to central Africa even more resolved to make a go of life on her own terms, as wife, mother, and model for refugee women.

Like Leah, the female protagonists of *Prodigal Summer* make the most of selfhood through ingenuity and perseverance. Deanna Wolfe, the outspoken forest ranger on Zebulon Mountain, refuses to compromise her ideal of the safe return of the coyote to eastern forests. When a summer affair with hunter Eddie Bondo leaves her pregnant and husbandless, she chooses to follow the example of her foster mother, Nannie Rawley, and rear the child without a father. Similarly resolved to succeed on her own terms, Polish-Palestinian neighbor Lusa Maluf Landowski is an outsider who is recently widowed and left with the Widener family homeplace. To stave off bankruptcy, she rejects tobacco as the only agricultural means of self-support. She relies on divergent thinking to come up with an ingenious product, goat meat for sale in New York City during Christian Easter celebrations and Jewish and Islamic high holy days. Each of the protagonists in *Poisonwood Bible* and *Prodigal Summer* relies on nature and human pluck rather than outside rescuers as a satisfying means to dignity and autonomy.

See also **ambition, community, journey motif, rescue, self-esteem, women**

- *Further Reading*

Cooke, Carolyn. "Review: *Animal Dreams.*" *Nation*, Vol. 251, No. 18, November 26, 1990, pp. 653–654.
Schuessler, Jennifer. "Men, Women, and Coyotes." *New York Times*, November 5, 2000, p. 38.
Tanenbaum, Laura. "Review: *Prodigal Summer.*" *Women Writers*, May 2001.

Axelroot, Eeben

The liberator of Rachel Price in *The Poisonwood Bible* (1998), Eeben Axelroot is an Afrikaner bush pilot and CIA operative who also smuggles diamonds, extorts cash from Nathan Price, and helps Nathan's daughter Rachel flee from the Congo to Johannesburg, South Africa. Eeben's surname implies his role in the C.I.A.'s axing of a tentative revolutionary root before it can take hold and sustain the Congo. He is physically and idelogically repulsive to the Price family. Upon the new missionary's arrival at Kilanga, Ruth May Price introduces Axelroot as the owner of a dirty hat. He lives in a shack on the runway between regular Monday flights, which arrive "Thursday, Friday, or not at all" (p. 33). Adah Price assumes that the pilot is the source of dynamite by which Nathan Price stupefies fish in a "high-horse show of force" intended to win converts to his Baptist mission (p. 69). To Orleanna, Nathan's wife, Eeben is "a sudden apparition in rotten boots and sweat-stained fedora, smoking Tiparillos in my doorway" (p. 91). To increase his earnings, he demands payment for items sent by the Mission League and sells the family's mail to them for cash, two mercenary actions that parallel his clandestine role as an enabler of U.S. subversives.

For all his shortcomings, Axelroot is a source of diversion for the bored Price girls. After Orleanna ends the family's association with Axelroot for spitting and cursing at dinner, the girls learn about him through illicit snooping. Ruth May rolls a bottle of red whiskey from under the plane seat and sits on bags of diamonds that the pilot smuggles. She conceals the discoveries from her parents after Eeben threatens her with her parents' illness and death. When Axelroot appears at the Price house, Ruth May fears that "He can see right inside like Jesus" (p. 273). Leah spies on him directly, hiding behind the lush banana plants that sprout behind his latrine. She observes his lengthy naps, tools, military attire, and a radio that carries English and French transmissions and his unprintable replies. Because she gains her view of him on the sly, she can't report the existence of a radio in the village. Thus, Kingsolver connects the pilot with despicable actions and forbidden knowledge.

As the Belgian Congo nears independence, Adah Price also observes Axelroot's furtive actions. After the elections of May 1960, the smuggler, like a reverse Santa Claus, continues cheating Kilangan women of a fair price for their manioc, bananas, and plantains, stuffs the produce into a sack, and speeds south to Katanga and Kasai on the weekly Thursday-to-Monday run. Adah broadens the image of colonial exploitation and self-interest with a wry observation: "The Belgians and the Americans who run the rubber plantations and copper mines, I imagine, are using larger sacks" (p. 174). Kingsolver's development of the pilot as a model of exploitation prospers from parallel comment on his body odor, unkempt shack and wardrobe, greed, and reprehensible conduct, especially around women. Congolese females are so revolted by him that they spit on his shoes.

Near the novel's climax, Axelroot gives a false impression of a rescuer by his courtship of Rachel to counter Tata Ndu's bid to add her to his harem. A walk into the outback allows the bush pilot to make advances. Rachel, who terms herself "a philanderist for peace," encourages him to bathe and, in her desperation to escape from the Congo, sees him as "very nearly almost … handsome" (pp. 269, 288). Her distorted perception quickly gives place to the truth. Axelroot's insinuating flirtation with married female Kilangans reminds her "you can't for one minute let yourself forget he is a creep" (p. 291).

The author creates the disheveled barnstormer by inverting the clichéd image of the cool, handsome white hunter, a stereotype common to Tarzan movies and furthered by Isak Dinesen's description of pilot Denys Finch-Hatton in *Out of Africa* (1937). In an urban setting, the filtered images of Axelroot as Rachel's lover living in Johannesburg on the edge of legality and respectability allow limited grounds on which to judge the pilot, who fades out of the novel after Kingsolver no longer needs him. In typical forgiving fashion, the author tones down his ill repute. In Rachel's last remembrance of him, he seems less criminal that he did in his Kilangan activities. He works as a security agent for the gold-mining industry as he continues weekly trips, "getting rich on one crackpot scheme after another that never did pan out" (pp. 402–403). By reducing him from foreign insurgent and smuggler to bumbling schemer, she makes him seem less mercenary.

See also **Patrice Lumumba**

• *Further Reading*

Kakutani, Michiko. "The Poisonwood Bible: A Family a Heart of Darkness." *New York Times*, October 16, 1998, p. 45.
Markels, Julian. "Coda: Imagining History in *The Poisonwood Bible*." *Monthly Review Press*, September 2003.

Barbie

A thief, counterfeiter, and woman-turned-doll in *Pigs in Heaven* (1993), Barbie is one of Kingsolver's less admirable eccentrics. Lacking adequate self-esteem, Barbie obsesses over the Barbie doll as her ideal woman and maintains an unhealthy body shape through gorging and vomiting. The bulimic character, a foil for protagonist Taylor Greer and a forerunner of the posturing Rachel Price in *The Poisonwood Bible* (1998), fleshes out the character of Brenda from *Animal Dreams* (1990), a bus passenger who coordinates three shades of eye shadow with triple watch bands. The author comments that "her hair looked as if each strand had been individually lacquered and tortured into position" (p. 318). The obsession with personal adornment embodies a neurosis resulting from the impossible standards of beauty forced on women by the media.

In addition to characters from prose, Kingsolver wrote "Reveille," collected in *Another America: Otra America* (1992), a verse diatribe against foundation garments, deodorant, perfume, hair plucking, makeup, violations of ethnic traits, and other evidence of "war with her mammalian origins" (p. 7). In a grimly sarcastic poem, "Elections, Nicaragua, 1984," she juxtaposes a media article on turmoil in Central American with an item remarking on coutourier Pierre Cardin's revitalization of femininity in women's fashions, a trivial non-event that passes for national news. Both poems prefigure the creation of Barbie as a repository of the author's distaste for decorative women.

Kingsolver uses Barbie's clothing fetish as a symbol of shallowness in fashionable females. Contributing to her airheadedness are an insistence on a full layer of makeup for daytime wear and a devotion to buying used clothing for "costuming," her word for the coordination of eye-catching garments as part of her Barbie look-alike charade (p. 202). To emulate the toy, she spends her pay from waitressing to acquire a wardrobe that parallels standard doll outfits, including a star-studded All-American ensemble that does little to enhance the stature of an adult woman. Taylor views Barbie's dress-up syndrome from a mother's angle and "wonders what it must have taken to turn someone's regular daughter into such a desperate, picture-perfect loner" (p. 204). The kindness in Taylor's response reflects her suitability for motherhood as well as an innate generosity toward a hanger-on and leech who cares little about the people she harms.

The novel pictures Barbie as comfortable in a circle of women, yet untouched by their humanity. With a black purse clutched close, she travels west from Las Vegas with Taylor, Turtle, and Alice Greer without revealing her need for flight. When curiosity goads Taylor into inspecting the handbag's contents, she discovers that Barbie stole a cache of one thousand silver dollars from a casino slot machine before skipping out on her employer. Later, Taylor reduces Barbie to "petty larceny waiting to happen" (p. 244). Critics question Kingsolver's creation of the character, who becomes Turtle's babysitter while Taylor drives the Handi-Van at their new home in Seattle, Washington. The humor of Barbie's self-absorption is so stretched that she seems ill-suited to play the role of either Kingsolver's typical motherly female or comic relief.

More troubling is Barbie's explanation of how her Xeroxed twenty-dollar bills stimulate the mall economy. The cover-up for criminality attests to a superego easily placated by dim-witted rationalization. Maintaining such close dependence on a morally corrupt female leaves in doubt Taylor's wisdom in allowing a six-year-old to bond with a bimbo. Taylor's misplaced trust results in the terrifying day that she discovers that Barbie vanished with a set of Taylor's sheets and the last of the cash that Alice gave her for moving expenses. Taylor's summation reflects on her pragmatism: "You don't adopt a wild animal and count it as family" (p. 214). Without spite, Taylor chalks up the loss to experience.

• *Further Reading*

Anderson, Loraine. "Barbie — More Than Just a Doll." Traverse City, Michigan *Record-Eagle*, March 26, 2000.
"Two Female Buddies on the Run." *Literary Review*, November 1993.

The Bean Trees

Kingsolver's bestselling novel *The Bean Trees* (1988) has found its way into book clubs, favorite titles lists, foreign book shelves, and high school and college curricula for its sincere statement of home truths. It succeeded because of her ability to interweave personal tenets into fiction. In *I've Always Meant to Tell You: Letters to Our Mothers: An Anthology of Contemporary Women Writers* (1994), she attempts to express to her mother, Ginny Kingsolver, all the controversial beliefs that clash with her family's philosophies: "refugees and human rights and the laws that are wrong, the terrible things men can do, the Problem that Has No Name, racism, poetry, freedom, Sisterhood is Powerful. All that" (p. 258). Kingsolver is surprised that a publisher found it readable and is gratified at her mother's response: "Barb, honey, it's beautiful. So good" (*Ibid.*).

The outgrowth of the short story "The One to Get Away," the text develops the journey motif by following Marietta "Missy" Greer in a '55 Volkswagen bug from Pittman County, Kentucky, on the way to nowhere in particular in Arizona by way of Homer, Sadorus, Cerro Gordo, Decatur, and Blue Mound, Illinois, and west to Wichita, Kansas; Ponca City, Oklahoma; and the Texas panhandle. Opening in winter 1979-1980, the plot pictures an adventuresome young woman willing to halt at Taylorville long enough to reincarnate herself as Taylor, a name change symbolizing her grasp of autonomy. Significantly, her mother named her for the town in which she was conceived; Taylor chooses a less frilly name "tailored" to an open outlook on what lies ahead.

The author picks up the pace by confronting her protagonist with a situation that bears no resemblance to ordinary life problems. At Cherokee County, Oklahoma, when a broken rocker arm necessitates repairs to the VW, she finds herself entrusted with a motherless baby girl whose aunt thrusts her into Taylor's Volkswagen. By sharing the ill luck of Lou Ann Ruiz, whose story appears in alternate chapters, Taylor forms an impromptu household comprised of two children and two single mothers. Because neither adult knows how to support a family, they do the obvious—rely on each other. The building of trust becomes the author's main theme as characters apply trial and error in managing unusual circumstances that include the Ruiz divorce, a refugee's attempted suicide, an assault in the park, unrequited love for a married man, and a fraudulent adoption.

Crucial to Taylor's success as a mother is her dependence on other women to form a matriarchal safety net, the backup that a working parent depends on. Kingsolver described the setting as "the down-in-the-heels neighborhoods ... where there are a lot of working poor and single mothers who know their neighbors because they have to, because in an emergency they'll look after the kids" (Ross, p. 287). Relying on the kindness and experience of older women, Taylor has an opportunity to grow into the role of parent without serious damage to Turtle, a three-year-old burdened with physical and emotional scars. Kingsolver exonerates Taylor of neglect after a mugger apparently seizes Turtle in the park. Under the care of blind Edna Poppy, the child survives the incident, but retreats blank-eyed into the trauma she bore from toddlerhood. Gradually, love and nurturance from the womanly circle retrieve Turtle, who emerges from terror like a turtle from its shell.

Kingsolver chooses fraud as a means of cutting through bureaucratic paperwork to assure Taylor the rights of an adoptive parent. By posing a Mayan couple, Esperanza and Estevan, as parents giving up their child, Taylor completes the necessary forms and rejoices that she is at last a legitimate mother. Following the book's publication, the author learned that such an adoption was not only fraudulent, but also illegal because of the transfer of a Cherokee child out of its ethnic background to a white parent. Kingsolver thrashes out the moral and legal technicalities in *Pigs in Heaven* (1993), which picks up the story three years later and carries it to a complicated, but satisfying end.

See also **beans, Cherokee, child abuse, Esperanza, Estevan, Alice Greer, Taylor Greer, Turtle Greer, Mattie, motherhood, Lou Ann Ruiz**

• *Further Reading*

Ross, Jean W. "Interview." *Contemporary Authors.* Vol. 134. Detroit: Gale Research, 1992, pp. 284–290.

beans

The bean is a worthy image in the hands of rural-reared naturalist Barbara Kingsolver. In *The Bean Trees* (1988), she makes use of the lowly bean as a double symbol of humility and of nature's building blocks. After Turtle's first laugh in Chapter 7, she pronounces a whole word—"bean" (p. 97). The setting is familial and informal: Taylor is helping to sow Mattie's summer garden with squash, pepper, and eggplant seeds. Taylor selects beans, which look most like the end product, and says, "These are beans. Remember white bean soup with ketchup? Mmm, you like that" (p. 97). The language lesson implies the working-class homestyle of a family that eats nourishing, but simple meals, which are all Taylor can afford. Turtle pipes up, "Bean

... Humbean," a suggestion of "human being," the focus of a novel that builds its conflict on the price exacted on humanity for its vulnerability (*Ibid.*).

The author rapidly develops the bean as a teaching tool. As the mother-and-daughter gardening team plants more seeds, which Turtle digs up to study, Mattie suggests giving Turtle her own seeds, a gesture toward establishing autonomy in the toddler. After a brief explanation of "playing-with beans," "putting-in-the-ground beans," and "eating beans at home," Taylor deduces that her daughter understands the complexities of purpose in each variety (p. 98). For a half hour, Turtle sits quietly at play with her own beans, which become a model for her perception of nature. On examining the child's growth and development, Taylor compares her to vegetables by remarking, "Turtle was healthy as corn," an indication of the author's placement of human life within the greater context of nature (p. 120).

The selection of bean trees for a title implies the importance of understanding life as a little child sees it. Turtle gravitates toward Burpee's seed catalog, *Old MacDonald Had an Apartment*, and the *Horticultural Encyclopedia*, which she reads with her mother at the Oklahoma City Main Library. The entry on wisteria explains the plant's endurance in unpromising soil and its reliance on rhizobia, a microbe that nourishes the roots just as the female support system helps Turtle overcome abuse and neglect.

By novel's end, Turtle is thoroughly engrossed in a "vegetable-soup song," stirred together from names of vegetables and from the people she loves: "Dwayne Ray, Mattie, Esperanza, Lou Ann and all the rest" (p. 232). Contented at last that her adoptive child is safe and content, Taylor adds herself to the soup stock and concludes, "And me. I was the main ingredient" (*Ibid.*). The jolly conclusion frees the novel of its weightier motifs by returning to Kingsolver's original scenario, the nurturing relationship of mother and daughter.

See also **nature, seeds**

• *Further Reading*

Hirsch, Marianne. *The Mother/Daughter Plot: Narrative, Psychoanalysis, Feminism.* Bloomington: Indiana University Press, 1989.

biblical allusions

Kingsolver makes enough references to biblical events and philosophy to establish her familiarity with scripture as a source of image and wisdom. For example, she has Eddie Bondo, the bounty hunter in *Prodigal Summer* (2002), refer to his obsession about killing coyotes as the result of "blood of the lamb," a reference to the Passover and the execution of Christ (Revelation 7:14). In *Pigs in Heaven* (1993), the author speaks of separating sheep from goats (Exodus 12:5) and refers to Solomon's classic court case in which he decided which mother deserved custody of a child (I Kings 3:16–28). The famous decision reflects on the placement of Turtle Greer, a thorny issue of motherhood versus tribal rights, which forms the novel's main conflict. In *Animal Dreams* (1990), Codi Noline supervises the Domingos children going trick-or-treat and watches their haul burgeon like loaves and fishes (Matthew 15:32–39). After engineer J. T. Domingos is exonerated for the derailing of a train and receives thirty days' probation from his job, Codi notes, "The railroad moves in mysterious ways," a witty restatement of one of William Cowper's Olney Hymns, "Light Shining out of Darkness" (1779), which many people mistake for scripture.

Even more chocked with bible figures and metaphors is *The Poisonwood Bible* (1998), in which Kingsolver organizes the first six segments as though they were biblical books. Threaded in and out of the exposition is familiar scriptural phraseology, e.g. the creation imagery of Genesis that results in "And so it came to pass that we stepped down there on a place we believed unformed, where only darkness moved on the face of the waters" (p. 10). Kingsolver uses biblical wording and allusions as a source of comedy and tragedy. She summons terror from the plague of ants and drollery from the cake mixes turned to muck in the jungle humidity like Lot's wife's transmutation into a pillar of salt for disobeying God. To transgress Pan Am's weight limits, Nathan orders his family to "consider the lilies of the field, which have no need of a hand mirror or aspirin tablets" (p. 14). In one absurd episode, the author reverses the parable of the loaves and fishes by depicting Nathan Price directing the Congolese to dynamite the river, an example of his witless role as proselytizer of Africans. After the jolt, their huge feast on fish satisfies for the moment, but turns to disaster as massive numbers of kill rot on the bank.

Biblical lore grows increasingly grim in the novel's third section. Nelson, the Prices' houseboy, tells Leah about Tata Chobé, the Kilangan name for Job, the Old Testament figure cursed by the Christian god with the pox and the death of all seven of his children. Because of the post–Independence Day fall of the Prices' fortunes in Africa, Nelson predicts that God will continue to test the family with ill fortune, beginning with Rachel. Nathan tries to stabilize the fearful family by citing "the only thing we had to fear was fear itself," a sonorous phrase from a speech by Franklin D. Roosevelt that Rachel misidentifies as a bible verse (p. 357).

At one point, the bible influences the Price family's struggle with the Kilangan power structure. Rachel and her sisters set a biblical trap similar to that of Daniel in the Apocrypha, who convinced King Cyrus that greedy priests and their families ate the foods presented to the statue of Bel. By spreading ashes around the altar, Daniel could point to the patterns of footsteps from a secret passage as an explanation of the missing food. The Price sisters' trap turns to tragedy after Tata Kuvudundu leaves a green mamba to strike Nelson in his henhouse lodging. One snap of the jaws quickly dispatches Ruth May. Critics use these perversions of bible events and images as evidence that Kingsolver maintained an anti–Christian, anti-scriptural subtext throughout the novel.

See also **Brother Fowles, Nathan Price**

• *Further Reading*

Birnie, Sue. "The Poisonwood Bible." *National Catholic Reporter*, Vol. 37, No. 32, 2001, p. 16.
Bromberg, Judith. "A Complex Novel About Faith, Family and Dysfunction." *National Catholic Reporter*, Vol. 35, No. 20, March 19, 1999, p. 13.

Charles, Ron. "A Dark Heart in the Congo." *Christian Science Monitor*, Vol. 90, No. 249, November 19, 1998, p. 20.

Glazebrook, Olivia. "Abandoning the Code." *Spectator*, Vol. 37, February 27, 1999.

Bondo, Eddie

Bounty hunter Eddie Bondo, a muscular, raven-haired, green-eyed Wyoming native, is the romantic interest in *Prodigal Summer* (2000). In the words of *Christian Science Monitor* reviewer Ron Charles, Bondo "struts into view and marches us across *The Bridges of Madison County*," a reference to the sexual electricity that blossoms between photographer Robert Kincaid and unfulfilled farm wife Francesca Johnson in Robert James Waller's smoldering bestseller novel (Charles). Kingsolver uses Bondo to create tension between opposing philosophies. The hunter hates coyotes as passionately as his lover, biologist and forest ranger Deanna Wolfe, loves balance in nature and the role of all creatures in ecology. By setting opposite sides to the preservation issue on a male-female perspective, Kingsolver muddles the debate with mutual attractions. The intensity of their views parallels the disagreements of Codi Noline and Loyd Peregrina in *Animal Dreams* (1990) and, to a lesser degree, Alice Greer and Cash Stillwater's interest in Turtle Greer's future in *Pigs in Heaven* (1993) and Leah Price and Anatole Ngemba's activism in Kinshasa in *The Poisonwood Bible* (1998). In each instance, a mutually satisfying physical relationship requires compromise on emotional and political issues.

Like the genial serpent in Eden, Bondo at first seems amiable and harmless. In his initial appearance, after overtaking Deanna on the trail, he is surprisingly courteous. A compact, twenty-something Adonis dressed in camouflage and armed with a rifle of serious caliber, he politely introduces himself to the ranger, who is hired to keep poachers out of the forest preserve. A northwesterner who hunted caribou in Canada the previous summer, he is "an outsider, intruding on this place like kudzu vines," whom Deanna dismisses with a curt rejection marked by a hillbilly twang (p. 4). For his own reasons, he steers clear of "a lady wildlife ranger with a badge," but reveals his passion for nature by envying her job of "keeping an eye on paradise" (pp. 10, 11). His devotion to natural beauty completes the thawing of Deanna's icy glare that her own hormones began at first sight of a gorgeous male in her domain.

The Bondo-Wolfe matchup draws significance from the imagery of their surnames. In their next meeting, both parties acknowledge a ferocious yearning, a feral lust that Kingsolver countenances as normal human sexuality. The visit extends to nine days, during which Bondo disarms the wary biologist and distracts her from regular jottings in her field notebook, a suggestion of the power of the libido to overcome the intellect. Eddie develops a lasting bond with Deanna, who bears the name of a predator and whose dedication to wild creatures keeps threatening a peaceful union. At a showdown over a pit fire, she declares her intent to convert Bondo's thinking toward coyotes. His reply is heartfelt: "I'm a ranching boy from the West, and hating coyotes is my religion" (p. 323).

The remainder of Bondo's purpose in the novel reveals Kingsolver's preference for motherhood over carnal dalliance as the height of womanly achievement. The author seems to side with Deanna during her response to early symptoms of pregnancy. Like a pirate concealing buried treasure, the ranger polishes off the summer fling with Bondo while deliberately concealing her mottled skin, darkness around the eyes, expanding waistline, emotional turmoil, and the deepening color of the aureoles of her breasts, all of which attest to impending maternity. Without giving him the option of knowing or helping to rear the child, Deanna concludes, "Better for this child, better for everybody, that he not know what he'd left behind — and so he never would" (p. 432). The possessive attitude parallels that of the Amazons, Homer's armed aggressors in the *Iliad*, who tolerate men like bulls in the pasture, then evict them after the females are bred.

Because Bondo is less likely husband material than Loyd Peregrina, Cash Stillwater, or Anatole Ngemba, Kingsolver lets him drift out of the picture as though his absence confers protection on both Deanna and the coyotes she shields from his rifle. An unusual image completes the parting: Deanna tears to bits the note he writes in her notebook and leaves the pieces in her sock drawer for mice to recycle as lining for their winter nests. Without regret, she turns away from her strapping lover and hermit's lodge to retreat to Nannie Rawley, the foster mother who raised her and who will provide Deanna with her own winter nest.

Further Reading

> Charles, Ron. "Mothers of Nature Howling at the Moon." *Christian Science Monitor*, Vol. 92, No. 230, October 19, 2000.

bureaucracy

Kingsolver's writings brandish ill-will at government meddling and institutional red tape. She rails at bureaucratic regulations that impede such transactions as adopting an abandoned Cherokee toddler, resettling political refugees in safe territory, hiring an uncertified biology teacher, pressing suit against polluters, receiving mail and packages from home, making telephone calls, purchasing produce in an African market, and proclaiming a desert community an historical treasure. In her first novel, *The Bean Trees* (1988), the routine medical questionnaires distributed by Jill, the nurse in Dr. Pelinowsky's office, reveal Taylor Greer's ignorance of the normal medical history that precedes a physical examination. Jill concludes that Taylor is Turtle's foster parent, although the term fails to describe the bizarre circumstances that advance Taylor in a matter of minutes from a childless traveler to a clueless single mother.

Similarly, the novel condemns the reams of paperwork necessary to guarantee an immigrant political asylum by picturing Mattie, the rescuer, going and coming on mysterious errands of mercy. Bypassing the obstacles to immediate protection for tormented Central American refugees, she resituates them in illegal sanctuaries unlikely to rouse suspicion in immigration investigators. Kingsolver thinks like the American abolitionists of the mid–1800s: when a life is endangered, altruism demands trust and action, not legalities. She speaks her disapproval of governmental rejection of terrorized people through Taylor Greer's complaint that people like Estevan and Esperanza are dubbed "illegals" (p. 195). Taylor fumes, "A human being can be good or bad or right or wrong, maybe. But how can you say a person is illegal?" (p. 195).

With *Animal Dreams* (1990), Kingsolver retreats from specifics. The protagonist, Codi Noline, not only receives a teaching job on emergency certification, but apparently continues in the post for the next two years. School authorities treasure her innovative methods and rapport with teenagers without making a fuss over her lack of a teaching license. The author also makes slick work of cleansing an Arizona river of poison. When male citizens press suit against the Black Mountain mining company to halt its pollution of the community's water source, they face a decade of litigation. The women, who raise money by selling piñatas in Tucson, pursue an end-run around the lengthy court battle by collecting photos and data that establish Grace, Arizona, an historic city worthy of listing on the national registry. The author's clever solution serves two purposes— exposure of the failure of legal systems to nab polluters and halt desecration of land and water and praise of grassroots methods of maintaining an American community in danger of annihilation.

The most inhumane of bureaucracy burdens post-revolution Zaire in *The Poisonwood Bible* (1998). Speaking through Leah Price Ngemba, Kingsolver presents from the peasant point of view Mobutu Sese Seko's criminal waste of revenues on palaces while the underclass starves. Living in a concrete-floored shack near an open-air sewage flow, she rages at the sufferings of the Congolese. The simplest transactions with postal clerks and passport offices require cash bribes that the poor can ill afford. To maintain ties with her husband while he serves prison sentences for treason, Leah learns the Kikongo language and the posture of the suppliant necessary for wangling information and mail privileges. In the privacy of home, she reverts into an American and vents her fury at Mobutu's faceless terrorism and extortion from his own people. With remarkable finesse, Kingsolver kills him off in a fictional scene that pictures him shriveling up with cancer, a suitable end to a regime that spread like a malignant growth over equatorial Africa.

See also **altruism, Cherokee,** *The Last Stand: America's Virgin Lands,* **Mobutu Sese Seko**

Cardenal, Ernesto

In her poem "The Monster's Belly" anthologized in *Another America: Otra America* (1992), Kingsolver grapples with the philosophy of a prolific Nicaraguan poet who espoused Christian Marxism and the utopian ideal. Born in Granada in 1925, Cardenal completed his education in New York City at Columbia University. After serving his nation as minister of culture, he studied under Thomas Merton at Our Lady of Gethsemani, Kentucky, and entered the priesthood at age forty. Rather than follow a theological career, he fostered literacy and art espousing political themes. Unlike Catholic propagandists, he uses verse to picture social injustice and materialism and to reclaim pre–Columbian history and culture dating to the Inca, Maya, and Nahuatl.

Kingsolver's poem parallels her growing-up years during the Cuban Missile

Crisis with the presence of Father Ernest at the Gethsemani monastery. The juxta-position points to a pervasive fact in history — that there are pockets of goodness and peace in the world contemporaneous with eras of threat and struggle. She hints that she would like to have learned from a priest "some greater love than the end of the world," an acknowledgement of her limited background in Christian principles (p. 25). The last stanza indicates that her life as an American prohibits a full under-standing of an idealistic priest who longed to "kill the monster" of Cold War aggres-sion (*Ibid.*).

• *Further Reading*

Darling, Juanita. "A Nation Tempered by Poetry." *Los Angeles Times*, July 26, 1999, p. A1.
Tamayo, Juan O. "Rethinking Option for Poor." *Miami Herald*, January 21, 1999.

Carlo

An emergency room doctor and the lover of Codi Noline in *Animal Dreams* (1990), Carlo is only partially outlined as a character. To enable her to ripen into a mature adult, Kingsolver withers the ten-year relationship, which began in a para-sitology class at Tucson medical school. After passing through a series of residences that took them as far away as Crete, Carlo lived in Tucson with Codi and her sister Hallie and bonded with Codi as "an orphan like me" (p. 10). Codi recalls their jobs of "[setting] broken legs on the steep slope of Mount Ida" and admires his tackling the job of reattaching severed limbs for a living, a metaphor that suggests her own feeling of detachment (p. 107). However, Carlo's expertise is purely mechanical. She gives up expecting him to provide guidance for her restless mind and relegates him to the army of shallow lovers she categorizes as "more of the same" (p. 47).

Carlo's weakness is an absence of heart. He diagnoses human frailty as a fault of neural synapses. After the decline of Doc Homer's mind from Alzheimer's dis-ease, Carlo's explanation leaves Codi feeling doubly abandoned by father and lover, who share a cold objectivity toward the practice of medicine. On a visit to Tucson before Christmas 1986, she reunites with Carlo, who returns from the late shift exhausted from reattaching a nose. He is sympathetic enough with Codi's home sit-uation to massage her feet and invite her to settle with him in Denver or Aspen. The image is significant of feet that find no resting place, even with Carlo. In a letter to Hallie, she admits that living with him is safe because she doesn't love him enough to miss him if they broke up permanently.

Kingsolver implies that the loss of Hallie, the third member of their trio, pro-duced a disharmony that clouded Codi's satisfaction with her lover. Without Hallie to provide compassion to their household, Codi must search anew for a sheltering nest. In June 1987, a quick switch from Carlo to Loyd Peregrina suggests the shallow nature of Codi's former relationship and the satisfying qualities of life with Loyd. The departure from the Tucson apartment to the vine-covered trailer in Grace also acknowledges Loyd's demands on Codi for a bond of love that moves beyond casual sex to a permanent commitment and eventual motherhood.

• *Further Reading*

DeMarr, Mary Jean. *Barbara Kingsolver: A Critical Companion*. Westport, Conn.: Green-
    wood, 1999.

Cherokee

Native Americans figure in Kingsolver's cast of characters from the first of her
career. Her point of view is pro–Indian and anti–Manifest Destiny, the philosophy
that exonerated European seizure of the New World, obliteration of the buffalo, and
the subsequent attempted genocide of Indians. In "Worlds in Collision," a 1990 book
review for the *Los Angeles Times*, she charges, "The history of Native Americans since
colonization is a fairly predictable story of betrayal and land theft," an opinion
expressed in Dee Brown's groundbreaking revisionist history *Bury My Heart at
Wounded Knee* (1970) (p. 3). Her novels illustrate the ongoing disruption of native
life by a government that tries to coerce tribes through dysfunctional bureaucracy
and disruptive land use policies that forced Cherokees west from the Appalachians
to Oklahoma over the Trail of Tears.

The author begins fictional characterization of the Cherokee with Great Mam,
the focus of the title piece in *Homeland and Other Stories* (1989). The elderly member of the Bird Clan relates to her great granddaughter Gloria St. Clair the importance of courageous ancestors who fought displacement from their tribal roots.
Symbolizing the loss of identity is Mam's renaming from the native Green Leaf to
Ruth, the biblical name carved on her gravestone along with a fabricated date of
birth. The author chooses the evocative name of a Moabite widow who lived apart
from her home with her Judean mother-in-law Naomi. Ultimately, Ruth remarried
Boaz, produced Obed, and became the great-grandmother of David. She is the only
female named on the lengthy genealogy of Jesus (Matthew 1:1, 5). The name imparts
additional honor to Great Mam, who is a modern-day version of the biblical matriarch.

Kingsolver elevates Great Mam as a vessel of native lore. Throughout her long
life, she honored Cherokee ritual and retained the dignity of the aboriginal past
through oral tradition, which a male character dismisses as "Great Mam's hobbledy-
gobbledy" (p. 16). Shortly before her death on a return trip to the touristy town of
Cherokee, she recoils from Chief Many Feathers, an exhibitionist dancing in a fluffed-
up bonnet that belongs in Hollywood movies rather than in aboriginal culture. A
cage displaying a mangy buffalo bears a sign identifying the pathetic beast as the last
of its species east of the Mississippi. The images are both shameful and stirring. At
Great Mam's urging, Gloria realizes the assault on the native past and takes seriously
her role in retaining the old narratives and relaying them to the next generation.

The author moves directly into Cherokee lore in *The Bean Trees* (1988) with
mention of the main character's great grandfather, one of the few Indians left in Tennessee when the government drove Appalachia's natives into Oklahoma territory.
Taylor Greer's mother speaks of this ethnic connection as "head rights," the family's
"ace in the hole" that entitles them to live among the Cherokee on reservation land

(p. 13). The great grandfather's ethnicity endows Alice with tribal membership. Although the racial tie is tenuous, it establishes her eligibility for government assistance to native Americans. The little security that she and her daughter cling to is ironic considering the loss of status and livelihood among Indians after the army ejected them from traditional Cherokee territory.

In *Pigs in Heaven* (1993), Kingsolver picks up the plot strand from *The Bean Trees* and explains more fully the value of head rights. She develops a unique form of American community standards among Cherokees who accommodate extended families by adding rooms and trailers to the parents' homeplace. Described by *New York Times* reviewer Karen Karbo, the native system gives "visions of the long-suffering Cherokee who knows the value of kith, kin, sacrifice and every other noble thing missing in American society" (Karbo, p. 9). The novel's conflict arises from the custody battle for Turtle Greer, who was born a Cherokee on reservation land and given away to an outsider by her aunt, Sue Stillwater. The author explains, "I had the option and the obligation to deal with the issue because the moral question was completely ignored in the first book" (*Ibid.*).

Kingsolver turns to America's past to explain the legal dilemma in which Taylor finds herself. The reason for the struggle, according to attorney Annawake Fourkiller, is historical: "We've been through a holocaust as devastating as what happened to the Jews, and we need to keep what's left of our family together" (p. 281). She summarizes the Trail of Tears, the forced removal of tribes from the southern Appalachians in the summer of 1838, when General Winfield Scott and his troops prodded the Cherokee to settle on "a worthless piece of land nobody else would ever want" (*Ibid.*). Incorporation of dark chapters in the nation's infancy offers the author an opportunity to remind Americans of the source of their ill-gotten prosperity in the New World.

To whites, the Cherokee outlook is less dire than Annawake's dramatic narration. The benefits are unique, especially to females. Karbo summed up the virtues of tribal life as "the rare sense of really belonging and, even rarer, the privileged place held by young girls in the spiritual life of the community" (Karbo, p. 9). Kingsolver exonerates the populace for poverty and slovenly homes by remarking how the government gave sixty-acre parcels of homestead land to families and how investors traded them out of their allotments with "a mule or a stove or ... a crate of peaches and a copy of *The Leatherstocking Tales*," a trumped-up native American series fictionalized by a white man, James Fenimore Cooper (p. 189). Reduced to subsistence on unpromising land, the Cherokee made do with the leavings and thrived outside the materialism of the white world. Taylor Greer sums up the native American ethic in folk terms: "Do right by your people," a simplistic phrase freighted with the responsibility of an extended family model, which seems burdensome to a white woman reared in a two-person nuclear family (p. 88).

As the predicament of Turtle Greer's parentage envelops Taylor, she admits that she doesn't know how to introduce her daughter to "which kind of Indians carved totem poles, which ones lived in teepees, which ones hunted buffalo, and which ones taught the Pilgrims to put two fish in the bottom of the hole with each corn-plant" (p. 206). The summary of images reflects the limited enlightenment about the first

Americans that students receive in public school. To relieve her ignorance, Taylor relies on people like Cash Stillwater, Turtle's loving grandfather, for the kindness and commitment necessary to round out the child's ethnic upbringing.

The author eases up on the heavy didacticism with some Cherokee fun. At a stomp dance, she inserts a scenario any Kentuckian knows well — the discussion of family line, which involves the unraveling of who married whom among Horn-buckles, Pigeons, Grasses, Goingsnakes, Fourkillers, and Tailbobs. After Alice and her friend Sugar work their way through the Dawes Rolls, Sugar admits that "being Cherokee is more or less a mind-set" rather than pure native ancestry or culture (p. 275). The concept of ethnic mind-set suits the falling action, in which Taylor is able to think of herself as mother to a child who can always rely on an elaborate and devoted tribal kinship.

See also **Annawake Fourkiller, Ledger Fourkiller, Greer genealogy, Cash Still-water, stomp dance**

• *Further Reading*

Chism, Olin. "Questions of Right; Author Presents Indians' Answers." *Dallas Morning News*, July 9, 1993, p. 1C.
Karbo, Karen. "And Baby Makes Two." *New York Times Book Review*, June 27, 1993, p. 9.
Myzska, Jessica. "Barbara Kingsolver: 'Burning a Hole in the Pockets of My Heart.'" *De Pauw Magazine*, Vol. 5, No. 2, Spring 1994, pp. 18–20.
Ryan, Maureen. "Barbara Kingsolver's Lowfat Fiction." *Journal of American Culture*, Vol. 18, No. 4, Winter 1995, pp. 77–82.
Shapiro, Laura. "A Novel Full of Miracles." *Newsweek*, Vol. 122, No. 2, July 12, 1993, p. 61.

child abuse

Kingsolver's interest in child welfare stems from deeply ingrained humanism as well as her own experiences with motherhood. Her inclusion of after-the-fact information on child abuse in *The Bean Trees* (1988) suggests the cruel and insidi-ous nature of child torturers and pedophiles without actually picturing them harm-ing the innocent. The author's omission of scenes of battery relieves the reader of graphic violence, particularly the fate of Ismene, the child of Esperanza and Estevan whom Guatemalan terrorists kidnap. The author includes enough detail to establish the criminality of Turtle Greer's first guardian, a legal term only peripherally reas-suring. From the unidentified aunt's hand-off of a terrified toddler to Taylor like a football in full play, the new mother grasps at understanding how an adult can jet-tison a child to a stranger. She knows instinctively that Turtle's death grip on the hair, shirt, and body of its protector indicates a desperate need for security.

Although Turtle appears to be a normal toddler, Taylor decides that a medical examination is in order in view of the child's history of abuse. After Dr. Pelinowsky x-rays Turtle and analyzes damage to her skeleton, Taylor realizes that "he looked just ever so slightly shaken up" (p. 123). The growth of hand and wrist cartilage is evidence of such vicious treatment that the child probably stopped growing in toddlerhood. He explains how trauma halts internal maturation and produces a syndrome known as "failure to thrive" (*Ibid.*). He mounts more of the x-rays in the window, saying things like "spiral fibular fracture here" and "excellent healing" and "some contraindications for psychomotor development" (p. 124). To Taylor, the abused baby resembles a bird outside the window building a nest in the inhospitable spines of a cactus. Dazed by more scary pictures than Taylor can comprehend, she concludes metaphorically, "You just couldn't imagine how she'd made a home in there" (*Ibid.*).

Kingsolver reprises Turtle's sufferings in Chapter 12, "Into the Terrible Night," an artistic blend of Taylor's pleasant evening witnessing life in the desert with arrival home to near tragedy. Before Taylor learns the facts, she senses terror in her roommate, Lou Ann Ruiz. One look at Turtle informs Taylor of the worst — bruises on the child's shoulders and an emotional response that reduced her eyes to "two cups of black coffee" (p. 165). Contributing to the horror of child abuse is the not-knowing. In the falling dark, Edna, the blind babysitter, heard sounds of struggle and struck with her cane. Whatever the crime, Turtle returns to her old habits, falls silent, and clings for twenty minutes to Edna's sleeve. The retreat reflects a child's method of withdrawing mentally into a catatonic state from a painful reality that overpowers her physically.

Both Taylor and Lou Ann have little choice but to wrestle with evil that they can't escape or overlook. Taylor confides, "I sat on my bed for hours looking up words. Pedophilia. Perpetrator. Deviant. Maleficent" (p. 169). Nearly immobilized with regret for another assault on Turtle and filled with "empty despair," Taylor becomes over-cautious: "At night I lay listening to noises outside, listening to Turtle breathe, thinking: she could have been killed. So easily she could be dead now" (p. 170). Lou Ann has her own problems understanding the perversion of Fanny Heaven, a porn house adjacent to the Jesus Is Lord Used Tires where viewers can see X-rated movies featuring sexual acts performed on young children. Cynthia, the social worker who investigates the assault in the park, worsens the gloom by reporting that "one out of every four little girls is sexually abused by a family member" (p. 173). Kingsolver indicates that the antidote to human evil is not found in books, medical offices, or bureaucracies— only in the heart.

In *Pigs in Heaven* (1993), a non-sequel, Taylor rechannels suffering by using past sexual abuse, maltreatment, and rejection as grounds for her right to keep Turtle. The Cherokee who contest the placement of a native child with a white parent are curt and dismissive in response to her charges against Sue Stillwater, the child's surrogate parent. Cash Stillwater, Turtle's grandfather, remarks that the federal government's discounting of local parenting and the removal of children to boarding schools disrupted their moral maturation. The author is careful to place little blame on Alma, Turtle's suicidal mother, who flips her car into the Arkansas River, or on Sue, the maternal aunt who suffers battering from a boyfriend and allows him to harm the child. In the end, compromise assures that Turtle will grow up Anglo-Cherokee from contact with two loving environments.

In-house child abuse in *The Poisonwood Bible* (1998) takes a quirky turn from pedophilia toward two incidents of more heinous disregard for child welfare, e.g., the smuggler Eeben Axelroot's threat and rough handling of Ruth May Price for spying whiskey and bags of diamonds in his plane and the prostitution of Elévée at age ten or eleven to earn money for her starving Congolese family. The first episode impresses, but does not traumatize Ruth May. In the second episode, Leah can do nothing to rescue Elévée. She bottles her fury and admires Anatole for "[expressing] his out-rage in more productive ways" (p. 451). Out of pity for people trapped by hunger and public venality, the author moves away from the image of a pre-teen hooker on the streets of Kinshasa, leaving the outcome to the reader's imagination.

A more insidious man-handler of girls and women is the Reverend Nathan Price. The vainglorious Baptist minister pictures himself baptizing the saved villagers of Kilanga at a ceremony held in the Kwilu River without realizing the threat the ritual poses to local children. Village mothers are so terrified "even on hearsay" of the tempting of crocodiles with the bodies of their children that they remain on the far side of the compound on Sundays to avoid the church and escape Nathan's baptism fetish (p. 46). At home, Price exhibits his punitive nature by bruising Leah's neck, yanking his wife's arm, and whipping five-year-old Ruth May with a razor strop that makes her "feel stripedy like a zebra horse" (p. 54). He verbalizes hostility through frequent denigration of his all-woman household as a burden of "dull-witted bovine females" (p. 73). On the night Leah rebels against his authority and escapes into the jungle, he strips off his leather belt and beats the tall grass for an hour, terrifying the rest of the family into protecting themselves with pots and lids.

During Chief Tata Ndu's courtship of Rachel Price, a barbaric form of ritual child abuse arises in the novel from the discussion of traditional African circumci-sion. Speaking the philosophy of female purity common to the Congo, he insists that, to curtail sensation during intercourse, his future bride undergo female geni-tal mutilation, a removal of the clitoris and perhaps labial tissue as well. By describ-ing the maiming of young girls from five-year-old Ruth May's frame of reference, Kingsolver delivers a stark denunciation of crude female surgery: "[Tata Ndu] told Father Rachel would have to have the circus mission where they cut her so she wouldn't want to run around with people's husbands.... They do it to all the girls here" (pp. 271–272).

- *Further Reading*

Banks, Russell. "Distant as a Cherokee Childhood." *New York Times Book Review*, July 11, 1989, p. 16.

community

Central to Kingsolver's fiction is the model of the individual and the family amid community, particularly those interdependent units that form from the least promising participants. Of the value of shared nurturing, she states in "Everybody's Somebody's Baby" (1992) that Americans are such traditional loners that "it's no sur-prise that we think of child-rearing as an individual job, not a collective responsi-bility" (p. 49). She contrasts the American nuclear home with village rearing, a tribal concept revered by the Cherokee (p. 49). In *The Bean Trees* (1988), protagonist Taylor

Greer, a new mother with no on-site family backup, must acclimate from the community paradigm of the Kentucky hills to the makeshift alliances of urban Arizona. She and her daughter flourish amid an informal matriarchal coterie after arriving in Tucson, where "there was nobody overlooking us all" (p. 47). To relieve Taylor's view of herself as parenting Turtle all alone, the author creates a touching image the night that Mattie stops her truck in the desert so a mother quail and her chicks can cross the road in safety. In similar fashion, Mattie shepherds both Taylor and Turtle, offering practical advice on rehydrating children in the desert air and feeding Turtle crackers and juice, the humble gifts of a woman who understands mothering.

Through the experiences of Lou Ann Ruiz, a divorced single mom, Kingsolver redefines the matriarchal community as a form of family. According to Lou Ann, the test of family is intimacy — going "through hell and high water together. We know each other's good and bad sides, stuff nobody else knows" (p. 231). To establish realism, the author illustrates the necessary balance of community and autonomy. While sharing space with Lou Ann and her baby son Dwayne Ray, Taylor fights for her newly gained adult status by ridiculing the Ruiz-Greer household as a model of the comic-strip paradigm of Blondie and Dagwood. Taylor emphasizes her disdain, "It's not like we're a *family*, for Christ's sake. You've got your own life to live, and I've got mine" (p. 85).

Kingsolver works out a balance between the support system and the mother's autonomy. The other characters remain committed to Taylor, but respect her centrality to Turtle's life, particularly after a mugger terrifies the child in Roosevelt Park. On the drive from Oklahoma City to Tucson, Turtle bobs her head hen-like and sings the vegetable soup song, an anthem to human nurturing and uniqueness. In response to Taylor's demand, the little girl accepts only Taylor as mother, her "main ingredient" (p. 232).

A prickly community forms in *Prodigal Summer* (2000) after the accidental death of Cole Widener, who expires from a broken steering column thrust through his ribs. His wife Lusa, an outsider, debates her position as inheritor of the Widener family homeplace. Slowly, through confrontations and admissions of false impressions, Cole's five sisters warm to their educated sister-in-law. Contributing to the tight network of family is Lusa's willingness to mother Crystal Gail and Lowell, the children of Jewel Widener Walker. Abandoned by their father Shel and soon to be orphaned by Jewel as cancer takes over her body, the children accept Lusa as the perfect off-beat mother. The coalescing of the Wideners' informal family circle echoes Kingsolver's communities in her earlier novels, including the circle of women who nurture Codi Noline in *Animal Dreams* (1990), the Cherokees of Heaven, Oklahoma, welcoming Alice Greer to the stomp dance, and the loving Congolese mothers and the missionary's wife in *The Poisonwood Bible* (1998) who gather at an African funeral for Ruth May Price. The author models how shared needs and losses offer disparate people reasons to empathize and bond with each other.

See also **cooperation, fable, family, motherhood, Cash Stillwater, trust**

• *Further Reading*

Aprile, Dianne. "Kingship with Kingsolver: Author's Characters Long to Belong, Something That Touches Readers." *Louisville Courier-Journal*, July 25, 1993, p. 11.

Murrey, Loretta Martin. "The Loner and the Matriarchal Community in Barbara King-
    solver's *The Bean Trees* and *Pigs in Heaven*." *Southern Studies*, Vol. 5, No. 1–2,
    Spring & Summer 1994, pp. 155–164.

compromise

Kingsolver's folksy plot constructions stress the value of flexible human relations built on trust and compromise. Within her own family, she reports in *I've
Always Meant to Tell You: Letters to Our Mothers: An Anthology of Contemporary
Women Writers* (1997) that, in summer 1996, she is not capable of tolerating shocking green and purple nail polish on nine-year-old Camille. Before school starts, the
author acknowledges her daughter's ability to form her own opinions about appearance. Kingsolver compromises on body adornment: the green fingernails must go,
but the toes may keep their purple lacquer. The choice of locations favors the mother's
position by drawing less attention to odd-colored nails.

The predicament at the heart of *Pigs in Heaven* (1993) reflects the quandary
Solomon faced in deciding which mother got the disputed infant (I Kings 3:16–28).
To allow Taylor Greer to keep her child and to satisfy Annawake Fourkiller's resolve
to rear Cherokee children within the culture, Kingsolver comes up with a viable
alternative — an impromptu marriage between Turtle's white grandmother and
Cherokee grandfather that will let Taylor continue mothering her foundling while
assuring Turtle the fostering of an ethnic community. Scholar Loretta Murrey characterizes the arrangement as a resetting of the Greek myth of Persephone, in which
the mother Demeter agrees to her daughter's residence in the underworld with her
husband Hades for half the year and a return for the remaining months on earth with
her mother.

The author's own ability to offset two sides of an issue dominates *Prodigal Summer* (2000), in which she pits evolutionist against creationist, organic gardener against
sprayer of defoliants and pesticides, tobacco growers against anti-smokers, and naturalist against coyote-hunting rancher. Kingsolver creates a sturdy devil's advocate
in Garnett S. Walker, III, a biblical fundamentalist and former vo-ag teacher and 4-
H adviser who accepts the fact that "the creatures of this earth came to pass and
sometimes passed on" (p. 139). He locates the bur that makes organic gardeners so
infuriating to him, their "placid, irritating sense of holier-than-thou" (p. 140). In an
extensive postscript to his letter to Nannie Rawley, he cites Genesis 1:27–30, the biblical account of creation, as evidence that animals are "gifts to [God's] favored children" to use as they see fit (p. 186). As their epistolary exchange picks up steam, he
sees himself as "a Soldier of God on the way to his mailbox, marching as to war," an
image taken from the crusader anthem "Onward Christian Soldiers" (p. 220). By
novel's end, arguments between Nannie and Garnett strike up more agreements than
variances of opinion. Kingsolver suggests that the compassion the neighbors feel for
each other far outweighs their intent to triumph one over the other.

See also **cooperation, Garnett Walker, women**

• *Further Reading*

Murrey, Loretta Martin. "The Loner and the Matriarchal Community in Barbara King-solver's *The Bean Trees* and *Pigs in Heaven*." *Southern Studies*, Vol. 5, No. 1–2, Spring & Summer 1994, pp. 155–164.

cooperation

Kingsolver's faith in positive alternatives in human relations points to the need for cooperation. In *The Bean Trees* (1988), the unusual relationship and behaviors of neighbors Virgie Parsons and Edna Poppy puzzle Taylor Greer and Lou Ann Ruiz until an unexpected encounter with Edna in the Lee Sing Market explains her reliance on Virgie. Taylor spies her neighbor's white cane and realizes that Virgie identifies people in the room and guides Edna by the elbow to compensate for Edna's blindness. By making no mention of handicap, Virgie respects Edna's dignity and need to appear normal.

As an illustration of interdependence, Estevan addresses "Tortolita" with an allegory about people in heaven using long spoons to feed each other rather than to attempt to feed themselves, as do the selfish, frustrated souls in hell. Kingsolver uses the story to offset Virgie's bigotry toward refugees. To demonstrate visually how the human family cherishes all members, he grasps a pineapple cube with his chopsticks and offers it to Turtle, who sits opposite him. Like a nested hatchling, she opens her mouth to receive it. The symbolism reflects the resolve of the matriarchal community to meet whatever need arises with clever solutions.

In a more community-oriented situation in *Animal Dreams* (1990), Kingsolver depicts the quick action of citizens of Grace, Arizona, to save their water supply. The men gather to work out a lawsuit to halt the poisoning of the nearby river and intervene in the copper company's damming of the only source of water. The women, who are ingenious in their homespun plotting, choose to sell feathered piñatas on the streets of Tucson. In addition to drawing media attention to the threat to their orchards and families, they acquire enough cash to pay for the background investigation preliminary to declaring the town a national heritage site. The methodology of male and female reflects on gender values: men rely on the law; women, who have long been marginalized by the justice system, cling to a homely, but effective matriarchy that has sustained the community for generations.

In the author's return to Taylor Greer's adoption of Turtle in *Pigs in Heaven* (1993), a third type of cooperation is necessary to settle the issue of who has the right to adopt a Cherokee foundling. Attorney Annawake Fourkiller, a fiercely tribal spokeswoman for her people, allows the pain of her twin brother Gabriel's adoption by whites to influence her resolve to return Turtle to the people of Heaven, Oklahoma. Kingsolver's transparent romance between Alice Greer and Cash Stillwater, the white and Cherokee grandparents, suffices as the basis for compromise. Thus, both ethnic groups cooperate in rearing the Indian child, who remains in Taylor's care.

Kingsolver takes cooperative efforts to a more complex level in her masterwork, *The Poisonwood Bible* (1998). The arrival of the ill-prepared Price family at a mission in Kilanga introduces the neighborliness of the Congolese, who greet the newcomers with a festive goat roast. Although the Reverend Nathan Price fails to exercise even the rudiments of courtesy and decorum in a foreign setting, village women make Orleanna welcome. Ruth May demonstrates the biblical concept of "a little child shall lead them" by playing with black children and teaching them "Mother, May I?," a favorite American game. The acceptance of the white child sets an example for the older Prices of the need to cooperate with village customs and to acknowledge the special needs of both races in the awkward situation that arises after the mission league stops supporting Nathan's work.

At the novel's climax, the death of Ruth May brings the women together for a demonstrative Congolese funeral. The placement of the shrouded corpse on an outdoor bier and the erection of a funereal arch of leaves and blossoms signals to village mothers an opportunity to pay their respects to the child in the local fashion. On their knees, they approach and keen as they would for their own babes. Frozen in anguish, Orleanna grasps oneness with other mothers as an opportunity to level differences in education and status. She distributes her goods and furniture to the have-nots. The cooperative efforts of white and black mothers ends a seventeen-month period of suspicion and gossip with mutual love and empathy.

Cooperation takes on a vital role in the survival of Leah Price, who departs with her mother and twin Adah on the long walk to civilization. Assisted in the pouring rain by two Congolese women, the five females press on amid swarms of mosquitoes over nearly impassable mud. The shelter of a crude hut rescues Leah from malarial fever; two charcoal makers carry her the rest of the way to Bulungu on a pallet. In her subsequent embrace of the African lifestyle, she learns to share misery and prosperity equally with others. In middle age, she grieves over the post-revolution burdens borne by the needy: "This world has brought one vile abomination after another down on the heads of the gentle, and I'll not live to see the meek inherit anything," a reference to the Beatitudes, in which Jesus declares that the "meek ... shall inherit the earth" (p. 522; Matthew 5:5). To do her part of a global rescue effort, Leah receives refugee women and children at a communal farm in Angola, where residents grow crops to sustain families who have survived the horrors of Mobutu's reign.

See also **compromise, fable, Mama Mwanza, women**

crime

Kingsolver's idealism impels her to fight a terrifying family of crimes, from local felonies and child abuse to Central American and African despotism and international war. In *The Bean Trees* (1988), Taylor Greer returns from a pleasant picnic to a traumatized three-year-old in a chapter entitled "Into the Terrible Night." The assault on Turtle in Roosevelt Park generates maternal despair at random crime on Tucson's vulnerable citizens. At the same time, the quick thinking of Edna Poppy, the blind babysitter, ennobles her efforts at swinging a white cane above Turtle's head toward the attacker and thwarting his evil intent. Edna's retaliation is a model of grassroots efforts that elevate ordinary people from victims to challengers of social chaos.

In "This House I Cannot Leave," a personal poem anthologized in *Another America: Otra America* (1992), Kingsolver pictures a friend alienated from her own dwelling after a burglar rifles her clothing and makes her flee to another neighborhood. The insidious image of a stranger wandering the rooms causes the owner to recoil from the house and abandon her fruit trees, which metaphorically stop growing. The breaking-and-entering that creates the woman's misery forces the poet to consider her own experience with date rape in 1974. A second poem, "Ten Forty-Four," accounts for the crumbling of innate trust after a man held her at knifepoint and eluded police investigators. In both instances, crime invades property and violates human trust, forcing victims to rebuild their lives around corrosive memories.

Kingsolver's diatribe against Mobutu Sese Seko in *The Poisonwood Bible* (1998) advances from crime against person and property to the rape of an entire nation. The dictator loses his Congolese values by adopting the methods of the rapacious Belgians and developing into a monster. Among his predations against the peasantry are brutal police strikes against the poor, unjust imprisonments and torture of political prisoners, and the formation of a corrupt bureaucracy that thieves from mail, telephone company, and the education system to deck a series of pretentious castles for the use of Mobutu and his sycophants. After Anatole and Leah Ngemba establish a cooperative farm, she recognizes that it is only "a tiny outpost of reasonable sustenance in the belly of Mobutu's beast" (p. 500).

See also **child abuse**

• *Further Reading*

Gergen, David. "Interview: Barbara Kingsolver." *U.S. News and World Report*, November 24, 1995.

desert

After settling in Tucson, Arizona, in 1979, Kingsolver began to incorporate the Sorona Desert in her writings as a model of the subtle strengths of life in a harsh climate. In "Lush Language," a 1993 book review for the *Los Angeles Times*, she observed that the American Southwest "is the enduring land of enchantment, of *curanderas* [healers] and Pueblo rain dances, of drought-stricken chile fields and a Spanish-speaking people whose tenure on that land precedes the arbitrary titles of 'United States' and 'Mexico'" (p. 1). Acknowledging late twentieth-century devolution, she is forced to add, "It is also a land of modern complications: polluted canals, food stamps, unemployment, and wide-screen TVs, which promise so much more, and so much less, than real life has to offer" (*Ibid.*). By turning her own backyard into a metaphor for the complicated interconnectedness of life, she builds immediacy into her commentary and a subtext of admiration for resilience in living things.

For all the hardships faced by the residents of the American desert, Kingsolver finds the environment uniquely suited to the sensibilities of a poet and fiction writer. She remarked to interviewer Jean Ross on the importance of Arizona's uniqueness to her point of view: "Living in the southwest makes you pay attention to color and contrast and hard edges, in terms of both physical landscape and human landscape" (Ross, p. 286). In the text of *Last Stand: America's Virgin Lands* (2002), she honors author Edward Abbey, a "prophet and visionary [who] planted his feet on the gorgeous, ravaged southwestern desert and burned her face into the nation's heart and conscience with his prose" (p. 17). By speaking of the desert as a feminine presence, Kingsolver alludes to ecofeminism, a maternal, nurturing attitude toward nature.

The fragility of life in an arid climate reminds the author's characters of nature's demands as well as the need to banish deserts in the soul. In *The Bean Trees* (1988), a night foray into the drought-choked suburbs of Tucson reminds characters that the lightning-charged scenario depicts all creation in a balance of living and dying. Through the observations of Codi Noline about polluters in *Animal Dreams* (1990), Kingsolver expresses the critical need for pure water to a desert community. During a long ride with Loyd Peregrina to Canyon de Chelly, Codi contrasts the "dinosaur skeletons of old machinery" at the abandoned Black Mountain mine to the subtle elegance of Arizona hills "pale brown grading to pink, sparsely covered with sage and fall-blooming wildflowers" (pp. 122, 123). Past galloping horses, evergreens, and "yellow flowers, punctuated by tall white poppies with silver leaves and tissue-paper petals," Codi takes in beauty as a prelude to lovemaking under a blue sky (p. 126).

Into the Christmas season, Kingsolver strengthens the link between Codi's love for Loyd and her appreciation of the desert. On the long drive north to Santa Rosalia Pueblo, she marvels at the pink and red striations of sandstone hills. The drive lulls her into blessed languor, "soaking into my body like blotter paper" (p. 209). Snow falls like powdered sugar on Codi's first view of the canyon at daylight and her introduction to Spider Rock, a mythic steeple that echoes through native oral stories. As though ushered into a cathedral, Codi absorbs the mystic religion of the North American past. Contributing to the sanctity of the landscape of Four Corners are the animal petroglyphs incised by preliterate people, an art show bearing scriptural reverence for nature.

See also **pueblo**

• *Further Reading*

Newman, Vicky. "Compelling Ties: Landscape, Community, and Sense of Place." *Peabody Journal of Education*, Vol. 70, No. 4, Summer 1995, pp. 105–118.
Ross, Jean W. "Interview." *Contemporary Authors.* Vol. 134. Detroit: Gale Research, 1992, pp. 284–290.

discontent

Like the author herself, Kingsolver's loners tend to suffer an abiding discontent that causes them to strike out on their own. In *The Bean Trees* (1988), Taylor Greer's flight from going-nowhere males in dead-end jobs frees her from having to marry from the small selection of potential mates in eastern Kentucky. Cash Stillwater, the Cherokee beadworker in *Pigs in Heaven* (1993), spends two years making Indian jewelry in Jackson Hole, Wyoming, but returns because he finds wealthy people unable to enjoy what they have without regrets or longing for more. Of the next generation,

Cash laments that they lack rural values: "Our kids had to work out what to do with liquor and fast cars and fast movies and ever kind of thing. For us, the worst we could do was break an egg" (p. 256).

The author reserves a more serious discontent for Codi Noline, protagonist of *Animal Dreams* (1990), who lacked adequate parental love in childhood. Her mind clouds the past, concealing people and events and replacing them with a pulsating sadness that overwhelms and paralyzes. Codi's inability to commit to a place, a job, or a lover rankles, threatening her stability and a budding relationship with Loyd Peregrina. He correctly accuses her of an inability to claim the things she loves. Symbolically, she lets go of the stillborn child from her teen years by exhuming the small black bundle and burying it in her mother's garden. The admission of the failed pregnancy relieves her anguish at the same time that it restores Doc Homer's love of his girls, whom his arms attempt to embrace once more as though Codi and Hallie were still babes.

Kingsolver builds irony out of more loss—first sister, then father—that liberates Codi from solitude and introspection and forces her into the loving arms of her fifty foster mothers in Grace, Arizona. An informal orchard funeral for Hallie restores tokens of the past as, one by one, friends recall the Noline girls in childhood. As though gathering her sister's remains, Codi enfolds the items in her security afghan, the crocheted embrace that warmed the motherless girls at difficult moments. The choice of town name suits the reclamation: Codi receives a touch of grace in each human contact she accepts at face value. Like the gift that doesn't have to be deserved, acceptance rids her of self-doubt and bonds her to a community, family, and the mothering of her unborn child.

In a more dangerous setting, discontent threatens to consume the Price women in *The Poisonwood Bible* (1998), the story of an ill-fated mission to central Africa. Given no voice in the family's future, Orleanna and her four daughters make the best of life in the village of Kilanga, a poor Congolese settlement on the Kwilu River. Kingsolver paces the female complaints with alternating chapters from varying points of view. Orleanna is the most pathetic in blaming herself for letting her misguided husband endanger his family and in shouldering guilt for the death of Ruth May from snakebite. The twins Leah and Adah recognize their father's phony righteousness as bull-headedness rather than sanctity. Rachel, the least contented and least changed by the family sojourn in the Congo, maintains an egocentrism that turns her into a caricature of American teen materialism. Into adulthood, she fends for herself through relationships and marriages that favor her enrichment. In her fifties, she sits at the bar of the Equatorial Hotel, smokes and drinks Singapore slings into the night, and reflects on a tenacious spirit that replaced the discontent of her young womanhood.

The simmering unhappiness in *Prodigal Summer* (2000) expresses normal shift in family life, beginning with the accidental death of Cole Widener in a truck jack-knifing. As the large rural family realigns itself, five sisters nearly overwhelm the widow, Lusa Maluf Landowski, with expectations for her behavior and use of the family homeplace. Parallel to her learning experiences are the mild disagreements between neighboring orchard keeper Nanny Land Rawley with next-door tree breeder Garnett

S. Walker, III. Above Zebulon Mountain, Deanna Wolfe, a forest ranger and naturalist, finds an idyllic life in a log cabin easily upended by the intrusion of rancher
and coyote-hating hunter Eddie Bondo.

The restoration of order to the Zebulon area involves interconnected actions:
Lusa learns from Garnett how to establish a goat farm; Nanny manages to lessen Garnett's hostility toward her organic apple orchard; and Deanna, carrying Eddie's child,
retreats to Nanny's farm to winter over while awaiting the birth of her first child in
spring. Critics were quick to point out the artificiality of so neat a resolution to each
character's complaints. The rapid-fire reconnection of characters to strands of contentment suits the author's essays on simplistic improvements to real life, such as
respect for nature by banning pesticides, respect for intellect by limiting family exposure to television, and respect for all life by ending wars and other forms of armed
violence.

See also **rescue, self-esteem, survival, Deanna Wolfe**

Domingos, Emelina

The high school chum of Codi Noline in *Animal Dreams* (1990), Emelina
Domingos epitomizes the welcome extended by Grace, Arizona. Her day-to-day existence revolves around an orchard, poultry and livestock, five sons, and a largely
absent husband, Juan Teobaldo "J. T." Domingos, who works for the railroad. On
her friend's arrival from Tucson, Emelina offers a guesthouse, a temporary residence
that confers family love as well as limited privacy. Set in Emelina's garden, the structure foreshadows the love that blossoms between Codi and Loyd Peregrina. Like Sugar
Hornbuckle in *Pigs in Heaven* (1993), Emelina is amiable, dependable, and devoted
to motherhood and domesticity. During a day away from motherhood and house-
wifely duties, she feels the tug from home that diminishes her delight in a moment
to herself.

Emelina is a model of sisterly friendship. She takes Codi to heart like blood kin
and shelters her through the hard times. At Hallie's funeral, Emelina shares with
Loyd the task of bolstering Codi, lending her strength to conduct the free-form
memorial service. When Codi chooses to depart Grace permanently, Emelina retreats
from words and communicates through tight, mute gestures. Kingsolver describes
her "unarmed rage" as "the worst thing she was capable of aiming at a friend" (p.
310). Emelina's hostility toward loss reflects the behaviors of other villagers, who
express their love for Codi without excess. Kingsolver implies that the Hispanic background of Grace residents produces ungenerous, yet loving gestures, including the
cool relationship between Codi and Doña Althea and between Doc Homer and his
emotionally needy daughters.

Domingos, Viola

The sixtyish widow of a steelworker and grandmother of J. T. and Emelina's five
sons in *Animal Dreams* (1990), Viola Domingos is like the petite, understated, and
resilient garden flower for which she is named. Beneath a matronly exterior, stereo-

typical in its black dress and tidy gray bun, she is savvy in the ways of a large-scale polluter in Grace, Arizona. To Codi Noline's naive assumption that an affidavit on the biotic death of the river will stir the Environmental Protection Agency, Viola is certain that the company will divert the river to free themselves of responsibility for poisoning the water. She informs Codi that owners of the Black Mountain mine will "dam it up and send it out Tortoise Canyon" to avoid harming residents, leaving them without a water source (p. 111). Because the community signed over water rights in 1939, citizens lack clout to halt the loss of their only source of water.

Viola's role in alleviating Codi's ignorance about the past elevates the old lady's importance from grandmother to sibyl. Viola is fatalistic, warning Codi, "We could all die tomorrow. Only the Lord knows" (p. 112). The annual celebrations of All Soul's Day enable Codi to nudge out tidbits of the past from Viola that gradually fill in family history that an emotional amnesia has shrouded. From a developing mother-daughter relationship with Codi, Viola feels obligated to tell her about the leave-taking on the hillside, when three-year-old Codi watched a helicopter alight to carry her dying mother away. The image burns away the amnesia, enabling Codi to relive the day she held Viola's hand and watched her mother's soul rise heavenward. As a fostering mother, Viola helps Codi ease back into village life and cope with greater losses of sister and father.

ecofeminism

Critics have attached to Kingsolver's works the term ecofeminism, a gynecentric attachment to nature that emerges from female nesting and nurturing of young to assure that life will thrive in subsequent generations. The subtext of *Animal Dreams* (1990) depicts a reverence for land and water in both the native American and Latino villagers of Grace, Arizona. To preserve their community, the women recycle peacock feathers as adornment for piñatas that they sell in Tucson. With the cash, they finance a campaign to declare their town a model of national heritage. For their battle against a copper-mining firm's poisoning of the river, critic Henry Aay depicts the novel as ecofiction, a genre "in which themes of environmental degradation, conflict, and restoration constitute important texts or subtexts" (Aay, p. 65).

The ennobling of women as stewards of the earth reaches a poignant height in *The Poisonwood Bible* (1998), in which a white missionary family observes at close range the struggle of Congolese women to survive. In a jungle setting along the Kwilu River, women make the most of native plants and animals to sustain hungry families and treat their ills. Mama Tataba, the Prices' housekeeper, demonstrates how to haul and purify water, split wood for the cookstove, deodorize the privy with ash, and kill snakes. Her knowledge of planting vegetables in hills derives from native experience with thin, unstable soil that quickly liquefies in monsoon rains.

Over thirty years later, Leah Price Ngemba cultivates vegetables on a communal farm in Angola and forges a oneness with Congolese women. Kingsolver pictures her as patient and experienced after years of living in a Kinshasa slum, where goats eat her poor garden patch under the clothesline. Away from the turmoil of Mobutu's dictatorship, she returns to planting and harvesting as the most sensible cycle of life.

Her ability to think like a native African helps her to understand transient people who refuse to plant fruit trees because they may not remain long enough to harvest a crop. She speaks the wisdom of the insider when she decries the European clear-cutting of jungle to plant in "fragile red laterite," a soil formed by the decomposition of rocks weathered by tropical heat and rinsed free of nutrients by monsoons (p. 524). She concludes that "Central Africa is a rowdy society of flora and fauna that have managed to balance together on a trembling geologic plate for ten million years" (p. 525). Out of respect for that balance, she becomes an "un-missionary" willing to learn from the land and its people (*Ibid.*).

See also **activism**, ***Animal Dreams***, **desert**, **Mama Mwanza**, **nature**, **pollution**, **Leah Price**, **pueblos**, **recycling**, **Mama Tataba**, **women**

• *Further Reading*

Aay, Henry. "Environmental Themes in Ecofiction: *In the Center of the Nation* and *Animal Dreams*." *Journal of Cultural Geography*, Vol. 14, No. 2, Spring/Summer 1994, pp. 65–85.

Eisler, Riane. "The Gaia Tradition and the Partnership Future: An Ecofeminist Manifesto," in *Reweaving the World: The Emergence of Ecofeminism*. San Francisco: Sierra Club, 1990.

Hile, Janet L. "Barbara Kingsolver." *Authors & Artists*, Gale Group, Vol. 15, pp. 73–79.

Eisenhower, Dwight D.

Dwight David Eisenhower (1890–1969), who served two consecutive terms as United States president from 1953 to 1961, recurs as a subtextual authority figure throughout *The Poisonwood Bible* (1998). During their seventeen-month sojourn at a mission in Kilanga, Congo, the Price family learns about an American conspiracy against Patrice Lumumba, a duly elected premier in equatorial Africa. In the description of critic Mike Gonzalez, the four Price women "come dramatically to the realisation that the cheerful, avuncular figure on the kitchen wall is a man willing to destroy a whole society, to impose a new barbarism in the name of civilisation" (Gonzalez). In late fall 1961, after Kilangans end their famine with the meat from a fire surround, Rachel, the least acclimated of the Price women, returns home sick with despair. While washing the ash from her body, she looks up at Orleanna's picture of the president as though glimpsing an amiable, white-haired father figure. Her attitude suits the idealistic teen girl who cares only for self by shutting out the social and political ills of the Congo.

Kingsolver weaves in and out of her text the paradox of the grandfatherly American head of government by revealing Eisenhower's concealed plot to murder Lumumba, the short-lived premier of the Congo. According to critic Jerome Weeks, the author was correct in her accusation: "Yes, he did order that assassination. As for his justifications—the Cold War, the prime minister's involvement with the Soviets—those are still up for debate," a mild disclaimer that presents the American justification for the killing (Weeks). Additional investigation suggests that Britain's Lord Home was Eisenhower's co-conspirator in reviving "the techniques of old-fashion diplomacy," a cynical euphemism for murder plots (Boateng). Joining Home and Eisenhower in sanctioning the plot to kill the Congolese premier were Belgian and United Nations leaders, including U.N. president Dag Hammarskjöld.

Crucial to an understanding of American involvement is Kingsolver's depiction of citizen disinterest in Eisenhower's meddling in global politics and the results of CIA-sponsored terrorism against the Congolese. While immured in the Central African mission in the early 1960s, Leah, the most politically astute member of the missionary family, admits to having "damned many men to hell, President Eisenhower, King Léopold, and my own father included" (p. 421). Critic Brad S. Born characterized Kingsolver's intent as a complex form of anti-patriarchy: "Immediately one encounters Kingsolver's heavy hand at work, hammering out the fearful symmetry of the abusive white male, the fundamentalist Christian zealot, and the ugly American, all incarnated in Nathan Price, the arch missionary villain ... a demonic trinity of Father Price, Father Christianity, and Father America," a reference to the two-term president (Born).

See also **Patrice Lumumba, Mobutu Sese Seko**

• *Further Reading*

Boateng, Osei. "United Against 'Satan.'" *New African*, No. 400, October 2001.

Born, Brad S. "Kingsolver's Gospel for Africa: (Western White Female) Heart of Goodness." *Mennonite Life*, Vol., 56 No. 1, March 2001.

Fahringer, Catherine. "Treat Yourself to *The Poisonwood Bible*." *Freethought Today*, June/July 2001.

Gonzalez, Mike. "Into the Heart of Darkness." *Socialist Review*, No. 261, March 2002.

Koza, Kimberly. "The Africa of Two Western Women Writers: Barbara Kingsolver and Margaret Laurence." *Critique*, Vol. 44, No. 3, Spring 2003, pp. 284–294.

"Review: *The Poisonwood Bible*." *Publisher's Weekly*, Vol. 245, No. 32, August 10, 1998, p. 366.

Weeks, Jerome. "Where Historians, Authors Part." *Dallas Morning News*, June 17, 2001.

Esperanza

A grieving Mayan mother fleeing Guatemala with her husband Estevan in *The Bean Trees* (1988), Esperanza hovers near the breaking point after losing home, country, and child. Kingsolver advances the irony of her name by calling her Hope, the English translation. The author depicts her in a severely depressed state compounded by attempted suicide after the kidnap of her daughter Ismene. On Esperanza's first sight of Turtle Greer, she blanches and stares at the Cherokee child, who resembles Ismene. Suitably, Esperanza chooses baby aspirin to end her misery, but survives. Making up an original axiom out of a pun, Taylor reminds her, "*Esperanza* is all you get, no second chances" (p. 148).

In a later conversation, Esperanza's limited comments relate her despair at rootlessness. She introduces Taylor to Mayan melodies, "songs older than Christopher Columbus, maybe even older than Christopher the saint" (p. 194). Worsening Esperanza's homesickness for her Mayan homeland is the burden of "not belonging in any place. To be unwanted everywhere" (p. 195). Kingsolver creates an ingenious escape valve for Esperanza in the playacting necessary to give Taylor permanent custody of Turtle. At the office of Jonas Wilford Armistead, Esperanza sheds honest tears of separation and confides, "Now is so hard. We move around so much, we have nothing, no home" (p. 214). As a blessing on Turtle as she enters the Greer family, Esperanza bestows her "medallion of St. Christopher, guardian saint of refugees" (p. 215). Estevan acknowledges that the catharsis offers his wife as much peace as she is likely to find.

Estevan

Fleeing political oppression in Guatemala City in *The Bean Trees* (1988), Estevan, an English teacher calling himself Steve, attempts to comfort his grieving wife and assuage the loss of their daughter Ismene to kidnappers. The couple chose between recovering the child or saving the seventeen surviving members of an illegal teacher's union. To Taylor Greer, he is remarkably noble and handsome. After he introduces chopsticks from the Chinese restaurant where he washes dishes, the author uses him as the conduit for a fable of cooperation, the story of people in heaven feeding each other with unwieldy spoons. A model of the native American oral tradition, the illustrative tale ripostes to Virgie May Valentine Parsons, a diner at the table who resents refugees coming to the United States.

While revealing his origin, Estevan divulges that one of the twenty-two Mayan dialects is his native tongue. He adds that the Maya flourished long before the European discovery of the New World and that their technology extended to astronomical observatories and brain surgery. He relieves Taylor's romantic notions of jungles bright with quetzels and women in vibrant dresses with the reality of political oppression and people fleeing for their lives from police who regularly burn homes and fields and torture people with charges from a crank telephone. With gentlemanly grace, he accords the worst of his family's sufferings to his wife by telling Taylor, "You cannot know what Esperanza has had to live through" (p. 135). With respect for both refugees' travails, Taylor remarks, "I can't even begin to think about a world where people have to make choices like that" (p. 137).

Estevan, like Anatole Ngemba in *The Poisonwood Bible* (1998), Loyd Peregrina in *Animal Dreams* (1990), and Eddie Bondo in *Prodigal Summer* (2000), is the outsider who develops into a problematic love interest. He engages Taylor's heart with gentleness and kind acts toward "Tortolita," but remains at arm's length out of devotion to his wife. His wisdom and guile aids the flight from immigration authorities in Tucson and the fraudulant handover of Turtle to Taylor at the magistrate's office in Oklahoma County. The attraction between Taylor and Estevan refuses to die, leaving her weepy and down-hearted at separation from a man who "wasn't mine to have" (p. 221). The author incorporates the possibility of illicit love to normalize political fiction that characterizes Estevan's fearful flight from home through the underground railroad in Tucson.

exclusion

Kingsolver's openness toward people emerges in positive scenarios of acceptance and cooperation as well as in the negative scenes of snobbery and exclusion. In a quiet talk in *The Bean Trees* (1988) between Taylor Greer and Estevan, a Guatemalan refugee, she states her feeling of alienation: "Sometimes I feel like I'm a foreigner too. I come from a place that's so different from here you would think you'd stepped right off the map into some other country where they use dirt for decoration" (pp. 135). The admission summarizes Taylor's sense of otherness among desert dwellers like Mattie, a rescuer of threatened Central Americans, who knows and loves the frightened survivors as though they were family members.

To express a childhood memory of exclusion, Taylor outlines for Estevan the cliques in her Kentucky high school, where a student could be a townie, jock, hoodlum, or nutter, the low-status group of rural and poor kids to which Taylor belonged. They received the ignoble nickname because they earned cash for school clothes by shelling and marketing walnuts, which darkened their hands with an indelible stain, a foreshadowing of the stain on their self-esteem. Estevan speaks from a scholarly interest in narrow social strata: "In India they have something called the caste system. Members of different castes cannot marry or even eat together. The lowest caste is called the Untouchables" (p. 133). His commentary helps her comprehend the suicide of nerdish Scotty Richey, a bright classmate who had no supportive social group equal to Taylor's nutters "at the bottom of the pile" (p. 134). The re-evaluation of her social life enables her to take comfort in the camaraderie of other nutters.

Exclusion takes the form of racism and exploitation in *The Poisonwood Bible* (1998). Leah Price, wife of Congolese freedom fighter Anatole Ngemba, faces the two-edged sword of hostile stares and rude remarks in the Congo as well as her home-state of Georgia. She weathers the silence of fellow shoppers in the Kinshasa market, where "a bubble of stopped conversation moves with me as I walk" (p. 472). From a mother's point of view, she regrets the ugliness directed at her four mixed-race sons and questions from the ignorant about the ritual scars on Anatole's face. Ending her reunion with the two surviving Price sisters are two more hurtful acts of exclusion — Rachel's lack of grief for the death of Pascal, one of their Kilangan friends from childhood, and her refusal to offer rooms to the Ngembas at her Equatorial Hotel, a whites-only bastion of decadent luxuries.

See also **Brother Fowles**

• *Further Reading*

Aprile, Dianne. "Kinship with Kingsolver: Author's Characters Long to Belong, Something That Touches Readers." *Louisville Courier-Journal*, July 25, 1993, p. I1.
Murrey, Loretta Martin. "The Loner and the Matriarchal Community in Barbara Kingsolver's *The Bean Trees* and *Pigs in Heaven*." *Southern Studies*, Vol. 5, No. 1–2, Spring & Summer 1994, pp. 155–164.

fable

Kingsolver elucidates the purpose of oral tradition to preliterate people with Loyd Peregrina's mythic tales of Spider Woman and the rearing of the War Twins in *Animal Dreams* (1990), Anatole's wooing fable in *The Poisonwood Bible* (1998), and a Mayan dining fable in *The Bean Trees* (1988). In the latter, Estevan's "South American, wild *Indian* story" explains the difference between heaven and hell while illustrating the importance of cooperation to human communities (p. 107). The choice of mutual feeding as a symbol of community and sharing suits Kingsolver's motifs of vegetables, flowers, nurturing, women's networking, and mutual assistance. The moral of Estevan's fable demonstrates how the human family must draw on patience and clever cooperative solutions to life-threatening difficulties, such as rescue of refugees, unloved women like Lou Ann Ruiz and Alice Greer, handicapped people like Edna Poppy and Angel Ruiz, and abused children like Turtle and Ismene. The allegory at the end of "How They Eat in Heaven" stresses the communal nature of the network of friends who give to each other, just as the characters in Estevan's exemplum feed each other with long-handled spoons (p. 90).

In *Animal Dreams*, Kingsolver reshapes explanations of multiculturalism through fable. Loyd Peregrina's eye-opening route to Santa Rosalia Pueblo becomes a visual education to Codi Noline on the beliefs and lore of desert peoples. Within the multi-hued canyon walls, Codi identifies a rock spire that resembles a steeple. Her recognition of a focal Indian landmark introduces Loyd's telling of the myth of Spider Woman. Like Arachne in Greek mythology, she uses her weaving skills to advantage and passes them on to Navajo women. Her importance to desert tribes resulted in variant sets of tales from Navajo and Pueblo mythmakers. No less structured than Spider Woman are the kachina dancers and the koshari, religious clowns, who pantomime in dance their role in universal stories of the cyclical renewal of nature. To Codi's questions about purpose, Loyd explains ritual dance as a form of prayer and a way to maintain balance.

The author returns to fable in the falling action of *The Poisonwood Bible*. In a scene that counters the early hungers and fears of the Ngemba family, Anatole lies in the dark and romances his wife of thirty years. Enjoying privacy and a comfortable bed at the agricultural station in Sanza Pombo, Angola, the two retreat to "the New Republic of Connubia" for his version of world history (p. 519). Through a fanciful retelling of the Portuguese exploration of Africa, he emphasizes the advanced civilization of the Kongo people, whom Europeans considered primitive. The story, which turns into a summary of their own marriage, soothes Leah during recurrences of malaria. She suffers the bad dreams of Africa's exploitation by slave traders and colonizers, but awakens to love for her family. The use of fable in this closing scene captures the idealism that Anatole and Leah share as a basis for a lasting love.

See also **Adah Price**

family

Kingsolver's concept of family bolsters isolated and lonely characters. The modified unit bends and stretches from the father/mother/child paradigm to include a variety of interdependent relationships. Just as Lou Ann Ruiz, Taylor Greer, and one natural and one foster child form a family unit in *The Bean Trees* (1988), so do Edna Poppy and her friend Virgie Mae Valentine Parsons, and Mattie and her refugees and support system of couriers, priest, and doctor. The emphasis is on trust and commitment rather than on a stereotype of people performing a predictable set of functions and conforming to a legalistic definition of wedded and blood kin residing in the same house. The fragility of human life makes the linkage that much more precious.

In an interview, the author asserted that the American family standard is a narrow model: "If you look anyplace else in the world that's simply not the case. It's an aberration, but we think of it as the norm" ("A Conversation"). By way of illustration, she created the story of Taylor and her unofficial daughter Turtle, who rely on Lou Ann and her son Dwayne Ray as well as on Virgie, companion and lead dog to blind Edna, Turtle's occasional babysitter. By telephone, Taylor maintains the link to home and birth mother, but the *ad hoc* community that buoys and supports her in Arizona offers the immediacy of non-blood kin living close and handy when Taylor needs help. From the experience of forming the family circle and embracing its members, in *Pigs in Heaven* (1993), Taylor acknowledges that the glue that holds them together is determination: "That's what your family is, the people you won't let go of for anything" (p. 328).

With *Animal Dreams* (1990), the novelist explores a motherless female character in Codi Noline, whose mother, Althea "Alice" Noline, died of kidney failure two months after giving birth to Hallie when Codi was three years old. When Codi produced a stillborn child after four hours' labor in the privacy of the bathroom, she demanded that Hallie fetch her mother's black sweater, an appropriate wrapping for the tiny bundle Codi buried in an arroyo of Tortoise Canyon. Similarly, the motherless sisters treasure their security afghan like woven arms wrapped around them. When Codi endangers her relationship with Loyd Peregrina, she "poked … fingers through the holes in the black-and-red afghan, a decades-old nervous habit," an image of grasping for mothering from a crocheted garment (p. 182). She cites Robert Frost's defensive line from "The Death of the Hired Man," issued in *North of Boston* (1914), in which the poet describes home as "the place where, when you have to go there, they have to take you in" (p. 182). Tearfully, Codi wishes for a place where she feels wanted.

Kingsolver demonstrates family love on Christmas Eve at Santa Rosalia Pueblo, where a loving mother, sisters, and aunts enfold Loyd Peregrina and welcome Codi in an ongoing conversation blended from English, Keres, and Spanish. To her questions about his Apache father, he explains the matrilinear arrangement that required him to live with Inez Peregrina, who met his father at a tribal dance. Loyd excuses his father's oddities as the result of life at a boarding school and a lack of family bonding that allowed him to desert "the old ways," which he never really learned (p. 233). The discussion causes Codi to reflect on her own unorthodox upbringing, which caused her to feel "undeserving of love and incapable of benevolence" (*Ibid.*).

The author enhances the irony of Codi's acceptance into Loyd's family at the same time that Doc Homer, her failing father, is receiving word that Hallie has vanished from a Nicaraguan field in the hands of Contra kidnappers. His *secuestrada* daughter inspires love from thirty locals, who search for her despite the danger of retaliation. The unidentified speaker on the telephone reminds Doc Homer that the Contras are a constant threat to family unity: "We're a nation of bereaved families. The only difference this time is that it happens to be an American" (p. 249). Appropriately, Kingsolver provides a community ingathering at Hallie's funeral to restore her place in their hearts and bolster Codi against the grief of her murder and the coming loss of Doc Homer, whose health lapses from Alzheimer's disease. Ironically, at the same time that her father is losing his own memory, Codi recovers her recall of community love from fifty foster mothers.

The image of family takes on more complexities when Kingsolver moves to the Congo to set *The Poisonwood Bible* (1998). The inclusion of villagers in an enlarged family results in the sharing of food in hard times and communal feasts to celebrate the arrival of a new missionary and his family. The Prices prove so inept at surviving in the jungle that Mama Mwanza, their neighbor, slips eggs and chickens into their henhouse as a surreptitious contribution. At the high point of crisis for Kilangans, a squabble breaks out after the villagers join in a fire surround, a communal kill of animals during an ongoing drought. The threat is manifold — a breaking down of kinships and neighborliness and an undermining of village cohesion, which depends on the family as its bedrock.

After Leah Price marries Anatole Ngemba and establishes a family of three mixed-race boys in Kinshasa, the household increases to seven with the addition of Aunt Elisabet and her daughter Christiane, all sheltering in a one-room house in the slums of Kinshasa. Leah's devotion to family requires constant discipline of funds and foodstuffs, which tend toward meal after meal of manioc. She acquires a new understanding of kwashiorkor, the disease that causes African children to produce bulging bellies as abdominal muscles lose the strength to bind heavy organs to their frames. She is able to feel that her family is blessed above other starving families because the Ngembas "have the option of leaving" (p. 455).

Kingsolver's expansive definition of family takes on new meaning in *Prodigal Summer* (2000), in which isolated people profit from inclusion in a network of loving people. The least involved in family is Deanna Wolfe, orphaned daughter of a farmer in Egg Fork. Her interest in the return of the coyote to the eastern mountains takes her into the wild as forest ranger. Her illusions about solitude and self-sufficiency collapse after a summer-long affair with hunter Eddie Bondo. Early symptoms of pregnancy and a terror of thunderstorms send her down the mountain to Nannie Land Rawley, a lone orchard keeper who had fostered Deanna after her mother's death.

The author revives memories of an unofficial family begun when Ray Dean Wolfe, Deanna's father, formed a relationship with Nannie and fathered her daughter, Rachel Carson Rawley. Nannie's isolation after Rachel's death from heart malformation subsides in part from the elderly woman's increasing fondness for a next-door grouch, Garnett S. Walker, III, who meddles in Nannie's lifestyle with unwanted advice. The third branch of the family takes shape at a nearby farm, where widowed goatherd Lusa Maluf Landowski offers a home to Crys and Lowell, Garnett's neglected grandchildren, whose mother is dying of cancer. The branches of the author's makeshift family reach out to relieve human need. The inclusiveness of families in Egg Fork forms a paradigm of Kingsolver's belief in the unity of all humankind.

See also **cooperation, ecofeminism, motherhood, women**

• *Further Reading*

"A Conversation with Barbara Kingsolver." http://www.readinggroupguides.com/guides/animal_dreams-author.asp.

Regier, Amy M. "Replacing the Hero with the Reader: Public Story Structure in *The Poisonwood Bible*." *Mennonite Life*, Vol. 56, No. 1, March 2001.

feminism

Reviewers hesitate to identify author Barbara Kingsolver as a bona fide, hard-charging feminist. Rather, she tends to choose women as having the most significant commentary on issues such as Mattie's aid to Central American refugees and Taylor Greer's experience with child abuse and adoption in *The Bean Trees* (1988) and *Pigs in Heaven* (1993); Orleanna Price and Leah Price Ngemba's survival of war and tyranny in *The Poisonwood Bible* (1998); and Deanna Wolfe, Nannie Land Rawley, and Lusa Maluf Landowski's fight for ecology. In the essay "His-and-Hers Politics" (1993), Kingsolver expounded on the dangers people face in a gender-fractured milieu: "The men's movement and the women's movement aren't salt and pepper; they are hangnail and hand grenade" (p. 70). Her diatribes in favor of family and full citizenship for women often focus on the distortions of the media. In "Between the Covers," a 1998 book review for the *Washington Post*, she railed against the absurd matings of Hollywood couples "in a world where nymphets and sexagenarian men in movie-love are beginning to wear down any other expectation" (p. 1). The examples reveal a tough point of view grounded in good sense.

In writing her first major publication, the feminist documentary *Holding the Line: Women in the Great Arizona Mine Strike of 1983* (1989), Kingsolver, then a free-lance journalist, allied with the women who supported striking miners. Crucial to assessment of a landmark standoff between labor and management was the determination of ordinary wives and mothers to remain on the picket line and fight a company that threatened workers with inadequate job security and benefits. The text delivers straightforward reporting of unconscionable behaviors, e.g., "On the picket lines, women complained of being spat upon, swerved at, and threatened with bodily harm while the police looked on but did nothing" (p. 128). False arrests and constant surveillance of the female auxiliary produced a surprising effect by turning amateur labor supporters into organizers and spokeswomen for fair treatment. The women's resolve grew out of daily experience with intimidation. At the book's conclusion, the author quoted their coming-to-knowledge about big business: "We're not dumb; we can see what's happening…. We're going to take care of ourselves now" (p. 190).

See also **motherhood, parenthood, women**

• *Further Reading*

DeMarr, Mary Jean. *Barbara Kingsolver: A Critical Companion*. Westport, Conn.: Greenwood, 1999.

flight

In Kingsolver's fiction, flight is one of the paradoxical sources of hope and unease
in displaced people. In *The Bean Trees* (1988), the novelist pictures the maturation
of Taylor Greer, a restless young woman in search of an adult life far from home.
Unlike characters who must run to survive, Taylor leaves home on purpose "just as
soon as I could get the tires of my car pointed rubber side down," as she states in
the non-sequel, *Pigs in Heaven* (1993) (p. 250). Juxtaposed with Taylor are Estevan
and Esperanza, a Guatemalan refugee couple escaping a murderous Central American regime that kidnapped their daughter Ismene. The refugees' relative contentment
in Tucson is temporary because of demands from anti-immigrant laws allowing only
those with documented proof of persecution to continue living in the United States.
When the pressures on Estevan and Esperanza call for immediate flight, Taylor volunteers to drive them to an Oklahoma safe house, where their native American col-
oring and made-up names allow them to blend in with Cherokees and to elude the
Immigration and Naturalization Service. The terrible parting from friends and familiar places is part of the price the emigrés bear for living in a safer land.

Pigs in Heaven moves from the Guatemalan couple's flight from the regime that
stole their daughter to American laws that threaten to repossess Turtle from Taylor,
who establishes claim to her by tricking an Oklahoma City magistrate into thinking
the adoption has the parents' blessing. Kingsolver assembles a full cast of characters
on the lam, beginning with Taylor, who eludes threats from the Cherokee nation to
her fraudulant claim on daughter Turtle. The non-sinister villain, attorney Annawake
Fourkiller, implies sympathy while brandishing a statute declaring the Cherokee as
the ultimate judge of adoption placement of native children outside the tribe. Rush-
ing to Taylor's assistance is her great-hearted mother, Alice Stamper Greer, who flees
a mismated second marriage. Her suitability for Cash Stillwater, a prodigal returned
to the native fold, enhances the happily-ever-after conclusion.

Critics credit the author with limited success in bringing all these characters
together through a far-reaching act of literary centrifugal force, initiated by the rescue of Lucky Buster, a retarded runaway, from a sluiceway of Hoover Dam. Strain-
ing the reader's credulity is the sudden romance of Alice and Cash, proof of Alice's
kinship to the Cherokee, and Annawake's emotional catharsis for the loss of her twin
brother Gabriel through an illegal adoption. The end of the protagonist's separation
from Tucson and her lover Jax Thibodeaux implies that Taylor can rest from constant shifts of residence and job and return Turtle to a normal home environment.

Flight in *The Poisonwood Bible* (1998), Kingsolver's most accomplished work, is
the self-preservation of four women bent on ridding themselves of the ogreish Nathan
Price, a self-important missionary to the African Congo. Prefiguring their fearful
escape is the abrupt departure of Methuselah, the parrot whom Nathan jettisons into
the wild to depend on atrophied wings frozen with terror at his moment of release.

After the death of Ruth May, the youngest child, from snakebite, Orleanna leads her three remaining daughters away from Kilanga. In the description of reviewer Julian Markels, the women flee because they "have no choice but to break out of their Southern Baptist female subservience" (Markels). Their routes back to civilization separate them in body, but not in family unity.

Freedom from patriarchy, like palimpsest, reveals the beauties of individuality and purpose that layers of Nathan's bullying had concealed. On return to Bethlehem, Georgia, Adah, the handicapped genius, marvels at concrete curbing and a ladies' magazine, both of which seem superfluous after months of penury in Kilanga. She retreats from ridicule to Emory University because she "needed to get out of Bethlehem, out of my skin, my skull, and the ghost of my family" (p. 409). Rachel, the self-centered teen queen, perpetuates her egotism in the pursuit of wealthy men to support an expensive self-indulgence in alcohol, cigarettes, clothes, and the aura of privilege. Leah, the sister most dedicated to the Congolese, uses freedom as a chance at education in Georgia. With the skills of an agronomist, she returns to the strictures of Mobutu's dictatorship to educate the peasantry in nutrition and sanitation.

For Orleanna, the wounds of the tragic Kilangan mission are too firmly rooted to her psyche for flight to make much difference. At her plywood shack in Georgia, she surrounds herself with vegetables, flowers, and vines as though recreating in a small plot the profusion of Africa. Her focus turns to the sea, the divider between continents, as her spirit wrestles with the loss of Ruth May. For characters like Orleanna, flight does nothing to relieve a host of self-imprisoning memories and regrets. Adah provides what comfort Orleanna is capable of accepting; Leah adds the joy of four grandsons on infrequent visits to America for schooling. In retirement, as though emotionally chained to Africa, Orleanna withdraws to Sanderling Island and maintains her somber gaze out to sea.

See also **opportunity, self-esteem**

- *Further Reading*

Markels, Julian. "Coda: Imagining History in *The Poisonwood Bible*." *Monthly Review Press*, September 2003.

Murrey, Loretta Martin. "The Loner and the Matriarchal Community in Barbara Kingsolver's *The Bean Trees* and *Pigs in Heaven*." *Southern Studies*, Vol. 5, No. 1–2, Spring & Summer 1994, pp. 155–164.

Willis, Meredith Sue. "Barbara Kingsolver, Moving On." *Appalachian Journal*, Vol. 22, No. 1, 1994, pp. 78–86.

Fourkiller, Annawake

A radical Native American attorney and skilled negotiator in *Pigs in Heaven* (1993), Annawake Fourkiller represents efforts of Cherokees to sustain their heritage and ideals against threats of disunion from the white world. Kingsolver found the character's name on two tombstones in Oklahoma and developed the earnest lawyer into a brilliant, brooding twenty-seven-year-old loner who bears the scars of losing a twin through adoption by white parents. In an interview, the author confessed her difficulty in picking up after *The Bean Trees* (1988): "I knew that 98.5 percent of my readers would feel a strong and instantaneous sympathy with Taylor, because that's our culture. My task was to somehow bring my readers around to an equal sympathy with Annawake, or not with Annawake, with the values she represented" ("A Conversation"). To enhance menace in her role as bringer of justice to the Cherokee people, the author allows Jax Thibodeaux, one of her more jocular figures, to describe Annawake as "the lurk-in-the-bushes and make-scary-noises type" (p. 245). Alice Greer sees her more perceptively as "a cross between a scared rabbit and the hound that hunts him" (p. 277).

The attorney's rather cardboard purpose in the action is to avenge wrongs that the white culture did to her twin Gabe and to speak for the Cherokee social system that seeks to rescue every native child from removal from the appropriate ethnic parentage. It's difficult for her to map out communal parentage to someone like Alice Greer, who has no sense of tribal belonging. Annawake recaps Cherokee history with a description of white-mandated boarding school: "Cut off their hair, taught them English, taught them to love Jesus, and made them spend their entire childhoods in a dormitory" (p. 227). Despite harsh Anglo bigotry from the past, the author allows her to accept Taylor Greer as a worthy mother, even though she is white.

Kingsolver is careful about separating human beings from faceless bureaucracies. To retrieve Annawake from stolid one-sidedness, the author fleshes out her feminine side with memories of brothers and loving, quilt-stitching aunts. In private, she is able to admit that "you can't just go through life feeding cats, pretending you're not one of the needy yourself" (p. 61). From her uncle Ledger Fourkiller, a medicine man, she learned logic and stage presence by following him about the sacred circle and imitating his sermons before stomp dances. With his encouragement, she developed scholarship into a post as ambassador for her people. By extending her range from mediator to matchmaker, she "hatches the most reckless plan of her life," a compromise that ends Alice's manlessness by introducing her to Turtle's grandfather, Cash Stillwater (p. 232). As is typical of Kingsolver, the emergence of feminine wiles in Annawake proves more effective than professional bluster.

- *Further Reading*

"A Conversation with Barbara Kingsolver." http://www.readinggroupguides.com/guides/animal_dreams-author.asp.

Ryan, Maureen. "Barbara Kingsolver's Lowfat Fiction." *Journal of American Culture*, Vol. 18, No. 4, Winter 1995, pp. 77–82.

Fourkiller, Ledger

The chief medicine man for Cherokees of Heaven, Oklahoma, in *Pigs in Heaven* (1993), Ledger Fourkiller represents tradition and stability in a native society that values both. He is already beloved for nurturing his niece Annawake before he appears in person in Kingsolver's text. As the community graybeard, he lives in seclusion on a houseboat on Tenkiller Lake, where children flock in summer to enjoy the water and adults come for counsel. Among his official duties is the task of blessing a truck in Locust Grove. Tapping a lifetime of wisdom, he is able to look into "the paper doll that is Annawake" (p. 332). He tells illustrative stories as a means of easing her frustration over the displacement of Turtle Greer from a Cherokee environment.

Ledger's official appearance in the novel is momentous. At the climactic stomp dance, Alice Greer glimpses an unassuming Cherokee man dressed in ordinary clothes. His name is indicative of his value as a source of aboriginal lore. As though drawing on male powers, he bears a scrotum-shaped pouch on his belt in which he stores herbs and tobacco, the source of his healing ministrations. At the beginning of the ritual, he speaks a blessing "so clear it seems to be coming from somewhere above his ears," a suggestion of sanctity from some heavenly source (p. 266). Elders line up around the fire to smoke the ceremonial pipe, which passes to all, even children. They gesture in a circle, the pervasive native American symbol of unity and wholeness that is the source of Ledger's sermon.

Kingsolver depicts Ledger's teachings as effective, even to those who don't understand Cherokee. His homily spins out from his prayers and words directed to the sky and fire as he paces the holy circle. Alice, who interprets the event from an English-speaker's point of view, absorbs the words like soothing syrup — "unbroken song, as smooth as water over stones" (p. 268). She experiences his phrasing as a tactile phenomenon sprouting from the ground like a crystal vase and broadening as it moves up through oak branches. The utterance concludes with the congregation's assent, which breaks the spell.

See also **stomp dance**

Fourkiller genealogy

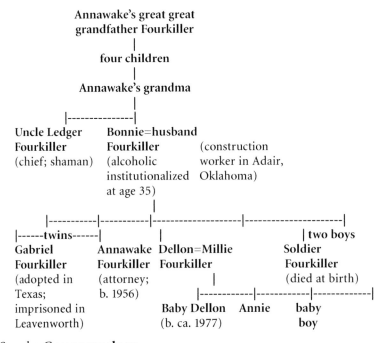

See also **Greer genealogy**

Fowles, Brother

In *The Poisonwood Bible* (1998), Brother Fyntan Fowles is the predecessor of the Price family in Kilanga village who "left some mystery in his wake" (p. 38). To the Prices' Georgian view, even though Fowles is a six-year veteran in the mission field, a New York–born Irishman like him deserves suspicion for being a Yankee. They suspect him of possible alliance with papist Catholicism, a heinous belief system to the Southern Baptist mindset. Among the enigmas of Fowles's departure from Kilanga are rumors of his "consorting" with black villagers (*Ibid.*). Among Fowles's requisites for redeeming Kilangans was an order that Tata Ndu disavow polygamy, a social institution that elevated his status as chief among his subjects. Aside from duties as moral guide, Fowles appears to have taken a naturalist's interest in Africa, an avocation that he followed through printed guides to butterflies, birds, and mammals. The study of local fauna contrasts Nathan Price's mule-headed disinterest in Africa and his immersion in scripture alone.

Fowles appears to have outshone his successor in pulpit skills. At one time, Fowles had most of Kilanga involved in Christian worship. Adding to the mystery of his tenure at Kilanga is the growl of his former African Grey parrot Methuselah, who learned to say "piss off" in some former life (p. 59). Adah Price considers the parrot "morally suspect"; Nathan declares him "a Catholic bird," the minister's most damning epithet (*Ibid.*). Leah innocently suggests Fowles's carnal interest in African females by repeating the parrot Methuselah's cry of "Sister, God is great! Shut the door!" (p. 66). Subsequent commentary reveals that he chose a Congolese woman for wife and established a healthy marriage and residency.

When Fowles reappears in the novel in fall 1960, local children welcome him as Tata Bidibidi (Mr. Bird), who chugs upriver in his boat along with his wife Celine and their biracial children. He asks about local people and takes the time to coddle Ruth May. To Leah's accusation of idol worship, he remarks diplomatically that "the Congolese have a world of God's grace in their lives, along with a dose of hardship that can kill a person entirely" (p. 247). For spiritual support, he avoids the hard-edged scripture that bolsters Nathan's resolve to baptize Kilanga's children. Instead of fundamentalist legalism, Fowles looks to nature. His method of instructing congregations is pantheistic, beginning with a seasonal Congolese hymn about seed yams and moving directly to the biblical parable of the mustard seed. To spread Christian practice, he debated husband-wife relations with Tata Ndu so thoroughly that village wife-beating declined. The fact reflects badly on Nathan, who strikes and browbeats his wife and daughters as his mood dictates.

In an interview with Michael Krasny of National Public Radio, the author identified Fowles, her favorite character in the book, as "a Jesus-like figure and he's actually married to a Congolese woman and he's in many ways the antithesis of Nathan Price" (Krasny). She describes their face-off as a kind of duel "using the Bible as sort of a sanction for their own views" (*Ibid.*). When the two men trade philosophies, Fowles chooses Romans 11:16–25 as a text, which speaks of grafting a wild olive shoot to a tree. Fowles warns of snobbery and elitism as looking down on the branches of God's tree and recommends Romans 12:3–5, which describes humanity as "one body in Christ" (p. 253). The inclusiveness of his philosophy is Kingsolver's snide comeuppance to Nathan, who is too proud and too judgmental to consider potential parishioners as friends and neighbors.

The crowning achievement of Brother Fowles as a missionary is his awareness of the needs of the body as well as of the spirit. The visit of the Fowles family is life-saving to the badly deteriorated Price family for the gifts of books, canned food, powdered milk, coffee, sugar, and quinine and antibiotics to battle Ruth May's malarial fever. More important to the Prices is Brother Fowles's loving interpretation of scripture in opposition to Nathan's punitive views of godliness. To Nathan, Fowles cannot rise above the level of "deluded purveyor of Christian malpractice" (p. 259). Overlooking his successor's scowls, Brother Fowles continues to supply the Price family with what he can spare.

Kingsolver withdraws from Fowles, supplying only snippets of future interaction with the Price family. While Leah shelters in a Central African mission, she tries to picture Jesus, but sees Brother Fowles, whose Christ-like behaviors endear him to his followers. He remains in touch with Leah and reports on Nathan's death. Both Fyntan and Celine Fowles maintain their support of the Ngemba family. In contrast to Nathan's madness and reputation for bizarre acts, Fowles holds steady to his theology of loving actions.

• *Further Reading*

Culp, Mary Beth. "Review: *The Poisonwood Bible*." Mobile, Alabama, *Harbinger*, February 2, 1999.
"Interview with Barbara Kingsolver." http://www3.baylor.edu:80/Rel_Lit/archives/interviews/kingsolver_intv.html.
Krasny, Michael. "Interview: Barbara Kingsolver, Author, Discusses Her New Book." *Talk of the Nation* (NPR), December 13, 1999.

Greer, Alice

The mother of Taylor Greer in *The Bean Trees* (1988) and *Pigs in Heaven* (1993), Alice Jean Stamper Greer Elleston is an older version of her daughter and a suitable spokeswoman for independent womanhood, marriage, and family. Unlike the self-serving mothers in Lillian Hellman's *The Little Foxes*, Amy Tan's *The Joy Luck Club*, and Tennessee Williams's *The Glass Menagerie*, Alice takes pride in her daughter's autonomy and fills an address book with crossed-out numbers as Taylor moves through a series of residences and jobs. Alice passed on to Taylor a strong work ethic, which Alice learned while growing up on a Mississippi hog farm, where she traded in cream, milk, and eggs. A hard-working housemaid and laundress, she was abandoned by Foster Greer, her first husband, shortly after Taylor was conceived.

Kingsolver, who values her own mother's example, describes Alice as an unwavering landmark to Taylor. Alice models the survivalism that strengthens her daughter from before birth into adulthood. In *The Bean Trees*, Taylor remembers her as believing "it was the moon I had just hung up in the sky and plugged in all the stars" (p. 10). To Taylor's dropping of Marietta, her birth name for the Georgia town in which she was conceived, Alice encourages her to be independent and think for herself. The advice is an outgrowth of lessons that the author learned from her own mother, Ginny Kingsolver.

Alice exemplifies a full range of human strengths and faults. Left alone when Taylor departs, she risks another relationship by marrying Harland Elleston, a poor choice for housemate. Symbolizing the lifelessness of their union is Harland's collection of antique auto headlights, which cast no beams on the couple's sterile relationship. Lacking warmth and intimacy, Alice chooses to give up on her second marriage, which offers only a warm body, little more than her abandonment by Foster Greer in the first marriage. In explanation of marital failure, she contends that the Stamper women have chosen to live manless for the past thirteen generations. The statement establishes her spunk in refusing to think of herself as a victim and in learning from her mistakes.

Kingsolver uses *Pigs in Heaven* (1993) as an opportunity to develop secondhand Harland's unappealing qualities, particularly his faith in television. He believes that watching events from his recliner is better than observing them in person because "you could see better on TV, because they let the cameras get right up close" (p. 264). Of the collapse of the marriage, Alice remarks that the Greers are "doomed to be a family with no men in it" (p. 231). In the earlier novel, she quipped, "My husbands went like houses on fire" (p. 328). Her reliance on humor is obviously the source of Taylor's wry observations about loss and defeat.

With no bitterness toward the male gender, Alice is willing to accept a date with a Cherokee man she has never met. Because of her resourcefulness and aggressive problem-solving, her daughter evolves a tough self-reliance that sees her through indecision. To assure her survival in the Southwest, she surrounds herself with wise matriarchs endowed with the traits of her mother, who becomes a spiritual guide during Taylor's hard times. Alice's voice and adages ring in Taylor's memory, raising an occasional longing for home. At times, the chiming of elements in the new setting harmonizes with memories of Alice at home in Kentucky and grips Taylor's chest so tightly that it hurts.

Part of Alice's legacy is the store of wise sayings that Taylor absorbed in her youth. Kingsolver uses Alice as a dispenser of countrified wisdom, e.g., "Hogs go deaf at harvest time" and "showing up at the party after they've done raised the barn" (pp. 87, 278). To the tears of Annawake Fourkiller, Alice passes her a handkerchief and reserves the thought that "heartbreak can catch up to you on any given day" (p. 285). As the mouthpiece for Kingsolver's disdain for modern media, Alice lambastes television for promising what people want, even before they want it: "TV does all the talking for you, and after a while you forget how to hold up your end" (p. 230). The statement establishes both her practicality and keen sensibilities grounded in a Kentucky mountaineer's pragmatism.

A more valuable set of sage counsel from Alice is the motherly advice that brings *The Bean Trees* full circle, reconnecting Taylor with the nurturing she left behind in Kentucky when she migrated to Arizona. With a mother's antennae, Alice recognizes distress in her child's voice three years later in *Pigs in Heaven*. Making an immediate flight from Kentucky to Las Vegas, she reunites with her daughter and granddaughter and murmurs the perfect maternal comfort; "You go ahead and fall apart. That's what I'm here for" (p. 128). Once the three refamiliarize themselves with each other, Alice is confident enough in her own parenting to recognize that, in the past three years, her daughter has become a true mother.

Alice's role as ameliorator helps solve the conundrum of who has rights to Turtle, the abused and unwanted Cherokee child. Alice's gift of twelve hundred dollars to Taylor is the kind of starting-over money her daughter needs to flee home in Tucson and work out her problem on the run. To rid her of constant stress, Alice does the spade work in the Cherokee Dawes Rolls of 1902–1905, a thick ring binder of tribal genealogy. She feels so cut off from her fleeing daughter that she mourns a relationship that must relay love by pay telephone. To her, "So much voice and so little touch seems unnatural, like it could turn your skin inside out if you're not careful" (p. 218). The tactile image suggests a mother's yearning to hold and comfort her child.

The alliance of unlike cultures comes together at the Cherokee Saturday stomp dance, a spirited midnight reunion that welcomes Alice after her trial of loneliness with a man who prefers silence to sound. Kingsolver hurries through the resolution of the plot with disjointed conversation between Alice and Turtle's uncle Ledger and Annawake, the tribe's attorney. True to her mothering role, Alice denies friendship and a budding romance by remaining loyal to Taylor. As her daughter faces the settling of legal matters, Alice cheers her on: "You never did yet let a thing slip away if you wanted it. I know you can do this" (p. 316). The confident voice supports Kingsolver's subtext of a model parent speaking eternal wisdom at a time when her daughter needs it most.

See also **motherhood, stomp dance**

• *Further Reading*

Hirsch, Marianne. *The Mother/Daughter Plot: Narrative, Psychoanalysis, Feminism.* Bloomington: Indiana University Press, 1989.
Murrey, Loretta Martin. "The Loner and the Matriarchal Community in Barbara Kingsolver's *The Bean Trees* and *Pigs in Heaven*." *Southern Studies*, Vol. 5, No. 1–2, Spring & Summer 1994, pp. 155–164.
Ryan, Maureen. "Barbara Kingsolver's Lowfat Fiction." *Journal of American Culture*, Vol. 18, No. 4, Winter 1995, pp. 77–82.

Greer, Taylor

A work in progress in *The Bean Trees* (1988) and *Pigs in Heaven* (1993), Taylor Greer learns from day-to-day challenge her strengths and principles, which reflect autobiographical elements in Barbara Kingsolver's life. As Mickey Pearlman describes the evolving heroine in *American Women Writing Fiction: Memory, Identity, Family, Space* (1989), Taylor is the solitary female who tests her endurance at age twenty-three by venturing beyond the familiar to try her luck with the unknown. In the first novel, she takes shape from an awkward teen "[dressing] like an eye test" and counting white cells through a microscope in the lab at Pittman County Hospital in Kentucky to a single mom in Tucson, Arizona. Abrupt motherhood in the form of an abandoned Cherokee child reveals reservoirs of compassion and good sense instilled by her own mother, Alice Greer. To supply the baby girl with temporary lodging, Taylor tackles the same unskilled employment that keeps her mother afloat — making motel beds, a womanly task that is repetitive, tiring, and unfulfilling. The unrelenting demands of a family force her to cook french fries at the Burger Derby and balance wheels at the Jesus Is Lord tire store, where employment requires her to overcome a fear of exploding tires (p. 4). She develops a spunky side by accepting the danger, remarking with John Wayne insouciance, "What the hell. Live free or bust" (p. 81).

Like the lone female characters in Carson McCuller's *The Heart Is a Lonely Hunter* (1941), *The Member of the Wedding* (1946), and *The Ballad of the Sad Cafe* (1951), Taylor chooses separateness over permanent alliance with a male. In *The Bean Trees*, she states a belief that there is no man who "could use all of my parts," an offbeat analogy that compares her to a toilet flapper ball (p. 88). She adds for good measure that the first parts that possessive men destroy are the woman's wings "right off the bat," a subtextual reference to an aggressive feminism she acquires through experience (*Ibid.*). The free-floating distrust of male support persists in the novel's nonsequel, in which Taylor hesitates to commit to Jax Thibodeaux, a gentle, loving soul who persistently batters her with proposals of a more stable arrangement.

With the least promising of omens at hand, Taylor spurns despair and refuses to accept defeat. Throughout, in frank Kentucky vernacular, she verbalizes the predicaments that perplex and stymy her, especially threats to the abandoned Cherokee child she mothers. At Dr. Pelinowsky's office, after accepting a medical form from nurse Jill, Taylor juggles questions that lie outside her knowledge, but she is wise enough in subtle forms of discrimination to fault the data sheet, not her mothering. Pragmatic from a rural logic she learned in the Appalachians, she searches for a source of courage. From Estevan, a Mayan refugee from Guatemala City, she acquires maturity that jerks her out of complacency. After learning how Guatemalan police use crank telephones to torture suspects, she admits, "I thought I'd had a pretty hard life. But I keep finding out that life can be hard in ways I never knew about" (p. 135). The author reprised the image of telephone torture in "On the Morning I Discovered My Phone Was Tapped," collected in *Another America: Otra America* (1992), in which she envisioned the connection of wires to tongue and genitalia as a means of "learning secrets" (p. 81).

Adversity threatens to drown Taylor in futility after Turtle is assaulted at Roosevelt Park. Taylor generalizes illogically that "the whole way of the world is to pick on people that can't fight back" (p. 170). She blames the president, Ronald Reagan, for generating a lack of respect for the downtrodden. Deep within, she recognizes the roots of depression, which a social worker worsens by insisting that Taylor make a legal claim to adopt Turtle. At the end of her emotional tether, Taylor loses the will to fight the bureaucracy. While battling for custody, she turns a venture to the Cherokee nation into a double rescue by ferrying two Mayan refugees away from immigration investigators. Her principles forbid her to act on a physical attraction to Estevan, who remains loyal to his melancholy wife Esperanza. The deliberate estrangement establishes Taylor's decency and her respect for a Guatemalan woman who has already lost too much in the flight from home.

In *Pigs in Heaven* (1993), Taylor accepts boyfriend Jax's opinion that she's a "damn proud little hillbilly" (p. 247). As her resolve begins to flag, her resilient self bobs to the surface and rejects his offer of two plane tickets home, but the struggle to support a child on minimum wages breaks her spirit. The admission that she needs family backup brings Taylor to a council hearing in Tahlequah, Oklahoma, to determine whether Turtle truly belongs in the custody of her grandfather, Cash Stillwater, whom the child remembers as Pop-pop. The bizarre proceedings so alarm Taylor that she was "ready to grab Turtle and run for it, except she knows where that road ends" (p. 340). Kingsolver uses Taylor as a model of brutal honesty who lucks into a happy ending after admitting failure. The jubilant return of Taylor and Turtle to their Tucson safety net exalts motherhood, family, and the hard-headed upbringing that Taylor ferries west with her from Kentucky.

• *Further Reading*

Hirsch, Marianne. *The Mother/Daughter Plot: Narrative, Psychoanalysis, Feminism.* Bloomington: Indiana University Press, 1989.

Murrey, Loretta Martin. "The Loner and the Matriarchal Community in Barbara Kingsolver's *The Bean Trees* and *Pigs in Heaven.*" *Southern Studies*, Vol. 5, No. 1–2, Spring & Summer 1994, pp. 155–164.

Pearlman, Mickey, ed. *Introduction to American Women Writing Fiction: Memory, Identity, Family, Space.* Lexington: University Press of Kentucky, 1989.

Greer, Turtle

April Turtle Greer, the abandoned Cherokee toddler in *The Bean Trees* (1988), travels from unwanted to fought over as she grows into young girlhood. She survives by hanging on and, at least at the start, by remaining unnoticed. After an aunt, Sue Stillwater, shoves the child into Taylor Greer's '55 Volkswagen bug, Taylor, still unaware of the child's gender, remarks that "it attached itself to me by its little hands like roots sucking on dry dirt" (p. 22). The image establishes both an infant's need and an allusion to female breasts that have no milk to offer. After Taylor rescues the child and establishes a home in Tucson, she names her Turtle and assumes she is about a year and a half old. Clues to serious trauma in her past emerge from a stony stare at nothing, a beloved flashlight named Mary, and "desperate, active dreams," a suggestion of unresolved conflict dating well into babyhood (p. 95).

In the new mother's estimation, Turtle "had to take practically everything on faith," particularly the parenting of an amateur mother (p. 97). After five months of caring for the child, in May 1981, Taylor discovers that the silent child is three years old. Dr. Pelinowsky's x-ray attesting to skeletal stunting from physical abuse jolts Taylor into a new mindset: "I thought I knew about every ugly thing that one person does to another, but I had never even thought about such things being done to a baby girl" (p. 23). Taylor's innocence elevates her above the seamy deviance of Fanny Heaven and predators who snatch little girls in a city park.

Turtle learns from Taylor that love has little to do with physical birth. The child begins to communicate by naming vegetables, beginning with "bean" and "humbean"

(p. 97). Her interest in seed catalogs prompts the name Shirley Poppy for her doll. After a mugger assaults her and reduces her to a catatonic state, the investigating social worker question's Turtle's custody. On Taylor's journey to Oklahoma City to gain further information about Turtle's background, the child manipulates a doll to act out her birth mother's burial, another clue to Turtle's mixed-up memories of pain that beset her before she had words to express it. Because of profound trauma and distrust of the world, she fails to make whole sentences until age four. Kingsolver's depiction of limited communication skills sheds light on the problems of other abused children, who begin life frustrated by the inability to demand help.

In *Pigs in Heaven* (1993), the non-sequel to *The Bean Trees*, six-year-old Turtle succeeds her mother as hero after reporting the fall of Lucky Buster, a retarded man, from Hoover Dam into a spillway the day before Easter 1983. Notoriety leads to a custody battle for Turtle drawn along ethnic lines. As the author explained, the vision of Madonna and child being forceably separated is dramatic: "These cases are given a lot of play here in the Southwest ... of a baby being ripped from its adoptive mother's arms. This is a religious image, an icon, in our culture" (Karbo, p. 9). The book develops the legal, social, and familial dynamics of a custody suit, which draws into play a mix of interests. Kingsolver adds, "The media view the basic unit of good as what is best for the child; the tribe sees it as what is best for the group. These are two very different value systems with no point of intersection" (*Ibid.*).

As the child emerges as the cause of an intercultural battle, she enters a win-win situation, a blend of aboriginal tribal stability with the hillbilly devotion of two Kentuckians, her mother Taylor and grandmother Alice, who is distantly Cherokee. Acquiring another strong female role model is significant to Turtle's evolving self-assurance. One slight obstacle to her progress, Alice's intent to leave her daughter and granddaughter, causes Turtle to rebel and toss the shoes of all family members into the toilet. The symbolism is obvious—shoes carry people away. To intensify serious misgivings, Turtle acts out her name by retreating to the bathtub and pulling a blanket over her head in a scenario that Taylor calls "a funeral for herself" (p. 183). The image recurs in "American Biographies," a poem collected in *Another America: Otra America* (1992), in which Kingsolver envisions the worldless victim "womb-curled in blanket darkness," a symbol of retreat from danger (p. 33).

Kingsolver restores to her young heroine an important voice in the development of the Greers' unorthodox family circle. Turtle's frank annoyance at her mother for being "always mad at something" alerts Taylor to the harm of a protracted tense situation (p. 287). Turtle suffers the ridicule of students for a limited wardrobe, a constant embarrassment that causes the child's physical distress at school. Assessment at the free clinic brings Taylor back to ethnic issues: Turtle, like other native Americans, is lactose intolerant. Lassoed by biological demands, Taylor must admit that there is no way to ignore Turtle's Cherokee roots.

• *Further Reading*

Karbo, Karen. "And Baby Makes Two." *New York Times Book Review*, June 27, 1993, p. 9.

Shapiro, Laura. "A Novel Full of Miracles." *Newsweek*, Vol. 122, No. 2, July 12, 1993, p. 61.

Greer genealogy

As the texts of *The Bean Trees* (1988) and *Pigs in Heaven* (1993) indicate, native American and Anglo strains interweave the Greer family tree. The eventual return of Turtle Greer, adopted daughter of Taylor Greer, heightens the irony of Alice Greer's limited memories of a Cherokee mother and her eventual engagement to Cash Stillwater, Turtle's Cherokee grandfather:

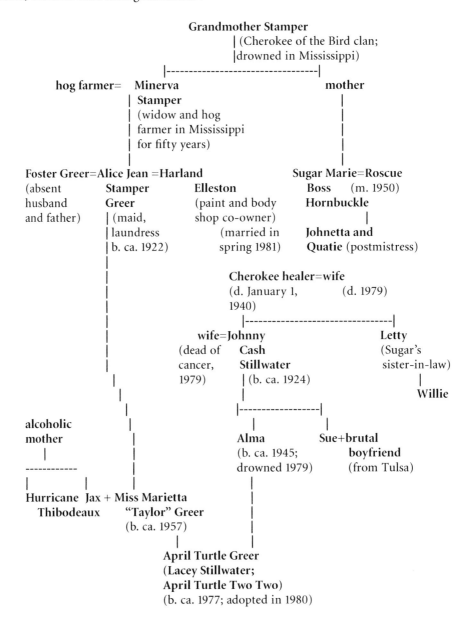

[N.B.: *The Bean Trees* names the Greer family's connection to the Cherokee as a great grandfather. In *Pigs in Heaven*, Kingsolver describes Grandmother Stamper as the full-blooded native American who establishes Alice's claim to head rights. There is no further mention of the great grandfather.]

See also **Fourkiller genealogy**

High Tide in Tucson: Essays from Now or Never

In 1995, Kingsolver issued a compendium of twenty-five lyric essays on natural instincts, family, and community, an amalgam her publicist called "the urgent business of being alive" (cover). The author remarked to Robin Epstein, an interviewer for *Progressive* magazine, on the difference between writing novels and composing essays: "Everything in *High Tide in Tucson* I think I've said before behind the mask of fiction, but this time I stepped out from behind the mask and said, 'I, Barbara Kingsolver, believe this'" (Epstein). In response to her candor, *New York Book Review* critic Casey King savored the author's ability to impart wisdom without ruffling the reader's spirit. He compared her essays to "quiet afternoons with a friend" and admired "language rich with music and replete with good sense" (King). Online reviewers Frederic Brussat and Mary Ann Brussat delighted in the book's attention to "the particularities of place, the play of the past, the challenges of parenthood, the vocation of writing, the pleasures of community, and the moral imperatives to speak out against palpable evil" (Brussat & Brussat). They summed up the author as a "national treasure" (*Ibid.*).

Kingsolver's balance of topics takes her from the human and fiscal costs of the Persian Gulf War to the numbing effects of a book tour and relaxation as keyboardist for a rock band. A skilled naturalist, she rejoices in the variety and beauty of nature. She visualizes the no-man's-land separating disparate views and offers her essays metaphorically as explorations of the desert spaces between. From an autobiographical approach, she writes of the issues that first grabbed her attention in college: child poverty, violence against women, the arms race, and pollution and other onslaughts against nature. From a mother's point of view, she battles the modern media, especially television, for perverting the minds and outlook of children. The topic that recurs in *Prodigal Summer* with Deanna Wolfe's complaints about Disney movies, in which "the bad guy is always the top carnivore, Wolf, grizzly, anaconda, *Tyrannosaurus rex*" (p. 317). Paul Trachtman, Kingsolver's former editor at *Smithsonian*, sums up the essayist's skill at maintaining a relaxed tone, even with dismaying subjects such as the lack of educational opportunities in Kentucky: "There is nothing artless about it, and the literary mind at work becomes visible now and then in the sudden splash of a figure of speech," a reference to Kingsolver's skill at creating imagery that immediately strikes home with the reader (Trachtman, p. 24).

See also **feminism, television**

• *Further Reading*

Brussat, Frederic, and Mary Ann Brussat. "Review: 'High Tide in Tucson.'" *Spirituality and Health,* http://www.spiritualityhealth.com/newsh/items/bookreview/item_5961.html.

Epstein, Robin. "Barbara Kingsolver." *Progressive*, Vol. 60, No. 2, February 1996, pp. 33–37.

King, Casey. "Books in Brief: Nonfiction." *New York Times*, October 15, 1995.

Stevens, Penny. "Kingsolver, Barbara. *High Tide in Tucson.*" *School Library Journal*, Vol. 42, No. 2, February 1996, p. 134.

Trachtman, Paul. "High Tide in Tucson." *Smithsonian*, Vol. 27, No. 3, June 1996, p. 24.

historical milieu

Kingsolver is a master at setting fictional events in a real period of history. During the Reagan administration, the stony-heartedness of conservative bureaucrats generated a selfishness and lack of compassion for the downtrodden, the motif of *The Bean Trees* (1988). Mounting racism and genocide in Latin America cast an ominous shadow over the fleeing underclass, whom Mattie, the auto parts dealer at Jesus Is Lord tire store, supports by arranging an underground sanctuary, clothing, medical attention, and escape route. Over a network of rescues, Estevan and Esperanza, a Mayan couple from Guatemala, escape anarchy and persecution by traveling through Arizona to Oklahoma, where their Indian features and skin tone blend in with local native Americans. The subterfuge necessary to their safety requires aliases, lies, appropriate disguises, interim jobs, and shifts in language to obscure the process.

For *Animal Dreams* (1990), Kingsolver draws on her journalistic experience covering a mining strike in Arizona that dragged on from July 1, 1983, to 1987, which she described in a feminist documentary *Holding the Line: Women in the Great Arizona Mine Strike of 1983* (1989). The courage of Anglo and Hispanic female villagers gave flesh to the fictional women of Grace, Arizona, who raise money to fight the Black Mountain copper-mining firm that recklessly endangers life by polluting the river. To conceal their violations of the environment and still comply with Environmental Protection Agency regulations, the owners attempt to dam the river and flood Gracela Canyon, an action that would cost Latino and native American villagers their homes, orchards, and local culture.

The author reaches a height of political commentary with *The Poisonwood Bible* (1998), which she sets in equatorial Africa at the time of the Congolese revolution against Belgian colonialism. The Price family, missionaries to Kilanga, remain oblivious to mounting tensions in the nation until the election of Premier Patrice Lumumba draws the village into the democratic process. Wisps of treachery drifting in from bush pilot Eeben Axelroot's short-wave radio inform Nathan's daughters of mischief afoot as American president Dwight D. Eisenhower engineers a CIA plot to execute Lumumba.

Kingsolver builds on familiar, social, and political tensions by setting the Price family adrift as the Congolese military initiates a country-wide backlash. The evil intent of strongman Mobutu Sese Seko, the American choice for dictator, puts a strangle hold on the poor as the Congolese currency drops in value and public and educational bureaucracies grow increasingly corrupt. As a result, bribery becomes the common currency for all seeking mail from the post office, operator-assisted telephone calls, or passports and visas from the office of foreign affairs. The author generates hatred for Mobutu through the outbursts of Leah Price Ngemba, who waits out her husband's two imprisonments for treason and wails against her own nati*on's involvement in the brutal crush of the Congo's abortive revolution.

For *Prodigal Summer* (2000), the author places a story of Zebulon Mountain and surrounding farmland in a time period when small farmers struggle against low-priced imported produce, a decline in tobacco markets, and increases in the cost of fertilizer, chemical sprays, and machinery. The growing relationship between the widow Lusa Maluf Landowski and her niece Crystal Walker reveals another worrisome aspect of the early twenty-first century, the younger generation's lack of knowledge of the natural world. To Crys, who entertains herself with "Game Boys and TVs that spew out cityscapes of cops and pretty lawyers," the study of grasshoppers and katydids is an awakening (p. 297). On a more positive note, the novel describes the return of the coyote to the southern Appalachians, a sign of hope in a time period when animal species were declining and vanishing at an alarming rate.

See also **Dwight Eisenhower,** ***Holding the Line,*** **Patrice Lumumba, Mobutu Sese Seko**

• *Further Reading*

Koza, Kimberly. "The Africa of Two Western Women Writers: Barbara Kingsolver and Margaret Laurence." *Critique,* Vol. 44, No. 3, Spring 2003, pp. 284–294.
Ognibene, Elaine R. "The Missionary Position: Barbara Kingsolver's *The Poisonwood Bible.*" *College Literature,* Vol. 30, No. 3, Summer 2003, pp. 19–36.
Weeks, Jerome. "Where Historians, Authors Part." *Dallas Morning News,* June 17, 2001.

Holding the Line

Kingsolver's feminist documentary *Holding the Line: Women in the Great Arizona Mine Strike of 1983* (1989) enabled the author to progress from strict scientific writing and newspaper reportage into an interim stage of fact-finding and theme development that informed later novels. By winnowing out the gist of a labor crusade from individual voices of the Chicana and Anglo women supporting workers of the Phelps Dodge Copper Corporation, she broke tradition calling for ponderous comments from Department of Public Safety officials, mine owners, union operatives, and law enforcement officers. Her text focuses on citizens of Ajo and Clifton-Morenci on a fork of the Gila River in southeastern Arizona and reports their struggles for civil liberties from several perspectives—cultural, gender, economic, and racial. While the men were enjoined from picketing and left the area to find work elsewhere, formerly non-confrontational housewives took charge of the struggle. By sustaining the picket line and facing down daily challenges and intimidation from June 1983 to December 1987, the heroines of the strike embraced an adversarial relationship and fought to the end, win or lose.

In 1984, Kingsolver and Jill Barrett Fein reported the developing confrontation in "Women on the Line," an article in the March issue of *Progressive.* The text cites Vicky Sharp, a resident of Morenci, for standing up to a wage freeze and cancellation of cost-of-living adjustments along with a reduction in dental, medical, and retirement packages that precipitated the strike. The thousand picketers who ousted scabs the previous August generated a ten-day cessation of operations, with women leading the tie-up in traffic and facing down state troopers toting machine guns.

To clamp down on unruly workers, officials suspended strikers from jobs, foreclosed on mortgages, and tossed families into the street. Among the women Kingsolver and Fein laud are Lydia Gonzales Knott, a single parent with three children who works as a mill repairer; Janie Ramon, whose employment dated to the equal opportunity lawsuit of 1969 forcing officials to hire women; and Gloria Blase, a Mexican-Papago whose father fought racist policies that limited benefits to native Americans. When women went to jail for picketing, they declared the arrest an on-site education to their children, who might one day face the same forms of discrimination.

Rather than an objective investigation, Kingsolver's case study is an on-the-scene chronicle of pro-union courage. In an interview, she explained, "You can't walk into a situation like that and pretend you don't know which side you're on" (Ross, p. 289). According to the introduction of *Holding the Line*, to establish trust after Huey helicopters, four hundred state troopers armed with tear gas, seven units of National Guardsmen, and goon squads armed with automatic weapons began moving into the strike zone, the author marked her truck with "Support the Copper Strikers" bumper stickers (p. xi). More vital to building rapport with local people were the lengthy talks she had with protesters "in bars, in cars, in their kitchens and back-porch swings, and on the picket line" (*Ibid.*). To protect one source, she changed a woman's name to honor a vow of confidentiality.

For women, the worst hardships were insidious scabs, violence, public apathy, dismissive and insulting media, false arrests, and the evictions and starvation that struck their families, especially those supported by female miners. Tenacious and vocal, the heroines survived by organizing food banks, battling the muck left by the flooding San Francisco River on October 1, 1983, and raising money and spirits with their unflagging cheer and belief in the right of workers to organize. Although the strike failed, the participants gained self-respect and public acclaim for their willingness to confront big business and to develop public speaking and organizational skills in full view of the world. To depict their metamorphosis, Kingsolver chose to present tableaux that concentrate on visual and auditory events.

In November 1997, a new edition of *Holding the Line* gave Kingsolver an opportunity to update the introduction with warnings gleaned from her own experience during the Reagan administration. She labeled her book a "cautionary tale" intended to remind Americans that civil liberties require constant vigilance and new challenges (p. xxiii). Her remarks echo the beliefs of Thomas Jefferson, who, in 1787, stated in a letter: "The tree of liberty must be refreshed from time to time with the blood of patriots and tyrants. It is its natural manure." Her regard for women who reshape their roles in a small Arizona community derives from idealism and an abiding humanism that values the individual's commitment to right and justice.

See also **feminism, women**

• *Further Reading*

Duval, Alex. "Shafted: How Phelps Dodge Strips Miners of Their Rights." *Tucson Weekly*, March 19, 1998.

Ross, Jean W. "Interview." *Contemporary Authors.* Vol. 134. Detroit: Gale Research, 1992, pp. 284–290.

Stegner, Page. "Holding the Line: Women in the Great Arizona Mine Strike of 1983." *New York Times Book Review,* January 7, 1990, p. 31.

Tischler, Barbara L. "Holding the Line: Women in the Great Arizona Mine Strike of 1983." *Labor Studies Journal,* Vol. 17, No. 1, Spring 1992, pp. 82–83.

Hornbuckle, Sugar

The link that joins the Greer genealogy to Turtle's Cherokee past in *Pigs in Heaven* (1993), Sugar Boss Hornbuckle is a gladsome earth mother who once posed for a cheesecake shot in *Life* magazine. The cousin that Alice Greer has not seen since 1949, Sugar fondly refers to her as "Alice Faye" and recalls how they "grew up together down in Mississippi, as good as sisters" (pp. 183–184, 274). Sugar, who was once the follower, asks no questions about Alice's intent, but serves as her guide into unfamiliar Indian territory. She leads Alice to the Cherokee archives and locates their Grandmother Stamper, listed on the Dawes Roll as 25844.

When Alice broaches the reason for her trip to Heaven, Oklahoma, Sugar discloses that she thought her cousin wanted a cure from Ledger Fourkiller, the local medicine man. With gentle compassion, Sugar comments, "Everybody's got their troubles, and their reasons for getting a clean start" (p. 276). At the council hearing that considers Turtle's placement, Sugar supports Alice by sitting on her side of the chamber, but chooses the closest seat to the Stillwaters, the contesting family. Physical placement expresses Sugar's intent to take no sides nor express hostility in the perplexing custody battle. After the settlement, she admits to engineering Alice's first date with Cash Stillwater and offers her home as the site of the post-wedding pig fry. Kingsolver uses Sugar's actions as an expression of life-long friendship as well as devotion to tribal values.

See also **Greer genealogy**

humanism

As a writer, mother, and citizen, Kingsolver's trust in human instincts is perhaps her finest trait. From an upbringing in rural Kentucky to experience covering a lengthy miners' strike in Arizona beginning in 1983, she developed an abiding faith in grassroots efforts to establish justice. Of working-class virtues, she remarked as though addressing ordinary readers, "Look, you're noble. The things you do in your life, from day to day to day, which you have probably never thought of as the stuff of literature, are heroic. And if it's not you, it's your mother, or your neighbor, or your sister" (Epstein). Her folksy faith in human nobility undergirds all of her essays, verse, and novels, particularly *Animal Dreams* (1990), in which the stodgy legal system prevents a community from gaining immediate justice in a suit against the Black Mountain mining company, a major polluter.

Against faceless bureaucracies and cruel governments, Kingsolver's writings exonerate individual clerks and workers, as with Cynthia the social worker in *The Bean Trees* (1988), who alleviates the terrors of Turtle Greer after a mugger assaults her in a public park. Another bureaucrat, Jonas Wilford Armistead, and his secretary, Mrs. Cleary, are moved by Taylor Greer's charade of adopting a Cherokee daughter. In *Pigs in Heaven* (1993), Annawake Fourkiller's summary of the Trail of Tears overwhelms Alice Greer with the horror of a forced march in summer from the southern Appalachians to Oklahoma. Along the way, some two thousand died, beginning with the youngest and oldest. Others suffered smallpox, malaria, and exhaustion. Alice concludes, "It's monstrous, what one person will do to another" (p. 282). To Annawake's crisis of faith, Alice reflects, "I wish I could say I always knew what was right" (p. 285).

Humanism undergirds the tragedy of the Price family in *The Poisonwood Bible* (1998), a novel set during Mobutu Sese Seko's takeover of the Belgian Congo. Kingsolver demonstrates the phenomenon of the poor helping the poor through the kindness of Mama Mwanza, a handicapped neighbor of Orleanna Price who slips eggs into Orleanna's henhouse and offers chickens to replace those cannibalized by swarming army ants. In the flight of the Price women from Nathan's monomania, two African women help Orleanna shelter Leah and Adah under elephant ear plants during a chilling downpour. Their sharing of a humble hut and the warmth of a fire helps Leah survive malaria and Orleanna and Adah return to Georgia. The author relates her belief that good deeds move outward like concentric waves by describing Leah's emergence as a teacher and aid to Congolese refugees.

In Leah's low moments as wife of freedom fighter Anatole Ngemba, his humanistic doctrine expresses the value of a man of principle. To his wife's despair, he offers hope in small victories. As he departs with the police for an undisclosed prison, he reminds her to be kind to herself, a beneficial blessing toward a woman who regularly shoulders blame for her nation's involvement in deliberate destabilization of the Congo's duly elected government. In middle age, she is able to reflect on living the day-to-day existence of a peasant wife and to share with fellow transients the gardening skills she learned at Emory University. Simultaneously, her twin sister Adah applies her skills as a researcher in communicable disease to the specific health needs of equatorial Africa.

See also **altruism, Cherokee, compromise, cooperation, ecofeminism, Annawake Fourkiller, Mama Mwanza, women**

• *Further Reading*

Epstein, Robin. "Barbara Kingsolver." *Progressive*, Vol. 60, No. 2, February 1996, pp. 33–37.
Goldstein, Bill. "An Author Chat with Barbara Kingsolver." *New York Times*, October 30, 1998.

humor

Kingsolver is keenly aware of the juxtapositions in human society that evoke humor. In *The Bean Trees* (1988), she locates the Jesus Is Lord tire store next to Fanny Heaven, a seedy porn shop denoted by "GIRLS GIRLS GIRLS on one side of the door and TOTAL NUDITY on the other" (p. 30). Contributing to the incongruity is the placement of an effulgent image of Jesus with a tire below his hand like a huge yo-yo. The acknowledgment of Bible Belt humor lightens the motif of haphazard travel from Mattie's tire store, a waystation for Guatemalans seeking political refuge.

At moments of crisis and indecision, Kingsolver salts in quick laughs as a means of refocusing each character. Lou Ann Ruiz's grief that her husband has abandoned the family concludes with a prolonged whoop at the sounds of turtles enjoying noisy sex at the zoo in Dog Doo Park, a cynical name for Roosevelt Park, the exercise yard the women use for relaxing with their children. In *Pigs in Heaven* (1993), Alice Greer, Taylor's mother, is pained to find that people packed into airplane seats remain aloof from each other and "behave like upholstery" (p. 126). Taylor reconnects with a witty mother-daughter repartee begun in her childhood by noting that the bleached-blonde waitress in a Las Vegas coffee shop has "accepted Barbie as her personal savior" (p. 135). A later sally comments that Las Vegas is "the only trash can for a hundred miles, so all the garbage winds up in it" (p. 144). At Taylor's coming to knowledge about trying to rear a child in poverty, she admits, "I've just fallen on some bad luck and landed jelly side down" (p. 290). The quip suits a story of Taylor rearing an abandoned child and their attempt to survive on such limited fare as peanut butter, jelly, and bread.

Against the threat of a dead river and dying community, *Animal Dreams* (1990) exudes frequent bits of incongruent imagery. In reference to a change in her outlook, Codi Noline recalls "the day I left Grace I bought a pair of gladiator sandals and my sex life picked right up" (p. 86). Her memories of living in an upscale Tucson neighborhood recalls Hallie's label: "Barrio Volvo" (p. 263). After the Latinas of Grace, Arizona, gain notoriety for their piñata campaign against the pollution of their river, CBS sends a crew into town "like Jesus into Jerusalem on Palm Sunday" (p. 264). Viola Domingos misunderstands their designation and calls them "the B.S. News" (*Ibid.*). Through frequent anti-climax and reduction to absurdity, the author indicates that wit and irreverent humor are a bulwark against despair.

Kingsolver's greatest *tour de force* is the tempering of humor from the Price girls in *The Poisonwood Bible* (1998). By characterizing Adah as brilliant and wry, Leah as rebellious and sharp-edged, Ruth May as innocently droll, and Rachel as dim-wittedly funny, the author sustains in the reader's mind the distinct point of view of each daughter as they weather their father's ditzy mission to Central Africa. Late in adulthood, the Price women perpetuate their skillful humor. Adah remains idiosyncratically pointed and edges toward bitterness by remarking on her recovery from hemiplegia: "How is it right to slip free of an old skin and walk away from the scene of the crime?" (p. 493). Of Orleanna's perpetual grief at Ruth May's death, Adah observes with a pun, "Mother is still *ruthless*" (*Ibid.*). During the surviving sisters' reunion, they enjoy chicken shish-kabobs and snicker at the image of their father's death, burned alive in a stilted hut much like meat on a stick.

Africa is particularly wearing on Leah, who is still the rebel after bearing four biracial children. She clings to resentment against the hardships of living like other Congolese women in a Kinshasa slum. As she boils diapers, she mutters, "Everything you're sure is right can be wrong in another place. Especially *here*" (p. 505). After migrating from the Congo, she imagines herself maimed by one of the landmines that dot Angola's roadsides. She retrieves her girlhood courage in finding a suitable haven: "If I have to hop all the way on one foot, damn it, I'll find a place I can claim as home" (p. 506).

The funniest and most pathetic of the Price daughters is Rachel, the unreconstructed materialist whose arrested development never frees her from teenage logic. At age fifty, as she gazes around the Equatorial Hotel, her idea of African heaven, she is vain about her age and paranoid that black employees are pilfering her inheritance. She rues the day that the mission took her from the teen scene of parties, cars, and music and misses "being a part of something you could really believe in" (p. 512). She recalls watching Dick Clark and *American Bandstand* on African television and grieves, "I *know* how to do those hairstyles. I really could have been something in America" (p. 512). Fortunately for her, shallow values protect her from the griefs that bow her mother toward the earth in search of redemption from the sins of failed motherhood. With the flip humor of girlhood, Rachel avoids the trap of self-blame and exults, "Oh, if Father could see me now, wouldn't he give me The Verse!" (p. 515).

• *Further Reading*

Higgins-Freese, Jonna. "The Kingsolver and I." *Grist*, July 16, 2002.
Karbo, Karen. "And Baby Makes Two." *New York Times Book Review*, June 27, 1993, p. 9.

journey motif

Kingsolver employs the traditional journey motif as a metaphor for life change. When Taylor Greer reaches for maturity and independence in *The Bean Trees* (1988), she departs from Kentucky in a 1955 Volkswagen bug minus a starter, a fault suggesting her ambivalence at leaving her home and mother. The journey west and south allows Taylor time to reflect on the multiple geographic and emotional states she passes on her way to Tucson, Arizona. The chance encounter with a desperate Cherokee aunt leaves Taylor with a seriously damaged toddler, the niece whose need for love and safety is the answer to Taylor's personal search for meaning and purpose.

On the road again, this time in Mattie's more luxurious Lincoln, Taylor ferries Mayan refugees to Oklahoma with an insouciance intended to fool authorities at a roadblock. Her brief respite in vacation cabins at Lake o' the Cherokee resets the friends in a more relaxed atmosphere, where Turtle's playacting produces another piece of the puzzle of her infancy. Significantly, the journey reaches resolution in the Oklahoma City public library, where Taylor learns wisteria's secret for thriving in poor soil. The image of purple-flowered vines absorbing nutrition through rhizobia suggests the future of the Greer family, with Taylor nurturing a child who didn't survive on native soil.

Kingsolver chose the theme of the prodigal child for *Animal Dreams* (1990), in which Codi Noline returns to her father's house after fourteen years' wandering. The renewal of acquaintance with Grace, Arizona, enables her to reflect on coming-of-age in a snug community and on childhood experiences with her younger sister

Hallie, who simultaneously journeys south to Nicaragua to aid peasant farm families of Chinandega grow more cotton. Because of Hallie's self-assurance and sense of belonging, Codi feels like the family's baby, "the one with no firm plans who's allowed to fiddle around forever keeping everyone young" (p. 32). The journey that takes Codi physically from Grace returns her spiritually and socially by reacquainting her with family, her stillborn child, an ailing father, and a female support system that sustained her from age three after her mother's death. Her search ended, Codi accepts Loyd Peregrina's love and settles in Grace to teach school and rear a family.

With *The Poisonwood Bible* (1998), the Reverend Nathan Price's mission to Africa generates separate journeys for each family member. The long-anticipated departure from a seventeen-month posting in Kilanga produces a crisis diaspora taking the surviving Price women away from an incipient revolution in the Congo and from starvation and misery in the nuclear family. The resulting polyphony tells the story in the round from the point of view of a mother, three teen-age girls, and a preschooler, who face what reviewer Sally Gabb calls "an Africa that is both vibrant and vicious, an Africa struggling to survive ubiquitous invasions, of army ants, jungle vines, colonizers and politics" (Gabb). Following the sudden death of Ruth May, the youngest, from snakebite, Orleanna positions her child's corpse on a makeshift bier, distributes the Prices' worldly goods to neighbors, and departs. The long walk takes Orleanna, Leah, and Adah away on foot. Simultaneously, Rachel expresses her own values by climbing into the cockpit of Eeben Axelroot's plane to fly south to Johannesburg, South Africa.

The three women's slog through rain, mud, and mosquitoes pushes them to their limit, arousing pity in two Congolese rescuers, Mama Boanda and Mama Lo. They leave Leah behind with Anatole, her African sweetheart, who tends her during a serious bout of malaria. The two remaining women press on to Bulungu's Belgian Embassy by banana truck and on foot. Rescued by the army, they have reason for gratitude as strangers help them board an evacuation flight to Fort Benning, Georgia. The return home seems magical after their months of deprivation and bewilderment in the Congo. Adah, the crippled daughter, rejoices that Orleanna remains true to her to "drag me out of Africa if it was her last living act as a mother" (p. 414).

Critical to Kingsolver's political novel is the lasting effect of Africa on all characters. Rachel, the petulant teen who demands to be taken home to Georgia, makes a place for herself in society as a butterfly bride and mistress and inheritor of a toney whites-only hotel. Orleanna bears a weighty onus of guilt that she left Ruth May buried in the Congo and returned to Georgia like a locust shell, drained of volition and pressed to the east as though looking across the sea toward the dark continent. Both Adah and Leah devote themselves to Africa — Adah as a Georgia-based medical researcher into contagious diseases of black Africa and Leah as the agronomist in an Angolan communal farm and mother of stout Congolese sons.

The post-mission journey must leave the missionary behind. The family's release of hatred for poor demented Nathan Price extends a slim blessing to the failed zealot who offered himself up as a sacrifice to immersion baptism, the ritual that kept him perpetually at odds with Congolese parents. Kingsolver's placement of the country within the characters' souls perpetuates the moral that the world's most backward continent refuses rejection by sojourners and exploiters. Old and wise, the cradle of human civilization maintains its hold on the Price family by nature of demands on outsiders unwary enough to dismiss Africa as primitive and inconsequential.

See also **Africa, Cherokees**

• *Further Reading*

Gabb, Sally. "Into Africa: A Review of *The Poisonwood Bible.*" *Field Notes,* Vol. 11, No. 1, Summer 2001.

Regier, Amy M. "Replacing the Hero with the Reader: Public Story Structure in *The Poisonwood Bible.*" *Mennonite Life*, Vol. 56, No. 1, March 2001.

Kilanga

The village of Kilanga, a Congolese settlement of two dozen families on the Kwilu River, presents a unique set of customs and challenges to the missionary Price family. Upon arrival, they begin to distinguish individuals from a sea of black faces that welcome them to a traditional goat roast. Each Kilangan demonstrates cultural and ethnic qualities of Central Africa:

Boanda, Tata a local fisherman who attends church with his two wives to seek divine intervention in the first wife's childlessness and the second one's problem with infant mortality. On the night of the army ant invasion, he rescues Orleanna and Adah in his boat. After the fire surround, he claims Anatole's bushbuck. While Leah and Anatole reside in Bulungu, Boanda brings money and a suitcase filled with the Price family's pitiful leavings.

Boanda Number Two, Mama Eba, Tata Boanda's broad-flanked younger wife, shows pride in her daughters by spiking their hair. She defends her husband in the argument over the bushbuck by slapping Anatole Ngemba. As the Price women depart Kilanga, she and Mama Lo share their elephant ear shelter from the rain.

Bwanga the tiny orphaned sister of Pascal, who was Ruth May's loyal playmate. Nathan forcibly baptizes Bwanga during the storm that follows Ruth May's death.

Gabriel and Nkondo two small boys in Anatole's school who drum on chairs rather than listen to a white female teacher explain long division.

Gbenye the oldest son of Tata Ndu. Gbenye claims the impala as his kill, even though his two arrows strike the animal's flank rather than a vital organ. The villagers oust him for his belligerence.

Kenge Tata Ndu's son, who replaces his father as chief of Kilanga.

Kili, Tata an elderly, one-armed villager who is joined by his two wives in claiming meat from the fire surround.

Kuvudundu, Tata Nganga a spiritual leader in Kilanga who sells aspirin on market day, casts bones to tell fortunes, and sometimes paints himself white.

Lakanga, Mama a mother of twins who attends Christian services to keep her from having more twins.

Lalaba, Mama a balding villager who prefers wading out among crocodiles to being attacked by army ants.

Lekulu, Tata a villager who rows Nathan Price to safety to protect him from army ants. While Nathan preaches, Lekulu stuffs leaves in his ears.

Lekuyu the Price family's houseboy, whom Anatole renames Nelson.

Lo, Mama chief hairdresser for Kilanga, Mama Lo is an elderly, unmarried entrepreneur who sells palm oil that she presses from palm nuts. She balances cans of oil on her head during the long walk to Bulungu and lives to advanced old age.

Lucien the orphaned half brother of Pascal, whom Nathan baptizes during the storm that follows Ruth May's death.

Mokala, Mama vendor of *malala* (blood oranges) at the weekly market.

Mwanza, Mama a critically burned housewife who tends to cooking, child-care, and laundry by scooting along the ground using her hands like feet.

Mwanza, Tata a local fisherman who flees from Leah for watching him weave fish traps.

Mwanza, the elder Tata a villager who sets out voting bowls on the church altar to receive pebbles to decide on Jesus as Kilanga's savior.

Ndu, Tata the chief, dressed in animal skins and a large sisal fiber hat, spreads his influence to neighboring villages, which reject Nathan's proselytizing. To increase respect for his office, Ndu considers adding Rachel Price to his harem as his seventh wife. He dies of an infected wound.

Nguza, Mama a villager whose neck is distended with goiter under her chin. She grows *mangwansi* beans in her garden and gladly shares her bananas with Mama Mwanza's children.

Pascal Leah's first Congolese *nkundi* (friend), Pascal, who is eight or nine, climbs trees with her, builds a miniature house of bark and mud, and teaches her names for weather and gender-specific terms. In exchange, he learns impudent Americanisms, e.g. "Man-oh-man! Crazy" (p. 218). He must give up play and help his family after his older brother dies of *kakakaka* (enteritis). In 1966 during the revolution, the Congolese army shoots Pascal near Bikoki.

Tataba, Mama an English-speaking house manager for the Prices who once served Brother Fowles during his six-year tenure

Zinsana, Tata a villager missing his fingers. He dislikes Tata Boanda, but allows his wife to accept Boanda's gifts of fresh fish.

See also **Africa, Tata Kuvudundu, Mama Mwanza, Tata Ndu, Nelson, poverty, Mama Tataba, women**

Kingsolver, Barbara

A winner with her first novel, Barbara Kingsolver is a master of theme and a perfectionist about setting, character, dialogue, and plot. Chief among her literary virtues is sincerity. She declared to interviewer Megan McMahon of the *San Francisco Chronicle:* "The things that I feel and care about and worry about most deeply find their way through my fingers onto the keyboard into the book" (McMahon). The author decks her characters in a mystic certainty of place, a quality she acquires from her own love of the earth and her need to sing the song of home. As she explains in the introduction to *Off the Beaten Path: Stories of Place* (1998), "Story is our grand explanation for ourselves, and it grows from place, as surely as carrots grow in dirt" (p. 19). The image reflects her agrarian upbringing in rural Kentucky and a feral need to write about place and emotion, which she describes in "In Case You Ever Want to Go Home Again" (1995) as a sharp-clawed ferret digging into her inner thoughts.

Kingsolver's touchstones of place — Arizona and the Appalachians — and native people shine through her verse and prose, for example, Taylor Greer's memories of her Kentucky home in *The Bean Trees* (1988), Loyd Peregrina's love of mythic rock formations in Canyon de Chelly in *Animal Dreams* (1990), and her own attempts to grow mountain-style hollyhocks on her four-acre desert plot in *High Tide in Tucson* (1995). In the estimation of critic Meredith Sue Willis, "She is consistently worth reading for her breadth of perspective and for a generosity of spirit that are particularly her own but quintessentially Appalachian" (Willis, p. 80). With a folk-based perception of need, the novelist honors suffering characters with tenderness, as in *Pigs in Heaven* (1993) with mountaineer Alice Greer's empathy for Cash Stillwater, whose daughter Alma committed suicide by driving her car off a bridge into the Arkansas River. Alice murmurs to herself, "There is nothing to say that can change one star in a father's lonely sky" (p. 256). Critic Kelly Flynn characterizes Kingsolver as "one of those authors for whom the terrifying elegance of nature is both aesthetic wonder and source of a fierce and abiding moral vision" (Flynn). The statement clarifies the link between homelands and the cast of characters that treasures them.

Kingsolver's works are characteristically non-confrontational. In the words of reviewer Paul Trachtman, her essays read "like conversations across a metaphoric fence," a homey image that reflects the writer's humanism and amiable style (Trachtman, p. 24). He pictures her text as "[flowing] by with as little turbulence as a clear stream" (*Ibid.*). Reviewer Russell Banks admires the human traits of her fictional casts: "There is a moral toughness in her characters — a determination to find value and meaning in a world where value and meaning have all but disappeared — that one sees in real people everywhere but rarely in recent American short stories" (Banks, p. 16). By stressing folkways and local networking, the author can address difficult issues — pollution, violence, child abandonment and abuse, gender inequities — without overtaxing the reader with negatives.

In reference to the real world, Kingsolver speaks of the terrible, the unthinkable — muggers in the park, a traumatized toddler with broken arms, the suicide of a despairing jewelry dealer, torture to the genitals with electric charges from a crank telephone, kidnap of Cherokee children, a concentration camp atmosphere in supposedly Christian boarding schools for Indians, death in Mobutu's prison, persecution of European and Middle Eastern Jews, a truck accident that leaves a twenty-eight-year-old woman a widow, organized slaughter of coyotes — yet observes the Greek concept of decorum by showing no villains in person. The characters who assault the Cherokee child, the kidnappers who wrest Ismene from her Guatemalan parents, the Contra murderers of Hallie Noline, the teachers who cause Cash Stillwater to cease speaking his native language, the mining company despoiling a community river, and the persecutors who steal Zayda Landowski's farm remain faceless

and out of view. Only their evil radiates into the reader's ken. To affirm that goodness will triumph, the author continually returns characters to reassuring locales, e.g.,
Grace, Arizona; Heaven, Oklahoma; Lake o' the Cherokees; Tucson's Jesus Is Lord
tire store; and the town of Egg Fork at the foot of Zebulon Mountain.

Through fiction, verse, and essay, Kingsolver aims to change social and political opinions by enlarging human compassion for the underdog and by rallying concern for nature. Reviewer Susan Lumpkin makes tongue-in-cheek fun of the author's
tendency to cram a single text with too many issues by "systematically [running]
down her list of environmental issues to raise. Invasive plants? Check. Logging?
Check. Poachers? Check. Pesticides? Check" (Lumpkin, p. 1). Maureen Ryan is more
openly critical of works that are "aggressively politically correct" (Ryan, p. 77).

These and other brickbats seem inconsequential to Kingsolver. She confided to
Michael Krasny, an interviewer for National Public Radio, her admiration for social
novelists Nikolai Tolstoy and John Steinbeck: "Steinbeck is one of the — sort of, kind
of the end of the line, in a way, of the great literary — the great writers who combined literature with social commentary as a matter of course, and who were
respected for it" (Krasny). She added, "When I sit down to stare at page one of a
novel on my computer screen, I have this real clear understanding that I'm sitting in
the same place where Tolstoy once sat" (*Ibid.*). Like previous social reformers, she
writes accessible works that academia can admire and the public can enjoy, even the
author's poorly educated kin and acquaintances of southern Appalachia.

For a working method, the author employs a question-and-answer method. She
explained, "I devise a very big question whose answer I believe will be amazing, and
maybe shift the world a little bit on its axis. Then I figure out how to create a world
in which that question can be asked, and answered" (Rubinstein, p. 254). She uses
characters as her personal minions to research the problem at hand and pursue redress
until it is solved. Her technique places heavy responsibility on people like Taylor
Greer and her mother Alice, who acknowledge the fragility of life and the need to
sustain the living with traditional customs and values. At the moment that Taylor
learns from Dr. Pelinowsky the degree of torment her daughter Turtle suffered in
infancy, Taylor looks out on a bird building a nest in a spiny cactus. As though congratulating Turtle for surviving, Taylor thinks, "You just couldn't imagine how [the
bird had] made a home in there" (p. 124). The image rounds out the scene with the
right amount of horror and admiration.

Kingsolver has garnered praise for carefully distilled imagery, quirky humor, lively
pacing, and faith in human actions, a humanism that caused her to describe herself as
"a pinko who wants to change the world" (Stafford, p. 88). To balance polemics with
everyday events, she sprinkles text with jolly folk sayings, e.g., "a chase around Robin
Hood's barn" (*Bean*, p. 217). In *Pigs in Heaven* (1993), she ridicules pretentious rock
stars "with limp hair and closed eyes and heads rolled back to the sounds of their own
acid chords, going for the crucifixion look" (p. 31). Less optimistic are poems such as
"The Loss of My Arms and Legs," anthologized in *Another America/Otra America*
(1992), in which she mourns the paralysis of a good Samaritan, the bombing of
Nagasaki, the rape of Central American women, and the dropping of napalm on children. Her final stanza requests the right to commiserate with the world's suffering.

Much of Kingsolver's wordcraft attempts to right elements of human society that have gone seriously wrong. For example, in the falling action of *The Poisonwood Bible* (1998), she remarks, "That's the Congo for you: famine or flood. It has been raining ever since" (p. 389). The terse, knowing quip leaves much to consider in the characteristic style of Kingsolver, who often crafts pithy comments for readers to ponder. To interviewer Michael Neill of *People* magazine, she explained, "I've always had this absolute belief in my ability to change things. I do what I do because that's the only moral option to me" (Neill, p. 110). A remarkably balanced populist, Kingsolver sets up idealistic themes of ecological responsibility and concern for the outsider while developing enjoyable human scenarios as true-to-life as a tape recording. Of note is her skilled poetic closure, a lyrical gathering-in of images and meanings.

Kingsolver flourishes by harvesting ideas and intersections of human history that her busy mind probes for potential subject matter. She informed *Book Page* interviewer Ellen Kanner, "What I love best about being a novelist is I get to do something different every time. When you're flying by the seat of your pants, you're never bored" (Kanner). She avoids the airs of the *artiste* by taking a laborer's view of the work at hand. The best part is revision to sharpen themes, particularly public service and respect for nature, two motifs that permeate her writings. Like the works of Ray Bradbury and Margaret Atwood, her images settle in the brain like lyric poetry, a quality that gentles her polemical outlook.

• *Further Reading*

Aay, Henry. "Environmental Themes in Ecofiction: *In the Center of the Nation* and *Animal Dreams*." *Journal of Cultural Geography*, Vol. 14, No. 2, Spring/Summer 1994, pp. 65–85.

Banks, Russell. "Distant as a Cherokee Childhood." *New York Times Book Review*, July 11, 1989, p. 16.

Flynn, Kelly. "The Rural Experience and Definitions." http://www.ruralwomyn.net/.

Kanner, Ellen. "Barbara Kingsolver Turns to Her Past to Understand the Present." *Book Page*, 1998.

Krasny, Michael. "Interview: Barbara Kingsolver, Author, Discusses Her New Book." *Talk of the Nation* (NPR), December 13, 1999.

Lumpkin, Susan. "Review: *Prodigal Summer*." *Smithsonian Zoogoer*, March/April 2001, p. 1.

McMahon, Regan. "Barbara Kingsolver: An Army of One." *San Francisco Chronicle*, April 28, 2002.

Neill, Michael. "La Pasionaria." *People*, Vol. 40, No. 15, October 11, 1993, pp. 109–110.

Rubinstein, Roberta. "The Mark of Africa." *World & I*, Vol. 14, No. 4, April 1999, p. 254.

Ryan, Maureen. "Barbara Kingsolver's Lowfat Fiction." *Journal of American Culture*, Vol. 18, No. 4, Winter 1995, pp. 77–82.

Stafford, Tim. "Poisonous Gospel." *Christianity Today*, Vol. 43, No. 1, January 11, 1999, pp. 88–89.

Trachtman, Paul. "High Tide in Tucson." *Smithsonian*, Vol. 27, No. 3, June 1996, p. 24.

Willis, Meredith Sue. "Barbara Kingsolver, Moving On." *Appalachian Journal*, Vol. 22, No. 1, 1994, pp. 78–86.

Kuvudundu, Tata Nganga

The healer-visionary of Kilanga in *The Poisonwood Bible* (1998), Tata Nganga Kuvudundu recognizes from his first glimpse of Nathan Price and his family the "price" they will pay for accepting a mission they little understand. Anatole Ngemba, the go-between of Chief Ndu, describes Kuvudundu as the alternate *nganga* (minister) to Kilanga. Because of his peculiar gait and association with local palm wine drinkers, Orleanna Nathan thinks of him as the "town drunk"; Nathan calls him a "witch doctor" (p. 131). In awe of his six toes on one foot, people believe that he solves practical male-centered problems, such as adulterous or barren wives. For women, he provides the *nikisi* (fetish) to bind a child's arm or neck to ward off evil, a stronger guardian than Nathan Price's promise of everlasting life in heaven for those who are baptized. Because the women prefer Kuvudundu's magic to that of Tata Price, the minister falsely concludes that Congolese families are less attached to their offspring than are Americans.

Kingsolver slowly reveals the witch doctor's power and indigenous wisdom. Anatole Ngemba insists that Kuvudundu is a counselor to the chief and a priest well versed in ancient tradition. Nelson, the houseboy, saves rotten eggs as ritual aids for Kuvudundu, who claims to know the secrets of raising the dead. Adah Price realizes the practicality of the animistic blessing of bushes used as shields for defecation far from sources of drinking water. She also perceives the menace in the calabash bowl of chicken bones that Kuvudundu leaves on the Prices' veranda. She hears him mutter *dundu*, the last two syllables of his name, which could be translated as antelope, a small plant, a hill, or "a price you have to pay," a repetition of the ominous pun on the white family's surname (p. 175). Kingsolver leaves little doubt which meaning is in store for Nathan's family. Within weeks, Nelson interprets the decline of Orleanna and Ruth May from malaria as *kibáazu* (a curse).

In late fall 1960, as drought consumes Kilanga, Kuvudundu uses bones to divine the future. After villagers vote to allow Leah to join local men in hunting, the shaman predicts turmoil in nature: "The leopards will walk upright like men on our paths," a metaphoric prediction of military incursions by Mobutu's army (p. 339). The shaman's summoning of the evil eye causes Kilangans to slaughter their poultry and livestock and protect their huts with severed animal heads, a reenactment of the biblical passover (Exodus 12:21–36). After the village fire surround lapses into a black-on-black melee, Kuvudundu uses the decline in civility to warn once more that nature plots against Kilangans because of their violation of tradition.

Kuvudundu undercuts his majesty with spite. Turned into a stalker in the falling action, he bears death in his hands in the form of a green mamba, which he places in the Price's henhouse to retaliate against Nelson for siding with Rachel at the hunt. Like the apocryphal story of Daniel, the image of a six-toed foot escalates from a sign of magic to proof of culpability. Ironically, Kuvudundu, like Nathan Price, betrays his position as spiritual leader and makes himself irrelevant to village survival. His reputation ruined among Kilanganas, Kuvudundu falls under the new chief's order of banishment and disappears from the text. The author engineers his gradual erasure from Kilangan life as a model of old-style ritual and fear-based religion giving place to European and American ideals.

• *Further Reading*

Gabb, Sally. "Into Africa: A Review of *The Poisonwood Bible*." *Field Notes*, Vol. 11, No. 1, Summer 2001.
Garner, Karen. "Review: *The Poisonwood Bible*." *Muse Newsletter*, September 2000.

Landowski, Lusa Maluf

A widowed lepidopterist of Polish Jewish–Palestinian parentage in *Prodigal Summer* (2000), Elizabeth "Lusa" Maluf Landowski's independence complements that of biologist Deanna Wolfe and Nannie Rawley. Fighting financial ruin in a clan of tobacco farmers, Lusa, in her late twenties, is a citified import from Lexington, Kentucky, to the southern Appalachians. She arrives in the town of Egg Fork by way of marriage to Cole Widener, a sensitive, woman-pleasing farmer who takes the time to break off honeysuckle branches for his wife's window sill jar. The effect is like the imprisonment of a rare bird in an isolated cage by a true bird lover.

Kingsolver creates Lusa as a champion of nature. Out of loyalty to ecology, she uses a bacterium rather than Sevin to kill hornworms and rails at the county extension agent, whose weekly newspaper column on gardening recommends a "stout chemical defoliant" to subdue honeysuckle, a wild climber that Lusa cherishes (p. 32). Her outrage masks the real vexation, feeling alone and alienated by staunch mountaineers, whose view of life clashes with the support system Lusa once had with lab partners Arlie and Hal. At the Widener farm, Lusa is surrounded by five back-biting Widener females, whom she maligns as a "hurricane of hateful women" (p. 40).

A feisty five-foot-one strawberry blonde and former postdoctoral research assistant on a National Science Foundation grant, Lusa brings to her marriage looks, brains, and a touch of humor from her Polish *zayda* (grandfather). Her specialty, moth pheromones, intrigues Cole, who translates her entomological research as moth sex. She violates local traditions by keeping her maiden name and by placing calf with milk cow overnight to end the pre-dawn milking ritual. Her wifely love takes the form of improvising a fresh cream of spinach soup recipe as a noontime treat for Cole. By imitating the mountain twang in her outburst, she alienates him with cyclical arguments that leave her feeling like a "frontier mail-order bride" (p. 46). Like the enveloping fog, her hostility arises in part from being "marooned" among Cole's sisters (p. 33).

After a truck jackknifing sends a steering column through Cole's ribs and leaves Lura a twenty-eight-year-old widow, she becomes "a woman men talked about" (p. 438). She makes peace with the demanding farm, vapory ghosts, and physical want, which strays toward her seventeen-year-old nephew Little Rickie. Erotic dreams of a moth-colored man assure that "words were not the whole truth," an adage that strengthens a progression of weary days overmanaged by the hovering Widener sisters (p. 80). Lusa rescues the family of her sister-in-law Jewel Walker, whose eventual death from cancer will leave two orphans. The fostering parallels canid behavior, which Deanna describes in detail. Like supportive female coyotes after the death of an alpha female, Lusa tends the motherless young. Kingsolver indicates that altruism becomes Lusa's salvation by offering her a ready-made family.

See also **Cole Widener, women**

• *Further Reading*

Bush, Trudy. "Back to Nature." *Christian Century*, Vol. 117, No. 33, November 22, pp. 1245–1246.
Eberson, Sharon. "Appalachian Romance Has Kingsolver in Top Form." *Pittsburgh Post-Gazette*, January 14, 2001.
James, Rebecca. "Booked Solid." *LETTERS from CAMP Rehobeth*, Vol. 11, No. 6, June 1, 2001.

Last Stand: America's Virgin Lands

Kingsolver's passion for nature is a pulsing drive that empowers a life dedicated to earth's bounty and goodness. By teaming with photographer Annie Griffiths Belt, the author completed a picture book, *Last Stand: America's Virgin Lands* (2002), as a project for the National Geographic Society. The lush photo album reminds readers of an alternate American history — a story of Manifest Destiny that threatens the natural wonders that amazed and delighted native Americans long before Europeans knew that North America existed. The text speaks eloquently of the tenuous remains of irreplaceable wilderness that "is its own reason for being" (p. 19).

The plan of the book calls for five divisions— wetlands, woodlands, coasts, grasslands, and drylands. In the first bioregion, the author exults in zooplankton, the tiny life forms that "[begin] a chain of provenance that ends in the farthest reaches of land and sky" (pp. 28–29). Her ability to swell prose passages like an organ diapason lures the reader into the secret society of species flourishing privately in the wild. She is careful to balance wonder with practicality by reminding the unwary that marshes, like blood purification filters, transform decayed matter into liquid nutrients and remove toxins that human hands so carelessly spread. She warns that the draining of natural water storage can "eviscerate our golden goose of a continent" (p. 30).

Kingsolver reaches a height of preservationist fervor in a paean to woodlands. She reminds readers that trees "[offer] silence to our noise, longevity to our hurried days, inspiration to our expiration," a lyric reference to the creation of oxygen to counter the human exhalation of carbon dioxide (p. 62). She personalizes the destruction of some ninety-six percent of the nation's virgin forests as the cause of broken-hearted trees. Indirectly, she lambastes the George W. Bush administration for reckless endangerment of national forests through logging, mining, and oil drilling.

Of the oceans, the author inserts a personal note of remorse that "we are in danger of loving our wild coasts to death" (p. 93). As a reminder of their importance to human happiness, she cites *The Yosemite* (1912) by preservationist John Muir, the first president of the Sierra Club and father of the American National Park system, who insists on "places to play and pray in, where Nature may heal and cheer" (p. 93). Just as Kingsolver writes of human regeneration in her novels, she urges Americans to ponder the impaired regenerative efforts of the seashore, where fishers may one day pull in empty nets.

In a prose style that reviewer Louis Bayard extols as "limpid streams of reverie and regret," Kingsolver's rejoicing in prairie grasslands reprises from a naturalist's standpoint the glory of the virgin barrens (Bayard). She remarks on agriculture's conversion of a pristine sea of grass to corn and soybean fields as "one of the most massive biological alterations humans have ever effected on our planet in such a short time" (p. 128). Similarly delighted in xeriscapes, she rejoices in the mating of the spadefoot toad, a dry-land amphibian that Mattie, the rescuer of Central American refugees, admires in *The Bean Trees* (1988) after a rejuvenating rain on the Sonora Desert. Of the treasure that nature stores in the arid wilderness, Kingsolver refers to Edward Abbey, the fierce advocate who fought a trend toward land "being paved over, ground to dust beneath automobile tires, or littered with the detritus left by … *Slobivious americanus*" (p. 159).

See also **nature**

• *Further Reading*

Bayard, Louis. "Last Stand: America's Virgin Lands." http://nature.org/magazine/books/misc/art9328.html.

Moreno, Sylvia. "Exploring Downtown; D.C. Students on Photo Expedition for National Geographic." *Washington Post*, July 18, 2003, p. B1.

Linder, Ben

Kingsolver dedicated *Animal Dreams* to Benjamin Linder, a twenty-seven-year-old hydroelectric engineer and humanitarian from Portland, Oregon, working in Nicaragua. For four years after his graduation from the University of Washington, he supported the Sandinista revolution and was building a dam in contested territory for the National Institute of Energy at the time of his death from the combined assault of hand grenades and shotgun and machine gun fire. U.S.-backed Contra guerrillas ambushed and slew him along with six other workers in San José de Bocay on April 28, 1983, at the project site of El Cua, where he was pouring concrete at a small weir.

Kingsolver honored Linder because of his dedication to volunteerism. In an interview, the author, an outspoken opponent of Ronald Reagan's covert Central American war, noted, "It makes me incredibly sad — more than sad — angry, that Ben's own nation has mostly forgotten him. I want people to remember him" ("A Conversation"). She reprised his altruism and execution in the character of Hallie Noline, an agronomist working on Nicaraguan pest problems.

In November 1989, a five-day memorial consortium in Central America honored the engineer. In view of the Santiago volcano, the Benjamin Linder Memorial Conference on Alternative Sources of Energy and Rural Electrification, held in Managua, Nicaragua, reflected the young peace volunteer's enthusiasm for grassroots efforts to help electrify peasant homes and businesses. Sessions covered solar and wind energy, small-scale hydroelectric plants, biomass, and other energy-saving projects.

• *Further Reading*

Atkinson, Barbara. "Nicaragua Hosts Ben Linder Alternative Energy Conference." *Earth Island Journal*, Vol. 5, No. 2, Spring 1990, pp. 22–23.

Cockburn, Alexander. "The Execution of Ben Linder." *Nation*, Vol. 245, October 17, 1987, pp. 402–403.

"A Conversation with Barbara Kingsolver." http://www.readinggroupguides.com/guides/animal_dreams-author.asp.

Kruckewitt, Joan. *The Death of Ben Under: The Story of a North American in Sandinista Nicaragua.* New York: Seven Stories Press, 1999.

"Setting the Record Straight." *Publishers Weekly*, Vol. 246, No. 38, September 20, 1999, p. 67.

Suchy, Angie. "Kingsolver Examines Issue of Governmental Injustice." *Oregon Daily Emerald*, April 25, 1997.

loss

Kingsolver is skilled at picturing characters suffering loss, from Esperanza and Estevan's failure to retrieve their kidnapped daughter Ismene in *The Bean Trees* (1988) and Annawake Fourkiller's regret at the adoption of her twin brother Gabriel in *Pigs in Heaven* (1993) to Orleanna Price's guilt and grief at the death of her youngest, Ruth May, from snakebite in the Congo in *The Poisonwood Bible* (1998). In the first novel, the author complicates the theme of loss with the separation of Taylor Greer and Estevan, a married man she has no hope of keeping for herself. In a rented boat on the Lake o' the Cherokees, the two contemplate a platonic romance that is doomed to end at the Reverend Stone's waystation, where the Mayan teacher and his wife will take on new identities. The loss of Estevan is a surprise obstacle to Taylor, who stumbles on love in an unlikely setting.

Unrequited love adds depth to the characterization of Taylor, a self-starter who tends to make her own way, yet who longs to nestle against Estevan's bare chest. He fondly calls her "mi'ija" (my daughter), but can offer only a high-minded farewell about making the world a better place (p. 220). With typical candor, she confides to him, "I've never lost anybody I loved, and I don't think I know how to" (p. 219). During a phone call to Alice Greer in Kentucky, the mournful tone in Taylor's voice reveals heartache. Her alert mother forces her to confess an illicit love for a man who "wasn't mine to have" (p. 221). The story honors Taylor's principles and her sympathy for Esperanza, both indications that Alice reared her daughter to respect herself as well as the rights of others.

With *Animal Dreams* (1990), Kingsolver examines the off-kilter life of Codi Noline, another independent woman who carries into maturity the estrangement from family and community that resulted after the death of her mother, Alice Noline, when Codi was three years old. The absence of warmth in the family from a too-professional father forces Codi to bond with her younger sister Hallie. On their own, the two girls remain close after Codi jettisons a medical career. They form a three-person household with Carlo, a practitioner of emergency medicine. Codi thinks of Hallie as "our center of gravity, the only one of us who saw life as a controllable project" (p. 10). Codi pictures Carlo as a fellow orphan. His expertise at reattaching severed body parts creates irony at his failure to restore her to emotional wholeness.

To heal Codi's fractured heart, the author forces her into a maelstrom of more pain and loss. Upon Codi's return to Grace, Arizona, she faces the task of easing Doc

Homer from his profession and tending his needs as he slides into the amnesia of Alzheimer's disease. As he strays from awareness of the present, Codi ventures farther into her past to grieve for her mother and for the stillborn child that Codi bore and buried in an arroyo in her teens. In a dream, Hallie urges her sister to lay down the burden and let the child's spirit rise to heaven. Complicating Codi's interior struggle is the execution of Hallie by Nicaraguan guerrillas, a shattering blow that leaves Codi numb at the loss of her one remaining bulwark. Grieving forces Codi into a living dream world: "Tears ran down to my collarbone and soaked my shirt and still I didn't wake up" (p. 306).

Mutual loss helps Codi bond with Loyd Peregrina, her high school sweetheart, who bears his own grief over the death of his twin Leander. Loyd's description of the "Zen of Southern Pacific" bears a subtext of personal struggle with jagged emotions. In describing how to maneuver a train over a hill, he adds that "every single run is a brand-new job," an image that suggests the uniqueness of each personal trial (p. 295). He listens to Codi's tearful discoveries from the family attic and eases her grief with simple arithmetic: "For everybody that's gone away, there's somebody that's come to you" (p. 297). From Loyd's strength and the mothering of local women, Codi recovers from loss, which she faces in the orchard memorial service for Hallie and buries in their mother's garden along with the exhumed remains of the stillborn infant. The ritual acts release the burden of separation and regret both from Codi and her father, who realizes how much he loves his daughters.

Kingsolver's feel for human longing and the ache of loss permeates her poetry anthology, *Another America: Otra America* (1992). "For Richard after All" channels personal emotion at the suicide of a friend who leaves her life like the impersonal return of a borrowed book. "Poem for a Dead Neighbor" expresses tenderness for an elderly widow who once watered the poet's neglected tomato plants. These intimate glimpses of grief precede Kingsolver's most poignant study of yearning, *The Poisonwood Bible*, which retains the lyrical description of death that begins the text and informs the action and themes until the last chapter's wistful benediction.

Set in the unforgiving equatorial jungle, Kingsolver's African odyssey pictures an entire family's sufferings as they give up materialistic American life in Bethlehem, Georgia, in exchange for the insecurities of a meager hut in Kilanga, Congo. Trivial inconveniences, such as the absence of hair spray and deodorant, arouse the rancor of Rachel, the most self-centered of the family. Orleanna, the discounted mother, loses self-respect as she remains silently acquiescent to her husband's snide remarks about women. More devastated than the bewildered housewives and mothers of the 1960s, she describes her hollowed-out self as "washed up there on the riptide of my husband's confidence and the undertow of my children's needs" (p. 8).

Already low on self-esteem, Orleanna suffers a life-long tribulation after losing Ruth May. At her Georgian refuge on Sanderling Island, she ponders grief like a puzzle: "It's as real as rope or the absence of air, and like both those things it can kill" (p. 381). The child's ghastly death from two tiny puncture wounds unshackles Orleanna from Nathan's demands and sets her on the path to independence. However, freedom comes at great price. She batters herself with blame for allowing him dominance over the family and faults herself for failing to protect her children from a hopeless situation. In daylight reveries, she returns to the eyes that watch her from African trees and to the small mound in the garden where vines cover Ruth May's remains. Trapped by revolving images of ruin, Orleanna confesses, "In perfect stillness, frankly, I've only found sorrow" (p. 385).

As in *Animal Dreams*, the suffering women of the Price family are able to uplift each other out of mutual experiences with hurt. Leah remains in the Congo and survives her husband's periods of imprisonment by tending her sons and fighting the oppression of Mobutu's regime. Adah, Leah's handicapped twin, undergoes a serendipity. In place of the pity and dismissal of Americans demanding perfection, the crippled sister earns acceptance among Africans, who are more tolerant of imperfection. As she recovers health and stature in adulthood, she is able to share her good fortune with Orleanna, who wearies with age and the constant guilt of her African experience. Infrequent visits with Patrice, Pascal, Martin-Lothaire, and Nataniel Ngemba confer grandmotherhood on Orleanna and give her joy in a new generation. In time, she accepts the grace conferred by Ruth May's spirit, which bids her mother to "Walk forward into the light" (p. 543).

The motif of loss remains strong in *Prodigal Summer* (2000), Kingsolver's fifth novel, which the author characterized as haunted by ghosts: "extinct animals, dispossessed relatives, and the American chestnut" ("Barbara"). The plot reveals the hurt in three strong women of the Appalachian town of Egg Fork. Nannie Land Rawley, an elderly orchard keeper, bears grief for her retarded daughter, Rachel Carson Rawley, who died at age fifteen from the failure of a malformed heart. Rachel's half-sister, Deanna Wolfe, retains happy memories of their play in childhood and returns to Nannie with her own emotional turmoil and the anticipation of a baby sired by hunter Eddie Bondo. More painful than Eddie's drift from Deanna's life is the early widowhood of Lusa Maluf Landowski. Her husband's death blindsides her with the anguish of terminated love and fear of financial ruin on the Widener family farm.

For all three of Kingsolver's female characters, love and ingenuity relieve anguish. Nannie exhibits a toughness to life's buffetings and supports herself from the organic apples she sells to a ready market. After a severe thunderstorm threatens Deanna's cabin, she abandons the false security of solitude in the mountains and returns to Nannie to receive the affection and support Deanna will need in the months preceding her child's birth. The reunion presages a trio bound in affection and hope for the future. Meanwhile, Nannie's friend Lusa forges bonds of sharing and trust with the stand-offish Widener sisters by turning the family tobacco farm into goat pasturage. With her new-found financial stability, she is able to foster Jewel Walker's two children, who face their own loss as their mother declines from cancer. The network of women helping women attests to the author's faith in females to hearten and aid each other through difficulties and to celebrate their triumphs over loss.

See also **love**

• *Further Reading*

"Barbara Kingsolver: Coming Home to a Prodigal Summer." http://www.ivillage.com/
books/intervu/fict/articles.

Danley-Kilgo, Reese. "Kingsolver's Latest Scores Hit." *Huntsville Times*, November 26, 2000.

Meadows, Bonnie J. "Serendipity and the Southwest: A Conversation with Barbara King-solver." *Bloomsbury Review*, November-December 1990, p. 3.

Tanenbaum, Laura. "Review: *Prodigal Summer*." *Women Writers*, May 2001.

love

Love is more than a constant in Barbara Kingsolver's fiction. As she explained its integral role in universal themes in "Poetic Fiction with a Tex-Mex Tilt," a 1991 book review for the *Los Angeles Times*: "The subject of love [is] inseparable from babies, hope, poverty, and escape" (p. 3). In *The Bean Trees* (1988), she juxtaposes varied types of love — Mattie's assistance to traumatized refugees, Lou Ann Ruiz's loyalty to an unfaithful husband, Alice Greer's love and pride in her daughter's independence, the bruised heart of Esperanza, mother of a kidnapped daughter, and Taylor Greer's doomed passion for a married man and her sustaining devotion to Turtle, an abandoned Cherokee toddler. For *Animal Dreams* (1990), Kingsolver builds a teenage fling into a mature love after Codi Noline returns to Grace, Arizona, and picks up a complicated match with Loyd Peregrina. The Pueblo-Apache railroad engineer romances Codi without realizing that she carries the emotional burden of their stillborn child, which she buried alone in the wild after giving birth unattended at age sixteen.

In balance with the grievous losses that stymy and confuse Codi, Kingsolver rejoices in the Hispanic Catholic tradition of All Souls' Day, when women and children serve food at family plots and deck tombs with chrysanthemums. To Codi, the tradition offers a respite from her life-long flight from domestication and a hint at her kinship ties to the community. The lavishing of comforts to the dead is a testimony to ongoing affection and to family continuity, a reassurance the Nolines lack. During grave cleaning, she observes, "In these families you would never stop being loved" (p. 163). The camaraderie of local women united in loving attention to the dead gives Codi a physical outlet for loss and a network of people to accept in the place of her dead mother.

Kingsolver turns Codi's observation of All Souls' Day into an epiphany freighted with personal connections to the souls of Grace. When she confronts her father with her discovery of a plot of Nolinas at the graveyard, rather than reply with information, he mutters distractedly to himself that "she is his first child, his favorite, every mistake he ever made" (p. 170). His revelations of love surprise her. The admission advances the rescue theme as Codi attempts to ease him out of his medical practice into the oblivion awaiting him in advanced Alzheimer's disease.

The author outlines a balanced love as Codi Noline gradually succumbs to Loyd's charm. Because Codi returns to town rootless and bewildered, the revival of their physical relationship offers diversion from her task of tending an ailing father and writing letters to her sister Hallie in Nicaragua. Beginning with need in both parties, their reunion revives the romance from their high school days with a mature trust and loyalty. After Loyd introduces Codi to close-knit Indian families residing in adjoined housing at Santa Rosalia Pueblo, he accuses her of being "scared to claim anything you love," an astute evaluation of her internal struggle (p. 220).

The mounting emotion that swamps Codi after Hallie's execution occludes her love for Loyd and sends her fleeing toward Colorado and a renewal of the makeshift relationship with Carlo. A brief, but essential catharsis on the Greyhound results from an outpouring of loss to Mrs. Kimball, a sympathetic stranger. Codi's choice to return to Grace enables her to bid farewell to her father and accept a delayed closure of mourning for the infant born dead when Codi was sixteen. With Loyd's help, she is able to let go of past losses and accept a permanent teaching job. She quells a need to flee commitment and Loyd's promise as lover and father of their unborn child.

In *Pigs in Heaven* (1993), Kingsolver pursues the concept of affection derived from the Greek *agape*, a love that doesn't have to be deserved. Models of loving relationships emerge in the Alice-Taylor-Turtle Greer triad of females and in Lucky Buster's place in a loving community under the watchful care of his mother, Angie Buster, the cafe owner, who accepts without reproach the oddities of the retarded. In Oklahoma, Annawake Fourkiller, the Cherokee attorney, speaks a philosophy of love that includes even eccentrics like Boma Mellowbug, the bottle tree lady: "You could love your crazy people, even admire them, instead of resenting that they're not self-sufficient" (p. 231). Ultimately, it is a love match between Grandfather Cash Stillwater and Grandmother Alice Greer that solves the dilemma of how to ally Turtle with her Cherokee past.

To expand on multicultural forms of love, Kingsolver examines biracial love matches in *The Poisonwood Bible* (1998), which is set in equatorial Africa. At first, the quandary Rachel Price faces on receiving Chief Ndu's gifts of food and local crafts creates comic relief from the family's suffering with malaria and a severely reduced supply of food. Nelson the houseboy puts the Congolese-style courtship in pragmatic terms favoring the girl's parents: "All those goats, *and* you won't have to feed her anymore" (p. 263). To Tata Ndu's benefit, Rachel's pale skin tone "would cheer up his other wives" (*Ibid.*). Realizing that she may face female genital mutilation and inclusion in his five-woman harem, Rachel turns to a sleazy, flirtatious bush pilot, Eeben Axelroot, a model of Mr. Wrong but the only hope for a girl desperate to flee polygamy in Kilanga.

Simultaneously, love beckons to Leah, Rachel's sister, in a more recognizable form. As Anatole Ngemba, the local teacher, draws her into his school to teach arithmetic to young boys, he introduces a subtler form of wooing, beginning with bestowal of a pet name, *béene-béene* (as true as the truth can be) (p. 287). In exchange, she offers him the world — a homemade globe fashioned on a calabash to fill in gaps in his understanding of geography. Their enduring love grows from a sounder basis than Tata Ndu's desire for a trophy wife or Rachel's need to escape Kilanga. Anatole offers calm reassurance during difficult times and a worldly-wise philosophy that helps Leah understand the revolution that grips the Congo. In exchange, she brings strength to their union and determination to her family of four boys while keeping alive love for Anatole during his imprisonments for treason. In a touching bedroom scene at the novel's close, Anatole turns their thirty-year love story into a fable. While fighting recurrent malaria, Leah is able to "lie in the crook of his arm and he comforts me this way, talking to me all night long to stave off the bad dreams" (p. 520).

The author's fifth novel, *Prodigal Summer* (2000), probes the theme of love muddled by loss. Most complex of three intertwined love stories is the phony bravado of Deanna Wolfe, a forty-seven-year-old forest ranger who appears to thrive on solitude at an isolated cabin on Zebulon Mountain. Her immediate sexual attraction to a stranger, hunter Eddie Bondo, belies her self-sufficiency as she morphs from a celibate, hermetic Artemis to a lusty Aphrodite. Through the summer, their physical relationship satisfies a need for touching and orgasmic release. Oddly, she seems relieved at his departure in late summer and at her ability to conceal the early symptoms of pregnancy, which she first mistakes for menopause.

A subtextual evaluation of conjugal love places it below motherhood in terms of fulfilling female emotional needs. As though yearning more for motherhood and a family than for a lover, Deanna retreats from her hermitage to "the genuine shelter of Nannie Rawley's place, the kindness of that leafy orchard" to wait out the months before the child's birth (p. 430). As though exalting Hera, goddess of parturient women, over Aphrodite, Kingsolver allies Deanna's response to motherhood with Nannie's devotion to a retarded love child fathered by Deanna's father, Ray Dean Wolfe, and to the foster mothering that Lusa Maluf Landowski offers her niece and nephew. Through formation of families lacking a strong male presence, all three women — Deanna, Nannie, and Lusa — achieve contentment and self-actualization.

See also **loss, motherhood**

• *Further Reading*

Judd, Elizabeth. "Review: *Prodigal Summer.*" *Salon*, November 17, 2000.
Ryan, Maureen. "Barbara Kingsolver's Lowfat Fiction." *Journal of American Culture*, Vol. 18, No. 4, Winter 1995, pp. 77–82.

Lumumba, Patrice

Kingsolver's introduction of Patrice Lumumba (1925–1961) to *The Poisonwood Bible* (1998) comes through the consciousness of Ruth May Price, the most naive and least interested in African politics. Seated in a Belgian doctor's office while he sets her broken arm, the child hears her father's glorified view of civilization and Christian salvation. The doctor retorts that Lumumba is "the new soul of Africa" with possibly more followers than Jesus, a dream as politically idealistic as Nathan's hope to save Africa's million souls (p. 122). Ruth May inserts an image of bugs drawn to a ceiling light "like something they want, and then they get trapped in there," a dire metaphor for the draw of Lumumba's genial speeches (p. 123).

Born in Kasai Province in the rural Belgian Congo, Lumumba was mission educated and employed as a nurse's aid, librarian, and postal worker and postal accountant in Stanleyville. At age thirty-four, he emerged from obscurity as a writer and radical political presence called the barefoot postman. Although his enemies imprisoned him on a trumped-up charge of embezzlement, peasants loved him for his charisma and for championing nonviolent revolution. Following Independence Day on June 30, 1960, a year after the Prices arrive in Kilanga, Nathan Price travels to Stanleyville and hears by radio that Lumumba supports neutrality and African unity.

Lumumba was inaugurated as premier of the newly liberated Democratic Republic of the Congo on June 28, 1960. Leah, who witnesses the swearing-in, pictures the thin leader like St. Francis of Assisi, whose compassionate words caused the birds to fall silent. Pressing his case like a fiery revival preacher, Lumumba rouses his hearers to cheers. Leah spies a rat running unnoticed under people's feet, an unsubtle symbol of the corruption that goes unreported during the power transfer. Meanwhile, Lumumba pledges "to make the Congo, for all of Africa, the heart of light" (p. 184).

The new premier's first major obstacle was Moise Tshombe, chief of the Lunda, who withdraws Katanga Province from the Congo. By setting himself up as leader of mercenaries, he controlled a region rich in cobalt, copper, diamonds, and zinc. To halt a split in the electorate, Lumumba called in the United Nations to reunite the Congolese. If they failed, he intended to beg Russian backup, a choice that established a lethal antipathy with the United States government.

In the novel, Eeben Axelroot, the sleazy bush pilot, divulges to Rachel the fact that Lumumba is "as good as dead," a fact Eeben intercepted in code from a radio transmission: "The King of America wants a tall, thin man in the Congo to be dead" (pp. 294, 297). Eeben adds that a hit squad will earn one million U.S. dollars by carrying out the mission. The author dwells on Rachel's disbelief, a position that American citizens of the period shared out of faith in Dwight Eisenhower, a beloved, grandfatherly, and highly trusted president. Leah, who is more astute than her older sister, recognizes the menace in Eeben and his bald-headed co-conspirator, who speaks into a radio over wire spilling out of its box like snakes. She concludes that the beloved Ike is a barbarian.

After General Joseph Mobutu imprisoned the new premier under house arrest on September 14, for inciting a riot, Lumumba remained out of play. Under cover of seasonal rains, he escaped on November 27 in a station wagon full of housemaids that mired on impassable roads. He fell into military hands and entered Camp Hardy at Thysville before being whisked away to Katanga, Mobutu country. Lumumba's keepers beat him savagely in a Katangan prison at Elisabethville, executed him by firing squad on January 17, and refused to return his remains to his wife Pauline. His corpse was located in an abandoned residence. In the novel, fifteen years after the fact, Orleanna Price chastises herself for being bogged in domestic troubles while feeling detached from revolution in the Congo.

See also **Dwight D. Eisenhower, Mobutu Sese Seko**

• *Further Reading*

Barrett, Sharon. "Kingsolver's Heart of Darkness." *Chicago Sun-Times*, October 25, 1998, p. 18.
Carman, Diane. "Kingsolver Hits Stride in Africa; Missionary's Muddling Creates Cultural Disaster." *Denver Post*, October 18, 1998.
"Patrice Lumumba." http://www.sci.pfu.edu.ru/~asemenov/lumumba/LUMUMBA.HTM.

malapropisms 116

Rubin, Sylvia. "Africa Kept Its Hold on Kingsolver." *San Francisco Chronicle*, October 30, 1998, p. Cl.

Rubinstein, Roberta. "The Mark of Africa." *World & I*, Vol. 14, No. 4, April 1999, p. 254.

Whitelaw, Kevin. "A Killing in Congo." *U.S. News and World Report*, July 24, 2000.

malapropisms

Kingsolver's joy in language spices her works with wit and humor. In addition to rural adages, puns, and palindromes, she favors malapropisms, inappropriate uses of diction that substitute an unfamiliar term with a familiar term that sounds like it. In *Pigs in Heaven* (1993), she develops the malapropism "millionaire typhoon" into a humorous exchange between Alice and Taylor Greer. Taylor corrects her mother: "Tycoon, Mama. A typhoon is a hurricane, I think. Or maybe it's that kind of snake that strangles you," a second malapropism confusing typhoon with python (p. 290). As the conversation turns to fearful matters, Alice warns her daughter to expect "Something Italian sounding. A semolina?" (subpoena) from attorney Annawake Fourkiller.

In *The Poisonwood Bible* (1998), Adah Price, one of the author's most adept wordsmiths, suffers Broca's aphasia, a congenital brain disorder that causes her to puzzle over the uniqueness of words. Contrasting her verbal conundra are the malapropisms of Rachel, her older sister, a self-absorbed teeny-bopper who ponders why native women must wear sarongs while Congolese men observe a "course of a different color" by dressing how they please (p. 44). Into adulthood, Rachel murders diction while congratulating herself for controlling her vervet monkeys, Princess Grace and General Mills, and for aging gracefully. Seated at the bar of the Equatorial Hotel while smoking a Lucky Strike, she weighs the importance of a fiftieth birthday: "It sure gives you something to compensate upon" (p. 511). She reflects on her late teens, when she could have scrounged plane fare "and then before you could say Jack Robinson Crusoe I'd have been back in Bethlehem" (p. 513). After thirty-five years in Africa, she realizes the impact on her lifestyle and outlook: "You have your way of thinking and it has its, and never the train ye shall meet!" (p. 516).

Mattie

A native of Tucson and the owner of the Jesus Is Lord tire store in *The Bean Trees* (1988), Mattie models Kingsolver's ideal of the resilient matriarch and earth mother. Mattie is the kind of woman who can balance the wheels of an ORV (off-road vehicle), drive a pickup to an impromptu picnic in the desert, and anticipate a child's need with peanut butter crackers and a spouted cup of apple juice. After mothering Turtle and offering Taylor Greer a job at $6.50 per hour, Mattie throws in two new tires and a repair to the ignition, enticements that force Taylor to accept. The deal attests to Mattie's ability to appease people by supplying what they most want.

Mattie is a believer in efforts put to good use, including planting unused turf with seeds, a symbol of her productivity and reverence for recycling. In her garden,

Taylor spies "heads of cabbage and lettuce sprouted out of old tires. An entire rusted-out Thunderbird, minus the wheels, had nasturtiums blooming out the windows" (p. 45). In addition to growing flowers and vegetables, Mattie straps on binoculars to go "bird watching" in her four-wheeled Blazer, a ruse for a volunteer post as human rights activist in a modern version of the Underground Railroad (p. 119). The author obviously approves of Mattie's civil disobedience by picturing her as a successful spearhead of the local operation.

The plot presents Mattie as a courageous middle-aged rescuer. By offering sanctuary to political refugees from Guatemala and El Salvador when Father William needs a safe house, she commits the crime of harboring illegal aliens in her upstairs quarters and incurs the unrelenting stalking of Immigration Service agents. The penalty is five years imprisonment and $2,000 in fines per assist to an illegal immigrant. She is cagey about danger, commenting, "If I don't like the smell of something … then it's not worth the risk" (p. 176).

Kingsolver avoids the self-importance of do-gooders in Mattie's make-up. In her non-judgmental way, she characterizes the difference between donating money to causes and doing the actual work: "Some folks are the heroes and take the risks, and other folks do what they can from behind the scenes" (p. 188). Reverting to a grandmotherly role, she bids farewell to Taylor on her first courier mission by hugging her and pressing cash into her hand. With a blessing — "Bless your all's hearts" — and finger kisses to Esperanza, Estevan, and Turtle, she sends them on their way. Mattie's heart-felt concern for the journey establishes love as her reason for helping people in distress.

• *Further Reading*

DeMarr, Mary Jean. *Barbara Kingsolver: A Critical Companion*. Westport, Conn.: Greenwood, 1999.

Methuselah

The emblematic African grey parrot of *The Poisonwood Bible* (1998), Methuselah is a thoughtless mimic, a three-dimensional mirror who apes the good and bad around him. Immured in a tall bamboo cage, he treads a section of yardstick that serves as a perch. His wing muscles atrophy, leaving him handicapped like the "Wreck of Wild Africa" (p. 137). Adah Price admires his "sharp skeptical eye," which reflects her own outlook (p. 58). Trained by Brother Fowles, the red-tailed bird lives outside arbitrary rules and enjoys his autonomy by muttering "damn" in Nathan Price's presence (p. 65). Adah describes him as "a sly little representative of Africa itself, living openly in our household," the image of the intractable villager (p. 60).

In August, Nathan Price recognizes in the bird's mimicry a potential heretic in the house. After riling Price with a repeated "damn," the parrot suffers banishment, but his wings are too stunted to carry him from the compound. He roosts in the outhouse and haunts the trees like a specter, glaring down on the family and demanding fruit, which Leah cuts into chunks for him. Ruth May feeds him "sour limes from the *dima* tree to make it sneeze and wipe its bill off" (p. 117). Like the Congolese, Methuselah lacks the mobility to escape gathering doom and the incentive to avoid the gifts of exploitive whites.

On June 30, 1960, the Congo's Independence Day, a civet cat slays the bird. Adah finds one red plume, then follows the wreckage down the trail from the latrine, but locates none of Methuselah's corporal remains. She prays for deliverance from a day of freedom for the Congolese, when death of an innocent and wordless parrot leaves behind "only feathers, without the ball of Hope inside" (p. 186). Brother Fowles, after learning that the parrot has gone to bird heaven, exults, "Best place for him, the little bastard!" (p. 258). Kingsolver appends Orleanna's reflection on the caged bird, a posthumous reminder that "though my soul hankered after the mountain, I found, like Methuselah, I had no wings" (p. 201). The extended metaphor pities not only Nathan's downtrodden wife, but all housewives and mothers of the mid–1900s who rejoiced in a "Maytag washer ... and called it happiness" (*Ibid.*).

• *Further Reading*

Ewert, Jeanne. "Shadows of 'Darkness': The Specter of Joseph Conrad's Classic Tale of Oppression Emerges Throughout Barbara Kingsolver's Latest Novel." *Chicago Tribune*, October 11, 1998, p. 6.

Mobutu Sese Seko

Two months before the death of General Joseph Désiré Mobutu (1930–1997), Barbara Kingsolver gave him an eerily accurate demise in *The Poisonwood Bible*, in which his name attaches to vile acts that target his own people. Ironically, both Mobutu and his victim, legally elected Premier Patrice Lumumba, were mission educated. The murderous Mobutu came to power after the Belgians recognized his strengths, which the novel summarizes as "wit and raw avarice—a useful combination in any game" (p. 318). He supplanted Lumumba in January 1961 as ruler of the Congo and may have ordered the premier's murder under the absurd justification that Lumumba threatened to create a Communist state. Under the name Mobutu Sese Seko and with American aid, the usurper earned the author's disdain for engineering a totalitarian government that lasted until only months before his death from prostate cancer in 1997.

In an interview with Michael Krasny of National Public Radio, Kingsolver spoke of American policy toward the successive regimes: "We didn't like the person (the Congolese) elected: Prime Minister Lumumba. So, President Eisenhower ordered his assassination. I mean, to put it very bluntly, that is what happened" (Krasny). In the novel, Kingsolver extends her denunciation of Mobutu through the experience of Anatole and Leah Ngemba, who "risk [their] head cracked open like a nut" for complaining about not being paid for their jobs as school principal and nurse (p. 434). By 1974, when the Ngembas and their three children live in the Kinshasa slums, Mobutu has channeled American aid into building his private castles in Brussels, Italy, Paris, and Spain. In anger at the lack of a decent hospital, Leah wonders, "Why doesn't the world just open its jaws like a whale and swallow this brazenness in one gulp?" (p. 448).

Mobutu's creative restructuring of the Congo includes renaming the nation Zaire and changing city and road names as well to wipe out the memory of the languages of European conquerors. Offering a purse of five million dollars each to two heavy-weight boxing champs, he stages the George Foreman–Muhammad Ali fight at Kinshasa's Stadium of the 20th of May, a notorious structure that houses political prisoners in its dungeon. Historically, the world-class bout took place on October 30, 1974, under the media-manufactured name "Rumble in the Jungle" (Pearlman, p. 4). As William Nack described in *Sports Illustrated* two decades after the fight, Ali, who was the underdog at odds of one to eight, "had been promising for weeks to pull off the greatest miracle since 'the resurrection of Christ'" (Nack, p. 48). Tickets for the epic matchup cost thirty dollars each, more than twice the monthly wage for the average Congolese citizen. After the brutal downing of Foreman in round eight, Ali trotted through Kinshasa with hosts of admirers and media flacks at his heels.

In the novel, the socio-political situation in the Congo pushes Leah near despair. Of the Foreman–Ali prizefight, which boosts business at Rachel's Equatorial Hotel, Leah grouses that "people from the world over will come watch this great event, two black men knocking each other senseless for five million dollars apiece. And they'll go away never knowing that in all of goddamned Zaire not one public employee out-side the goddamned army has been paid in two years" (p. 451). She admires the aver-age person's survival skills under Mobutu's tyranny. She ponders, "How can I begin to describe the complexities of life here in a country whose leadership sets the stan-dard for absolute corruption?" (p. 452). Since the murder of Lumumba, bureaucrats replace nonexistent paychecks with bribes from citizens seeking to collect their mail, make long-distance telephone calls, and apply for passports and visas. With much satisfaction, the author kills off Mobutu with a permanent sleep that lets "the mur-dered land [draw] a breath" (p. 540).

See also **Africa, Patrice Lumumba**

• *Further Reading*

Cullen, Paul. "What Mobutu Learned from King Léopold." *Irish Times*, August 12, 2000.
Goldstein, Bill. "An Author Chat with Barbara Kingsolver." *New York Times*, October 30, 1998.
Krasny, Michael. "Interview: Barbara Kingsolver, Author, Discusses Her New Book." *Talk of the Nation* (NPR), December 13, 1999.
McGee, Celia. "'Bible' Offers Two Good Books in One." *USA Today*, October 22, 1998, p. 6D.
Nack, William. "Muhammad Ali." *Sports Illustrated*, Vol. 81, No. 12, September 19, 1994, p. 48.
Ognibene, Elaine R. "The Missionary Position: Barbara Kingsolver's *The Poisonwood Bible*." *College Literature*, Vol. 30, No. 3, Summer 2003, pp. 19–36.
Pearlman, Cindy. "A Rumble to Remember." *Chicago Sun-Times*, February 23, 1997, p. 4.

motherhood

The nurturing instinct in females is one of Kingsolver's predominant motifs, which she characterizes in Alice and Taylor Greer, Mattie the tire dealer, the refugee Esperanza, orchard keeper Nannie Land Rawley, cancer victim Jewel Widener Walker, and Leah and Orleanna Price as well as in personal essays about her own family. The author indicates in the dedication to *Last Stand: America's Virgin Lands* (2002) a mother's concern for the "wild places that will forever stir your hearts" (p. 5). By publishing a pictorial work on remnants of the nation's scenic bounty, she hopes to preserve "the American childhood" for her two daughters and their progeny that they "may grow up to inherit something of this world I have been lucky enough to love" (p. 14). The statement illustrates a pervasive point of view in her writing that derives from her own experiences as a parent.

In *The Bean Trees* (1988), the author heightens the irony of Taylor Greer's fleeing a dead-end marriage and potential motherhood in Kentucky by escaping to Arizona, where she receives an abandoned Cherokee toddler shoved into the front seat of her '55 Volkswagen bug. Out of concern for the baby girl's survival, Kingsolver forms a circle of women who protect and assist Taylor in establishing a two-member family with the child, whom she names Turtle. Mrs. Hoge, the innkeeper at the Broken Arrow Lodge, hires Taylor through the New Year on the pretext of needing domestic help. The real reason, her longing for a grandchild, inspires an impromptu three-generation triad repeated later in Tucson with Mattie the tire dealer, Virgie Parsons, and Edna Poppy in the senior roles. To visualize the warmth of their mothering and the vulnerability of their charge, the author describes a magic moment at night when a female quail shuttles to safety dozens of baby quails that "looked like fuzzy ball bearings," a sight the author drew from the nestlings she watched in her own back-yard (p. 96).

Despite a mutual bond, childcare becomes a pressing issue for Taylor and Turtle. While working in Mattie's Jesus Is Lord tire store, Taylor depends on her employer as well as on Edna and Virgie as babysitters. Taylor also relies on her roommate, Lou Ann Ruiz, who accepts Taylor like a sister and loves and protects Turtle as much as she loves her son Dwayne Ray. As Taylor approaches Oklahoma City with the intent to acquire adoption papers, she turns to another devoted mother, Esperanza, a Mayan refugee who masquerades as a Cherokee and sings child-pleasing songs to make the trip less boring for Turtle. The staged act of giving up Turtle for adoption at the magistrate's office becomes all too real for Esperanza, who is recovering from a suicide attempt triggered by her despair at losing her own daughter, Ismene, to Guatemalan kidnappers. Knowing the pain the couple must feel, Taylor offers the slim comfort that stability may give Estevan and Esperanza another chance at having a family.

In addition to providing food and domestic comforts, Taylor is at times overwhelmed by the world's menace to her child. She "[wonders] how many other things were lurking around waiting to take a child's life when you weren't paying attention," like dehydration in the desert climate of Tucson (p. 45). At the zoo, she imagines elephants gone mad and unidentified beasts snapping off children's hands. It takes an unforeseen threat to Turtle's safety to jolt Taylor into accepting Mattie's dictum that "nobody can protect a child from the world" (p. 178). By her appearance at age six in *Pigs in Heaven* (1993), Turtle has maneuvered her impromptu mother toward a more laid-back philosophy "that everything truly important is washable" (p. 14).

Kingsolver complicates the mothering issue in the non-sequel by acknowledging the rights of the Cherokee nation to one of their own, even though Turtle's family broke her bones and tossed her to an unknown party like a bag of laundry. To establish the importance of ethnic belonging to Turtle's sense of self, the author stated, "I understand the gut-wrenching attachment and nuclear family relationship that seem to supersede all others. But clearly there was another view, and I wanted to bring readers to sympathize with the tribe, too" (Myzska, p. 20). At Taylor's lowest point, she acknowledges the torment of poverty for a single mother, when she accepts dates just to have complete meals. To threats from attorney Annawake Fourkiller, Taylor declares, "I have no bargaining chips: there's just Turtle, and me. That's all" (p. 292).

The author turns to the topic of miscarriage in *Animal Dreams* (1990). By juxtaposing Emelina Domingos, mother of five sons, with her friend thirty-two-year-old Codi Noline, Kingsolver develops Codi's secret suffering and loss at age sixteen, when she miscarried a fetus in the sixth month before learning to think of herself as a mother. In her mind, the "tape broke" and "life started over" (p. 296). She mourns privately, "I'd lost what there was to lose: first my mother and then my baby. Nothing you love will stay," a rephrase of poet Robert Frost's title "Nothing Gold Can Stay" (1913) (p. 233). The abiding grief suggests the emotional self-battery she bears in silence, in part from guilt that she starved herself to conceal her pregnancy. She sees herself "watching mother-child rituals from outside the window," an image of alienation that explains her inability to settle into a career or marriage (p. 215).

To Codi, motherhood is a constant state of alert. She dreams of misplacing an infant on the creek bank. Her rescue instinct saves Mason Domingos from choking on a pinto bean. Emelina's protracted jitters that night are understandable to Codi, who interprets the overreaction as a recognition that "life held possibilities she couldn't handle alone" (p. 117). Later, Codi acknowledges, "It's not the practical side of things that breaks us up," a reference to the unspoken, unimagined terrors that threaten the innocent (p. 208). The steady stream of insecurity and fear attests to her motherless childhood and single parenting by a father who showed more concern for his daughters' orthopedic shoes than for their emotional needs.

Kingsolver expands Codi's view of parenting by introducing her to another culture. While visiting Santa Rosalia Pueblo, she witnesses an extended-family version of motherhood among native women who clasp Loyd Peregrina like a long-lost child. Amid a kitchen furor of cooking and baking, constant chatter in Keres and Spanish, and much admiration of female family members for Loyd, the author implies that unflagging mother love from so many people helped him to grow up feeling self-assured with women. Although he is an independent adult, he winces when Codi threatens to divulge to Inez, his mother, that he was a cockfighter, a brutal hobby out of sync with the home side of his life.

At difficult passes in Codi's coming to knowledge, she reverts to childhood coping mechanisms. She clings to the black-and-red afghan that she and Hallie used as a security blanket after their mother died. To Codi's surprise, she later learns that Uda Dell, the girls' caregiver and surrogate mother, crocheted the wrap. Its value to Codi's past and to the release of suppressed memories turns the afghan into a palpable link to a lost mother and to the community of women who replaced her in the Noline children's lives. Its fervent colors, warmth, and snuggly texture translate into a faceless, nameless form of mother love.

In her masterwork, *The Poisonwood Bible* (1998), the author reveals the hardscrabble existence of third-world parents, a topic she broached in *The Bean Trees* with the hard-luck story of Esperanza, the suicidal refugee mother of a kidnapped daughter named Ismene. Kingsolver chooses as models the Congolese women who live alongside Orleanna Price in the wretched African village of Kilanga. The Georgian newcomer performs some of the same demanding chores, including shrouding her youngest in mosquito netting and placing her small body on a homemade bier. After Orleanna falls ill with malaria, the three oldest girls realize the extent of her responsibility for feeding and tending the family. When *kakakaka* (enteritis) afflicts the neighbors, Leah, Orleanna's perceptive daughter, describes a Kilangan funeral for a deceased mother: "Skinny and forlorn," the children appear devastated by loss of their mama (p. 146). When the epidemic takes village children, the mothers stagger down the road behind small shrouded corpses, "mothers crazy-walking on their knees, with mouths open wide like a hole ripped in mosquito netting" (p. 296). At night, they crawl the raw gravesites, trying to eat the dirt that covers the corpses. Their grief trounces insensitive American assertions that jungle dwellers are unable to love like normal parents.

Kingsolver's novel muses on other forms of tortured womanhood. The pose of missionary's wife forces Orleanna Price from a pagan intensity to "the higher plane of Motherhood" (p. 56). On recognizing the multiple threats in equatorial Africa, including the deaths of thirty-one children in Kilanga within seventeen months, she suffers insomnia. In snatches of sleep, she dreams of children "drowned, lost, eaten alive" (p. 95). The absence of someone to talk to saps her self-confidence, robbing her of support. From brief discussions with local wives, she learns about Belgian brutalization of miners and plantation workers, which often leaves women as lone supporters of their children. Without good news to counter the bad, Orleanna sinks irrevocably into despair.

Years after returning to Georgia, Orleanna blanches at a scent that reminds her of Africa and accuses her of her youngest child's death. Sad memories flash back to the soft flesh and fuzzy scalps of her suckling daughters. The worst times in her young motherhood occurred after the birth of twins when Rachel was just learning to walk. Orleanna recalls the fatigue of tending three small girls: "One mouth closed on a spoon meant two crying empty, feathers flying, so I dashed back and forth like a mother bird, flouting nature's maw with a brood too large" (p. 381). In a loving eulogy to Ruth May, Orleanna reshapes the biblical drama of Ruth 1:16–17, a familiar passage often recited at weddings, into a farewell: "My baby, my blood, my honest truth: entreat me not to leave thee" (p. 382).

Orleanna's tenderness strengthens Leah in 1985, a quarter century after the family's mission to the Congo. Driving down a rutted road in the Kimvula District of

Zaire, she is jostled into contractions a month early and gives birth to Nataniel, whom his father delivers by the roadside. The child's fever and inability to nurse terrify Leah, who broods over "a lethargic little bundle of skin-covered bones and a gaunt, skin-covered skull" (p. 498). Too weak to cry, the baby boy hovers for a week in his parents' arms, requiring two instances of mouth-to-mouth resuscitation. While dropping sterile water between his lips, Leah has a sudden memory of Orleanna's crazed words and prayers to Ruth May during the child's bout with malaria. The warming sense of Orleanna's arms around Leah strengthens her. She muses, "If God is someone who thinks of me at all, he must think of me as a mother" (p. 499).

See also **beans, Alice Greer, Taylor Greer, love, Mama Mwanza, parenthood, Lou Ann Ruiz, Spider Woman, Mama Bekwa Tataba, women**

- *Further Reading*

Hirsch, Marianne. *The Mother/Daughter Plot: Narrative, Psychoanalysis, Feminism.* Bloomington: Indiana University Press, 1989.

Lyall, Sarah. "Termites Are Interesting But Books Sell Better." *New York Times*, September 1, 1993.

MacDougall, Ruth Doan. "Becoming Mother to a Little Turtle." *New York Newsday*, March 13, 1988, p. 18.

Myzska, Jessica. "Barbara Kingsolver: 'Burning a Hole in the Pockets of My Heart.'" *De Pauw Magazine*, Vol. 5, No. 2, Spring 1994, pp. 18–20.

Murie, Adolph

The detailed studies of coyote habits conducted by Adolph Murie (1899–1974) aid Deanna Wolfe, a wildlife biologist in *Prodigal Summer* (2000), who analyzes the animal's return to the southern Appalachians. From 1934 to 1939, Murie, a native of Minnesota and younger brother of naturalist Olaus Johan Murie (1889–1963), provided the National Park Service with data on the coyote's role in the ecological system of Yellowstone National Forest. In 1940, he published his findings on the coyote's diet of smaller animals, including elk and deer carrion, pocket gopher, field mice, marmot, muskrat, and showshoe hare. Because he refuted widespread belief in ranchers that coyotes prey on domestic herds, the Yellowstone staff began a predator protection program. For his interest in wildlife management, the National Park Service presented him the John Burroughs Medal and a Distinguished Service Award.

In 1945, Olaus Murie, an eminent scientist and author, published his findings on predator eradication, a policy of the United States Biological Service for over a quarter century. He rejected respected beliefs that suppression of predators aided both ranchers and the balance of nature. One of the four founders of the Wilderness Society, he promoted an integrative approach to animal life. In 1959, he received the Audubon Medal for his championing of the National Park Service and for support of political action leading to the establishment of the Arctic Wildlife Range and passage of the 1964 Wilderness Act.

• *Further Reading*

Murie, O. J. *A Field Guide to Animal Tracks.* Boston: Houghton Mifflin, 1954.
Murie, Olaus. *Food Habits of the Coyote in Jackson Hole, Wyoming.* Washington: U.S. Department of Agriculture, 1935.
"A Short History of the Murie Family." http://www.muriecenter.org/family.htm.

Mwanza, Mama

A pathetic, hard-working cripple in *The Poisonwood Bible* (1998), Mama Mwanza is Kingsolver's model of the open-hearted African villager with an instinctive understanding of charity. After a catastrophic fire, Mama Mwanza's reduction to a crawling freak fails to daunt her spirit. She feeds her family by swapping oranges for eggs and rejoices in having a fisherman for a *bákala mpandi* (strong husband), a promise of security lacking in the white missionary household. Two of her children die of *kakakaka* (enteritis). Even in sorrow, she can find the heart to pity the cashless Price family, to whom she offers oranges and a benevolent belief that "whenever you have plenty of something, you have to share it with the *fyata* [poor]" (p. 206). The model shatters the philosophy of the arrogant Nathan Price, who contends that the Congolese are heathens in need of Christianity. Like the paradigm of womanly virtue in Proverbs 31:10–31, Mama Mwanza extends "her hand to the poor; yea, she reacheth forth her hands to the needy" (Proverbs 10:20).

As the older Price girls attempt to hold together their crumbling family, Leah studies Mama Mwanza as a model of womanly courage and discovers one of her strengths, the ability to delegate. While cooking over a dented can, the handicapped mother orders her sons to help with chores and supervises a pair of daughters pounding manioc in a mortar. The harmony and cooperation in the Mwanza family overcomes Leah, who "envied them with an intensity near to love, and near to rage" (p. 234). On the night of the ant attack, Leah fears that Mama Mwanza's sons may fail to rescue her. The author indicates the concern her family feels for her by picturing Tata Mwanza carrying her on his back toward the boats. On the sly during a drought, she continues to slip eggs under the Prices' hens to save the family from starvation and offers them two laying hens after the ants recede. Nelson reveres her as the savior of her son from the strike of a green mamba, a feat accomplished by neutralizing venom with milk.

Because of Mama Mwanza's numerous kindnesses, it is not surprising that the Price women turn to her to help lay out Ruth May's body under the traditional palm frond and flower funeral arch. The generosity of the Price's neighbor triggers an ingathering of women, many of whom had lost children and who share Orleanna's suffering. The gift of her best skillet is an appropriate kindness to Mama Mwanza, as are blouses and dresses for her children. As the Price girls flee Kilanga, Mama Mwanza's daughters bring them oranges and water for their journey. Reflecting on Mama Mwanza's devotion to motherhood, Orleanna honors her as "the backbone of a history" (p. 383).

nature

Kingsolver's love and trust of nature invests all of her writing. In an interview, she commented, "I grew up with both feet planted in nature and a house full of field guides.... Natural history is my avocation" ("Barbara"). She relieves the tension of an urban background in *The Bean Trees* (1988) with pleasant excursions into the Sonora Desert and to the Lake o' the Cherokees. The novel uses nature imagery as lyric statement and commentary on themes. As Taylor steers Mattie's white Lincoln toward Oklahoma City, Estevan breaks the monotony with a description of the Guatemalan national symbol, the quetzal, a spectacular tropical bird decked in red and green iridescent feathers and a long, curving tail that extends more than twice the length of its body. The species is so freedom-loving that it dies in captivity. In ancient times, Mayan shamans used the plumes to adorn ceremonial robes and head-dresses. In contrast to their majesty, Taylor imagines the alligator as the American symbol, an unsubtle dig at national rapacity and ruthlessness.

Kingsolver makes thorough use of her title by turning the wisteria vine into a controlling metaphor for the struggle for survival. In contrast to her suspicion of human institutions and bureaucracies, Taylor takes solace in the natural world, where the night-blooming cereus perfumes the air only once a year on a Tucson porch, Queen Anne's lace bobs in the Oklahoma wind, the rare desert rain of Arizona sparks life in tiny frogs, and king and silver salmon labor up fourteen steps of a fish ladder to spawn in a Seattle lake. A similar vision of a rattlesnake climbing a tree in search of a tender meal suffices as a reminder of the battle for sustenance. After she formally takes possession of Turtle and settles into permanent motherhood, the final scene in Oklahoma City again puts the child and her official mother in the public library, where books on horticulture broaden the theme of the bean trees with details of wisteria cultivation in poor soil. The image parallels Turtle's triumph over child abuse and her new life with a parent who is willing to lie to a magistrate to gain custody of her daughter.

For *Animal Dreams* (1990), set in Grace, Arizona, nature informs much of the action. The author anchors the story among apple, pecan, pear, plum, and quince orchards that line highways on both sides of a dying river. Within the clusters of trees are free-roving peacocks, which drop their bright-eyed tail feathers on the grass. Nature's generosity becomes the source of feathered piñatas, the local craft that Latina women sell in Tucson to keep their town alive and the river flowing with clean water. The recycling of feathers reflects the author's admiration of humble people who make the most of the earth's bounty.

Nature imagery expresses human tethers to earth in *Another America/Otra America* (1992), Kingsolver's first poetry anthology, rendered in English and Spanish. The poem "In Exile" personifies a cluster of mountains in Chile into human knuckles that press residents into their homeland. Another human rendering, "Apotheosis," uses the hen's daily egg production as a model for the writer's ideal of a steady turnout of pages. In the essay "High Tide in Tucson" (1995), she extols her belonging to earth's habitat: "What a stroke of luck. What a singular brute feat of outrageous fortune: to be born to citizenship in the Animal Kingdom" (p. 16).

In *Pigs in Heaven* (1993), nature again contrasts the human element of the author's fiction. Kingsolver accords a dignity to the salmon horde as they "curve and buck and thrust themselves against the current, dying to get upstream and pass themselves on" (p. 150). The cyclical behavior of fish expresses Kingsolver's respect for animal urges to protect species from extinction. A grotesque scenario in which a female coyote leaps in a tree to devour dove eggs points up the complexities of mothering vulnerable young, a parallel to Taylor's internal war against attorney Annawake Fourkiller, spokeswoman for the Cherokee, for wanting to enfold her daughter into an ethnic community.

The author again examines human behavior from its primitive side in *Animal Dreams* (1990). Codi Noline, who is well versed in zoological behaviors from her years of medical training, recognizes in herself the involuntary prickle of scalp and neck at the howling of a coyote pack. In another passage, she remarks that animals depend on the instincts of "desire and yawning and fear and the will to live" (p. 319). In identifying her sexual yearning for Loyd Peregrina, she remarks, "We're born like every other mammal and we live our whole lives around disguised animal thoughts. There's no sense pretending" (p. 118). Her acceptance of libido as a normal human urge is an initial step toward wholeness and recovery from too little love in childhood.

Because of her training in ecology and a dedication to the finite chain of life, Kingsolver erupts in frequent surges of protectiveness toward nature's bounty. Codi's disgust at human profligacy ignites in the high school classroom as she hacks her way through an impromptu tirade on how clear-cutting of virgin timberland to make paper is reducing forests and cluttering the world in waste. To a teenaged questioner she glowers, "Your life is the test. If you flunk this one, you die" (p. 254). The outburst derives from Codi's awareness of the tenuous state of Grace, a town named for God's gift to humankind.

Kingsolver turns nature into a character in *The Poisonwood Bible* (1998), where nothing progresses without taking into consideration the fast-growing jungle, swards of green vegetation, and the crocodile infestation of the Kwilu River. As described by book critic Nancy Pate, "The tropical landscape is omnipresent in both its pleasures—frangipani, exotic birds and butterflies, golden oranges—and its perils—venomous snakes, torrential rains, voracious driver ants, malarial fevers" (Pate, p. 4). The author describes Brother Fowles's tedious progress upriver in his houseboat and the slow task of transporting a tally of votes in the national election by canoe to Léopoldville. Through Rachel, the author remarks on buzzing bugs, red birds in the long grass stalks, and elephant grass tall enough to overarch a shaded tunnel. The concept of living with wild fruit trees as well as the menace of the poisonous insects and crocodiles in the river inhibit Anatole Ngemba's understanding of Georgian farming methods. To a native who knows no other habitat than jungle, the picture of rolling acreage lined with even rows of grain is impossible to imagine.

As rumors from Léopoldville and Stanleyville report the worsening political backdrop, Kingsolver uses nature to create atmosphere in Kilanga. To Rachel, the "muggy waiting-for-it days" that precede the annual rainy season abrade human behavior like the scratching of a persistent itch (p. 291). In the middle of the night, *nsongonya* (army ants) invade every surface, boiling over the setting "like black flowing lava in the moonlight" (p. 299). The late fall drought turns the creek bed to "dry cradles of white stones" and yellow leaves (p. 327). The barren state of manioc fields and fruit trees echoes the devastation of the Price family's henhouse and the fruitlessness of Nathan's ministry.

On the day of the village hunt by fire surround, natives turn to a last resort for sustenance. They pit themselves against nature by beating back head-high elephant grass with sticks and by lighting torches of greenheart wood topped with rags soaked in palm oil. The results of burning out a circular area is a variety of meat. It ends "hunger of the body" for protein, which Adah describes as "altogether different from the shallow, daily hunger of the belly" (p. 345). Her quick bites of caterpillars, crickets, grasshoppers, and locusts begin to stave off the pangs of famine, illustrating how a girl brought up among Georgia mammal-eaters can adapt to the insect-eating habits of the Congo.

The scenario is one of Kingsolver's most existential—a finely honed tableau of human will inflicted on nature through application of fire. Birds ignite like bottle rockets; baboons debate their options and realize there is "no choice but to burn with their children" (p. 347). Adah summarizes the effects of such dramatic carnage—Rachel turns to vegetarianism, Leah celebrates bagging an animal larger than herself, and Ruth May forages for crispy insects. Adah, the most contemplative and far-sighted of the Price sisters, accepts the law of nature that insists that "all animals kill to survive" (*Ibid.*). Kingsolver looks beyond Kilanga in the final book with an image of land clearing in Central Africa, which threatens nature's balance. Leah predicts: "Stop clearing, and the balance slowly returns," a tribute to the jungle's resilience (p. 525).

The author embraced the positive aspects of nature more fully in *Prodigal Summer* (2000) than in past books. She dedicated the text to "wildness, where it lives," an indication of her intent to preserve nature in pristine form against a tide of polluters, bounty hunters, and sprayers of harmful chemicals (p. vii). In limpid descriptions of the Appalachians, she claims that Zebulon Mountain breathes with "one long, slow inhalation every morning" (p. 31). The animistic thrust suits a tripartite story of the survival of goats, coyotes, and organic apple trees in an area overrun with natural and human predators. In response, reviewer Jenny Jones of the *New Zealand Herald* stated that the author "makes you feel the expiry of life" (Jones).

Prodigal Summer, the author's fifth novel, grips readers with its exultation of nature's wholeness and its ability to assure "persistence of life on earth" (p. 258). Reviewer Gary MacEoin of the *National Catholic Reporter* described the novel's "enhanced awareness of the profound interrelatedness of all creatures great and small, of our dependence as humans on the plants and animals of whose existence we city dwellers are only vaguely aware" (MacEoin, p. 19). In the front matter, Kingsolver acknowledges the importance of the American Chestnut Foundation for a breeding plan to re-establish the American chestnut in national woodlands. In the text, Garnett S. Walker, III, dubs his family "chestnut people" for their success at selling nuts and using lumber for tough, rot-proof cabins and barns (p. 129). He reveres old chestnut stands and the "great emptiness their extinction had left in the world" after the blight of 1904 brought them down (p. 128). Re-establishing them requires his crusade to hybridize a disease-resistant strain.

The novel's rhapsodic carnality draws instant comment from most reviewers, some of whom praise Kingsolver's frank observations, such as the power of the moon to regulate human ovulation and the joy in spontaneous intercourse between strangers. Copulations begin with bats aggressively mating under the porch eaves and range to fluttery lacewings, grappling red-tailed hawks, sleepy Io moths, and the trill of the magnolia warbler, a sound that protagonist Deanna Wolfe describes as "males drumming up business" (p. 13). The coyote, a newcomer to the southern Appalachians, is her chief concern, but the thrill of Eddie Bondo's hand on hers results in an impromptu invitation to a night in her cabin. Kingsolver acknowledges their shared electricity with images of the scrotal shape of lady's slippers and mushrooms pushing through leaf mold "announcing the eroticism of a fecund woods" (p. 20). She excuses the risky, on-the-spot touching of bare skin as "the body's decision," as though will and second thoughts have no vote in the abrupt coupling. A lyrical afternoon delight occurs two weeks later during the full of the moon after Bondo returns to a tryst with Deanna in a giant hollowed-out chestnut trunk. The image unites human intercourse with the forces of nature, much as estrus regulates the mating of other mammals.

In the words of reviewer Reese Danley-Kilgo, "Kingsolver is at her best in creating scenes in which the natural world lives and breathes" (Danley-Kilgo). For *Prodigal Summer*, she uses the survival of the fittest as an organizing principle. The concept lies at the heart of conflicts between Cole Widener and Lusa Maluf Landowski, Nannie Land Rawley and Garnett Walker, and Deanna and Eddie Bondo. To the latter pair, the idea of sheltering lamb-eating predators ignites Eddie with a sheepman's ire. After he shoots a Thanksgiving-in-July tom turkey for Deanna, he is shocked that she accepts the gift. To his surprise, she answers, "Predation's a sacrament, Eddie; it culls out the sick and the old, keeps populations from going through their own roofs. Predation is *honorable*" (p. 317). The statement relieves Deanna of a fanatic pro-life stance and acknowledges the normal demands of the food chain.

In her latest book, *Last Stand: America's Virgin Lands* (2002), a picture album of natural wonders, Kingsolver issues a lyric reply to critics who label her a ditzy tree hugger. She marvels at the uniqueness of the "natural world that proceeds by its own rules, for its own reasons, apart from any measure of utility to human need" (p. 17). The sparse text and grand photo spreads remind readers that "our continent is making its last stand" as asphalt and housing developments gradually displace wildflowers and animal species (p. 19). In a more personal vein, the author queries "the arrogance of the agenda we've inherited from our forebears," who lacked the capacity to value nature for its intrinsic worth (p. 15). The loss, to Kingsolver, is unthinkable, both for the current generation and the unborn, who may live in a world greatly denuded of earth's wonders.

See also ecofeminism, *Last Stand: America's Virgin Lands,* Methuselah, pollution, pueblos, seeds

• *Further Reading*

Aay, Henry. "Environmental Themes in Ecofiction: *In the Center of the Nation* and *Animal Dreams*." *Journal of Cultural Geography*, Vol. 14, No. 2, Spring/Summer 1994, pp. 65–85.

"Barbara Kingsolver: Coming Home to a Prodigal Summer." http://www.ivillage.com/books/intervu/fict/articles.

Danley-Kilgo, Reese. "Kingsolver's Latest Scores Hit." *Huntsville Times*, November 26, 2000.

Finkel, Mike. "The Ultimate Survivor." *Audubon*, Vol. 101, No. 3, May-June 1999.

Jones, Jenny. "Review: *Prodigal Summer*." *New Zealand Herald*, February 10, 2001.

MacEoin, Gary. "Prodigal Summer: A Novel." *National Catholic Reporter*, Vol. 38, No. 3, November 9, 2001, p. 19.

Pate, Nancy. "Five Distinctive Voices Narrate Kingsolver's Remarkable 'Bible.'" *Tulsa World*, November 1, 1998, p. 4.

Ndu, Tata

The traditionalist chief of Kilanga village in *The Poisonwood Bible* (1998), Tata "Undo" Ndu is a power to be reckoned with. He impresses others with a grand outfit, which Ruth May Price describes as "cat skins and everything and a hat," a tall crown of sisal fiber complementing his lens-less glasses, high-domed forehead, and powerful physique (p. 51). To her sister Adah, he's a "comic-book bully" who imposes his will through physical intimidation and who spreads a false report that a lion has eaten her (p. 135). To Leah, Adah's twin, he's the power broker who manipulates village opinions through an elaborate system of discussions intended to maneuver citizens to his way of thinking. In retrospect, she recalls that Ndu was arrogant, but "almost incomprehensibly polite," a combination necessary to the savvy politician (p. 453).

Because of the Prices' mission, Tata Ndu becomes concerned with the moral decline of villagers from attending Nathan's services, which encourage them to neglect traditional ancestors and gods. From a front-yard throne, Ndu listens impatiently to Price's proposals and resurrects the command of the previous missionary, Brother Fowles, that the chief marry only one wife. Ndu warns his people to resist the offer of baptism in river water teeming with crocodiles. He seethes at Nathan's superiority toward local people and his treatment of them as "*mwana*, your children, who knew nothing until you came here" (p. 333). Kingsolver stresses the incongruities of democracy to a tribal society by describing the chief's outrage that Nathan disrespects village elders by allowing each resident an equal vote in a democratic election.

To the Prices' amazement, in August 1960, Ndu suddenly begins offering food and other gifts to the Prices, a gesture of courtship. He woos Rachel and intends to add her to his harem because of her light color. Orleanna grouses that the chief wants the girl "like she's an *accessory* he needs to go with his outfit" (p. 263). The courtship scenario is more complex than it appears on the surface. By pursuing the fair-haired Rachel Price for his harem, the chief flatters his masculine ego at the same time that he performs a selfless act on behalf of Nathan Price. In Leah's opinion, "Tata Ndu was gently suggesting we'd become a burden to his village in a time of near famine;

that people here accommodate such burdens by rearranging families" (p. 453). In the view of critic Julian Markels, the gesture is meant "to relieve her family's hunger by one mouth through an act of philanthropy for his Christian antagonist" (Markels). The irony of the gesture reflects both on Ndu's steadfast rejection of the missionary version of Christianity and on the discourtesies of Price, who bears little altruism to parishioners in his religious outpost.

According to a go-between, Anatole Ngemba, Ndu is content for Nathan to draw the most luckless Kilangans to worship services, but the chief worries that proselytizing more stable citizens will draw disaster on the village. At the novel's climax, Kingsolver orchestrates a dramatic irony — Kilanga's embrace of the Western-style ballot box. Ndu's appearance on the front row of Nathan's Sunday service is ominous. Unfortunately for the minister, the choice of a fearful sermon topic from the Apocrypha — a Semitic hero tale extolling the prophet Daniel and belittling the Babylonian idol worship of Bel — does not bode well for the locals' decision on whether to accept Jesus as the village deity.

The chief grows in stature among his people with the delivery of his own sermon. He uses Nathan's outrage as proof that whites think the Congolese are incapable of evolving social and political structures. In an ironic twist of American ideals, he proposes a democratic election on the advancement of Jesus to village god. To the fanatic minister's charge of blasphemy, Ndu insists that a vote is the fair method of choosing a god: "You say these things are good. You cannot say now they are not good" (p. 33). When the congregation finishes casting ballots, Jesus garners a little over 16 percent out of sixty-seven voters.

With a surprise plebescite that overthrows Nathan's influence, Ndu ironically violates his beloved African traditions, thus setting a precedent for further choice of democratic methods to settle disputes. After he demands a subsequent vote on the matter of allowing a woman to hunt with the men, he is dismayed to that over 53 percent favor Leah and her bow and arrow. Because the hunt raises a rumble of discontent over possession of bush meat, Ndu chops off the hindquarter of the impala that Leah shoots and throws it at her. She reciprocates by tossing the shank at Gbenye, Ndu's eldest son, who claims the kill. The undercurrent of tempers causes Ndu to insult Anatole, a black who sides with whites.

The character of Chief Ndu continues to reflect a canny leader of Kilangans. After the Price family's dissolution, Ndu deals with local troubles, including skirmishes between Lumumbists and the National Army. To his credit, he threatens to banish Kuvudundu for placing the snake in the henhouse and causing the death of Ruth May. On learning of the chief's death from complications of a wound, Rachel sneers at "my would-be husband" (p. 484). As a gesture of respect to Tata Ndu, Adah reminds her, "You could have done worse" (*Ibid.*).

See also **Rachel Price**

• *Further Reading*

Carman, Diane. "Kingsolver Hits Stride in Africa; Missionary's Muddling Creates Cultural Disaster." *Denver Post*, October 18, 1998.

Jones, Elin. "From the Sublime to the Ridiculous." *Marietta Leader*, November 3, 1999.
Markels, Julian. "Coda: Imagining History in *The Poisonwood Bible*." *Monthly Review Press*, September 2003.

Nelson

A twelve-year-old houseboy at the Price family compound in *The Poisonwood Bible* (1998), Nelson offers delightful remedial training to white Americans who resist learning firsthand Congolese attitudes, outlooks, and customs. After Nelson's parents, brothers, and baby sister drown in a canoe mishap, Anatole Ngemba ostensibly sends the orphaned boy as a hostess gift to acknowledge a dinner invitation. In exchange for meals, a room in the henhouse, and a weekly basket of eggs to sell, Nelson takes over the chores once performed by Mama Tataba, including scraping manure from roosting boxes and rigging up an oil drum swing. His knowledge of wildlife blesses the household with homemade nostrums and warnings about poisonous snakes; his very presence intrigues five-year-old Ruth May Price to peep at his nakedness. His multiple talents turn allegorical after he rigs up a bamboo frame for the family's one mirror. Leah describes it as "Kilanga's one looking glass," an objective judge that even-handedly reflects the faces of all, black and white (p. 142).

In the estimation of Ruth May, Nelson is savvy to the theological warfare in Kilanga, which pits Nathan Price against centuries of ancestor worship. Nelson knows that villagers hover at the threshold of Christianity, but will retreat to their familiar pantheon of gods if anything bad happens under the aegis of Jesus. Nelson interprets the Prices' financial collapse as a supernatural curse and relates a widespread prejudice toward *báza* (twins), a concept that Kingsolver may have adopted from Chinua Achebe's Nigerian novel *Things Fall Apart* (1958). The idea of abandoning twins to die in the jungle is so ingrained in Nelson that he sits four feet from Adah, Leah's twin, while she teaches her silent lessons. To protect Ruth May from harm, he offers a *nkisi* (fetish) in a matchbox for *Bandu* (the littlest one), but later assumes that her zombie-like stare is the result of an owl's theft of her soul. His nonchalant explanation of Tata Ndu's courtship of Rachel astounds Orleanna, but seems like a sensible bargain to Nelson, who knows how close the family is to starvation.

Nelson makes himself useful. He teaches Leah to shoot her bow and arrow. He is the family runner, bearing boiled eggs to Leah at the school and returning with news that Anatole has seen a green mamba by his bed, a sign of *kibaazu* (a curse). On the day of the fire surround, Nelson repudiates the chief's son Gbenye for claiming that he killed the impala that Leah shot in the neck. For all his courage in defending the rebellious female, Nelson's stout-heartedness fails him after he locates a snake in the henhouse, a sign of evil stalking him. Kingsolver reduces him to a whimpering voice crying to be admitted to the Price house for the night "over and over like a poor starving dog that's been whining so long it doesn't know how to stop" (p. 358). In the falling action, he rises once more in villagers' esteem for revealing Kuvudundu's plot that caused the death of Ruth May. A survivor of the Congo's harsh environment, Nelson later marries and sires five children.

See also **Adah Price**

• *Further Reading*

Koza, Kimberly. "The Africa of Two Western Women Writers: Barbara Kingsolver and Margaret Laurence." *Critique*, Vol. 44, No. 3, Spring 2003, pp. 284–294.

Ngemba, Anatole

The noble Congolese freedom fighter and Christ figure in *The Poisonwood Bible* (1998), Tata Anatole Ngembe is the outsider and rescuer who dedicates his life to uplifting the poor. He was born in Stanleyville and, after his parents' death when he was a child, worked on a rubber plantation and then in a diamond mine. Education is the salvation that moves him up from certain death at manual labor to professional status as trilingual teacher of village males. At Kilanga, his intimate relationship with the missionary family takes varied forms: he translates into Kikongo the inept sermons of Reverend Nathan Price, befriends Leah, and helps the family survive army ants by placing Leah and Ruth May in a boat. At a dark hour in Leah's sorting out of spiritual beliefs, Anatole's sensible explanation of ant behavior reduces her fear that the invasion was a punishment from God. His reason for aiding Nathan is pragmatic — Anatole provides villagers with "full disclosure" of all information to allow them a chance to form an opinion on Christianity (p. 453).

At age twenty-four, Anatole, like Loyd Peregrina in *Animal Dreams* (1990), becomes both romantic interest and counterpoint, despite slanted eyes and thin tattooed lines on his ebony face. He delights Rachel as the rare bachelor invited to dinner and mediates between Nathan Price and Chief Ndu, who considers church attendance an element of moral decline. As a go-between, Anatole helps the Prices comprehend local people, whose superstitions revile Leah's pet owl as a gobbler of dead souls. In addition to providing the Prices with rabbit for dinner, he consoles families for the schoolboys who died of *kakakaka* (enteritis), secretly guides the Communist boy scouts toward revolution, and refuses to allow Nathan to proselytize them with bible classes.

By training villagers in how to select candidates and cast their votes, Anatole becomes a herald of freedom, a male awarded the honorific of "Monsieur" (p. 337). Like Apollo, the bringer of light and skill in Greek mythology, he introduces Leah to archery with a bow he carves from greenheart wood, asks her to teach arithmetic to his youngest pupils, and helps her comprehend the harm that colonialism has done to Africa. In one of Kingsolver's subtle ironies, Leah muses that "Anatole could be my father's friend, if only he had a better grasp of the Scripture" (p. 144). The antecedent of the pronoun "he" opens to question which man is less adept at biblical interpretation.

Advancing from friend to Anatole's protector, Leah shifts loyalties from father to lover. She retreats from the bible-thumping idiocies of her father and, with Anatole's help, rebuilds her world view toward a more positive image of equatorial Africa. Unlike propagandists and missionaries, Anatole seeks a fair presentation of new ideas to the Congolese to enable them to choose for themselves which proposals to retain and which to discard. In his opinion, "Some of these things seem very handy, and some turn out to be not so handy. It is important to distinguish" (p. 286). His open-mindedness nudges Leah from friend to sweetheart to wife.

With Anatole's skill at sniffing out the social and political situation, the couple avoids anti-white sentiment in Bulungu and Stanleyville by crossing into the Central African Republic. For a time, they attempt to live American style in Georgia. At Emory, Leah studies agricultural engineering and Anatole enrolls in political science and geography. However, life in comfort fails to counter the thrum of the distant continent that permeates their spirits. Most painful are the Georgian bigots who gawk at Anatole's facial scars and alienate their three biracial children "as advertisement for our sins" (p. 468).

The departure from Southern racism offers Kingsolver an opportunity to elevate Anatole to the level of people's champion. On return to Zaire after Leah's third trip to Georgia, he suffers the capricious arrest common to dictatorships—airport authorities seize his passport and pass him into the custody of Mobutu's thugs. During years of separation while Anatole serves a prison sentence for treason in Thysville's Camp Hardy, Leah rears three children on a communal farm before resettling the family in Angola. A year after Anatole's return, he delivers their fourth son, Nataniel, during a drive down a rutted road and saves him from dying in the first week by breathing into his frail lungs. A mature couple happy in their choices of mates, Anatole and Leah are the most promising of characters from *The Poisonwood Bible* for their loyalty to the Congolese and their trust in education and cooperative efforts to relieve the peasants' misery.

See also **Leah Price**

• *Further Reading*

Fletcher, Yael Simpson. "History Will One Day Have Its Say: New Perspectives on Colonial and Postcolonial Congo." *Radical History Review*, Vol. 84, 2002, pp. 195–207.

Koza, Kimberly. "The Africa of Two Western Women Writers: Barbara Kingsolver and Margaret Laurence." *Critique*, Vol. 44, No. 3, Spring 2003, pp. 284–294.

Markels, Julian. "Coda: Imagining History in *The Poisonwood Bible*." *Monthly Review Press*, September 2003, p. 1.

"Review: *The Poisonwood Bible*." *Timbrel*, September-October 1999.

Rubinstein, Roberta. "The Mark of Africa." *World & I*, Vol. 14, No. 4, April 1999, p. 254.

Skow, John. "Hearts of Darkness: Matters of Race, Religion and Gender Collide as a Missionary Family Moves to the Congo in 1959." *Time*, Vol. 152, No. 9, November 9, 1998, p. 113.

Noline, Cosima "Codi"

The thirty-two-year-old daughter who takes charge of a sickly father in *Animal Dreams* (1990), Cosima "Codi" Noline models the internal angst of the unreconciled prodigal. She arrives home feeling "emptied-out and singing with echoes, unrecognizable to myself" (p. 9). Out of persistent despair, she admits to looking for the ideal nest "where trains never wrecked and hearts never broke, where no one you loved ever died" (p. 236). Unlike Taylor Greer, the protagonist in *The Bean Trees* (1988) and *Pigs in Heaven* (1993), Codi is the motherless daughter who must make a place for herself in a community matriarchy. Bearing one of the two intellectual names her father chose for his daughters, she is the underachieving drifter, the cynical individualist who left home in 1972 at age eighteen. Her puzzling resume includes doing research for the Mayo Clinic after fleeing from a difficult breach birth and abandoning the last two months' work on a medical degree. Subsequent employment placed her on the graveyard shift of the 7-Eleven and a three-year teaching job in Biology I and II at Grace High School.

Codi's rootlessness derives from a need for unconditional love and acceptance. She admits to having been a loner, outsider, and victim of a dream that blinds her, leaving her "nowhere at all," a memory from infancy when Doc Homer photographed her unusual marbled eyes (p. 204). Rather than talk truth, she perennially lies, particularly to strangers on buses and planes, "making things up so there would be no discussion of what I was *really*" (p. 203). When faced with small-town gossip, she complains that she's not used to "a place where everybody's into everybody else's business" (p. 151). The scrutiny ends her dependence on a series of aliases and forces her to deal in truths.

The novelist uses naturalistic terms to describe Codi's behaviors, which include a ready supply of smart-mouthed comebacks, but a lack of insight into her role as Hallie's surrogate mother. Their father remembers Codi in childhood as "pretty and stubborn as a wild horse, but without an animal's instincts for self-preservation" (p. 19). On return from Tucson for the first time since 1972, she protects herself from emotional battery with a "hope for nothing at all in the way of love, so as not to be disappointed" (p. 117). In time, her rejection of intimacy becomes a habit, which she breaks by making the first move toward Loyd Peregrina, her high school sweetheart. After a pleasant afternoon of love-making in the open air, she feels "renewed" like "a patch of dry ground that had been rained on" (p. 130).

Codi, who is three years older than Hallie, identifies herself as "the sister who didn't go to war" (p. 7). Codi contrasts her altruistic sibling by refusing to commit to a profession, social issue, lover, or family as though she were an alien from outer space uncertain of how to proceed on earth. While reflecting on Hallie's commitment to a real cause in Nicaragua, Codi admits that she studied medicine solely "to win love, and to prove myself capable" (p. 36). Her hunger for acceptance dates to her mother's death in 1947. The loss causes Codi to muse on the superstitions of youth: "Children robbed of love will dwell on magic" (p. 50). She pictures herself as a stark loner symbolized by an architectural monolith — "a grain elevator on the prairie" (p. 128). Walking among strangers back in Tucson for a visit allows her to smile while feeling "anonymous as a goldfish" (p. 200). These images disclose serious issues in Codi's personality concerning honesty and trust.

The decision to resettle in Grace causes Codi to do some cynical stock-taking: "I had no real attachment to selling lottery tickets at 7-Eleven; Doc Homer was going off the deep end; Carlo was Carlo; Hallie would be leaving at summer's end" (pp. 54–55). After quitting a dead-end job and leaving her lover, Codi accepts the task of teaching school while ending the medical practice of her father, who is too ill from senile dementia to trust himself in treating the sick. She is able to put into perspective the retirement, deterioration, and future demise of her only parent. Both father and daughter fear his death, but lack the words and rituals for sharing deep concerns and mutual love.

Complicating the letting go are Codi's unaddressed feelings for the dead fetus she miscarried one night nearly two decades past, when she bolted herself in the bathroom for four hours. In secret, she wrapped her child in her mother's black sweater and knelt to bury the small bundle in Tortoise Canyon "with the dignity of an old woman" (p. 141). She blames Loyd for "[cutting] me to the edge of what a soul will bear" (p. 131). Guilt later emerges for dieting and ultimately starving the fetus "*in utero*, rather than risk known disaster," a parallel to the emotional starvation that the girls suffer at the hands of their distant father (p. 207). In dreams, Codi hears Hallie say, "You can put her down now," a tender gesture of support (p. 301).

Simultaneously, Codi evolves a hands-on classroom style that reveals her skill at problem solving. She incorporates student findings about the high pH of river water and damaged biota to solve the problem of a dying river. She teaches about "poor countries and rich countries and DDT in the food chain, and the various ways our garbage comes home to us" (p. 262). To combat a high teen pregnancy rate, she risks being fired by lecturing on birth control. In her free time, classroom objectivity fails her, leaving her on edge when interacting with others, especially Doc Homer. She bristles at the intrusion of the citizens of Grace, Arizona, her hometown, "a memory minefield" (p. 46). In preparing for a first date with Loyd Peregrina, she mutters darkly, "I can get into a mood when I annoy myself no end" (p. 119).

The falling action coordinates a series of healing relationships, including Doc and Loyd, the two testy, combative men in her life. Friend Emelina Domingos's memory of Codi as the organizer of a boycott is prophetic. After befriending the matrons of the Stitch and Bitch Club and educating them on river pollutants, Codi begins to feel the motherly support that her early life lacked. On her last day in Grace, she seems to have "fifty mothers," who lighten the burden of tending to Doc after he takes to his bed (p. 311). On her last flight from home, she encounters Mrs. Kimball, a willing listener, and completes a talk cure by disburdening herself of the pain of losing both mother and child. The cleansing enables Codi to return to Grace, mourn the passing of sister and father, and accept Loyd's love on a permanent basis. Her second pregnancy is the author's blessing of the union and a prediction of happiness for the couple.

See also **discontent, journey motif, loss, love, Halimeda "Hallie" Noline, Homer Noline, self-esteem, women**

• *Further Reading*

Murrey, Loretta Martin. "The Loner and the Matriarchal Community in Barbara Kingsolver's *The Bean Trees* and *Pigs in Heaven*." *Southern Studies*, Vol. 5, No. 1–2, Spring & Summer 1994, pp. 155–164.

Ryan, Maureen. "Barbara Kingsolver's Lowfat Fiction." *Journal of American Culture*, Vol. 18, No. 4, Winter 1995, pp. 77–82.

Willis, Meredith Sue. "Barbara Kingsolver, Moving On." *Appalachian Journal*, Vol. 22, No. 1, 1994, pp. 78–86.

Noline, Halimeda "Hallie"

The unseen sister in *Animal Dreams* (1990), twenty-nine-year-old Hallie Noline is the "blossom of [the] family," the optimist who believes "you can't let your heart go bad" (pp. 49, 223). The other half of a *doppelgänger*, she is sister to Codi, who wars against adversity at home while Hallie volunteers in August 1985 to assist cotton farmers in Chinandega, Nicaragua. Kingsolver later pondered close sisterhood in the poem "Street Scenes," collected in *Another America/Otra America* (1992). The parting in the first stave describes the fear of permanent separation, which she pictures as "a lock about to be forced" (p. 9). The third stave reflects the power of sibling unity to fight back against a male stalker. After they turn on their attacker, inspect his body, and laugh, he flees from a united front as strong as the camaraderie of Codi and Hallie. The scenario characterizes the growing-up years of the Noline sisters before life sent them on two rescue missions— Codi to comfort her father during the onset of Alzheimer's disease and Hallie into a war zone guarded by "men in uniforms decorated with the macho jewelry of ammunition" (p. 31). Both Noline sisters face formidable adversaries— Codi familiarizes herself with love and trust, Hallie challenges the bullies who threaten the lives of innocent peasants.

For Codi, who is three years older, Hallie was the stabilizer of a living arrangement in Tucson that included Codi's lover Carlo. Hallie is sensible, "perversely honest," abnormally happy, and radically idealistic (p. 34). She reminds her sister that "libraries are the one American institution you shouldn't rip off" (*Ibid.*). Codi thinks of her as the only one of the trio "who saw life as a controllable project" (p. 10). Codi acknowledges that men tended to prefer Hallie before settling for Codi. The situation might have spawned jealousy, but Codi admits, "I loved her too" (*Ibid.*).

Hallie is an expert in integrated pest management. To aid Nicaraguan farm families, she leaves her job staffing a hotline for the extension service and departs south in a Toyota pickup. She displays a determination and courage that Codi calls a "cross between Johnny Appleseed and a freedom fighter" (p. 30). Hallie rejects being idolized and asserts, "What keeps you going isn't some fine destination but just the road you're on, and the fact that you know how to drive" (p. 224). Her wants are simple — kindness, enough food for all, and a peaceable life for children. Prophetically, she writes, "I don't think I'll ever be going back. I don't think I can" (p. 300).

The author uses Hallie's letters as a means of voicing her own contempt for United States involvement in destabilizing Nicaragua through guerrilla warfare illegally financed by the Reagan administration. Living on hope and solving one local problem at a time, she intends to improve the nation's harvest as a way of insuring children's health. Her character takes on an incandescent valor and nobility because of the huge task of uplifting so poor and hopeless a nation. Her letters abound with affection and blessing. She denies that she wants to rescue the Third World, yet explains that she must leave the homeland that subsidizes the murder of Central Americans. The fictional abandonment suggests that Kingsolver considered the issue of expatriation at least a year before she and her daughter Camille settled in Santa Cruz in the Canary Islands to protest President George H. W. Bush's entry into the Gulf War.

Persistent images suggest that Hallie can't survive so destructive a war as the one the United States conducts in Nicaragua. When Codi returns to an empty apartment, she finds a head-sized white balloon floating at eye level, an omen of Hallie's death that brazenly stares Codi in the face. Intermittently before Hallie's demise, she sends letters jubilant with her activities "in seventh heaven" riding from field to field past land mines on her gray-spotted white horse named *Sopa del Dia* (Soup of the Day) (p. 120). The menacing presence enhances the reader's image of Hallie as a cheerful, altruistic risk-taker. When Codi reports the death of the river in Grace, Arizona, Hallie posts a pep talk, "You can't live through something like that, and not take risks now" (p. 149).

At the same time that Codi learns bits about her family history and begins helping local matrons understand the danger of polluted river water, Kingsolver builds tension in Hallie's distant adventures. The news that American National Guardsmen in a helicopter strafed and killed three teenage girls forces Hallie to protest carnage from the sky as grotesque. Contributing to the hideous story is the name of one of the children, Alba (white), a symbol of innocence. Clinging to shreds of tainted nationality, Hallie demands to know how the event played in American news, a subtextual suggestion that Americans can't depend on the media to inform them of shocking events involving the U.S. military.

Ironically, news of Hallie's fate comes to her befuddled father long distance and in Spanish, a tragic model of the failed communications that permeate the story. After her kidnap and murder during the Sandinista revolt, sister Codi realizes Hallie's bravery in supplying peasant farmers with agricultural advice in the face of menace from right-wing Contra guerrillas. Sarcastically, Codi envisions Hallie eating military C-rations and mutters from a taxpayer's perspective, "Dinner was on me. So were the land mines" (p. 262). In a conciliatory moment with Doc Homer, Codi finds the strength to bury the bundled leftovers of her stillborn child and to celebrate her sister's life: "We still gave the world a lot, Pop. We gave it Hallie" (p. 333). The intense hero worship suggests that part of Codi's emotional problem is her unfavorable comparison of herself to Hallie.

Kingsolver's commiseration with Hallie's tragic death echoes from an essay, "Personal Perspective," published in September 2001 in the *Los Angeles Times* following the World Trade Center disaster:

> Every life that ends is utterly its own event — and also in some way it's the same as all others, a light going out that ached to burn longer. Even if you never had the chance to love the light that's gone, you miss it. You should. You bear this world and everything that's wrong with it by holding life still precious, each time, and starting over [p. M1].

She uses the tragedy of the sister's murder to express outrage that the Contras flourished with tax dollars the Reagan administration dispatched to manipulate Central American politics.

See also **Cosima "Codie" Noline, Homer Noline**

• *Further Reading*

Siegel, Lee. "Sweet and Low." *New Republic*, Vol. 220, No. 12, March 22, 1999, pp. 30–37.
Smiley, Jane. "In Our Small Town, the Weight of the World." *New York Times Book Review*, September 2, 1990, p. 2.

Noline, Homer

The sole doctor of Grace, Arizona, in *Animal Dreams* (1990), Homer Noline lives a persnickety anal existence aloof from the humble community until he reaches a pitiable crossroads of his life. Born Homero Nolina, he returned to his hometown of Grace after World War II to a hostile, disapproving environment. After his wife Alice died following the birth of her second child, he was left the widowed father of two girls, three-year-old Codi and the infant Hallie. He deliberately stripped the family of Latino ancestry in a desire to elevate the girls socially, causing Codi to think of herself as a member of "The Nothing Tribe" (p. 213). In 1986, the elder girl returns to help him cope with Alzheimer's disease, which he diagnosed in himself two years before, but she considers him "an unwilling candidate for rescue" (p. 10). She recalls his emotional remoteness and fierce protection in their childhood, when he ruled out collecting peacock feathers to protect the girls from bird mites. The precisely stacked food boxes in his refrigerator symbolize his unbending rules for health while imparting a stark absence of emotional involvement with his motherless girls.

Doc Homer is both physician and researcher. After delivering a number of local infants born with Gracela syndrome or marbled irises, he collected photos and data on a recessive gene that caused the anomaly, even in his daughters. He published the findings in the *American Journal of Genetics* and stored project papers and photos in the attic. Clinically, he treats his daughters more as patients than as offspring or even distant family members. He regrets not cutting down the poisonous oleanders when his first daughter was born. He is skilled enough at diagnosis to recognize without an examination that sixteen-year-old Codi's unannounced pregnancy is nearing the end of the second trimester. He surmises that "she was so malnourished, he could have predicted toxemia, even placenta abruptio" (p. 142). During her delivery of a stillborn infant, he is torn between objectivity and fatherly concern, but opts to respect her privacy. In retrospect, he regrets not counseling her about the predicament and "would sell his soul to back up the time" (p. 141). The depth of regret in Doc Homer's brief commentaries on family suggests a pervasive theme in the failing minds of Alzheimer's patients.

In considering how he has managed a badly conflicted parenthood, Doc Homer fears that "he's failed them uniformly" (p. 141). When his mind derails while he examines Rita Cardenal, a teen pregnant with twins, he returns to the past and weeps for Codi. In decline after a diagnosis of terminal illness, he takes to his bed and mourns that he "turned out to be a brute beast after all," a suggestion of the high ideals he maintained during his prime, when he tried to redeem his family from ignominy (p. 287). Of his extremes of autonomy as father and physician, Codi observes, "I hadn't thought before about how self-sufficiency could turn on you in old age or sickness" (p. 69). Her remark reflects an inability to reach far enough into the past to make things right between herself and her dad.

See also Cosima "Codi" Noline, Halimeda "Hallie" Noline, parenthood

• *Further Reading*

DeMarr, Mary Jean. *Barbara Kingsolver: A Critical Companion.* Westport, Conn.: Greenwood, 1999.
Smiley, Jane. "In Our Small Town, the Weight of the World." *New York Times Book Review*, September 2, 1990, p. 2.

Noline genealogy

Animal Dreams (1990) is the story of the Noline family and the reason its ancestral line was sabotaged a quarter century before the story begins, when Homero Nolina married his second cousin Althea. The action describes the homecoming of Codi Noline, the lost daughter from "a marooned family, shipwrecked on three separate islands," an image of the father and his two daughters, alienated by Codi's adolescent angst and the stillbirth of her child (p. 139). In a confrontation about the family's stunted background, she typifies them as "auburned-haired and angry, living in exile in our own town" (p. 260).

```
      one of the        Conrado Nolina,
      nine redhaired    one of the
      Gracela sisters = local miners
(Althea, Camila, Carina   |
Estrella, Hilaria, Julietta, |
Renata, Ursolina, and     |
Violetta come from        |
Spain as bartered brides) |
          |-----cousins-----|
      mother (with      Doña Althea
      pot-black kitchen)  (and her sisters)
        |
Dr. Homer = Alice Carlisle          |----------|------|
   Noline  | (Althea Nolina,     father=Inez    Tía brother + Maxine
  (Homero  | second cousin;     (Apache;  | Peregrina  Sonia      Shorty
  Nolina;  | d. 1957 of         cockfighter |       (orchard keeper  (Loyd's
  d. 1988) | kidney             from Jicarilla)|      in Grace)     Navajo aunt)
           | failure)                       | identical
   |--------------------|            |-------- twins ----------|---------------|
Halimeda    Carlo + Cosima + Loyd = Cissie        Leander    Birdie
"Hallie"   (her lover "Codi" | Pere-  Ramon       (killed by    |
Noline     from age  Noline | grina  (left him)   a drunk)   daughter
(b. 1957)  24 to 34)  (b. 1954)| (Apache-                        |
                             | Pueblo; b.                     Hester
                             | ca. 1951)
                             |--------------------|
                   miscarried child          unborn child
                   (b. 1969)
```

Paine, Robert T.

Winner of the 2000 Eminent Ecologist Award, Robert T. Paine (1933–   ) has directed global attention to the dangers of species decline and extinction. A respected professor emeritus of zoology at the University of Washington and past president of the Ecological Society of America, he has won numerous fellowships and honoraria for his defense of nature's intermeshed systems. Deanna Wolfe, a wildlife biologist in *Prodigal Summer* (2000), refers to his 1966 experiment that led to the keystone predator theory. By removing starfish and sea otters from intertidal pools, he generated a caroming imbalance in nature after the top predators no longer controlled populations within an ecological system. Deanna comments, "No one had known, before that, how crucial a single carnivore could be to things so far removed from carnivory" (p. 62). Scientists apply Paine's paradigm to such ecological threats as the loss of lions to distemper on the African veldt and the removal of mountain lions from the Grand Canyon.

• *Further Reading*

Levin, Simon, and Marty Peale. "Beyond Extinction: Rethinking Biodiversity." *SFI Bulletin*, Winter 1995–1996.
Paine, R. T. "Food Web Complexity and Species Diversity." *American Naturalist*, Vol. 100, 1966, pp. 65–75.
_____. "A Note on Trophic Complexity and Species Diversity." *American Naturalist*, Vol. 103, 1969, pp. 91–93.

parenthood

Kingsolver examines parenthood from a variety of perspectives, all of which elucidate the uniqueness of the American family. Of the industrialized world's recoil from children, Kingsolver observed, "Children are an aberration in late capitalism. They're also a liability, because they're not productive. So that's why capitalism treats them like toxic waste" (Epstein). In a poignant contrast with American attitudes, in *The Bean Trees* (1988), she creates a pair of Mayan refugees fleeing Guatemala and leaving behind their daughter Ismene, a pawn the oppressive government holds in a deadly game of cat and mouse. Rather than cause the death of seventeen members of a teacher's union, Estevan and Esperanza chose to leave Ismene in the hands of monsters and, with bruised hearts, to seek safety in the United States. The decision reveals the multiple complexities of parenthood in terms of what is best for the child, who is at least alive and safe rather than on the run like her parents.

The Bean Trees also examines a pair of mother/daughter relationships by presenting Taylor Greer from both vantage points. In her telephone conversations with Alice, her mother, Taylor demonstrates a wholesome search for fulfillment and a fondness and trust in her only parent, a humble Kentucky washwoman and domestic. As the mother of a toddler, Taylor shows promise in immediate bonding and fierce determination to retain her daughter. The job is tough, as Kingsolver indicates in the essay "Stone Soup: What Does It Mean to Be a Family Anyway?" (1995): "I know of no one who really went looking to hoe the harder row, especially the daunting one of single parenthood. Yet it seems to be the most American of customs to blame the burdened for their destiny." Despite obstacles, the closeness Taylor develops with Turtle suggests that Taylor capitalizes on the mothering she received from Alice and passes it along to Turtle. Both relationships evolve from Taylor's first person dialogue, a structural force in Kingsolver's skillful fiction.

With *Pigs in Heaven* (1993), the non-sequel, the author pictures Cash Stillwater, a grieving father who retreats from his Cherokee community to spend two years making jewelry for tourists in Jackson Hole, Wyoming. He carries with him heavy anguish at the death of his unnamed wife from cancer and guilt for the suicide of his daughter Alma, who drives her vehicle into the Arkansas River. In despair at the time from two losses, he allowed his granddaughter Lacey Stillwater to slip away after his surviving daughter Sue gave the child to a passing motorist to protect her from Sue's brutal boyfriend. The serendipity that allies Cash with Alice Greer brings new love to his declining family as well as a second chance to rear Lacey, now named April Turtle Greer. Kingsolver depicts him as the right parent for a difficult familial situation as well as a worthy husband for Alice and stepfather for Taylor.

Parenthood is a dominant theme in *Animal Dreams* (1990), a novel that pictures fathers as well as mothers doing their best for their families. In Grace, Arizona, where matriarchal culture thrives, male characters require open-minded understanding. Doc Homer Noline, the community physician, withdraws emotionally at the death of his wife Alice and offers his tiny daughters a stiffly objective upbringing devoid of hugs and cherishing. Grating on his flagging memory is his role in sixteen-year-old daughter Codi's premature delivery of a stillborn child. Pacing about the kitchen, he diagnoses pain and bleeding and offers her medication without comment. Years later, while Codi reinters the small bundle in the family garden, he regrets his lack of overt affection for his girls.

Kingsolver presents a similar absence of support in Loyd Peregrina, a village lothario who charmed girls with his Pueblo-Apache good looks. His brusque treatment of Codi left little room for love. The text indicates that he may have learned the lady-killer pose from his Apache father, a skilled cockfighter who deserted his Pueblo wife Inez. In Loyd's defense for offering no help during her pregnancy is the fact that Codi shut him out of the situation and kept her predicament to herself. After they reunite as mature lovers, she reveals his teen parenthood and is surprised to find him remorseful at the loss. Perhaps in atonement for immaturity, he hovers over Codi during the first months of a subsequent pregnancy and gives indications of being a worthy husband and father.

In *The Poisonwood Bible* (1998), parenthood is a serious consideration in an African nation rapidly collapsing following a failed democratic election. Anatole Ngemba, a model husband and parent, thrives by defusing his wife's fears and restoring calm, even in dire situations of hunger and threat from Mobutu's corrupt police. During the family's drive to Kimvula District in Zaire, he has the presence of mind to send his three sons on ahead with the truck while easing Leah into a comfortable position on damp leaves to deliver her fourth baby. As contractions indicate that the infant is indeed arriving a month early, Anatole arranges a grass mat and clean garments for cushioning his wife while she makes the final push to deliver Nataniel. In token of his delight in a fourth son, the father does "a laughing, backward-hopping dance of congratulation" (p. 498). He aids Leah in a round-the-clock watch on the weak infant and breathes into his failing lungs to keep him alive during the tenuous first seven days of the child's existence.

See also **motherhood, Homer Noline**

• *Further Reading*

Epstein, Robin. "Barbara Kingsolver." *Progressive*, Vol. 60, No. 2, February 1996, pp. 33–37.

Peregrina, Loyd

A hunky hoghead (locomotive engineer) and best friend of J. T. Domingos, Loyd Peregrina is a suitable mate for Codi Noline, heroine of *Animal Dreams* (1990). Born in Santa Rosalia Pueblo of Apache-Pueblo parentage, he grounds his life on working-class ideals and on the earthy native American philosophy that evolved from the cliff dwellers of the Southwest's Great Basin. He is loved by his aunt Maxine Shorty and his sisters and mother, whom he gave an antique Navajo pot he discovered in ruins at Canyon de Chelly while summering at his aunt's sheep farm. The gesture suggests a male persona who is comfortable in acknowledging female roles. Like Codi, he is a recovered native son who lived at Ghost River with his father before returning to Grace, where his Aunt Sonia gave him a peach orchard. Codi's main complaint with "Loyd-with-one-L" is his choice of cockfighting as a hobby, a thrill he shared with his first wife Cissie Ramon, a wild choice of mate who left him (p. 115).

Loyd's personal philosophy tends toward the simplistic: "Nobody can be good all the time. Or bad all the time" (p. 215). In another bestowal of wisdom, he instructs Codi about life: "It's one thing to carry your life wherever you go. Another thing to always go looking for it somewhere else" (p. 236). He honors his heritage and, in recognition of familial love, reveals to Codi two handprints that he and his twin Leander placed on a sandstone wall in early childhood. In his first serious discussion with her, he claims that the one thing he would die for is the land that draws him back. His words typify the earth-first outlook that ties first nations to plants and animals, weather, and topography. Living the concept of topophilia or love of land, he echoes the attitudes and passions of the Stitch and Bitch Club, who refuse to sit still while their community is poisoned by greedy mining officials.

Loyd recalls the disconnect of his high-school relationship with Codi and admits he hurt people. To her commentary on animal dreams, he delivers one of Kingsolver's oft-cited lines: "If you want sweet dreams, you've got to live a sweet life" (p. 133). The recipe for calm sleep precedes Codi's gentle slumbers when he shares her bed. She confesses in a letter to Hallie, "He's better than Sominex" (p. 181). Codi's description quickly palls after he sums up her demand for a smart, degreed, well-paid mate "like every other woman alive," a hasty generalization that Codi later disproves (p. 182). Using cockfighting as his claim to macho skill, he indoctrinates Codi at a session on the reservation, then voluntarily gives up his hobby out of deference to her and to his memories of Leander's death from puncture wounds in a bar fight.

Kingsolver explores the physical relationship between Loyd and Codi more than mates in her earlier novels. In the estimation of Diana Abu-Jaber, a reviewer for the *Oregonian*, writers like Kingsolver "rely more on evoking the experience than their counterparts in women's fiction, re-creating it through sensory detail, careful observation, and close psychological description" (Abu-Jaber). The scenes take the pair from the ancient Pueblo ruin at Kinishba to Codi's residence, a volcanic hot springs, a bed at Loyd's mother's house, and, eventually, to Loyd's trailer. Comments on his job as locomotive engineer perpetuate an undercurrent of sexuality that, like a powerful engine, is both urgent and controlled. The author contrasts his strength of character with the failed engine on the plane from Arizona to Colorado, which halts Codi's journey back to Carlo in Telluride.

Because of Loyd's steady presence in Codi's jangled life, she comes to count on Loyd as her emotional backstop, much as the Southern Pacific depends on his control of trains. Significant to their relationship is Loyd's Christmas gift to her of a burden basket, an empty receptacle that suggests the native Pueblo woman's method of shouldering sorrows. When Codi allows regret and self-blame for Hallie's execution to overstress her, he reminds her that each life, like a train, gains momentum until "it's heavier than heaven and hell put together and it runs on its own track" (p. 304). Their union bodes well for both parties and for the second child they conceive.

- *Further Reading*

Abu-Jaber, Diana. "Women's Fiction Tends to Congregate at the Middle of Things." *Oregonian*, July 25, 1999.

Gray, Paul. "Call of the Eco-Feminist." *Time*, Vol. 136, No. 13, September 24, 1990, p. 87.

Willis, Meredith Sue. "Barbara Kingsolver, Moving On." *Appalachian Journal*, Vol. 22, No. 1, 1994, pp. 78–86.

Pigs in Heaven

Kingsolver wrote the novel *Pigs in Heaven* (1993) as a comedic non-sequel to follow the characters and journey motif in *The Bean Trees* (1988). In the traditional sense of comedy, everything works out for all concerned, but not until major players undergo intense heartache. According to *Newsday* reviewer Dan Cryer, the story is a "tribute to spunky independent womanhood" (Cryer, p. 46). The action contrasts a mother's love for her adopted child against a strong ethnic strand of tribal cultural responsibility to its offspring. In an interview, the author explained: "I got into this question of individualism and communal identity — which is not just a thematic question, but also a very real and delicate political one — I realized I had already set up a situation in an earlier novel and hadn't even touched on the political ramifications of taking a Cherokee baby away from her tribe" ("A Conversation"). The ethical question fueled Kingsolver's search for an answer.

The novelist named her bestseller after an Indian myth on the origin of the

Pleiades constellation and based the action on the 1978 Indian Child Welfare Act, which banned adoption of Indian children without tribal permission. Written in third person omniscient point of view, the story produced what reviewer R. Z. Sheppard termed "folksy delivery with gentle pokes at America's media-driven culture" (Sheppard). Of her use of fiction to characterize the battle between the tribe and the individual, Kingsolver attested in *Newsweek* magazine to faith in the novel: "Fiction creates empathy, and empathy is the antidote to meanness of spirit" ("A Science," p. 61). The immediacy of realistic characters causes "something inside [to shift] a little," her term for the reader's identification with human struggle (*Ibid.*).

The story of the tribal challenge to Turtle's adoption involves an unlikely trek from Tucson west to Las Vegas, northwest to Seattle, and southeast to Tahlequah, Oklahoma, the Cherokee heartland. However, the crux of the action is more interior than exterior geography. Alice Greer departs from Kentucky to aid her daughter and to search out the family's link to the Cherokee nation. Taylor, on the lam from possible removal of Turtle to a native home, departs from her boyfriend Jax Thibodeaux to provide for herself and her daughter without a familial or economic safety net. Upon Taylor's confession that Turtle is suffering from their tenuous home situation, the conflict begins to slide into a neat resolution.

The falling action brings out the human qualities of Kingsolver's characters. Taylor blames herself for the looseness of personal relationships in her life: "When you never put a name on things, you're just accepting that it's okay for people to leave when they feel like it" (p. 328). She adds that family consists of "people you won't let go of for anything" (*Ibid.*). To save the conclusion from too much soul-searching, the author depicts Cash Stillwater shooting a hole in his television set, a nonverbal statement before witnesses of his love for Alice.

• *Further Reading*

"A Conversation with Barbara Kingsolver." http://www.readinggroupguides.com/guides/animal_dreams-author.asp.
Cryer, Dan. "An Unexpected Miracle and a Conflict of Roots." *New York Newsday*, June 21, 1993, p. 46.
Fleming, Bruce. "Woolf Cubs: Current Fiction." *Antioch Review*, Vol. 52, No. 4, Fall 1994, p. 549.
"A Science to Her Fiction." *Newsweek*, Vol. 122, No. 2, July 12, 1993, p. 61.
Shapiro, Laura. "A Novel Full of Miracles." *Newsweek*, Vol. 122, No. 2, July 12, 1993, p. 61.
Sheppard, R. Z. "Little Big Girl." *Time*, Vol. 142, No. 9, August 30, 1993.

The Poisonwood Bible

Covering events spanning a quarter century, Kingsolver's most controversial book, *The Poisonwood Bible* (1998), provoked an outpouring of critical response. According to *Time* magazine critic Paul Gray, the novel is "a long, incantatory meditation, filtered through the memories of an American mother and her four daughters, on the evils of Western colonialism in Africa" (Gray, p. 90). The novel bears a title redolent with spiritual gravity, prophecy, and death. From memories of her own year in the Congo, Kingsolver worked at language that would capture the sensory uniqueness of equatorial Africa: "I retrieved the olfactory memory of my childhood. The fish, the bananas and onions and tomatoes and peanuts and caramel-colored soap on market day in the villages. The bougainvilleas, orange trees and coconut palms" (Hoback, p. 1e). Her skill at evocative diction creates an immediacy that removes the foreignness of Africa and shortens the distance between the American and Congolese outlook.

The diary-like text has been called a "saga of hubris and deliverance" and a "heart of darkness" for its reflection of themes in Joseph Conrad's novel (Seaman, p. 1922; Goudie, p. K5). Like Marlowe, Conrad's naive outsider, and Adam and Eve in Eden in the book of Genesis, the Price family in Kingsolver's text arrives in Africa in all innocence to serve the "First Baptist Church of Kilanga" and scour surrounding villages for potential converts (p. 72). In scenarios of a patriarchal Freewill Baptist family half-heartedly supported by the Southern Baptist Mission League, the action suggests the leap of faith that brings the Reverend Nathan Price with wife and daughters to the extremes of outback Africa. The title derives from his mispronunciation of the Kikongo word for "precious" and reflects a monomaniac who is incapable of ministering to the needs of real people.

The author equates the era's colonial domination with a hard-handed 1950s marriage sabotaged by a husband at war with his own sexuality. At the Price family's home along the Kwilu River in Kilanga, Congo, the wife, Orleanna Price, and the four daughters of the inflexible missionary live out a seventeen-month sojourn unsanctioned by mission officials and merely tolerated by Kilangans. To the minister's wife, her family shrinks to "messengers of goodwill adrift on a sea of mistaken intentions" (p. 323). As the author explains in the introduction to *Off the Beaten Path: Stories of Place* (1998), these characters are "deeply embedded in the culture and sense of a place ... [and] are moved by some outside force that is set upon the land" (p. 18).

As described by Amy M. Regier, the novel follows a Faulknerian narrative structure molded by "points of view shaped by history, familially-inherited vision, and resistance to exterior realities rather than within an objective form of knowledge" (Regier). The Price women suffer more deprivation from the narrow-minded, lack-logic head of household than from the heat, monsoons, insects, reptiles, and jungle. Nathan's authoritarian interpretations of scripture support verbal abuse and physical violence toward his daughters and wife, who considers herself more primeval conquest than mate. He doles out to his children stroppings, slaps, or "The Verse," a bitter punishment that forces them to copy one hundred bible verses, such as a grim jeremiad for the Old Testament that ends in a baleful prediction of doom (p. 59). In summation of the family's predicament in summer 1960, Leah reflects on "Mother against Father, Rachel against both of them, Adah against the world, Ruth May pulling helplessly at anyone who came near, and me trying my best to stay on Father's side" (p. 230).

As external terrors loom, the fragile familial structure has only a short time to survive. During the last of their fractious term of service, they experience various levels of involvement in a momentous pass in Congolese history, a brief embrace of democratic election. Leah, the sensitive seeker of redemption, struggles with the knowledge that President Dwight D. Eisenhower has called for the assassination of rightfully elected Premier Patrice Lumumba. On the night of an army ant invasion, she longs for home, "the easy land of ice-cream cones and new Keds sneakers and *We Like Ike*, the country where I thought I knew the rules" (p. 309). The author uses Orleanna's introduction of Book Four as a thinly disguised speech accusing Allen Dulles, head of the CIA, of setting in motion the subsequent assassination and coup that removed Lumumba from office while elevating Colonel Mobutu to dictator. Of the Prices' moral and ethical crisis, Kingsolver asks the reader: "What have we done as a nation, as a culture, to Africa? There is a cultural arrogance, a spiritual, agricultural and political invasion. How do we make our peace with that?" (Hoback, p. 1e).

Following a momentous election that ousts Jesus as Kilanga's deity, Kingsolver sets up another power struggle. This time, she pits the austere Chief Ndu and his elders, shaman Kuvudundu, and Anatole Ngemba, a symbol of the educated youth, in a discussion of tradition. Because Leah Price proposes to join males in the hunt, elders reject a violation of womanly roles. Nathan, who has already lapsed into irrelevance along with his god, attempts to inject piety into the colloquy, but finds himself ignored as the juggernaut rolls over his parish like an elephant squashing an anthill. Rachel comments with her usual smirk, "It's just lucky for Father he never had sons. He might have been forced to respect them" (p. 337). The comment elucidates Nathan's stiffnecked opinions as well as his gender prejudices.

The situation lapses into chaos after the fire surround, a primitive method of killing game by burning off a circle of its habitat. Instead of a traditional village feast shared by all after serious hunger, individual Kilangans shout and tussle over gristly, drought-shriveled carcasses, a to-do that suggests the fight of European colonists over African provinces. During a night of rancor, Rachel admits that the Price family's life among the Congolese has demeaned them: "Being American doesn't matter and nobody gives us any special credit" (p. 358). Leah, the most intuitive member of the family, admits that "we've all ended up giving up body and soul to Africa" (p. 474). The resolution proves her right by describing the post-mission lives of the survivors— Nathan, Orleanna, Rachel, Leah, and Adah.

Reviewers poured out lyric commentary on the novel, including Jenny Jones of the *New Zealand Herald*, who marveled that 13,000 New Zealanders bought the book. Jeff Giles, a *Newsweek* reviewer, summarized the novel as "a forest fire of a book about the Belgian Congo's struggle for independence: gripping, blazingly smart, ferociously angry, out of control at times" (p. 82). Speaking for the *Boston Globe*, Abby Frucht felt a tense juggling act in the background as the novel "[straddled] a sometimes uncomfortable line between fiction and textbook, dogma and entertainment, poetry and platform" (Frucht, p. K1). To Yael Simpson Fletcher, a critic writing for *Radical History Review*, the novel is a "profoundly American parable of enlightenment" relating "the literal transformation of a Christian consciousness of original sin to an awareness of the oppression of Africans by Europeans and of women by men" (Fletcher, p. 198). Her precise summation comes closest to the religious, political, economic, and gender crosscurrents that alternately buoy and repress the main characters.

As described by Kimberly Kozo, "[Kingsolver's] Africa seems to function as a backdrop for working out essentially American concerns," particularly its burden of wrongdoing in the 1960s after President Dwight D. Eisenhower okayed the assassination of Lumumba (Kozo, p. 294). As the action extends from the turbulent 1960s into the 1980s, the Price women, like socialized slaves in the American antebellum South, become unwitting enablers of Nathan Price's depredations to Kilanga. Realizing her position as a colonizer's accomplice, Orleanna Price reaches an epiphany: "A foreign mother and child assuming themselves in charge, suddenly slapped down to nothing by what they all saw us to be. Until that moment I'd thought I could have it both ways: to be one of them, and also my husband's wife" (p. 89). Late in the text, the preacher's wife continues to shoulder guilt for her role in Nathan's ogreish evangelism.

Kingsolver respects individual speakers of the story by assigning them opportunities to state their observations and memories of the tragic mission. In the view of Celia McGee, columnist for the New York *Daily News*, Kingsolver's intent with her complex novel was "to exorcise a host of personal, historical, and political ghosts" (McGee, p. 6D). McGee faults the writer with appending to the original novel a lengthy history of the five original voices—Nathan's daughters and wife—as they retreat from domestic tyranny and national revolution. In McGee's opinion, the two stages "don't quite work together as a single, overstuffed volume of fiction" (McGee, p. 6D).

Other critics lauded the novel's alternating speakers as an ingenious narrative device. Reviewer Colleen Kelly Warren ranked the author's voicing as "stunning": "The poetic utterings of hemiplegic Adah, who thinks in palindromes, reads backwards and walks with a 'slant' are in stark contrast to the hilarious asides of Rachel, who barrels through the English language with disdain for spelling or pronunciation. Orleanna is sparse with her words, but eloquent" (Warren, p. C5). Olivia Glazebrook, a British critic for *Spectator*, agreed that the point of view of children relieves the novel of cant. However, she declared comments from their adult years lacking in vitality and spontaneity because the author chose to "[reflect] the nature of growing up, the realisation that being an adult is even more horrid than being a child rather than less" (Glazebrook). Because Kingsolver harmonizes the growing-up years of Nathan's hapless daughters simultaneously with the maturation of equatorial Africa, some reviewers chose the novel as one of the masterworks of the late twentieth century.

See also **Africa, Eeben Axelroot, Dwight D. Eisenhower, Brother Fowles, Kilanga, Tata Kuvudundu, Mama Mwanza, nature, Tata Ndu, Nelson, Anatola Ngemba, Adah Price, Leah Price, Nathan Price, Orleanna Price, Rachel Price, Ruth May Price**

• *Further Reading*

Douthat, Ross. "Kumbaya Watch: Barbara Kingsolver's America." *National Review*, September 26, 2001.

Fletcher, Yael Simpson. "History Will One Day Have Its Say: New Perspectives on Colonial and Postcolonial Congo." *Radical History Review*, Vol. 84, 2002, pp. 195–207.

Frucht, Abby. "'Saving' the Heathen Barbara Kingsolver's Missionary Goes Into Africa, but He Just Doesn't Get It." *Boston Globe*, October 18, 1998, p. K1.

Giles, Jeff. "Getting Back to Nature." *Newsweek*, Vol. 136, No. 18, October 30, 2000, p. 82.

Glazebrook, Olivia. "Abandoning the Code." *Spectator*, Vol. 37, February 27, 1999.

Goudie, Jeffrey Ann. "Poisonwood Bible Delivers a Powerful Tale." *Kansas City Star*, November 29, 1998, p. K5.

Gray, Paul. "On Familiar Ground." *Time*, Vol. 156, No. 18, October 30, 2000, p. 90.

Hoback, Jane. "Kingsolver's Holy Grail Mythic in Tone." *Denver Rocky Mountain News*, October 18, 1998, p. 1e.

Jones, Jenny. "Review: *Prodigal Summer*." *New Zealand Herald*, February 10, 2001.

Koza, Kimberly. "The Africa of Two Western Women Writers: Barbara Kingsolver and Margaret Laurence." *Critique*, Vol. 44, No. 3, Spring 2003, pp. 284–294.

Krasny, Michael. "Interview: Barbara Kingsolver, Author, Discusses Her New Book." *Talk of the Nation* (NPR), December 13, 1999.

McGee, Celia. "'Bible' Offers Two Good Books in One." *USA Today*, October 22, 1998, p. 6D.

Regier, Amy M. "Replacing the Hero with the Reader: Public Story Structure in *The Poisonwood Bible*." *Mennonite Life*, Vol. 56, No. 1, March 2001.

Rubinstein, Roberta. "The Mark of Africa." *World & I*, Vol. 14, No. 4, April 1999, p. 254.

Seaman, Donna. "Review." *Booklist*, Vol. 94, No. 22, August 1989, p. 1922.

Smiley, Jane. "In the Fields of the Lord." *Washington Post*, October 11, 1998.

Sullivan, Patrick. "'Poisonwood Bible' Makes a Departure." *Sonoma County Independent*, October 22, 1998.

Warren, Colleen Kelly. "Family Tragedy Plays Out in Congo." *St. Louis Post-Dispatch*, October 18, 1998, p. C5.

pollution

Kingsolver, a leader of the ecofeminist fiction from the late 1980s and into the twenty-first century, makes an impression on readers with her stark picture of the era's arrogance and reckless disregard for nature. According to Paul Gray, reviewer for *Time* magazine, the evolution of the era's female-driven anti-pollution movements resulted from gender differences in regard to the environment: "Women, relying on intuition and one another, mobilize to save the planet, or their immediate neighborhoods, from the ravages— war, pollution, racism, etc.— wrought by white males. This reformation of human nature usually entails the adoption of older, often Native American, ways" (Gray, p. 87). His description fits Kingsolver's early themes and her second novel, *Animal Dreams* (1990). The latter draws on the Phelps Dodge violation of the Clean Water Act that she disclosed in her feminist documentary *Holding the Line: Women in the Great Arizona Mine Strike of 1983* (1989). Among the company's crimes against the community was the release of dissolved arsenic, copper, manganese, and zinc into the San Francisco River, which earned the company a fine of four hundred thousand dollars and additional penalties of five thousand dollars a day until the pollution ceased.

The author's activism developed a serious bent in *Animal Dreams*. As Codi Noline returns to her hometown of Grace, Arizona, in 1986 and adapts to changes in people and places over a fourteen-year absence, she spies dead alfalfa fields and recognizes the threat to pecan orchards from fruit drop. At a Labor Day party, she overhears a conversation on the declining fortunes of the local copper mine, where the remaining staff leach gold and moly from the tailings with sulfuric acid. She thinks of the insult to nature as "a mountain cannibalizing its own guts" (p. 240). With a pH "a hair higher than battery acid," the process poisons local trees, the major source of income to former mine employees (p. 110). The seriousness of the situation comes home to Codi during a lab exercise in which she examines samples of highly acidic river water: "Our water was dead. It might as well have come from a river on the moon" (p. 110).

Kingsolver keeps in mind the rootedness of people in the American Southwest and their devotion to place. Upon witnessing the crusted salts in fallow alfalfa fields, Codi considers the cropland "murdered" by Black Mountain Mining, a company notorious for digging and dumping at will (p. 123). When managers came for a ground-breaking ceremony for a new dam, they acted as though they supervised "some kind of community-improvement project," but to Codi, it looks like "a huge grave" or shipwreck (pp. 161, 122).

One slick escape for the company is to divert the river before owners face charges from the Environmental Protection Agency. With the river redirected, Grace, Arizona, would lose its heart, a lifeline to homes backed up against canyon walls in arid terrain. The settlement dates to a mythic clutch of nine Spanish sisters whom their father dispatched from Iberia to marry the womanless miners of Arizona. The women contribute a culture of homes and children, orchards, and peacocks, the birds that drip rich blue feathers on the ground. The one-eyed feathers symbolize the consciousness of the community that something must be done to stave off disaster. Critic Henry Aay describes the homeland as "a kind of Garden of Eden to which people need to return to receive 'grace,' an environmental harmony, a personal sense of security, and an identity related to community and environment" (p. 74). With the poisoning of the river, they would be homeless, their culture dispersed as they set out in search of safer homes and jobs.

In *The Poisonwood Bible* (1998), the author turns to a more insidious pollution of peasant culture in equatorial Africa, the human source of epidemics and chronic infestation from parasites. Adah Price, the brilliant daughter of missionary Nathan Price, recognizes the value of the Kilangan witch doctor, Tata Kuvudundu, who enforces rules about where villagers can deposit sewage and which part of the river they can use for laundry, bathing, and drawing drinking water. She points out his short-sightedness in failing to consider pollutants above Kilanga: "Downstream is always someone else's up," a wry observation that skewers short-sighted examination of water contaminants (p. 173). Her observation may reflect the source of *kakakaka*, the enteritis that afflicts during the rainy season and kills village adults and children.

Leah, Adah's twin, sharpens her knowledge of the jungle and Congolese farming with classes at Emory University. On return to her adopted homeland, she teaches nutrition and sanitation to native women. Her immersion in local problems offers insights into the desecration of the jungle. She realizes that clear-cutting leaves the fragile laterite soil open to savage monsoons, "like stripping an animal first of its fur, then its skin. The land howls" (p. 524). The image of suffering denuded land explains why soil collapses and the earth erodes "into red gashes like the mouths of whales," the preface to topsoil depletion, rutted roads, and clogged waterways (p. 525). To prevent loss of the soil base, she advises that people "return to the ways of the ancient Kongo," by which families traveled on foot, grew their own vegetables for local trade, and abandoned the idea of driving crops to distant markets (*Ibid.*). Her suggestion contradicts centuries of colonial efforts to convert African communities to European urban planning.

The author's fifth novel, *Prodigal Summer* (2000), perpetuated her method of impregnating fiction with stiff lessons in earth management. The prominence of nature lore causes critics to reject Kingsolver's heavy didacticism, which tends to overburden the fictional mode with sermonettes on ecology. Deanna Wolfe, the wildlife biologist who is eager to see coyotes returned to the southern Appalachians, describes the gradual disappearance of mussels, moths, and stoneflies. The extinction of the acornshell, forkshell, leafshell, and sugarspoon mussel she blames on "pesticide runoff, silt from tilling, cattle in the creek" (p. 63). She anticipates that the return of a keystone predator might restore balance to nature and aid the mussel in reestablishing itself.

Simultaneously, down in Zebulon Valley, Nannie Land Rawley squabbles with Garnett S. Walker, III, a proponent of chemical control of agriculture. Their neighbor, Lusa Maluf Landowski, launches a personal war on tobacco. She states to her two brothers-in-law: "The government's officially down on it, now that word's finally out that cancer's killing people" (p. 106). The novel awards her a small victory in turning tobacco acreage into goat pasturage, the open-air classroom in which she teaches her foster children the glories of nature. Small victories for each of the three female protagonists illustrate Kingsolver's belief in the human war for a clean environment, one skirmish at a time.

See also **activism, Viola Domingos, ecofeminism, *Last Stand: America's Virgin Lands*, nature, Cosima "Codi" Noline**

• *Further Reading*

Aay, Henry. "Environmental Themes in Ecofiction: *In the Center of the Nation* and *Animal Dreams*." *Journal of Cultural Geography*, Vol. 14, No. 2, Spring/Summer 1994, pp. 65–85.

Gray, Paul. "Call of the Eco-Feminist." *Time*, Vol. 136, No. 13, September 24, 1990, p. 87.

Neill, Michael. "La Pasionaria." *People*, Vol. 40, No. 15, October 11, 1993, pp. 109–110.

Rubinstein, Roberta. "The Mark of Africa." *World & I*, Vol. 14, No. 4, April 1999, p. 254.

poverty

Kingsolver uses various family situations as springboards to commentary on poverty. The struggle of America's working poor burdens characters in the short story "Homeland" (1989), in which Great Mam, a Cherokee matriarch, witnesses the squalor of native settlements in Tennessee. Likewise overwhelmed by need is Taylor Greer, protagonist of *The Bean Trees* (1988) and its non-sequel, *Pigs in Heaven*

(1993). In the former, she willingly makes up beds and cleans a motel along the way from Kentucky to Arizona to pay board for herself and her foundling daughter Turtle. Worse off than Taylor are donors earning cash from the Red Cross plasma center and Sandi, a worker at Burger Derby who must "[chase] off drunks and broke people who went around the tables eating nondairy creamer straight out of the packets" (p. 50). Sandi is so poor that, in lieu of a babysitter, she dumps her toddler at Kid Central Station, a child care facility at the mall. Taylor's personal knowledge of the plight of Estevan and Esperanza, illegal aliens from Guatemala, comes closer to breaking her heart. On their flight to a safe house in Oklahoma, Taylor observes the small suitcase that holds all they own.

In a spiral of rent, utilities, insurance, car, and child care, Taylor, a single mom living in "the projects" in *Pigs in Heaven*, is one disaster away from homelessness. On a date with Kevin, she tours the tonier section of Seattle, Washington, far from where she lives, and ponders having "a passport to come over here from the other side of the hill" (p. 208). In a desperate phone call to boyfriend Jax Thibodeaux, she sums up the situation in two words: "Poverty sucks" (p. 245). In a more pictorial image, she compares herself to king and silver salmon swimming against a current and regrets "working yourself for all you're worth to get ahead, and still going backward" (p. 251). The scene sums up the author's concern for the working poor.

Although Taylor needs assistance in paying for rent and food, she hesitates to spend anything from the ill-gotten funds of Barbie, a hanger-on during the drive from Nevada. The tension between providing for Taylor's two-person family and honoring principles increases her loneliness and need of emotional support. She is disappointed in a first paycheck as Handi-Van driver of the handicapped because so much of the total goes to taxes and Social Security (p. 207). On a dinner date with Steven Kant, Taylor notices that menu prices add up to more than she spends on food for a week. She swallows anger at Kevin, a workmate who spouts the standard line that poor people are at fault for their own misery because of "poor money-management skills" (p. 210). A more compassionate opinion comes from Alice Greer, Taylor's mother, who fears that poverty causes people to "start thinking they're no good" (p. 229).

Kingsolver's fictional approach to poverty is tutorial. She explains her intent to enlighten the reading public about their misperception of need: "It has to do with our mythology in this country that if you are smart enough and work hard enough, you will make it. It allows us to perpetuate this huge gulf between the well-off and the desperately poor" (Karbo, p. 9). Worsening the plight of the poor is the other half's tendency to blame them for their penury: "If you fall through the cracks you must be stupid or lazy or both. It's a trap because poverty is viewed as shameful. In this culture, it's more honorable to steal than to beg" (*Ibid.*). In a 1993 address to the American Booksellers Convention, she extended hope that writers can bridge the gap between reality and faulty perception: "What the writer has to do is find a way to carve those enormous truths down to the size of the personal, to the size of individual reality, something that can fit inside a heart. The amazing power of fiction is that it can do that. It can create empathy" ("An Address").

The subject of poverty in the Congo occupies a central chapter of *The Poisonwood*

Bible (1998), Kingsolver's masterwork. The novel, according to critic Sally Gabb, is "seen through eyes of white bantu, Euro-American souls" (Gabb). After Leah Price joins Anatole Ngemba's teaching staff, the two discuss differences in their two nations. To her claim that most American families have one or more cars, Anatole is incredulous. She tries to explain why transportation needs differ in large American cities from the demands of everyday life in Kilanga, but the discussion begins to press for a more detailed exchange. While gazing out on the jungle, Leah realizes that "In the Congo, it seems the land owns the people. How could I explain to Anatole about soybean fields where men sat in huge tractors like kings on thrones, taming the soil from one horizon to the other" (p. 283). To his questions about Nathan Price's interest in evangelizing a poor Congolese community, she must admit, "It's like he's trying to put rubber tires on a horse" (*Ibid.*).

Overall, Kingsolver presents an existential view of Africa, where the "struggle of life is not won or lost, but experienced, endured, survived" (Gabb). In the novel's resolution, Leah and Anatole form a team, mates and partners dedicated to uplifting the Congo's peasants through education. Leah is proud to share slum conditions in Kinshasa, yet must reflect on poor sanitation, which threatens her sons Pascal and Patrice with hookworm from free-flowing sewage in their backyard. After the Ngemba family's move to a communal farm in Senza Pombo, Angola, they still struggle to grow crops, but share the burden with refugee families not much different from their own household. They spread the word about cooperative efforts as a commitment to hope for black Africa, which European exploiters and dictators like Mobutu weaken by stripping natural resources for their own enrichment.

• *Further Reading*

Gabb, Sally. "Into Africa: A Review of *The Poisonwood Bible.*" *Field Notes,* Vol. 11, No. 1, Summer 2001.

Gergen, David. "Interview: Barbara Kingsolver." *U.S. News and World Report,* November 24, 1995.

Karbo, Karen. "And Baby Makes Two." *New York Times Book Review,* June 27, 1993, p. 9.

Price, Adah

The source of title for *The Poisonwood Bible* (1998), Adah Price, fifteen-year-old daughter of fundamentalist minister Nathan Price and his wife Orleanna, is the family's acid-voiced skeptic, math whiz, and oracle. Dark-eyed and chestnut-haired like Leah, she is physically shorter than her twin, whom Adah claims cannibalized her in the womb. She thinks of herself as Quasimodo, a "mental freak," because she is impaired by hemiplegia, a one-sided brain anomaly that leaves her body lame (p. 73). She mocks herself as "slowpoke poison-oak running-joke Adah" and recalls an epiphany in childhood when a Sunday school teacher's cruelty caused Adah to stop believing in God (p. 171). Leah, who regularly explains her twin's shortcomings, dismisses Adah's peculiarities as normal: "Staring at somebody without making a peep is her idea of a conversation" (p. 289). To avoid such judgments, Adah takes to creeping about Kilanga by night.

Because Broca's aphasia turned Adah's tongue mute, silence left her mind obsessed with puns (His punishment is the Word, and his deficiencies are failures of words), palindromes ("Bats stab!" and "Sun o put o not upon us!"), and reverse phrase formation ("*Erom Reven!*") (pp. 213, 295, 56, 55). In an opening line, she rhymes, "Sunrise tantalize, evil eyes hypnotize" (p. 30). She muses on idiosyncrasies of the Kikongo language and discovers that *mbote* means both hello and goodbye. She recognizes what reviewer Sally Gabb calls her father's "relentless spiritual and cultural imperialism" (Gabb). Adah quips about his evangelism, "Oh, that Bible, where every ass with a jawbone gets his day!" (p. 217). She admits to reading many times Robert Louis Stevenson's *Dr. Jekyll and Mr. Hyde* (1886), a victorian tale of the duality of a human soul that she ranks for plot above John Bunyan's *Pilgrim's Progress* (1678) and John Milton's *Paradise Lose* (1667). She confides, "I have a strong sympathy for Dr. Jekyll's dark desires and for Mr. Hyde's crooked body" (p. 55). Her compassion for suffering foretokens her training in adulthood in researching the communicable diseases of equatorial Africa.

Early on, Kingsolver uses Adah as the veiled seer, who views the self-important Nathan as "Our Father," a sarcastic reference to his self-righteousness and its effect on the Price family during their seventeen-month immurement in the jungle (p. 55). In the Congo, she feels free to unleash pent-up darker selves, "the wicked hoodoo Adahs" (*Ibid.*). Gradually distancing herself from the house and her mother's watchful eye, Adah progresses slowly into the forest, where limited speech enables her to observe in silence women cultivating manioc fields, elephant herds and Pygmies. Farther afield, she locates a cult graveyard and the paradise flycatcher and commiserates with the crippled parrot Methuselah, whom she follows into the wild and feeds bits of fruit.

In wordless reflection, Adah ponders the truths in the poems of Emily Dickinson and Edgar Allan Poe and realizes that her missionary father is a self-indulgent absolutist in matters of religion. In an adolescent shaping of faith, Adah recognizes the arbitrary nature of fundamentalist beliefs that those who accept Jesus are the only ones God will save from perdition. Although her parents shun her handicap, the Congolese, lacking a demand for perfection, call her *bënduka* (crooked walker) and accept her without criticism, a "benign approval ... I have never, ever known in Bethlehem, Georgia" (p. 72). The town's evocative name enhances the irony a pilgrimage from Bethlehem to live among pagan Africans, who are less critical of her than white Southern Baptists.

At a significant turn in the action, Adah's delivery from a stalking lion is interpreted in the village as a miracle. Only a week after Nathan preaches on Daniel in the lion's den, Adah unknowingly returns home unharmed by a beast she never saw. Kilangans become so excited by the omen that they increase church attendance. Nelson the houseboy sets the event in mythic form, with a magical metamorphosis of Adah into a bushbuck, which replaces the girl in the lion's mouth. His version ends with Adah returning unharmed to the family porch. His skill at oral interpretation reprises the circumstances that generate parables and fables of preliterate people like the Kilangans.

Kingsolver uses Adah as a model of the recycling of a human being. Upon her flight from Kilanga and emergence from aphasia, in 1962, she flourishes at Emory University in science courses, gains relief from a twisted body, and develops into a neonatal pediatrician and medical researcher. Abandoning Baptist dogma, she claims the Periodic Table as her liturgy and exams as her Holy Communion. Her mind ponders the choices of the past and the loss of Ruth May, her little sister, to snakebite. Adah's spirit wrestles with feelings of worthlessness until Orleanna explains that she values Adah as her youngest child. Suitably, Adah becomes her mother's comfort in old age, her physician, and her solace from the guilt of Ruth May's death.

• *Further Reading*

Barrett, Sharon. "Kingsolver's Heart of Darkness." *Chicago Sun-Times*, October 25, 1998, p. 18.
Gabb, Sally. "Into Africa: A Review of *The Poisonwood Bible*." *Field Notes*, Vol. 11, No. 1, Summer 2001.
Koza, Kimberly. "The Africa of Two Western Women Writers: Barbara Kingsolver and Margaret Laurence." *Critique*, Vol. 44, No. 3, Spring 2003, pp. 284–294.
Rubinstein, Roberta. "The Mark of Africa." *World & I*, Vol. 14, No. 4, April 1999, p. 254.

Price, Leah

A curious, energetic tomboy and fawning daddy's girl in *The Poisonwood Bible* (1998), fourteen-year-old Leah Price is the first daughter to speak her family's miseries at a Congo outpost. Of the five female points of view, she is also the first to learn the Kikongo language, the bravest in domesticating the chameleon Leon, and the most sincere, straightforward narrator of the missionary family's downfall. To lighten the atmosphere, she catalogs in mock–Homeric style the packing of worldly needs—cake mixes and deviled ham, thimble and scissors, plastic mirror, number-two pencils, band-aids, over-the-counter cures, and a thermometer "like bright party favors" (p. 14). The list expands with antibiotics, iron frying pan, yeast, pinking shears and handleless hatchet, and latrine spade, "the full measure of civilization's evils" (*Ibid.*). To her older sister Rachel's complaints about the loss of beauty aids to the needs of the "lilies of the field," Leah remarks that her sister "never does grasp scripture all that well" (p. 15).

Leah, as described by reviewer Sally Gabb, is "politically and socially precocious" (Gabb). On the first day of residence in equatorial Africa, Leah helps her father search for nails to pound, but discovers that the village is nailless. She takes as her responsibility the planting, watering, and tending of his "Kentucky Wonder beans, crookneck and patty-pan squash, [and] Big Boy tomatoes," a garden allegory drawn from Jesus's parable of the seeds (Matthew 13:3–9) (p. 35). Her inadvertent description of Nathan's "big goose steps" in stepping off the garden creates a subtext of the Nazi storm trooper father who tromps over family and village alike as his conquests (p. 36).

For her own reasons, Leah cultivates her father's attention and love. As he gestures the meaning of scripture, she "[covets] the delicious weight of goodness he cradles in those palms" and views his bullheadedness as "steady as a stump" (pp. 37, 39).

To her skewed thinking, his tendency to frighten people with sternness is the result of "such keen judgment and purity of heart," both gifts of God (p. 41). She divulges her own desire for "heaven and to be my father's favorite," a suggestion of adolescent need rather than budding sanctity (p. 66). Upon meeting the houseboy Nelson, she compares the plight of Congolese children under Belgian rule to that of the "Price girls," who stand no chance of going to college, primarily because of their father's disaffection for females (p. 143).

While Leah thinks of herself and her twin as "onions in the petunia patch," Adah envies the "hunt-goddess twin" her physical perfection, with "muscles working together like parts of a clock" (pp. 149, 278, 63). Like a modern Artemis, Leah violates the Congolese gender restrictions on women by joining a hunt, which begins with a fire surround. In the view of Marxist critic Julian Markels, Leah "thereby challenges the native gender tradition from within in a manner quite opposite to that in which her father challenges the native religion from without" (Markels). The threat to the opinions of elders sets off squabbles and family unrest that ends in the Price family's dissolution.

Unlike Nathan, who disdains Africans as ignorant heathens, Leah looks to the Congolese themselves for answers to her mental and emotional turmoil. Friendship with Anatole Ngemba and Nelson opens her mind to doubts that white Christianity values African welfare. In this same period of abstract exploration, Leah develops a mature fantasy life that pictures Nancy Drew descending to the basement to meet a man with a scarred face, a thinly concealed image of Leah's sexual interest in Anatole. Because he teaches her archery, Kilangans refer to her as *bákala*, which translates as lumpy potato, hot pepper, or penis. The latter indicates a pejorative cast on women who venture into male-dominated weaponry. From a jaundiced point of view, Adah imagines her twin marked like Hester Prynne with the letter "D for Dramatic, or Diana of the Hunt, or Devil Take Your Social Customs" (p. 278).

Leah's maturation is a masterful element of Kingsolver's novel. As reality sets in for the lone missionary family, Leah attempts a feat of logic: "If [Nathan's] decision to keep us here in the Congo wasn't right, then what else might he be wrong about?" (p. 244). At an emotional extreme while coping with disaster the night of the army ant attack, she declares her love for Anatole, a climactic point in their relationship that concludes Book Three. The invasion twists Leah's thinking in another direction as she rushes to safety without giving thought to her family, even her hobbling twin. Leah's epiphany is biblically grounded: "Once in the womb, once to the lion, and now like Simon Peter I had denied her for the third time" (Luke 24:34, 60–61) (p. 300). To atone for the lapse, Leah utters an eloquent prayer for heavenly intercession.

Leah's fiery rebellion against Nathan in Book Four suggests a normal abandonment of the father preceding claim of the lover, but the author builds the shift in family alliances toward a greater clash over patriarchy. At the fire surround, a primitive method of hunting involving all of Kilanga's starving villagers, Leah contests the rule of Chief Ndu, Tata Kuvudundu, and Nathan, who cling to gender-specific traditions. Only Anatole is willing to stake his reputation on her defense. After Ruth May's death from the bite of the green mamba, Leah, like Electra to Nathan's

Agamemnon, is so disillusioned that she turns against her father for his pride and bigotry. Following recovery from her bout with malaria and years of imprisonment for Anatole, Leah retreats to a Central African mission at Bangassou. Still opinionated and moody, she marries him and lives at Bikoki, where she mourns the loss of her family, particularly Ruth May.

After settlement with Anatole and their sons in Kinshasa, Leah gains the experience and insight that the Price family lacked upon arrival in the Congo. Rachel, the materialist, complains that the Ngembas "evidently have chosen to live like paupers" (p. 477). Still a white American outsider, though married to a Congolese husband, Leah silently mourns January 17, the anniversary of Ruth May's death. In 1968, the twin sisters reunite in Atlanta, where Adah meets nephew Pascal Ngemba. While visiting her mother, Leah's study of agronomics is a pragmatic use of the trip to acquire skills to aid her adopted country. On return to a slum in Kinshasa, she suffers repetitive dreams of guarding children, a nightly terror that Anatole chalks up to the aftereffects of her battle with malaria. Their marriage, despite its obstacles, is one of the most successful in Kingsolver's five novels.

See also **Anatole Ngemba, rescue, trust, wisdom, women**

• *Further Reading*

Bromberg, Judith. "A Complex Novel About Faith, Family and Dysfunction." *National Catholic Reporter*, Vol. 35, No. 20, March 19, 1999, p. 13.
Charles, Ron. "A Dark Heart in the Congo." *Christian Science Monitor*, Vol. 90, No. 249, November 19, 1998, p. 20.
Fletcher, Yael Simpson. "History Will One Day Have Its Say: New Perspectives on Colonial and Postcolonial Congo." *Radical History Review*, Vol. 84, 2002, pp. 195–207.
Gabb, Sally. "Into Africa: A Review of *The Poisonwood Bible*." *Field Notes*, Vol. 11, No. 1, Summer 2001.
Glazebrook, Olivia. "Abandoning the Code." *Spectator*, Vol. 37, February 27, 1999.
Markels, Julian. "Coda: Imagining History in *The Poisonwood Bible*." *Monthly Review Press*, September 2003.
Ognibene, Elaine R. "The Missionary Position: Barbara Kingsolver's *The Poisonwood Bible*." *College Literature*, Vol. 30, No. 3, Summer 2003, pp. 19–36.
Smiley, Jane. "In the Fields of the Lord." *Washington Post*, October 11, 1998.

Price, Nathan

A close-minded rote-spouting proselytizer, the Reverend Nathan Price of Bethlehem, Georgia, carries wrongheadedness to tragic extremes in *The Poisonwood Bible* (1998). Because the author allots him no first-person remarks, critical opinions vary widely on his characterization, which pictures him striking his pregnant wife shortly before she gives birth to their first child and threatening Leah with a leather belt. Critic Jane Smiley, writing for the *Washington Post*, regretted that "he is a cause and an effect, but never a man" (Smiley). In a *Publisher's Weekly* review, the critic elevates the minister to villainy as a "domestic monster" ("Review," p. 366). Dr. Mary Beth Culp, critic for the Mobile, Alabama, *Harbinger*, takes a more compassionate view that Nathan is a "tortured soul whose own sense of unworthiness and failure makes him incapable of empathy or love for anyone" (Culp). The text supports her view of a cold-hearted man who refuses to hold Leah's hand in the inauguration day crowd in Léopoldville. Leah expects the brush-off: "Father wouldn't have held my hand for the world — he isn't like that" (p. 181). His wife Orleanna summarizes his possessiveness as a father who owns a daughter "like a plot of land. To work her, plow her under, rain down a dreadful poison upon her" (p. 191).

Out of respect, Price's three daughters and wife call him Father, but Kingsolver gives him no clear identity. During World War II, he was an army infantryman who hovered in a pig sty to avoid being herded on the Bataan death march. In a post-war malaise, he returned from the Pacific theater with a heart "[curled] like a piece of hard shoe leather" (p. 196). The only member of his regiment to survive, he received a purple heart and developed into a manic crusader intending to rid the world of cowardice and sin. His zealous lunacy distances him from the people he intends to save, including his own unbaptized baby girl, whose death leaves him babbling. In the estimation of reviewer Jane Smiley, "Nathan goes unloved — by his daughters, his wife, himself, his 'congregation,' his God and his author. As a character, he never comes alive" (Smiley). As a result, he relieves frustration by becoming more judgmental and abusive.

Leah, his devout follower, describes his red-blond crewcut, broad shoulders, wide freckled hands, and Scots vigor, good looks, and righteous temper, which he vents with high-toned language more suited to a pulpit jeremiad. Rachel, who is less impressed than Leah, recognizes the trip-wires to his explosive personality and ridicules him as "the Father Knows Best of all times," a reference to a syrupy television serial that ran from 1954 to 1962 and featured a comic, but wise father, played by Robert Young (p. 131). Because of a war wound incurred in the Philippines, his vision is compromised in the left eye, a physical suggestion of his emotional, intellectual, and social limitations. In the author's words, "Nathan stands for the conqueror and for the hyperbole of our cultural arrogance. Our process as readers is to examine him and take our positions" (Doenges).

The fact that the Mission League originally turned down Nathan's request for a mission post is prophetic. His obstinence forces his family and ministry into chaos, beginning with his damning of casual nudity, which Rachel refers to as the "little dress-code problem" (p. 47). Because he spouts scripture like missile launches and prefers sarcasm and pompous oration to dialogue, he stunts his children's growth in faith by forcing them to think of bible verses as punishment and Christianity as punitive and confining. As Rachel describes his tirades, "Here comes Moses tromping down off of Mount Syanide with ten fresh ways to wreck your life" (p. 26). She later characterizes his efforts as "out somewhere looking for trouble as usual" (p. 246). Nathan treats his black parishioners with similar arrogance and lops off their questions and concerns with brief legalistic axioms derived from the white world. Curiously, he finds spiritual comfort from the Apocrypha, which he wants added to Baptist readings.

Kingsolver creates infuriating paradoxes in Nathan — bravery and cowardice, charisma and repulsive monomania, brilliance and tedium. He embraces the role of head of household and ennobles himself as "the captain of a sinking mess of female minds" (p. 36). His thinking is so convoluted that his decline seems eminent before he leaves the States. He responds with increasing diatribes and physical abuse, including the execution of Orleanna's only china plate as though it were guilty of sacrilege. The rate of Nathan's slide into tyranny increases after the missionary board cuts off the family from spiritual and financial support and urges their immediate withdrawal from the Congo. With no thought to his wife's fears for herself and the four girls, he vows that he and his family will stay. The author retrieves him from the brink of villainy with compassion. Her view of human frailty, as stated in "Mormon Memories," a 1989 book review for the *Los Angeles Times*, is comforting: "We're flawed creatures: less noble, perhaps, than chinchillas, but more interesting to know, and lovable, not for the righteousness of our lives but the immensity of our hopes" (p. 13).

On the precipitous Sunday morning when Tata Ndu forces an on-the-spot vote concerning the selection of Jesus as the village deity, Nathan finds himself outfoxed. Because he can't deny the importance of a democratic election, he angrily pounds his pulpit of palm fronds, causing them to collapse. The image illustrates the ephemeral nature of his ministry, which falls apart like dry chaff after Jesus loses, "eleven to fifty-six" (p. 334). After losing a second vote concerning Leah's joining the village men in a hunt, Nathan retreats quietly to his porch to read the bible. Rachel's snide summation captures a prime aspect of Nathan's ego-shielding maneuvers: "With Father, life's just one surprise after another" (p. 341).

After Orleanna and the three surviving girls flee Kilanga, scraps of Nathan's demise filter out to Leah, who learns from Brother Fyntan Fowles that her father lives alone in poor health at a forest hut he calls the New Church of Eternal Life. After making his way to the Kikongo mission for treatment of malaria and parasites, he fled to the forest. Because he annoyed local people with demands to baptize their children in the Kasai River, he fled their anger, climbed a coffee plantation watch tower, and was burned to death. Adah concludes a discussion of his death with a lengthy citation from Second Maccabees that describes a similar punishment. She and Leah snicker over a snack of chicken kabobs that were cooked the same way that Nathan met his fiery end. According to critic Roberta Rubinstein, only in retrospect do family members realize that "Nathan's error was in trying not only to deliver the word of God but to assume His place" (Rubinstein, p. 254).

• *Further Reading*

Barrett, Sharon. "Kingsolver's Heart of Darkness." *Chicago Sun-Times*, October 25, 1998, p. 18.
Culp, Mary Beth. "Review: *The Poisonwood Bible*." Mobile, Alabama, *Harbinger*, February 2, 1999.
Doenges, Judy. "The Political Is Personal — Barbara Kingsolver's Novel Measures Tragedy in the Congo in Terms of Intimate, Individual Costs." *Seattle Times*, October 29, 1998.
Frucht, Abby. "'Saving' the Heathen Barbara Kingsolver's Missionary Goes Into Africa, but He Just Doesn't Get It." *Boston Globe*, October 18, 1998, p. K1.
Glazebrook, Olivia. "Abandoning the Code." *Spectator*, Vol. 37, February 27, 1999.
Higdon, Barbara. "Nathan Responds to God's Call, But Not His Family's." *San Antonio Express-News*, October 18, 1998, p. 4G.

Ognibene, Elaine R. "The Missionary Position: Barbara Kingsolver's *The Poisonwood Bible*." *College Literature*, Vol. 30, No. 3, Summer 2003, pp. 19–36.

"Review: *The Poisonwood Bible*." *Publisher's Weekly*, Vol. 245, No. 32, August 10, 1998, p. 366.

Rubinstein, Roberta. "The Mark of Africa." *World & I*, Vol. 14, No. 4, April 1999, p. 254.

Smiley, Jane. "In the Fields of the Lord." *Washington Post*, October 11, 1998.

Price, Orleanna

Defeatist and dutiful to a fault, Orleanna Wharton Price is the quiet culprit whose "passivity keeps her from speaking up against the crimes of others" (Kakutani, p. 45). A native of Pearl, Mississippi, and the submissive wife of a fundamentalist missionary in *The Poisonwood Bible* (1998), she lies meekly in the path of her husband Nathan's steamrolling juggernaut, the light fading from her eyes to blankness. Too late, she sees herself as "an inferior force" and realizes, "There are no weapons for this fight" (pp. 192, 191). As a parent, she softens the tone of the household by calling her girls "sugar" and by pitying black children their scars, which she considers a "map of all the sorrows in their lives" (p. 123). Of her own girls' relationship with Nathan, she anticipates the day that they "[turn] away hard, never to speak to him again" (p. 191). However, she remains faithful to the mid-twentieth century I-Love-Lucy concept of wifehood that confers no volition to begin or end a marriage, even one so brutal and debilitating as the Price union.

Africa lops Orleanna's life into three eras—before, during, and after. Growing up motherless in Pearl outside Jackson, Mississippi, during the Great Depression, she realized disparities of haves and have-nots. She knew in girlhood that Nathan was stubborn and "contemptuous of failure" (p. 96). He returned from the war a changed man, an embittered survivor while the rest of his company succumbed during the Bataan death march. Her daughter Adah recalls a fun-loving woman in the first third of her mother's life "laughing blue-eyed in the grass, child herself" as her daughters decked her in purple clover (p. 56). To Nathan's shame, he never realizes that his wife and daughters are his treasure. In contrast to his ignorance, Mama Tataba, the housekeeper, proffers an ironic compliment by calling Orleanna "Mama Prize" (p. 90).

In the second stage of her married life, Orleanna is so moved to help Nathan succeed that she falls to willful conquest. She manages to conceive three daughters in under two years and marvels, "I cannot believe any woman on earth has ever made more babies out of less coition" (p. 199). In Kilanga, she abandons parental non-violence and threatens to thrash her four girls if they disgrace her at the first-night goat roast. Reshaping her from limp doormat to self-actualized individual are scenes informed by her principles, particularly the rejection of monkey meat for dinner because it looked "like kinfolk" (p. 46). She retreats from a last straw with a roar of "Damn!" at sight of Betty Crocker cake mixes transformed into cement, the end of her hopes for a sweet sixteen party for Rachel on August 20 (p. 68). In the night, Orleanna consoles Nathan in her arms as his uncompromising heart slowly turns to stone.

Under Nathan's vicious patriarchy, Orleanna tolerates cascades of contempt and chastisement for failing to close curtains or letting her slip show. In her husband's relentless glare, she pictures herself as skewered on the head of a pin, like a butterfly under glass. Powerless to claim the rights of wife and parent, she introduces the text with a forbidding image of slithery snakes, ravenous ants, murderous spiders, and "forest [that] eats itself and lives forever," a description that introduces a subtext of perverted Christian communion (p. 5). Her children describe her pagan apprecia-tion for scripture and grieve for the times that they can't protect her from Nathan's court of no appeal.

Kingsolver depicts Nathan as oblivious to the role of his helpmeet. Her contri-butions, particularly the donation of chickens, which she slaughters and fries for a church picnic, go unnoticed by the Reverend Price, whose monomania, like that of the self-righteous Reverend Abner Hale in James Michener's *Hawaii* (1958), causes Nathan to mourn the lack of converts to baptize but to observe no human needs among the unsaved. Significantly, Orleanna, like Michener's Jerusha Bromley Hale, grows apart from Nathan and misses coffee more than she misses his "physical pres-ence" (p. 91). In 1974, Leah is able to look back on her mother and award her a ver-bal crown: "My pagan mother alone among us understood redemption" (p. 456).

The third segment of Orleanna's adult life begins after her month-long battle with malaria, which reduces her to a wide-eyed zombie. In July 1960, she suddenly deserts her cot to teach Rachel to cook. Out of motherly devotion she promises to take her children out of the Congo, even if she has to pay the extortionate price demanded by bush pilot Eeben Axelroot. The epiphany spreads to Leah, who retreats from her adoration of Nathan to the safety of a parent willing to rescue her from the revolution. In retrospect, Orleanna envisions the downfall of equatorial Africa as an amusing chess game played between an American and a Belgian, two insouciant males who sip brandy as they make their moves without regard to the game's murderous subtext.

Kingsolver builds a symphonic tribute to Orleanna's motherhood and to her inhuman solitude in a "moldy corner of hell" that costs her a favorite child (p. 164). Orleanna refers to her religiosity as "Southern Baptist by marriage" later "[conse-crated] in the public library" and blames her faulty union for the coercion of four daughters in a wretched jungle setting and the death of the youngest and most inno-cent (p. 7). Orleanna conceals with effort her daily struggle not to run away from "the gloom, the humidity, the permanent sour breath of rainy season ... the fresh stench of night soil in the bushes" (p. 91). By Thanksgiving, she prays for deliver-ance.

Speaking in retrospect from her retirement cottage in Sanderling, Georgia, Orleanna thinks of herself as "Lot's wife" and recalls the stress of "waiting for that ax to fall," a free-floating dread that clouded her married life (pp. 98, 323). She grieves over her life's strange turn every time a fragrance reminds her of the scent of Africa, which accuses her of allowing Ruth May to die. Orleanna recalls her isolation among black vendors on market day. The only white outsider, she stood "pale and wide-eyed as a fish" before black women who chastised her for violating marketplace decorum (p. 88).

In a plywood shack in Bethlehem, Georgia, Orleanna rehabilitates herself with a garden that fills two acres with a burst of blossoms. Upon learning from Adah that

Nathan died as he would have wanted in "a blaze of glory," Orelanna maintains the spunk to mutter, "I don't give a damn what he would have wanted" (p. 494). Kingsolver bestows on the tormented mother a touch of grace from Ruth May's spirit, which offers her mother a blessed life: "You will forgive and remember.... Move on. Walk forward into the light," a metaphoric path that leads Orleanna from the shadowed nightmares of Africa to a semblance of peace (p. 543).

See also **self-esteem, survival, trust, women**

• *Further Reading*

Fletcher, Yael Simpson. "History Will One Day Have Its Say: New Perspectives on Colonial and Postcolonial Congo." *Radical History Review*, Vol. 84, 2002, pp. 195–207.

Green, Gayle. "Independence Struggle." *Women's Review of Books*, Vol. 16, No. 7, April 1999, pp. 8–9.

Kakesako, Gregg K. "'America's Storyteller' James Michener, Dies: Author Came to Love Isles While Writing 'Hawaii.'" *Honolulu Star-Bulletin*, October 17, 1997.

Kakutani, Michiko. "The Poisonwood Bible: A Family a Heart of Darkness." *New York Times*, October 16, 1998, p. 45.

Ognibene, Elaine R. "The Missionary Position: Barbara Kingsolver's *The Poisonwood Bible*." *College Literature*, Vol. 30, No. 3, Summer 2003, pp. 19–36.

Skow, John. "Hearts of Darkness: Matters of Race, Religion and Gender Collide as a Missionary Family Moves to the Congo in 1959." *Time*, Vol. 152, No. 9, November 9, 1998, p. 113.

Price, Rachel

A touch of comic relief in *The Poisonwood Bible* (1998), Rachel Rebeccah Price offers a satiric picture of the self-centered Barbie-style going-on-sixteen-year-old developing into an Ugly American and voice for commercialism. While still in Georgia, she suffers a lashing from her father for painting her fingernails a glowing bubblegum pink, "trying to work in just one last sin before leaving civilization" (p. 16). Upon setting foot in the Congo, she doesn't feel that the family is "in charge of a thing, not even our own selves" (p. 22). In a "heathen pandemony," she immediately regrets taking for "granite" the "flush commodes and machine-washed clothes" of home and considers selling her "soul for a dry mohair sweater and a can of Final Net hairspray" (pp. 23, 460). She regrets that Nathan's Fourth of July celebration of Easter Sunday brings no new outfits and muses over the missionary barrel donations worn by local men. Some of Rachel's antics sound like the author's confessions to her mother in an entry in *I've Always Meant to Tell You: Letters to Our Mothers: An Anthology of Contemporary Women Writers* (1994), a suggestion that the author put a heavy autobiographical touch on the character.

Kingsolver illustrates the ethnic parameters of beauty and freakishness by noting that villagers are less likely to ridicule Adah, her handicapped sister, and more intent on staring at Rachel, the posturing egocentric with mediocre intelligence whom Adah calls "our family's own Queen of Sheba" (p. 62). Adding to Rachel's absurd opinions and behaviors is the sibling rivalry with Adah's twin sister Leah, whom Rachel reviles for learning archery to gain attention. While avoiding household chores, Rachel obsesses over her waist-length cottontop hair, colorless lashes, blue eyes, and pink, easily burned skin, which earn her the name *mvúla* (termite) among Kilangans. Villagers feel free to yank on her hair. Her own father considers her "blonde as a white rabbit" (p. 52). In five-year-old Ruth May's estimation, "Rachel was Miss Priss and now she is a freak of nature" (*Ibid.*). When Tata Ndu honors Rachel with courtship, she goes into a frenzy and considers "filing for an adoption" when the family returns to Georgia (p. 268). In Book Four, she is so traumatized by Ruth May's death that she abandons her usual prattle and admits that she can never return to life as she knew it in Bethlehem, Georgia.

Ironically, the teenager who longs to quit the Congo develops into a lifetime resident of Africa as replete with American smugness as the worst of colonial expropriators. She considers repatriating to Georgia, but realizes that Africa has matured her outlook: "My high school friends would still have been whining over boyfriends and fighting for carhop jobs at the A & W. Their idea of a dog-eat-dog world was Beauty School" (p. 513). Eeben Axelroot's dramatic wooing by lighting a cigarette and placing it between her lips feeds her vanity. After she resolves privately to use feminine wiles to get him to fly the family out of the Congo, he mocks her for believing that she is "the epicenter of a continent" (p. 293). On the night of the army ant attack, Rachel shows her true colors by abandoning clothes and bible and grabbing her mirror as the one personal item worth saving. While her father yells about Moses and the plagues of Egypt, Rachel cradles her mirror to keep it safe, but fails to protect it from destruction.

In adulthood, Rachel develops into what interviewer Michael Krasny calls "a South African Leona Helmsley," who casually shrugs off responsibility for a national nightmare of smuggling and intrigue that enriches her with payola (Krasny). After an illicit alliance with Axelroot in "Joburg," she marries him and lives among the poor, whom she belittles as "people [who] don't have any perspective of what good scenery is" (p. 424). She becomes mistress, then wife of Daniel Duprée, a French diplomat, but must admit that "a man who leaves his wife for his mistress is no catch" (p. 461). After a subsequent marriage, she inherits from her dead husband, Remy Fairley, the Equatorial Hotel, an insular retreat advantageously located on the road from Owando to Brazzaville. Of her managerial role, she marvels, "[It] isn't just a hotel, it's like running a whole little *country*" (p. 512). Her motto changes little from her outlook at age fifteen: "The neck you save will be your own" (p. 516).

Celia McGee, reviewer for *USA Today*, describes Rachel as self-absorbed racist, "a vamp practiced in bigotry and seduction" (McGee, p. 6D). She exults in *prix fixé* dinners and a swimming pool and flaunts her bikini-clad figure among hotel guests. In widowhood, she thinks often of family, but rejects her biracial nephews and black brother-in-law and denigrates Leah as "the Bride of Africa" (p. 465). Rachel complains that Leah is only "a hop, skip, and jump away" in Kinshasa, but the distance measured in social strata is too great to allow Leah a visit. Rachel explains the lack of family get-togethers as her sisters' wish to "go on thinking they are the brains of the family and I am the dumb blonde" (p. 464).

Kingsolver depicts Rachel as the least astute of the three surviving Price sisters. During the 1984 reunion of the Price sisters, she drives the Ngembas' Land Rover from Senegal to Zaire. She grows testy and suspicious from failing to keep up with conversation between Leah and Adah: "It was very hard to concentrate while my sisters were giving me a pop quiz on world democracy" (p. 478). She registers no sympathy for the death of the houseboy Pascal, but attempts to comfort Leah over the news that natives immolated Nathan in a wooden tower. As unforgiving as ever, Rachel recalls their father as "mean as a snake. There's nothing he got that he didn't deserve" (p. 486).

See also **malapropisms**

• *Further Reading*

Bromberg, Judith. "A Complex Novel About Faith, Family and Dysfunction." *National Catholic Reporter*, Vol. 35, No. 20, March 19, 1999, p. 13.
Glazebrook, Olivia. "Abandoning the Code." *Spectator*, Vol. 37, February 27, 1999.
Higdon, Barbara. "Nathan Responds to God's Call, but Not His Family's." *San Antonio Express-News*, October 18, 1998, p. 4G.
Krasny, Michael. "Interview: Barbara Kingsolver, Author, Discusses Her New Book." *Talk of the Nation* (NPR), December 13, 1999.
Markels, Julian. "Coda: Imagining History in *The Poisonwood Bible*." *Monthly Review Press*, September 2003.
McGee, Celia. "'Bible' Offers Two Good Books in One." *USA Today*, October 22, 1998, p. 6D.
"Review: *The Poisonwood Bible*." *Timbrel*, September-October 1999.
Smiley, Jane. "In the Fields of the Lord." *Washington Post*, October 11, 1998.

Price, Ruth May

Only five years old when her fundamentalist family moves to the Congo, Ruth May Price adds poignance and charm to the text of *The Poisonwood Bible* (1998). Her understanding of religion is highly visual, e.g. the description of Jesus "with long brown hair and sandals, size extra-large" (p. 155). She is given to eavesdropping on adults, who seem unaware of her presence, and ventures for a glimpse of the burned legs of Mama Mwanza. With a child's understanding of Georgian segregation, Ruth May believes the bible allots black children a special day to visit the zoo and remarks on "Jimmy Crow," who "makes the laws" (p. 20). Her naive commentary includes predictions that black people will dig up rocks turned to gold after all the white people die, but she puzzles over the Tribes of Ham and the purpose of racial killings. She is clear on one matter: after Nathan flies to Léopoldville on June 28, 1960, she says, 'Mama, I hope he never comes back" (p. 215).

In retrospect, Orleanna remembers her curly strawberry-blonde favorite in images of glass-eyed okapi stuffed and mounted at the New York Museum of Natural History. Ruth May receives more attention than her sisters because she was born nine years after the twins and has little competition. A foreboding of the child's demise occurs with an episode of vomiting into her Donald Duck comic book and, on arrival in Léopoldville, fainting from heat and humidity on the plane's off-ramp. She repeats the swoon upon the family's greeting by pungent-smelling Congolese. Because she is given to rambling beyond the yard, Leah warns that she might be sliced by a machete or bitten by a snake, a prophetic comment that recurs as though preparing the reader for the child's death.

Unlike her three sisters, Ruth May is young enough to let go of her Georgia roots, even her monkey sock doll, and find beauty and solace in the jungle. With a spirit bound for "all or nothing," she happily makes friends and enjoys a rope swing that Nelson makes from an oil drum (p. 106). Aiding her acclimation to equatorial Africa are a pet mongoose named Stuart Little, Leon the chameleon, and a penchant for climbing trees, the author's metaphor for rising above the moment to take in a fuller picture of her new home. Ironically, the author pictures the child teaching Congolese friends Bangwa, Mazuzi, Nsimba, and Tumba to play "Ma-da-meh-yi?" (Mother May I?), a game reflecting the authoritarian, top-down order of the Price family (p. 111). It is significant to Kingsolver's theme that the child brags about confining the chameleon to a box and poking it "to show him who's boss," a child's version of the patriarchal white colonial (p. 118).

Ruth May extends love and acceptance to natives who suffer malnutrition and physical impairments. For an open-hearted embrace of the village, she earns the affection and admiration of Kilangans. She is fearless around wildlife and wants a pet snake. She confides to Leah that she can climb a tree and blend in just like a green mamba, a mental scenario Ruth May relives on the night of the army ant attack. While spying on the Communist boy scouts, Ruth May falls from a tree and breaks an arm, an accident Orleanna prefers to snakebite, a comment that echoes in various forms throughout the text. Anatole remembers her as having "the heart of a mongoose," an ironic choice of a small animal that kills vermin and snakes (p. 430).

The child's decline from malaria precedes Orleanna's discovery of a cache of quinine squashed on the wall behind her bed. Ruth May is still hollow-eyed from sickness and hunger on the day of the fire surround. Kingsolver pictures her as a *muntu* (spirit), a complex being that critic Amy M. Regier describes as "paradoxical combination of the living spirit of a person translated by death into another form of environmental being beyond individuality" (Regier). Kingsolver pictures the fragile ghost "chained to this briefly belligerent child through forelife, life, and afterlife, peering out through her sockets" (p. 346). At her death at age six from the strike of a green mamba at her left shoulder, she is the only member of the Price family whom the Congolese mourn.

In death, Ruth May influences the choices and regrets of family members. The loss triggers the arrival of life-giving rain, but ends her sisters' hopes of returning to their former lives with family intact. Nathan uses her sacrifice as the mystical moment to baptize the children who cluster around the homemade bier chanting "Mother May I?" For water, he uses the abundant rain that ends Kilanga's drought. At her coastal home in Georgia, Orleanna retreats into an extended period of mourning that causes her to train sad eyes across the sea to Africa. They meet the gaze of Ruth May's disembodied spirit, which blesses the mother with forgiveness.

• *Further Reading*

Ewert, Jeanne. "Shadows of 'Darkness': The Specter of Joseph Conrad's Classic Tale of Oppression Emerges Throughout Barbara Kingsolver's Latest Novel." *Chicago Tribune*, October 11, 1998, p. 6.

Regier, Amy M. "Replacing the Hero with the Reader: Public Story Structure in *The Poisonwood Bible*." *Mennonite Life*, Vol. 56, No. 1, March 2001.

Price genealogy

The Price family tree contains the irony of Nathan Price's ill-advised mission to Congo and his depersonalized treatment of blacks in Kilanga. After the family's seventeen-month ordeal and the death of Ruth May, the four female survivors turn away from Nathan. Rachel becomes a life-long resident of southern Africa. Leah marries Anatole Ngemba, bears four mixed-race boys, and helps her husband retrain peasants for survival under Mobutu's tyranny.

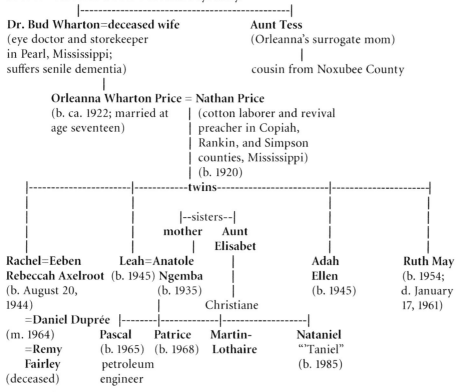

```
         |---------------------------------------------|
Dr. Bud Wharton=deceased wife              Aunt Tess
(eye doctor and storekeeper                (Orleanna's surrogate mom)
in Pearl, Mississippi;                          |
suffers senile dementia)                   cousin from Noxubee County
            |
      Orleanna Wharton Price = Nathan Price
        (b. ca. 1922; married at  | (cotton laborer and revival
        age seventeen)            | preacher in Copiah,
                                  | Rankin, and Simpson
                                  | counties, Mississippi)
                                  | (b. 1920)
  |--------------------|-----------twins-----------------------|--------------------|
  |                    |                                       |                    |
  |                    |        |--sisters--|                  |                    |
  |                    |        mother    Aunt                 |                    |
  |                    |                  Elisabet             |                    |
  |                    |           |                           |                    |
Rachel=Eeben      Leah=Anatole     |                         Adah              Ruth May
Rebeccah Axelroot (b. 1945) Ngemba |                         Ellen            (b. 1954;
(b. August 20,         (b. 1935)   |                         (b. 1945)        d. January
1944)                              |      Christiane                           17, 1961)
   =Daniel Duprée |--------|-------------|------------------|
(m. 1964)        Pascal   Patrice   Martin-           Nataniel
   =Remy       (b. 1965) (b. 1968)  Lothaire          "'Taniel"
  Fairley       petroleum                             (b. 1985)
(deceased)      engineer
```

Prodigal Summer

Set in farming country in the southern end of the Appalachian chain, *Prodigal Summer* (2000) is a threefold paean to urgent, uninhibited sex. In the essay "A Forbidden Territory Familiar to All" (2000), Kingsolver confessed to readers her involvement in a steamy new novel:

> I'm having a good old time writing about it, too. I've always felt I was getting away with something marginally legal, inventing fantasies for a living. But now it seems an outright scandal. I send my kids off to school in the morning, scuttle to my office, close the door, and hoo boy, *les bons temps roulent* [the good times roll]! [p. E1].

The result is what Colleen Kelly Warren of the *St. Louis Post-Dispatch* calls "a large, lush celebration of life in its myriad manifestations" (Warren, p. F10). Polly Paddock Gossett, book editor for the *Charlotte Observer*, concurs with praise for a "lovingly drawn — and achingly beautiful — hymn to the natural world" (Gossett).

In a "season of extravagant procreation," copulation commands attention at every turn in Kingsolver's novel, including the post-funeral erotic dreams of widow Lusa Maluf Landowski following the tragic death of her husband, Cole Widener, in a truck accident (p. 51). The author refuses to let loss overrule life. Described by critic Amanda Cockrell, Kingsolver's theme is "people sex, bug sex, coyote sex; about pheromones and full moons, and the drive to pass on your genes" (Cockrell, p. 1). As a balance, the theme of failed ambition gains steam from the hardships of Zebulon Valley farmers from "bad luck, bad weather, chestnut blight, change, economics, the antitobacco lobby," a daunting list of threats to food production and livelihood (pp. 180–181).

The author explained on National Public Radio to interviewer Linda Wertheimer that the bases of the work derive from evolutionary biology and cultural anthropology: "Because this novel is about the human food chain, among other things, it's about the connections between humans and our habitat and our food chain. And there's a lot of information in this book about small farming and the difficulties faced by small farmers" (Wertheimer). Of the overt carnality in the story, she reflected, "There are difficult things about it because the language of coition has pretty much been divvied up between pornography and the medical profession" (*Ibid.*). The author manages to reclaim that language and use it tastefully in description of a summer rife with couplings.

There is a homey quality to Kingsolver's writing. Of her return to familiar folkways and language of Appalachia after the exotics of *The Poisonwood Bible* (2000), she remarked in an interview that she was "coming home to my own language and culture. The ways these characters speak, their idioms and understated humor, the things they do— stripping tobacco, bringing casseroles to a wake, counting on relatives and looking askance at outsiders— are all utterly familiar to me" ("Barbara"). According to reviewer Jeff Giles of *Newsweek*, the text is "clearly the product of lifelong fascinations and of a deeply held world view. Human beings are just one species among many here — mating, traveling alone or in packs and always fighting for territory" (Giles, p. 82). Writing for the *Washington Post*, book critic Daniel Woodrell took offense at the author's reduction of men to bundles of primitive urges while female characters view the intrinsic value of the cosmos at large. The overall effect is less accusatory. In Woodrell's words, "Human characters meld into the tapestry of nature, become threads in the necessary entanglements of our world, which is exactly the big picture Kingsolver wants us to recognize" (Woodrell, p. X6).

In a mode that James Shilling, reviewer for the *London Times*, calls modern American pastoral, the novel opens in early May, a "time of birthing and nursing," when wildflowers begin to blossom and mushrooms to cluster in bright-hued colonies (p. 29). The author tracks animal and human characters through sense impressions, mostly scent. Her description of spring moving up the elevation of Zebulon Mountain concludes with a flame sweeping to the pinnacle, a parallel to Deanna's blush on first encountering hunter Eddie Bondo and a portent of the body heat of their first night in her log cabin. Shifts to the other two strands subtly reconnect to familiar themes and events, e.g., a huge downed chestnut tree hollowed out over time, a honeycomb in a church wall, and the den of coyotes that Deanna spies and Herb Goins shoots to keep predators from ravaging his dairy herd. However, observes *Smithsonian* reviewer Susan Lumpkin, the author is more faithful to the characterization of the Appalachian mountains than to her *dramatis personae*.

Kingsolver develops conflict through a trio of love matches, beginning with the unlikely pairing of sheep farmer Eddie Bondo and Deanna, bounty hunter and wildlife protector. The lovers cool their amours long enough to share personal information, including opposing views on the return of coyotes to the wild. The author depicts Deanna's conflict in wanting to know, yet wanting to leave unsaid Bondo's enmity toward predators accused of raiding sheep herds. Her view of sport hunting is simple: "I'd never kill just for fun" (p. 187). Bond's view elevates the animal to the level of mythic marauder: "A coyote is just something you can blame. He's nobody's pet; he doesn't belong to anybody but himself" (p. 176). Oddly, the description acknowledges an animal mythos that dates to animistic Indian lore and adventure stories of the Old West.

To Deanna, Bondo's answer perpetuates the great Western cliché of male toughness and supremacy over all comers, be they human or some aspect of nature. She summarizes his view as a romanticized myth, like Little Red Riding Hood and the wolf. The truism that coyotes are destructive is specious and, as an overt element of manhood, self-perpetuating — "a bunch of macho ranchers scared of a shadow" (p. 180). She pictures Bondo's hobby of traveling North America to hunt coyote as "prolonged adolescence," the protracted boyhood of a man destined to inherit his father's fifteen-hundred-acre sheep ranch.

Kingsolver is expert at presenting the laws of nature through dialogue. Deanna summarizes the value of the predator coyote to the balance of nature. Nannie Land Rawley, in spirited lectures to neighbor Garnett S. Walker, III, delivers a series of explanations of Darwinian principles — survival of the fittest, natural selection, evolution — as well as the Volterra principle, which explains why spraying insecticide on plant-eating bugs increases their population and why chemical manufacturers capitalize on the farmer's ignorance of the harm they do. Lusa, the third protagonist, concurs with the other two by inveighing against the use of herbicides to control honeysuckle. The lessons in ecology form a gossamer network that is both readable and entertaining. In the opinion of reviewer Kelly Flynn, Kingsolver "may have inherited Thoreau's mantle, but she piles up riches of her own making, blending her extravagant narrative gift with benevolent concise humor" (Flynn).

At the novel's conclusion, the author downplays the wilderness theme to dwell on the human family. Lusa's contribution to the biological motif makes an unusual connection with motherhood, the secondary theme, by intriguing her niece, Crystal Walker, with information about moths, a beneficial hobby that distracts her from fears of her mother's losing battle with cancer. Kingsolver allows parenting to win out in the resolution as Lusa eases into the role of surrogate parent and Deanna, overcome by the nesting urge, returns to the valley to reside with Nannie, her foster mother, until the birth of Deanna's child. Like a grand motet, theme melds with theme as Kingsolver builds to a parting observation: "Every choice is a world made new for the chosen" (p. 444).

See also **Eddie Bondo, Lusa Maluf Landowski, Nannie Rawley, Garnett Walker, Walker genealogy, Cole Widener, Jewel Widener, Widener genealogy, Deanna Wolfe, Wolfe genealogy**

• *Further Reading*

"Barbara Kingsolver: Coming Home to a Prodigal Summer." http://www.ivillage.com/books/intervu/fict/articles.

Charles, Ron. "Mothers of Nature Howling at the Moon." *Christian Science Monitor*, Vol. 92, No. 230, October 19, 2000.

Cockrell, Amanda. "Luna Moths, Coyotes, Sugar Skulls: The Fiction of Barbara Kingsolver." *Hollins Critic*, Vol. 38, No 2, April 2001, pp. 1–15.

Flynn, Kelly. "The Rural Experience and Definitions." http://www.ruralwomyn.net/.

Giles, Jeff. "Getting Back to Nature." *Newsweek*, Vol. 136, No. 18, October 30, 2000, p. 82.

Gossett, Polly Paddock. "Review: *Prodigal Summer*." *Charlotte Observer*, November 29, 2000.

Judd, Elizabeth. "Review: *Prodigal Summer*." *Salon*, November 17, 2000.

Lane, Tahree. "A Lust for Nature." *Toledo Blade*, November 26, 2000.

Lumpkin, Susan. "Review: *Prodigal Summer*." *Smithsonian Zoogoer*, March/April 2001, p. 1.

Rosen, Judith. "Kingsolver Tour Helps Indies Clean Up." *Publishers Weekly*, Vol. 247, No. 48, November 27, 2000, pp. 26–27.

Shilling, James. "Animal Instincts." *London Times*, December 23, 2000, p. 25.

Warren, Colleen Kelly. "Literature, Biology Fuse in Kingsolver's Novel About Life." *St. Louis Post-Dispatch*, October 15, 2000, p. F10.

Wertheimer, Linda. "Interview: Barbara Kingsolver Discusses Her Latest Novel, 'Prodigal Summer.'" *All Things Considered* (NPR), October 23, 2000.

Woodrell, Daniel. "Ah, Wilderness." *Washington Post*, November 19, 2000, p. X6.

pueblo

Kingsolver depicts pueblo lifestyle as a model of sensible uses of natural resources and recycling as a means of living in harmony with the land. In *Animal Dreams* (1990), she introduces Codi Noline to "prehistoric condos" through the tutelage of a date, Loyd Peregrina, an Apache-Pueblo, who drives through cottonwood stands, sage, and fall wildflowers in "God's backyard" on the way to Kinishba (Brown House) (p. 127). At the ruins southwest of Whiteriver on the Fort Apache Reservation in Yavapai County, Arizona, she learns that the Pueblo people built the community dwelling entirely out of native stone in the late 1100s. Archeologist Byron Cummings discovered the remains in 1931 and attempted to restore and preserve them. Loyd reveres Kinishba as a special place that he visits only with his dog Jack. By guiding her room by room through the structure, he shares his love of place and an admiration for prehistoric lifestyles. He confides to Codi that the land is something he would die for.

In an image that echoes her life struggle for direction, Codi familiarizes herself with the intricacies of Kinishba. Its two hundred rectangular, dirt-floored rooms cluster in the stone building like a maze that once offered three times that many rooms in three stories. The thick walls, resembling cell structure under a microscope, serve as gravesites for family members, who buried dead children in earthen walls or floors to keep their bones close to the living. Unlike Anglos, pueblo dwellers lived simply and without competition for bigger, better, grander housing than their neighbors. In Loyd's opinion, his ancestors "[built] something nice that Mother Earth will want to hold in her arms" (p. 126). The totality illustrates an integrative concept of dwellings that blend organically with the rugged landscape.

After the introduction to pueblo living, Loyd invites Codi to spend Christmas at Santa Rosalia Pueblo, a fictional desert setting near Canyon de Chelly overseen by "godheads of red sandstone" (p. 209). The author introduces the village as a stone structure so similar to outcroppings that it blends in with the mesa. Codi discerns that earth tones come in an infinite number of hues, an image that precedes her recognition of villagers as individuals. At the home of Inez Peregrina, she connects the smell of cedar smoke, jars of hominy, and fresh globes of bread from the outdoor adobe oven with genial hugs, teasing, and welcome. From her vantage on the roof, Codi watches Christmas Day festivities, which involve an all-day dance in the plaza and entertainment by the koshari, a ritual clown. The sight of parts of the dwelling collapsing with age surprises her, but Loyd explains that houses, like people, are expected to totter, collapse, and return to the earth. His image explains why the Pueblo structured residences in comfortable alliance with nature: "We're like coyotes…. Get to a good place, turn around three times in the grass, and you're home" (p. 325).

• *Further Reading*

Go, Kristen. "Tribe Works to Guard Sacred Kinishba Ruins." *Arizona Republic*, July 18, 2003.
Hoffman, Dillene. "Photographer at Kinishba." *Expedition*, Vol. 37, No. 1, 1995, p. 67.
Negri, Sam, and Jerry Jacka. "Kinishba: The Ruin That Refuses to Go Away." *Arizona Highways*, Vol. 69, No. 2, February 1993, pp. 52–55.

Rawley, Nannie

A seventy-five-year-old farmer and beekeeper in *Prodigal Summer* (2000), Miss Nannie Land Rawley is a voluble, but well-meaning neighbor. Biologist Deanna Wolfe recalls from childhood Nannie's generous gifts of Arkansas blacks from her apple orchard and her mothering and love for Deanna's widowed father, Ray Dean Wolfe. Cole Widener also enjoyed the apples when he played with Nannie's daughter Rachel, a victim of a deformed heart and Down syndrome. To Deanna, Nannie is a blend of affability and selfhood, "staking out her independent old-lady life but still snatching conversation wherever possible" (p. 53).

The spirited orchardist extends both soothing and sharp words, depending on the situation. At Cole's wake, Nannie, her head wrapped in gray plaits, confides the death of her love child to widow Lusa Maluf Landowski and observes, "You learn to love the place somebody leaves behind for you" (p. 73). At other times, Nannie's keen-edged criticism can wound, as with her description of Mary Edna Goins as having "about the worst case of herself I've ever seen" (p. 337). The ins and outs of these examples of Nannie's commentary lend spice to the text when it threatens to take itself too seriously.

Nannie is a friend-maker who writes to Deanna in her mountain hermitage and wins the gossipy Oda Black with apple pies, but fails with vo-ag teacher Garnett S. Walker, III. In the words of reviewer Sharon Eberson, "Everything about Nannie eats away at the fabric of all that Garnett believes in" (Eberson). The combative next-door neighbor berates her for believing in "evolution, transcendentalism, things of that nature" (p. 131). In the words of reviewer Kelly Flynn, the two "seem bent on thrashing out the countless intimate lessons of biology as only an irascible traditional farmer and a devotee of organic agriculture can" (Flynn). In addition to despising free-thinkers like Nannie, he grudgingly admires her for having borne an illegitimate child without shame. Less acceptable is Nannie's Unitarianism and her pride in being a certified organic fruit grower and enemy of Sevin dust. Garnett grumbles at the hand-painted plywood sign declaring a no-spray zone that she hoists before the county spray truck arrives to spew 2-4-D herbicide along the right-of-way. She is the laughingstock of Egg Fork for buying salamanders from Grandy's bait shop and setting them free to perpetuate an endangered species.

Like Kingsolver herself, Nannie lives an uninhibited life free of concern for other people's titters and jeers. She chastises Garnett for his cavalier attitude toward the extinction of species and calls him "a regular death angel" (p. 273). Like parent to small child, she patiently explains the Volterra principle, a mathematical paradigm accounting for the increase of plant-eating bugs after spray kills their natural predators. In her opinion, "Everything alive is connected to every other by fine, invisible threads" (p. 216). She also disdains clear-cutting of forests, destroying cropland to make pastures, consumer demand for foods out of season, and shipping produce to places where it isn't native. According to her philosophy of the universe, "We're that foolish, to think we know how to rule the world" (p. 217).

In addition to being what reviewer Elizabeth Judd calls an "an earthy-crunchy, Unitarian-church-going, Rachel Carson–loving orchardist," Nannie is the soul of kindness (Judd). After wounding Garnett by charging that his spraying may have caused fatal lung cancer in his wife, Nannie moves on to address her neighbor's loneliness and isolation. Getting right to the point like a surgeon's scalpel to diseased tissue, she charges, "You self-righteous old man. Do you ever wonder why you don't have a friend in the world since Ellen died?" (p. 279). Realizing that she transgresses on private territory, Nannie quietly lays a hand on Garnett's arm and apologizes. In a subsequent meeting at the creek, she diagnoses his dizzy spells as nystagmus, a disruption of normal eye movements, and teaches him the Epley maneuver, a self-treatment that repositions crystalline particles in the inner ear to restore balance. To free him from embarrassment at contact with her hands, she informs him that he has rocks in his head.

Kingsolver favors the smart-mouthed septuagenarian because of her good-heartedness and spunk. Nannie meets Garnett, a fellow "old chestnut," head-on over his

charge that her no-spray sign is high-handed and her shorts are immodest. By expressing the obsolence of human beings in old age, she states a biological fact. Her choice
of terms, however, insults his manhood and sense of decorum. Nannie is quick to
make amends. An aggressive embrace of the man she labels a "sanctimonious old fart"
cinches what reviewer Ron Charles terms "the most refreshing and funny love affair
of the year" (p. 427; Charles).

- *Further Reading*

Charles, Ron. "Mothers of Nature Howling at the Moon." *Christian Science Monitor*,
    Vol. 92, No. 230, October 19, 2000.
Eberson, Sharon. "Appalachian Romance Has Kingsolver in Top Form." *Pittsburgh Post-
    Gazette*, January 14, 2001.
Flynn, Kelly. "The Rural Experience and Definitions." http://www.ruralwomyn.net/.
James, Rebecca. "Booked Solid." *LETTERS from CAMP Rehobeth*, Vol. 11, No. 6, June
    1, 2001.
Judd, Elizabeth. "Review: *Prodigal Summer*." *Salon*, November 17, 2000.

recycling

Recycling is a subtle subtext in Kingsolver's works, which reflect ingenious ways
of using discarded items, such as the torn page in *Prodigal Summer* (2000) that ranger
Deanna Wolfe leaves in her sock drawer as material for mice to line their winter
lairs. In *The Bean Trees* (1988), the confines of Mattie's junkyard garden and afternoons at Roosevelt Park become Turtle's classroom as she learns names for plants
and practices growing seeds and trusting adults. In *Animal Dreams* (1990), the Stitch
and Bitch club turns a harvest of peacock feathers into piñatas for sale in Tucson to
raise money to halt the pollution of the river from the local copper mine. The examples illustrate simple measures that draw humans close into the circle of life that
embraces all living things.

In *The Poisonwood Bible* (1998), Kingsolver notes the skill of Kilangans in getting full use of missionary donations, particularly oddments of clothing. At a dramatic moment, she turns a wake for Ruth May Price into Orleanna's spread of worldly
goods among the thrifty Congolese, who transform the white family's leavings into
treasure. She anticipates how dresses and curtains will be reshaped, a tea towel turned
into a diaper, and "empty food tins ... pounded into palm-oil lamps, toys, plow-
shares maybe," a biblical allusion to Joel 3:10, which anticipates demilitarization as
technology turns from the mercenary to the agricultural (p. 382). By divesting her
home of materialism, Orleanna rids the Price family of some of the guilt they have
borne for living above the level of dirt-poor female villagers. On return to Bethlehem, Georgia, she puts into practice the thrift of African women by hoeing her two-
acre lot and planting peanuts and sweet potatoes, two standard food items in the
Congo, and "four dozen kinds of flowers" (p. 408). For fertilizer, she hauls manure
from a nearby goose and pigs to nourish flowers that she sells by the roadside.

A more ingenious form of recycling energizes the resolution in *Prodigal Summer*. Among the mundane methods—Nannie Rawley's mulch pile, Jewel's filling of

canning jars with cherry pie filling and green beans— sparkles Lusa Maluf Landowski's ingenious notion of turning a tobacco farm into a breeding ground for prize Spanish meat-goats. The idea takes shape during her conversation with a nephew, seventeen-year-old Little Rickie, who is stuck with two goats left over from a 4-H project six or seven years earlier. Kingsolver stresses that, not only is recycling good for the earth, it can also solve agricultural dilemmas, such as the decline of cigarette smoking from health warnings and the replacement of tobacco with a livestock plan that provides meat for followers of three disparate religions— Christianity, Islam, and Judaism — to celebrate their uniqueness.

See also **Mattie, seeds**

• *Further Reading*

Judd, Elizabeth. "Review: *Prodigal Summer.*" *Salon*, November 17, 2000.
Uschuk, J. "Green Light: Barbara Kingsolver's New Novel Fights for Life and Love in the Natural World." *Tucson Weekly*, November 2, 2000.

religion

Kingsolver's theology is a homemade patchwork based on experience rather than scripture or such foolish ministers as the "nudnick" Brother Leonard in *Prodigal Summer* (2000) (p. 74). In "Mormon Memories," a 1989 book review for the *Los Angeles Times*, she states that "Religion is so much more than belief" (p. 13). Her fiction muses steadily on the human yearning for a faith suited to idiosyncratic needs. In *The Bean Trees* (1988), Taylor reflects on a Cherokee great-grandfather "who believed God lived in trees" (p. 195). Lou Ann Ruiz's Appalachian-born mother hums constant tuneless repetitions of "All our sins and griefs to bear," the second line of the hymn "What a Friend We Have in Jesus" (p. 53). The dismal cadence is suitable background music for Granny Logan's gift of a bottle of Tug Fork Water, the fundamentalist equivalent of holy water for baptizing the infant Dwayne Ray to cleanse him of original sin. The offering loses its meaning with Lou Ann, who has decided to have her child blessed in a Catholic ceremony, a gesture intended to please his Hispanic relatives. To keep peace with her Kentucky relatives, she says nothing about her intent to deviate from Appalachian protocol. The baptism exemplifies compromise, one of the author's favorite themes in motifs involving human clashes over personal values and customs.

In *Pigs in Heaven* (1993), the author brings two cultures together over the issue of interracial adoption. Alice Greer observes the introit to a Cherokee stomp dance, a call to worship in Cherokee that makes her reflect on glossolalia in "holy-roller churches in Mississippi" where members of the congregation babbled in tongues (p. 264). Because the religious ad lib sprang from individual ecstasy rather than from an established language, "it was more or less every man for himself" (*Ibid.*). In contrast to the frenetic evangelical services of her girlhood, she is entranced by Ledger Fourkiller, medicine man for Heaven, Oklahoma, who conducts a dignified ritual, prayers, and folksy homily urging all participants at the stomp dance to be good and avoid envy. Kingsolver implies that frenzied wailing in gibberish is more temporal exhibitionism than faith and that the native American way of addressing local misbehavior has a lasting effect on participants at the dance.

Although religion isn't a controlling theme among the Hispanics and Indians that populate *Animal Dreams* (1990), Kingsolver illustrates the pervasiveness of thoughts about deity. Of particular worth is Codi Noline's feeling of sanctity as she enters the sacred confines of Canyon de Chelly and hears Loyd Peregrina's stories of Spider Woman and her importance to local tribes. Rather than a lesson in complicated theology, Codi reacts to the majesty of nature, which impresses visitors with its austerity and beauty. From responses of the first canyon dwellers came a mythic series that clarified the relationship between humans and landscape and furthered the Indian philosophy of reverence for earth.

Kingsolver introduces more complex figures on Christmas Day. While Codi and Loyd look out on a December Corn Dance at Santa Rosalia Pueblo, she absorbs the prayerful postures and the value of kachinas both as native spirits and as human actors playing the parts of divine beings. The koshari, an entertainer from a holy clown society, lightens the tone of worship with pranks, buffoonery, and satire. Loyd interprets for Codi the source of his belief: "The spirits have been good enough to let us live here and use the utilities, and we're saying: We know how nice you're being … and we'll try to be good guests" (p. 239). He explains that the importance of the festival is its ability to restore balance in human thinking and behavior. As a gesture to Codi's worry over Hallie in a troubled Central American land, Loyd sends a small eagle dancer winging to the south, a kinetic liturgy that seeks heaven's blessing.

To Pueblo worship style Codi contrasts the Anglo thinking on God, whom arrogant whites assume gave them earth as "a special little playground" (p. 240). She recalls how the Black Mountain mine fouled the earth with poisons and realizes that "it was such an American story," an allusion to the pollution, land grabbing, extinction of the buffalo, genocide, and rape of the earth that followed European colonization of the New World (*Ibid.*). At the end of a long pilgrimage back to her hometown, dying father, and truncated motherhood, she realigns herself with the forces of nature through two ceremonies, beginning with a free-form funeral for her sister Hallie. Codi also reburies her "knotted bundle" in the backyard and acknowledges an epiphany that "It's what you do that makes your soul" (pp. 331, 334). The physical act of reinterment helps rid her conscience of blame for self-starvation that may have precipitated the death of the fetus. The informal ceremony also serves as a catharsis for Doc Homer, who realizes how much he has loved his daughters without verbalizing their importance to him.

In contrast to the downplaying of religion in Kingsolver's first three novels, the question of short-sighted evangelism dominates much of the action in *The Poisonhood Bible* (1998), a literary *tour de force* in which the author studies the arrogance of religious missions to so-called "heathen" nations. In the text, Leah Price ponders the scenario of "Grandfather God sending the African children to hell for being born too far from a Baptist Church," a reference to a fundamentalist belief that only baptized Christians will be saved from the fires of hell (p. 298). In reference to strict orthodoxy, Brother Fyntan Fowles, a Christ-like missionary, offers a restrained criticism of zealotry: "There are Christians and then there are Christians" (p. 255). In an interview for the Arts & Souls program at Baylor University, Kingsolver indicated her agreement with Fowles's great-hearted approach to sanctity. In her opinion, the most dangerous of religious practitioners are those like Nathan Price, who "reduce [God] to a sound bite" ("Interview").

For Nathan, taking his family to Kilanga in the equatorial Congo is a certainty he grasps like "paying in cash and sticking the receipt in your breast pocket," a sure-fire relief from the guilt that has dogged him since the rest of his company died at Corregidor during World War II (p. 96). He has no inkling that he threatens Kilangan children with death by crocodile when he offers "the Kingdom and the Power and the Glory" of Christendom through baptism in the Kwilu River (p. 174). He fails to understand the nuances of attendance at his services until translator Anatole Ngemba explains that the villagers following Christianity are the *lenzuka*, "people who have shamed themselves or had very bad luck," such as the Boandas, whose children tend to die in infancy (p. 128). According to houseboy Nelson, the congregation of losers includes twin-prone women, lepers, families hard hit by *kakakaka* (enteritis), and killers of a child or clansman. Adah, Nathan's mentally acute daughter, is quick to perceive that Nathan "cannot imagine that he is still merely serving the purpose of cleaning up the streets, as it were" (p. 212).

Kingsolver creates irony and droll humor over apostasy in Nathan's own household. To his dubious wife Orleanna, following him to the mission site is expected of a spouse, but believing his Christian tenets lies beyond her. Faced with the struggle for cleanliness, nutrition, and safety, she ponders: "I could never work out whether we were to view religion as a life-insurance policy or a life sentence" (p. 96). A significant event in her family occurs after Adah survives being stalked by a lion. Because her safety elevates Christianity over the animism of Tata Ndu, the village chief, Adah muses, "One god draws in the breath of life and rises; another god expires" (p. 141). Kingsolver's bit of drollery suggests her belief that human squabbling over the identity of God is more annoying than enlightening.

Orleanna elucidates the dangers of haphazard scriptural interpretation. She attempts to follow Christian teaching by turning to the bible for answers to her misery in Kilanga. After reading the curse on woman in Genesis 3:16, she moans for mercy and confesses, "If it catches you in the wrong frame of mind, the King James Bible can make you want to drink poison in no uncertain terms" (p. 192). Her doubts presage a grand coming-to-knowledge after Africa claims her youngest child, Ruth May, from snakebite. In retrospect, Orleanna blames herself for weakness because she "couldn't step in front of my husband to shelter [the girls] from his scorching light" (*Ibid.*). Leah's revelation that Nathan planned to turn Ruth May's baptism in the Kwilu River into religious grandstanding further diminishes the minister in his family's estimation.

After her success at describing the plight of Kilangans choosing between indigenous beliefs and the teachings of missionaries, Kingsolver used the Polish Jewish–Palestinian Lusa Maluf Landowski in *Prodigal Summer* (2000) to express the difficulties of people born into multiple religious traditions. Lusa's Judaic streak from the paternal side is largely cultural because her father abandoned practicing the faith.

She was left with the active Islam of her mother. As an adult, Lusa has little interest in piety and thinks of herself as a religious mongrel.

To Little Rickie, her nephew, Lusa explains the tenets of Islamic worship, particularly cleansing of the hands before the five-time-daily prayers toward Mecca. At his surprise, she remarks, "You haven't *seen* religious. You're not supposed to touch alcohol or cigarettes, and women cover themselves up totally, all but their eyes" (p. 152). The author's choice of Islamic elements reflects American prejudices and omits such important beliefs as charity toward the poor, monotheism, abstinence and fasting during Ramadan, and the sacred once-in-a-lifetime *hadj*, which combine with ritual prayers to form the five pillars of the faith. Additional tenets for the ideal Muslim include giving up gambling, usury, pork in the diet, sex out of wedlock, and infanticide and cultivating peace and fellowship with all Muslims.

The author uses Lusa as a model of religious compromise that brings out the best in variant ethnic traditions. The trade-offs between her mismatched parents resulted in "[skipping] the guilt-and-punishment stuff" and replacing legalism with festivals involving good food and dancing with relatives (p. 153). Rickie's response to Lusa's tutelage is an immature extreme: "I thought people that didn't believe in God just mostly worshiped the devil and stuff" (*Ibid.*). She upbraids him for ignorant assumptions by reminding him that Arabs and Jews spend more time on theology and less on gossip than the people of Zebulon Valley. She tempers the theological discussion with childhood memories of Id-al-Adha, the post–Ramadan feast, which features milk-fed kid and other memorable recipes.

In bringing together the disparate lives and philosophies of characters, Kingsolver rounds out the tripartite novel by accounting for Deanna Wolfe's love of Nannie Land Rawley, her surrogate mother. Nannie instilled in Deanna an appreciation of nature's ability to grow and adapt. In a discussion of human mating, Nannie uses Deanna and her half-sister Rachel as examples of extremes of human genetics— Deanna with her brilliance and Rachel suffering mental retardation and a faulty heart. The impromptu lesson concludes a description of evolution with a paean to variety in living things: "That was the *world*, honey. That's what we live in. That is God Almighty" (p. 390).

See also **Ledger Fourkiller, Brother Fowles, Nathan Price, stomp dance, Garnett Walker**

• *Further Reading*

Byfield, Ted, and Virginia Byfield. "The Evil Missionary." *Alberta Report/Newsmagazine*, Vol. 26, No. 7, February 8, 1999, p. 35.
"Interview with Barbara Kingsolver." http://www3.baylor.edu:80/Rel_Lit/archives/interviews/kingsolver_intv.html.
Markels, Julian. "Coda: Imagining History in *The Poisonwood Bible*." *Monthly Review Press*, September 2003.

rescue

In tandem with innocence, the theme of rescue recurs in Kingsolver's writings as a height of humanistic attainment. *The Bean Trees* (1988) describes Mattie the tire dealer's role in helping political refugees flee Guatemala and El Salvador and elude immigration officers by passing from one safe house to another. Similar to the Underground Railroad that directed runaway slaves to freedom during the American Civil War, the chain of waystations provides necessities to people who escape persecution with little more to carry with them than memories of terrorism. The rescuer thinks of herself as grandmother to the children of emigrés. Their gifts of drawings reflect the terrors of oppression: "Practically all ... had guns in them somewhere, and huge bullets suspended in air" (p. 146). Adding to the martial atmosphere are "men in turtle-shaped army helmits" and "a helicopter streaming blood," all elements of children's nightmares of the Contra war, which the Reagan administration illegally bankrolled (*Ibid.*). Taylor Greer's selfless act of ferrying a Guatemalan couple to safety attests to her empathy for others, a quality that Mattie encourages.

Several types of rescue activate the novel's non-sequel, *Pigs in Heaven* (1993). The initial event is Turtle Greer's witness of a retarded man's fall into the sluiceway of Hoover Dam. Because she appears on Oprah Winfrey's television show as a rescuer, Annawake Fourkiller presses for custody of the Cherokee child, forcing Taylor to flee Arizona for Seattle, Washington. The choice to run rather than stand and fight is problematic. As Kingsolver noted in "Widows at the Wheel," a 1989 book review for the *Los Angeles Times:* "Beauty, let's face it, is there or it's not, but adventure is in the eye of the beholder" (p. 1). Without the skills or connections to locate a job paying a living wage, Taylor finds herself seeking advice from her mother and from boyfriend Jax Thibodeaux, who offers plane fare home. With the pride of an Appalachian native, Taylor states her position on rescue and self-reliance: "I always knew I could count on myself. If I bail out here, I won't even have that" (p. 247).

In between the two novels, Kingsolver published *Animal Dreams* (1990), a story of self-rescue. In the exposition of the father figure, Dr. Homer Noline grapples with shifting time zones in his head after he is stricken with Alzheimer's disease. He imagines rescuing his two daughters, Codi and Hallie, who spend a half day by themselves in a flooded arroyo of Tortoise Canyon trying to save seven coyote pups. When he arrives, they scream with "mouths stretched open like the mouths of fledgling birds" (p. 20). Like their ambitious plans, the paper bag holding their store of prickly pears shreds, leaving the sisters weeping and fearful that the babies died. The episode characterizes extreme idealism as the downfall of the neophyte rescuer.

In college, Hallie perpetuates her role as savior by welcoming to her apartment Central American refugees—"kids scared senseless, people with all kinds of damage" (p. 35). The scenario prefigures her adult crusade for Nicaraguan farm families, which ends tragically in her roadside execution at the hand of rebels. In a first letter home, she describes the Guatemalan army's "new scorched-earth campaign," which sends people "running across the border with the clothes on their backs and their hearts in their throats" (p. 88). To Hallie, American children are blessed with "the privilege of a safe life" (*Ibid.*). The *doppelgänger* outlook of her sister Codi suggests the anti-idealistic approach to terror: "To run hell for leather in the other direction" (p. 88). In the opinion of Bill Mahin, reviewer for the *Chicago Tribune*, Codi considers Hallie a saint, a "grand-scale heroine," but later acknowledges in people like Codi a "daily heroism, in our seemingly ordinary acts and choices…. Heroes are no longer beyond reach, unattainable. They are us" (Mahin).

Codi proves her own heroism in numerous scenarios, beginning with dinner at Doña Althea's restaurant by saving seven-month-old Mason Domingos from choking on a pinto bean. The instinctive protocol for unblocking a windpipe attests to Codi's background in medicine, which she downplays as "no big deal" (p. 117). Her sense of human safety impels her to lecture on birth control to teens likely to conceive babies before they are ready for parenthood or marriage. Finally, she begins a no-win campaign to save Doc Homer from Alzheimer's disease and confesses, "We're the blind leading the blind here" (p. 153). The breaking point of her resolves comes from Doc's admission about losing his nerve "a dozen times a day" (p. 156). Kingsolver implies that Codi's willingness to tackle the impossible discloses a heroism that she is too self-punishing to perceive.

The concept of rescue takes on central importance in *The Poisonwood Bible* (1998), in which a misguided missionary attempts to save the Congolese of Kilanga village from heathenism. The Reverend Nathan Price is so inept at understanding himself that he is unable to preserve his family or his ministry. Because he sees himself as the elevated prophet, he fails to communicate with people on a human level. The decline of membership in the African community reaches a critical point the night of the army ant invasion. While Orleanna tries to carry Ruth May and lead Adah toward the river, the minister uses widespread terror as a tutorial opportunity to impress on the unsaved the heroism of Moses during the ten plagues of Egypt — river water polluted with blood, frogs, gnats, flies, cattle disease, boils, hail, locusts, darkness, and the deaths of all firstborn sons. With no thought to family or neighbors, Nathan spouts his scriptural message over the turmoil in Kilanga's streets.

According to Adah, the family's least able child, the powers of the Prices to guard and preserve a family collapse irrevocably during the plague of ants. As she stumbles and rolls over and over in the crush of fleeing villagers, Anatole Ngemba, the local schoolmaster, carries her to safety at the shore of the Kwilu River. Face to face with Orleanna, Adah stares at the woman who left her behind and experiences her "life's dark center, the moment when growing up ended and the long downward slope toward death began" (p. 306). For all its terror, the night is an epiphany that prepares Adah for the final retreat from Africa in Book Five, "Exodus," when her mother clings to her hand with parental determination to return her safely home. Radiant from her mother's love, Adah knew that Orleanna "would drag me out of Africa if it was her last living act as a mother" (p. 414).

Kingsolver's female characters vary in their response to withdrawal from Kilanga. Rachel leaves with joy by accepting a plane ride to Johannesburg with mercenary Eeben Axelroot. Orleanna, battering her conscience for Ruth May's death from snakebite, leaves Africa in body, but not in spirit. A model of forgiveness and filial devotion, Adah remains at Orleanna's side in Georgia and helps her return to normal life. Leah, Adah's twin, whom Anatole rescues from malaria, has the best experience with rescue because she is willing to cherish a Congolese man. She finds herself enveloped in a love that lessens the burden of being "a foreigner in the eye of a storm" (p. 416).

Still living under straitened means after their marriage during the Congo's revolution and seizure by Mobutu Sese Seko, Leah survives Anatole's imprisonment, which requires a retreat to Mission Notre Dame de Douleur in the Central African Republic. Under the name Soeur Liselin, nurse trainee, she lives among Benedictine nuns until her family reunites in Kinshasa. Even after marriage, Leah bears guilt for being rescued and leaving Ruth May behind in a jungle grave. Anatole continues to be his wife's savior by delivering their fourth son in a hasty birthing at the roadside and by lulling her during nightly recurrences of malaria and talking "all night to stave off the bad dreams" (p. 520). The events confirm that rescuer is a character type that best describes Anatole.

With *Prodigal Summer* (2000), Kingsolver stresses the importance of self-rescue. The intertwined stories of three female protagonists— a forest ranger, an entomologist, and an orchardist — recognizes strengths in each that makes them equal to challenge. Nannie Land Rawley, a strong-minded ecologist and grower of organic apples, takes hold of her crotchery neighbor, Garnett S. Walker, III, and delivers him from spells of dizziness with a simple hands-on method. He acknowledges that she was equally tough in the matter of bringing up a fatherless retarded daughter, Rachel Carson Rawley, sired by Ray Dean Wolfe. Wolfe's first daughter, Deanna Wolfe, wildlife protector for Zebulon Mountain, is the second protagonist. She exerts vigilance and care to assure that coyotes will return to the eastern wilderness. When she recognizes early signs of pregnancy in herself, she abandons her job to return to Nannie, her foster mother, and accept mothering until the baby is born.

Kingsolver seems to reserve the most respect for Lusa Maluf Landowski, the widowed entomologist, who finds herself husbandless and saddled with farm debt. After making friends with his hostile sisters, she discovers a way to avoid planting tobacco and still make a profit. By raising goats for slaughter, she establishes her independence and manages enough energy and funds to accept a niece and nephew, who need mothering. She explains to their dying mother, "It just seems right to do that" (p. 383). Lusa's chutzpah, like the self-effacing courage of Taylor Greer, suggests elements of the author's personal philosophy, which extols self-reliant women.

See also **journey motif, Anatole Ngemba, Nathan Price, survival, Mama Bekwa Tataba**

• *Further Reading*

Mahin, Bill. "Review." *Chicago Tribune*, June 23, 1989.
Pate, Nancy. "Faith in the Future: Kingsolver Finds Hope in Natural World." *Orlando Sentinel*, April 7, 2002, p. F8.

Ruiz, Lou Ann

The single mother and former employee of Three Bears Day School in *The Bean Trees* (1988), Lou Ann Ruiz is the loving, motherly foil of Turtle Greer's abusive aunt Sue. Lou Ann's husband, ironically named Angel Ruiz, leaves home on Halloween in her eighth month of pregnancy to join a rodeo in Montana, leaving her to face impending childbirth alone. Her pregnancy and the possibility of giving birth to a daughter epitomize the shadow that engulfs unwanted women from conception. As the single parent of an infant, she describes her husbandless predicament as "just lumping along here trying to get by" (p. 76). In "Mormon Memories," a 1989 book review for the *Los Angeles Times*, Kingsolver sums up Lou Ann's situation as a gender dilemma: "The conservative tradition promises women a lifetime of safety if only they will stand by their men, then deals out the cards of abandonment and poverty" (p. 13). The author's acerbic comment explains her dedication to woman- and child-centered ideals.

Kingsolver develops the theme of self-denigration in women who allow society's devaluation of the less-than-perfect specimen to rob them of self-worth. In Appalachian style, Lou Ann compensates for Angel's absence by calling on mountain folk, Granny and Ivy Logan, Lou Ann's grandmother and mother, to make the three-day Greyhound trip from Kentucky to help out. The circle of women who love and support Lou Ann and infant includes Taylor Greer, who believes that Lou Ann chooses to err on the side of caring too much for her baby boy Dwayne Ray by reading about disasters and being prepared for the unlikely. Another stalwart female, Angel's Mexican mother, speaks no English, but manages to exonerate her daughter-in-law of fault for the failed marriage and values her as "worth five or six of Angel" (p. 229).

Significant to Kingsolver's canon is the placement of Lou Ann among poverty-stricken workers who can't support their families. The author rebuts beliefs that the poor are responsible for their own sufferings by picturing Lou Ann's sincere efforts to make a home for Dwayne Ray and her teamwork with Taylor to care for Turtle. Of the power of fiction, Kingsolver explained,

> In this story, you move through that woman's life in real time. You hear the things she hears, you touch the things she touches, you think her thoughts, and you watch the face of your child and you struggle with the pain and shame you feel because you're doing all you can and it's still not enough ["An Address"].

The author's identity with Lou Ann as a struggling single mother enlightens readers as it opens the way for empathy: "When you finish that book..., you still have that mother inside you somewhere" (*Ibid.*).

Ruiz genealogy

The Ruiz family tree illustrates Kingsolver's interest in intercultural marriage and the melding of racial, ethnic, and religious customs and traditions:

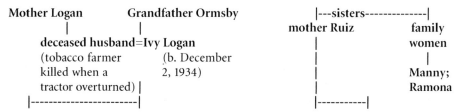

brother=She-Wolf Who Hunts by the First Light	Lou Ann =Angel Ruiz (rodeo rider) (married ca. 1976; separated October 31, 1980)	two brothers (moving to San Diego)
│ four daughters with Eskimo names	│ Dwayne Ray Ruiz (b. Jan. 1, 1981)	

seeds

Kingsolver applies her training in biology by creating images in nature that parallel human conception and growth. In *The Bean Trees* (1988), she turns mundane plant propagation into a miraculous form of education. An urban garden milieu in Tucson offers Turtle Greer, a traumatized three-year-old, a means to learn and communicate. Avoiding human interaction, she focuses on seeds, purple beans, and flowers in Mattie's junkyard garden, where nasturtiums grow out of a rusty Thunderbird, cabbages and lettuce grow out of old tires, and cherry tomatoes vine over a tepee of CB antennas. The motif of turning trash into treasure characterizes Mattie's intent to make the most of her assets to help distressed people.

The value of seeds to Turtle is significant. After she learns to talk, her childhood reading focuses on a Burpee seed catalog and a storybook, *Old MacDonald Had an Apartment House* (1969), written by Judith Barrett and illustrated by Ron Barrett. The comfort of beans returns after the child's reenactment at Lake o' the Cherokees of her mother's burial. With the free-form thinking of a pre-schooler, she adds to the heap of dirt a handful of pine needles and says of her handiwork, "Grow beans" (p. 211). In the novel's falling action, Taylor takes Turtle to the Oklahoma City library and reads that wisteria vines are legumes that thrive in poor soil. The secret to their miraculous profusion is rhizobia, a hidden network of enzymes, a metaphor for Turtle's human safety net, which enables her to overcome child abuse and assault by a mugger.

As symbols of human connectedness, vegetable seeds parallel the sowing of human concern for abandoned and fatherless children and for illegal aliens, regardless of how relationships form or upon what basis they are maintained—friends, strangers, rescuers, roommates, grandparents, employers and employees, doctor and patient, social worker and client, or couples and their children. Turtle and Taylor evolve a strong sense of family by including Esperanza, Esteban, Mattie, Mrs. Parsons, Edna Poppy, Dwayne Ray, and Lou Ann Ruiz. Like a collection of vegetable seeds, they complement each other to form the soup that is the human family. Turtle's perceptions of life, as echoed in her silences and her vegetable litany, comprise both good and bad, including the aborted assault on her under the bean trees in the park. The triumph of wholesome beans over menace epitomizes born-in strength, the will to flourish that keeps Turtle centered in her own love garden.

A prominent image in Kingsolver's fiction, seeds also demonstrate the human intrusion in nature. In *The Poisonwood Bible* (1998), the stubborn, unteachable Nathan Price overrules African planting styles by flattening the mounds Mama Tataba raises around his Kentucky Wonder bean seeds, squash, and Halloween pumpkins, and by returning his garden to parallel rows. The level sowing leaves tender seedlings at the mercy of a Congo downpour, creating an image of his cut-and-dried theology, which lacks the humanity of his forerunner, Brother Fowles. Similar to his gardening method is his inept missionarying, which begins with the premise that he is saving Africans from ignorance and idol worship.

Because of his superior attitude toward Kilangan natives, Nathan denigrates Mama Tataba's knowledge with patronizing: "She's only trying to help, in her way" (p. 41). His intention, according to garden helper Leah, is to demonstrate an American miracle of grand harvest and supply of vegetables and seeds, but the subtext reveals his true purpose as self-glorification. Ultimately, a July monsoon gouges out the "Reverend Farmer's flat-as-Kansas beds" (p. 63). The lesson learned, he returns to the garden to hoe up rectangular raised beds "exactly the length and width of burial mounds" (*Ibid.*). The image prophesies destruction and death following the social and political deluge that turns his naive fundamentalist mission into catastrophe.

See also **beans**

• *Further Reading*

Carman, Diane. "Kingsolver Hits Stride in Africa; Missionary's Muddling Creates Cultural Disaster." *Denver Post*, October 18, 1998.

self-esteem

Self-esteem is an element of survival in Kingsolver's most resilient characters, as demonstrated by Taylor Greer and her mother Alice in *The Bean Trees* (1988) and *Pigs in Heaven* (1993), striking workers in the feminist documentary *Holding the Line: Women in the Great Arizona Mine Strike of 1983* (1989), and Orleanna and Adah Price, a downtrodden mother and handicapped daughter in *The Poisonwood Bible* (1998). One of the author's major self-bashers is Codi Noline, the failed medical student in *Animal Dreams* (1990). In reflecting over three decades of life, she compares herself mercilessly with her younger sister Hallie, a volunteer agronomist in Nicaragua. To Codi, there is no way to acquire Hallie's panache and mystical humanism. Recalling school days among the Mexican-Americans of Grace, Arizona, Codi recalls herself as "ugly and embarrassed to be alive" (p. 259). By carrying teen burdens into her early thirties, she exhibits an unhealthy absorption in unresolved issues.

In outlook, Codi takes the fatalistic approach in mourning her "stupidity in trusting that life could be kind" (p. 261). Although she teaches vulnerable teens about birth control, tends her ailing father, and aids the town of Grace, Arizona, in recovery from river pollution, she gives herself no credit for tackling serious problems with energy and ingenuity. A surprising boost to her self-image is the serendipitous letter from the school board renewing her contract and lauding her for innovation and relevance. Codi considers the letter and a vote of teacher of the year a "gold star" (p. 290). Her lover, Loyd Peregrina, interprets the compliment as proof that "you're real good at what you do" (p. 292).

With *The Poisonwood Bible*, Kingsolver moves into more serious emotional stunting in the late middle age of Orleanna Price. Like wives and mothers of the 1950s, she once believed that marriage and children were the pinnacles of her being. Valuing Nathan Price, a seriously flawed husband, who returned from World War II with daunting battle fatigue, she observes, "Nathan was changed, I could see, but he only seemed more devout, and it was hard to name the ruin in that" (p. 197). She follows him to a disastrous mission in the Congo and continues supporting him through a litany of failures, which include rejection by Congolese church members and an invasion of army ants that destroys the family's foodstuffs and devours their hens. The false face that she wears turns on her, forcing a showdown with her principles of right and truth.

At a cataclysmic moment in Nathan's worsening arrogance, brutality, and bull-headedness, Orleanna chooses children over husband. The last straw, the tragic death of Ruth May from snakebite, leaves the mother grieving for her youngest and unable to maintain a facade of approval for Nathan's foolishness. Engulfed with sadness, she flees from suffering but discovers "It wasn't the spirit but just a body that moved me from one place to another" (p. 382). On return to Georgia with Adah, the handicapped daughter, Orleanna berates herself for leaving Leah behind to recover from malaria and for abandoning Ruth May's pitiful grave mound at the jungle's edge. In later years, Orleanna relives that dreadful day when she laid out Ruth May's body and worked like a drudge at emptying the house of its furnishings. Of woman's lot, Orleanna mourns: "We whistle while Rome burns, or we scrub the floor, depending" (p. 383). By seeing herself as the perennial victim of patriarchy, she limits her ability to recover.

Looking back rather than forward, Orleanna shreds her self-esteem for staying seventeen months in a losing situation. She queries Ruth May's spirit, "I wonder what you'll name my sin: Complicity? Loyalty? Stupefaction?" (*Ibid.*). Reuniting with her African daughters, Rachel and Leah, elevates Orleanna to the status of mother to adult girls and grandmother to four grandsons. Still, her self-confidence shattered, she looks toward the ocean that separates her retirement home on Sanderling Island, Georgia, from Africa and mutters, "I have my own story, and increasingly in my old age it weighs on me" (p. 8).

See also **Barbie, exclusion, *Holding the Line: Women in the Great Arizona Mine Strike of 1983*, Motherhood, Lou Ann Ruiz, Deanna Wolfe**

• *Further Reading*

Hollands, Barbara. "Languid Eco-Drama." *New Zealand Dispatch*, June 2, 2001.

Small Wonder

A beacon of comfort begun the day after the 9/11 catastrophe, Kingsolver's *Small Wonder* (2002) is a lyric essay collection covering twenty-three topics ranging from raising chickens, rearing teens, rescuing an Iranian child lost in a cave and found by a bear, treasuring the Grand Canyon, and avoiding television. For the author, as an antidote to overwhelming sorrow, writing essays became the equivalent of donating blood in a crisis, an image suggesting heart-felt emotions for the nation's anguish. Her intension was to "carve something hugely important into a small enough amulet to fit inside a reader's most sacred psychic pocket" (Ciolkowski). Strongly liberal themes elicited a variety of critical descriptors ranging from gentle and thought-provoking to insanely naive. Analyst Harriet Malinowitz summarized the compendium as "sometimes blandly laudable and consequently a bit toothless" (Malinowitz, p. 36). A harsher view from Anne Gibson of the *New Zealand Herald* summarized the collection as a "self-righteous concoction of anti-technology, anti–American ramblings" (Gibson).

On a more positive note, other critics found emotional sustenance in Kingsolver's essays. Polly Paddock, book editor for the *Charlotte Observer* described the collection as "a delightful, lucid gathering of 'parables and reveries' to dip into during a troubling time" (Paddock). Drusilla Modjeska, reviewer for *The Australian*, exonerated Kingsolver's tone and purpose: "While there is something earnest, almost evangelical, about her tone and her call to fellow Americans to look beyond their immediate emotional responses to last September's attack, you can't deny the genuine depth of her feeling" (Modjeska). Pamela LeBlanc championed Kingsolver's courage in fighting America's "strip-mining mentality" (LeBlanc). LeBlanc summarized the essay series as a klaxon "warning us about what our country is doing to its natural resources and the people who share the world with us" (*Ibid.*). LeBlanc came close to summarizing Kingsolver's ethnical foundations, which undergird her novels, journalistic writings, book reviews, and verse as well as the essays in *Small Wonder*.

• *Further Reading*

Ciolkowski, Laura. "Review: *Small Wonder*." *New York Times*, May 5, 2002.
Gibson, Anne. "Review: *Small Wonder*." *New Zealand Herald*, October 1, 2002.
LeBlanc, Pamela. "Kingsolver Reacts to the Pain of Sept. 11 with Small Wonders and Big Messages." *Austin American-Statesman*, April 21, 2002.
Malinowitz, Harriet. "Down-Home Dissident." *Women's Review of Books*, Vol. 19, No. 10–11, July 2002, pp. 36–37.
Modjeska, Drusilla. "Writing as Incest." *The Australian*, September 28, 2002.
Paddock, Polly. "Pages Hold Hope for the World." *Charlotte Observer*, April 14, 2002.
Pate, Nancy. "Faith in the Future: Kingsolver Finds Hope in Natural World." *Orlando Sentinel*, April 7, 2002, p. F8.

Spider Woman

The myth of Spider Woman, a symbol of human creativity, is anchored to Canyon de Chelly National Monument in Arizona, one of the world's holiest places predating Columbus by millennia. In *Animal Dreams* (1990), Codi Noline realizes the sanctity of the stratified walls to Indians: "The place did not so much inspire religion as it seemed to be religion itself" (p. 210). Elegant twin sandstone verticals, the world's tallest free-standing columns, serve the Hopi and Navajo as the residence of Tse-che-nako or Spider Woman, a vengeful cannibal who nets naughty children and devours them. To the Pueblo, she is Sussistanako or Thinking Woman, the planner of the universe who formed the earth and its people, who were born through a birth canal called a sipapu and nourished on corn milk. Her role as a spinner explains the umbilical cord, the life tether that binds infant to mother. Because of the connection between Spider Woman and birth, natives hold her in reverence as a cosmic mother figure, the foundation of human life.

In the womb-like canyon walls of Four Corners, native dwellers first learned life skills—fire-making, hunting, healing, gardening, weaponry, worship, and carving sacred pictographs. At Spider Rock, the mythic wisewoman, mate of the sun god Tawa, created the Navajo and taught them pottery-making and weaving on the cosmic loom. To the Anasazi-Hopi, Spider Woman resembles the Greek Apollo, god of light and life and disseminator of mystic chant, ritual, song, and dance. Loyd Peregrina, Codi's Apache-Pueblo lover, summarizes the myth's importance to Navajo women: "One day she lassoed two Navajo ladies with her web and pulled them up there and taught them how to weave rugs" (p. 210). The scenario suggests the value of the female enclave to the preparation of women for doing their share of the division of labor.

Kingsolver uses the myth of Spider Woman as a subtextual explanation of Loyd's vulnerability. He mentions that, to the Tewa, Spider Woman's paired spires were the home of a grandmotherly deity who reared sets of human twins. Loyd explains the need for fostering: "When twins are born people say there'll be a poor rainy season or grasshoppers or some darn thing" (p. 207). The link to ancient customs that required parents to abandon twins to relieve the tribe of bad luck and to Loyd's personal grief at the death of his twin Leander in a bar brawl supplies two reasons for Loyd's reverence for the culture heroine.

• *Further Reading*

Bierhorst, John, ed. *The Way of the Earth: Native America and the Environment.* New York: William Morrow, 1994.

Kelley, Klara Bonsack, and Harris Francis. *Navajo Sacred Places.* Bloomington: Indiana University Press, 1994.

McCoy, Ronald. "Spider Woman's Legacy: The Art of Navajo Weaving." *World & I*, September 1990.

McPherson, Robert S. *Sacred Land, Sacred View: Navajo Perceptions of the Four Corners.* Salt Lake City, Utah: Signature Books, 1992.

Milne, Courtney. *Sacred Places in North America: A Journey Into the Medicine Wheel.* New York: Stewart, Tabori & Chang, 1995.

Reichard, Gladys A. *Spider Woman.* Tucson: University of New Mexico Press, 1997.

Stillwater, Cash

On the advice of a female Alaskan attorney, Kingsolver added to *Pigs in Heaven* (1993) a positive model of the Cherokee spokesperson for tribe and family. The resulting shaman and beadworker, Cash Stillwater, according to the author, fulfilled the role of "integrating the needs of the individual and the collective" ("A Conversation"). The son of a healer, Cash came of age during a difficult time for Cherokees when the government sent their children to white-run boarding schools, which Alice Greer describes as "prison for children" (p. 257). To Cash, native students took shape in dormitories like biscuits lined up in a pan. At age sixteen, he learned nothing about his father's death on New Year's day 1940 until January 17, when he returned home to assist his mother. The cruel severance of Cash from his family accounts in part for his failures as husband and father.

Like many of the author's *dramatis personae,* Cash is a restless fugitive. Gnawing at his contentment is the memory of a beloved wife, who died of cancer in 1979, and of their daughter Alma, who killed herself shortly afterward, when her daughter Lacey was only three years old. He blames himself indirectly for not knowing what to tell them or how to cope with adversity. He sets up a jewelry-making business during a two-year sojourn in Jackson Hole, Wyoming, but retreats from the tourist-motivated area after his employer kills himself at his desk. The second suicide sends Cash back to Oklahoma in search of the peace of an inclusive tribal community.

Kingsolver creates in Cash a human figure who is honest about his shortcomings. He confesses his earlier error in judgment: "I had this idea you can get ahead by being in a place where everybody's rich" (p. 255). The author suggests that Cash's thinking is better suited to materialistic whites than Indians. After a three-year jaunt away from home, he is happy to resettle in the run-down burg of Heaven, Oklahoma. The author accounts for his contentment as the result of tribal ritual and family inclusiveness in a community where he can count on "a place at the table" (p. 112).

As a means of assuring Turtle Greer, the unwanted Cherokee child, of the ethnic grounding and love of two devoted grandparents, Kingsolver makes an unlikely match between Alice Greer and Cash. By pointing the intrusive Letty Stillwater toward the potential for a loving mate for her brother, Annawake Fourkiller stands back and allows the nosy sister and community pressures to bring Alice and Cash together. Without warning, he invites her to pick huckleberries and to attend the Saturday night stomp dance. His optimism and candor impress her by negating the doldrums of marriage to Harland Elleston, a man who lives vicariously through television. Cash's impromptu proposal during a council hearing shocks Alice, but ends the problem of sending a small girl to Oklahoma three months of the year to live with virtual strangers. At Cash's log cabin, he moves gracefully from stove to sink making *kunutche,* which requires the pounding of nuts into powder to add to hominy, a union of two compatible foods that reflects the couple's human marriage.

See also **stomp dance**

- *Further Reading*

"A Conversation with Barbara Kingsolver." http://www.readinggroupguides.com/guides/
    animal_dreams-author.asp.

stomp dance

In the falling action of *Pigs in Heaven* (1993), the novelist points toward ritual as an answer to the question of how to restore love to the three Greer females, Alice,

Taylor, and Turtle. Driven away in Cash Stillwater's penny-colored pickup near midnight on a Saturday night, Alice arrives at her first Cherokee stomp dance in a clearing near Heaven, Oklahoma. The organizing principle of native American symbolism is the circle of life, family, tribe, and earth cycles. At the core of the dance floor lies the log tepee holding an altar. Burning brightly are the remnants of a fire dating to their ancestral home in the Appalachians before the Trail of Tears uprooted them to Indian Territory. A pulsating heart as alive as the Cherokee spirit, the fire centers a four-point compass of logs that reminds all of their place in nature. To Alice, the flame is "like a quiet consciousness presiding" (p. 270). Kingsolver absolves the old antagonisms between white newcomers and American aborigines with a mutual commitment to the source of heat and light: "The beloved old fire that has lived through everything since the beginning, that someone carried over the Trail of Tears, and ... someone will carry home and bring back again to the church of ever was and ever shall be, if we only take care of it" (p. 272).

A merger of themes takes shape as several hundred participants gather around the fire, listen prayerfully to Ledger Fourkiller's homily, and join the circles that shuffle around the fire. Alice perceives the movements as graceful and restrained, with only the shackle-bearing girls making noise with their terrapin-shell rattles. Joined by a drummer, the dancers progress to "music that sounds like the woods," growing hypnotic in its cycle of repetitions (p. 269). When Sugar urges her old friend into the line, Alice experiences an epiphany, an appreciation of community participation that thrills her from fingertips to the roof of her mouth, which she characterizes as "a Stairmaster [workout] with a spiritual element" (p. 270). By 2:00 A.M., she feels herself "completely included" in a fairy tale aura that brings peace and an ineffable understanding (p. 271).

See also **Cherokee, community, Ledger Fourkiller**

• *Further Reading*

Jackson, Jason Baird. "The Opposite of Powwow: Ignoring and Incorporating the Intertribal War Dance in the Oklahoma Stomp Dance Community." *Plains Anthropologist*, Vol. 48, No. 187, 2003, pp. 237–253.

survival

Threats to vulnerable creatures permeate Kingsolver's fiction. She introduces the motif in *The Bean Trees* (1988) with the catatonic states into which toddler Turtle Greer retreats to escape physical abuse and the recreation of her mother's burial by playacting the scene with a doll. On a grander scale, the novelist depicts Mattie the tire dealer as savior and foster mother to Turtle as well as to streams of illegal aliens. Taylor, Turtle's mother, encounters a pathetic Spanish-speaking woman at the apartment over the tire dealership and is stunned by the toll survival has taken on her frame: "I had never before seen anyone whose entire body looked sad. Her skin just seemed to hang from her" (p. 147).

Involvement with the rescue of two of Mattie's aliens, Estevan and Esperanza, a Mayan couple fleeing political persecution and the kidnap of their daughter Ismene, introduces Taylor to the terrible price people pay to cling to life. She agrees to ferry the couple northeast to Oklahoma and concludes the journey at the Pottawatomie Presbyterian Church, a waystation and safe house. Far from home with only a small suitcase of personal items, Estevan states his intention to survive the tragedy in Central America: "Think of us back in Guatemala with our families. Having another baby" (p. 219). Idealistically, he maintains the will to live and looks forward to a time "when the world is different from now" (Ibid.).

In Animal Dreams (1990), the author returns to the theme of survival, which she examines in one main character. In Grave, Arizona, interlinking threads of survival and death entrap Codi Noline in a difficult time in her life. In peripheral action, her lover, Loyd Peregrina, tells her about the killing of twin infants in early Indian practice and confides that he and his brother Leander were identical twins. To express the hardships of his childhood, Loyd describes his father, an Apache from Ghost River, as a skilled breeder of fighting cocks, which regularly slice and pierce each other in the ring with their talons. In a childhood memory of his parent's disrespect for life, Loyd recalls how the father drowned six mongrel coyote pups in a cement sack. Because the seventh hid and survived, Loyd adopted him and named him Jack, a macho name that suits the dog's toughness. Because of Jack's loyalty and spunk, Loyd and Codi reward him with affection.

The loss of life in Animal Dreams weighs heavily on Codi, who turns to Loyd and community women for solace. Following the execution of her sister Hallie in Nicaragua, Codi leads two ceremonies to close miserable chapters in her life, beginning with a free-form funeral for Hallie. Codi moves on to other unfinished business, the reinterment of her stillborn child from the arroyo in Tortoise Canyon to the garden of her mother Alice, who died when Codi was three. The will to survive multiple tragedies helps Codi cope with Doc Homer's decline and death from Alzheimer's disease. Kingsolver stresses Codi's mettle three years later when she accompanies Viola Domingos into Gracela Canyon to celebrate All Souls' Day with festive bunches of marigolds and creek rock to outline Doc Homer's grave. Codi abandons her former despair to adopt a new attitude toward survival: "It was something like tucking children into bed. I was their historian and their guardian angel" (p. 339). Slowing her movements on the steep hillside is the fatigue of early pregnancy, a promise of the continuation of the Noline line in the children of Codi and Loyd.

The novelist offered her most stirring comments on survival in The Poisonwood Bible (1998). At the height of danger to a Congolese village, she characterizes a fire surround as the epitome of threat to animals, which hunters intend to kill and eat. Like the primates and bushbucks that attempt to leap the flames, Orleanna Price and her daughters resolve to live through the family's failed mission to the Congo. After the youngest, Ruth May, dies of snakebite and the Reverend Nathan Price loses touch with reality, Orleanna realizes that it is her duty to free herself and two of her three living daughters, from certain death in equatorial Africa. In a driving rain and resultant muck, Orleanna leads her handicapped daughter Adah and Leah, the twin suffering malaria, toward Bulungu. The mother admits, "By instinct rather than will,

I stayed alive" (p. 382). Her statement links her to jungle animals, who rely on inborn compulsions to sustain them.

Taking courage from the daily example of Mama Mwanza, a severely handicapped Kilangan housewife, Orleanna joins two village women on the way upstream along the Kwilu River. Battling rain, fatigue, and mosquitoes, the women shelter at the hut of Mama Boanda's parents, where the gift of a boiled egg seems like treasure. Leah is so ill that her "mind ached like a broken bone" (p. 393). Her memories of the extended flight from the jungle and Anatole Ngemba's treatment of her fever with boiled concoctions merges with the memory of his kisses and their emerging love. Kingsolver fuses the two, love and healing, as Leah's source of survival. She returns the favor during her husband's two prison sentences by keeping the family together and awaiting Anatole's safe return.

In retrospect, the four Price women react individually to the threat of living with Nathan as they do to their clutch at life without him. Rachel, the most easily rescued, makes her way to Johannesburg with Eeben Axelroot, a bush pilot and mercenary. Leah, a bride-to-be at age sixteen, clings to Anatole as savior and eventual husband. Adah and Orleanna, who make their way home to Georgia by truck and a mercy airlift, are too traumatized by Africa to perceive that they are safely delivered to their hometown of Bethlehem. In a reversal of the Virgin Mary's flight from Bethlehem with the Christ Child in Matthew 3:19–21, Orleanna brings Adah safely home, where the single twin grasps at the realization that her mother chose her as the one to rescue.

Kingsolver extends the terrifying flight from Africa in memories too dire to dismiss. The mental anguish and regrets that impede Orleanna's contentment cause her to "[want] to wash herself clean, but she clings to her clay and her dust" (p. 493). Her retirement to Sanderling Island allows Adah, like Leah, to return the gesture of rescue. It is Adah who divulges the facts of Nathan's death and who visits monthly to walk the beach with Orleanna and to treat the results of "schistosomiasis, Guinea worms, and probably tuberculosis" (p. 531). Despite Adah's faithful ministrations, it is the mystic return of Ruth May's spirit that bears healing after war and border closings keep Orleanna from closing the door on the past by returning to the jungle grave to honor her dead child with a marker. The hospitable spirit offers peace and relieves her mother of pain by pointing out, "The teeth at your bones are your own, the hunger is yours, forgiveness is yours" (p. 543). Ruth May's ghost directs her mother toward the beneficent symbol of light.

See also **child abuse, crime, rescue**

Tataba, Mama Bekwa

A friendly Congolese woman in Kilanga in central Africa in *The Poisonwood Bible* (1998), Mama Bekwa Tataba is the maternal rescuer and stabilizer of the Price family during their disastrous sojourn. Small, half-blind, and jet black, she holds her arms like wings and walks with regal grace, a suggestion of her self-assurance, a quality she shares with Mattie in *The Bean Trees* (1988), Viola Domingos and Doña Althea in *Animal Dreams* (1990), Angie Buster and Alice Greer in *Pigs in Heaven* (1993), and

Nannie Land Rawley in *Prodigal Summer* (2000). Mama Tataba aids Orleanna Price and her daughters as she had Brother Fyntan Fowles, the former missionary for six years. Daily, she tends to jobs common to the jungle outback — hauling water, supplying splits to the cook shed, making a spread from groundnuts and butter from goat fat, cleaning kerosene lamps, freshening the outhouse with ash, and killing hookworms and snakes. In counterpoint to labor, she mutters during the unending tasks of cleaning and cooking for the family and stops to slap Orleanna's hand before she can light a fire of *bängala* (poisonwood) sticks, which would have produced a toxic smoke. According to Rachel, who calls the housekeeper her "Mama Tater Tots," Mama Tataba is best at haggling for dinner meats and at firing up the stove to roast the entree, usually tenderized antelope meat (p. 51). The family does not fully appreciate well-rounded meals until Mama Tataba has abandoned them and famine sets in during a lengthy drought.

In the view of scholar Sally Gabb, Mama Tataba "[recognizes] the blind ineptitude of these pale invaders," yet does what she can to simplify their acculturation to the Congo (Gabb). Like others of her race, she has wisdom to offer the inexperienced newcomers to equatorial Africa, which she distributes in pidgin English. She drills Orleanna in Kikongo words, pampers the girls, and "[curses] our immortal souls as evenhandedly as she [nourishes] our bodies" (p. 94). She introduces the overconfident Nathan Price to dangers of poisonwood sap and to African-style planting in hills rather than rows, a necessity in thin jungle soil. When he disobeys, with the patience of a mother, she returns the vegetable plot into a neat arrangement of raised beds, a method of directing monsoon rains away from seedlings. The irony of her forgiveness of the willful missionary is evident in his failure of extending the same gesture to his parishioners.

Unlike the Price females, Mama Tataba is not cowed by the minister's bluster. After Nathan delivers his first August sermon, she shocks the family by chastising him for suggesting a river baptism among crocodiles, which is the crux of his difficulty among Kilangans. With the dignity of a citizen embracing Independence Day, she stalks away into the jungle, leaving the good reverend to unravel for himself the faulty reasoning that alienates potential converts from his church. The departure suggests the lessons that the dark continent offers white insurgents: Natives proffer advice briefly, then withdraw it when the proud and unwary fail to heed warnings. To Orleanna, Tataba's absence "left a pitched wake in which I felt I would drown" (p. 94). The water imagery suits a situation brought on by Nathan's insistence on baptism by immersion.

• *Further Reading*

Arten, Isaac. "Review: *The Poisonwood Bible*." *Midwest Book Review*, December 2001.
Gabb, Sally. "Into Africa: A Review of *The Poisonwood Bible*." *Field Notes*, Vol. 11, No. 1, Summer 2001.
Ognibene, Elaine R. "The Missionary Position: Barbara Kingsolver's *The Poisonwood Bible*." *College Literature*, Vol. 30, No. 3, Summer 2003, pp. 19–36.

television

Kingsolver's disdain for modern media crops up regularly in her essays and novels. In *Animal Dreams* (1990), Emelina Domingos, a devoted mother in Grace, Arizona, blames satellite television for encouraging her modish boys to demand fad shoes rather than hand-me-downs. Codi Noline later notes that children have lost "the Spanish-flavored accent of Old Grace" because of their exposure to the generic speech on television (p. 56). A more serious indoctrination in *Pigs in Heaven* (1993) convinces Harland Elleston that acquiring culture from a home screen is more valuable than actually experiencing life in the company of his wife Alice. She grows so alienated from her second husband that she abandons him and settles in Oklahoma. Her test of beau Cash Stillwater is his relationship to a kitchen TV set. To prove his love, he shoots the television with his rifle, "a little right of center but still fatal" (p. 343). The outrageous act is typical of the author's blend of humor and political statement.

Kingsolver has numerous bones to pick with the popular media. In *Small Wonder* (2002), she blames televised news for projecting a fallacious image of constant turmoil in the world. In the title essay, she complains that "we now know so very much about the world, or at least the part of it that is most picturesquely exploding on any given day, that we're left with a desperate sense that all of it is exploding, all the time" (p. 15). She remarked in an interview for the *Progressive* on the media's divisiveness in idolizing the rich and in giving the impression that average Americans kowtow to a ruling class.

To avoid these false impressions in her own home, the author prides herself on rearing a daughter who wastes no time watching "the one-eyed monster," which could replace more profitable activities (*Small Wonder*, p. 131). In an interview, Kingsolver justified a family-style executive decision: "I'm sure the absence of television in my life also caused me to invest more time in both reading and writing. Because I think this was a very good thing in the long run, I've made it a point to keep TV to a minimum in my own children's lives" ("Barbara"). Nonetheless, Kingsolver took part in a statewide literacy effort in spring 2001, when one hundred KET affiliates inveigled ninety-seven hundred participants to read *The Bean Trees*.

• *Further Reading*

"Barbara Kingsolver: Coming Home to a Prodigal Summer." http://www.ivillage.com/books/intervu/fict/articles.

Barkley, Tona. "KET Reading Program Takes First Place in National Competition." *Commonwealth Communique*, April 2003.

Epstein, Robin. "Barbara Kingsolver." *Progressive*, Vol. 60, No. 2, February 1996, pp. 33–37.

Thibodeaux, Jax

Jax Thibodeaux, the rock keyboardist and melodic lover of Taylor Greer in *Pigs in Heaven* (1993), is one of Barbara Kingsolver's more developed male loners. Jax is secure in his manhood and independent enough to grant Taylor the time she needs to settle a major problem, the securing of her daughter Turtle's adoption against Cherokee tribal demands. Early on in the relationship, Jax acknowledges that the source of motherly instincts is "not an answerable question" (p. 155). He accepts Taylor's womanly love of him as second in intensity and focus to parental devotion to Turtle. His acceptance is an authorial gesture toward a softer, less macho image of males.

In part, the author clarifies the genesis of affection as outgrowths of need. Jax needs a woman to love and to complement his life; Taylor reciprocates by blossoming in a normal male-female relationship. However, before Taylor met Jax, Turtle needed a mother to provide familial support, but even more to protect her from the abusers who halted her physical and emotional development when she was a toddler. With those two magnets pulling Taylor north and south, it is not surprising that Turtle's draw far exceeds that of Jax. The author reprises the pecking order of love relationships in *Prodigal Summer* (2000), in which Deanna Wolfe willingly gives up hunter Eddie Bondo, her summer lover, and conceals the resulting conception to concentrate her efforts and attention on pregnancy and motherhood.

As with Bondo, Kingsolver depicts Jax as a male with a strong mating urge. After Taylor's hasty withdrawal from Tucson to avoid losing custody of Turtle, Jax inhabits a lover's limbo that he tries to escape with carnal encounters with Gundi, the free-spirited landlady at Rancho Copo. He fantasizes about siring a child, whom he and Turtle could introduce to the ducks in the park. He sees himself in animal terms—a father "[wearing] one of those corduroy zipper cocoons with the baby wiggling inside, waiting for metamorphosis. He likes the idea of himself as father moth" (p. 146). In tears at a low point, he weeps and struggles with the source of his loss. The author juxtaposes sympathy for Jax while Taylor and Alice converse in Sacramento about women's loss of patronyms when they marry. Alice interjects, "Either he's your boyfriend or he isn't, but don't just sit on the fence and run him down" (p. 182).

To maintain her theme of female self-actualization through independence, the author sacrifices Jax by refusing to grant him the role of *deus ex machina* to her protagonist. When Taylor phones him with a woeful tale of facing more home expenses than her job as cashier in intimate apparel can cover, he begs her to return to Tucson and offers money for plane fare. To her idealistic belief that a single mother should be able to provide for a family of two, he replies, "Horatio Alger is compost, honey. That standard no longer applies to reality" (p. 246). In her delight at ending the novel with a victory for Taylor's adoption, Kingsolver makes no further reference to the Taylor-Jax liaison, which continues to rate second in the scheme of things.

• *Further Reading*

Murrey, Loretta Martin. "The Loner and the Matriarchal Community in Barbara Kingsolver's *The Bean Trees* and *Pigs in Heaven*." *Southern Studies*, Vol. 5, No. 1–2, Spring & Summer 1994, pp. 155–164.

trust

Whether in reference to confidence in nature, relationships, or self, trust is a powerful motivator in Kingsolver's works, including her latest, *Last Stand: America's Virgin Lands* (2002), a photographic journey through picturesque settings that confirms her belief that nature is trustworthy. When small-town girl Taylor Greer moves from the Kentucky mountains to Tucson in *The Bean Trees* (1988), she develops a distrust of the city, in part out of concern for her daughter Turtle, whose foster parents abused her. To neutralize abnormal fear in Taylor, Kingsolver underscores intergenerational harmony in Taylor's extended family circle, which welcomes an unlikely blend of strangers— blind Edna Poppy and her guide Virgie Parsons, roommate Lou Ann Ruiz, Mattie the underground railroad conductor at the Jesus Is Lord tire service, and Estevan and Esperanza, refugees fleeing political persecution in Central America. The counter forces of trust and distrust generate tension in Taylor, whose most pressing need is faith in self and acceptance of her skill at mothering and supporting a family.

The trust-distrust tension remains at the forefront in Kingsolver's next two novels—*Animal Dreams* (1990), the story of Codi Noline's lack of connectedness to home, family, lover, and community, and in *Pigs in Heaven* (1993), the non-sequel to *The Bean Trees*. In the former, Codi Noline has borne a heavy burden of misgivings since the death of her mother when Codi was three years old. Linked with her younger sister Hallie, Codi attempted to handle a serious situation on her own by concealing a pregnancy at age fifteen, giving birth alone in the sixth month in the family bathroom, and burying the stillborn child in the arroyo without informing either sister or father. On return to Grace, Arizona, to care for her ailing parent, Codi rediscovers love with her baby's father and confides how she kept secret the baby's birth and death.

By revealing Codi's inability to trust others, Kingsolver pictures a woman who fails to engage in life to the fullest. As Codi builds trust in her scientific expertise among high school biology classes and the local citizens battling serious water pollution, she develops a mature attitude toward family and community. Her first inclination of success comes from the school board, which indicates that faculty and students have voted her teacher of the year. At an intimate moment with Doc Homer, Codi expresses a renewed faith in humanity with her belief in utility: "I've about decided that's the main thing that separates happy people from the other people: the feeling that you're a practical item, with a use, like a sweater or a socket wrench" (p. 334). By pouring her energies into loving Loyd and belonging to the community, she recovers a sense of utility, the ingredient that rids her of self-doubt.

In *Pigs in Heaven*, Kingsolver inserts a question about blind trust of strangers. In flight from Arizona, Taylor and her mother Alice inadvisedly add Barbie, the larcenous waitress from Las Vegas, to their traveling trio. In phone calls to Alice, Taylor is vague about the money that Alice gave her for the trip and conceals that Barbie stole all that was left. Alice says nothing, but ponders a truism: "Trust only grows out of trusting" (p. 217). Her philosophy emerges from experience, the testing ground for a lifetime of human relationships.

In the author's masterwork, the emotionally and politically complex *The Poisonwood Bible* (1998), trust underlies the theme of dysfunctional family and international relations. Orleanna Price, the persistent voice of self-doubt and guilt, loses faith in self after she fails to protect her youngest daughter from a menacing green mamba at their mission post in the Congo. More serious to the mother's tremulous view of her place in the world is self-blame for marrying a religious fanatic, Nathan Price, a controlling zealot and life-long wife and child abuser. In their mother's shadow, the three surviving daughters grow up to place their confidence in variant forms of rescue — Rachel in feminine wiles, materialism, and a capitalistic venture, Adah in scholarly research, and Leah in an idealistic husband and four sons. To Leah's credit, although her children grow up in the chaotic world of Congolese politics, they maintain wholesome values and more realistic expectations than their white grandmother had.

Similar to Leah are the three female protagonists in *Prodigal Summer* (2000), who shrug off reasons to doubt other characters as they establish fulfilling lives. Nannie Land Rawley, the orchard keeper in Zebulon Valley, discovers goodness in Garnett S. Walker, III, the next-door curmudgeon, who offers rare heart-shaped shingles to repair her roof. With more difficulty, Lusa Maluf Landowski discerns glimmers of kindness and acceptance in her four judgmental sisters-in-law, who ease the task of accepting widowhood and responsibility for a debt-ridden farm. Less successful at trust is Deanna Wolfe, the forest warder and watcher of a coyote family, who is unable to convince lover Eddie Bondo that killing predators is detrimental to nature.

Kingsolver relieves the text of failure by revealing a new self-confidence in Deanna, who transfers her maternal instincts from phoebe chicks on the porch and infant coyote pups in a forest den to her unborn child, which Eddie sires. Without revealing her condition, Deanna separates from her lover and from her mountain hermitage. The downhill journey toward the town of Egg Fork reunites Deanna with a milieu that once alienated her. The choice to leave nature to its own devices and to trust surrogate mother Nannie with supporting her during a transformation from wilderness keeper to parent is an essential of Deanna's blossoming as a character.

See also **compromise, survival**

• *Further Reading*

Hollands, Barbara. "Languid Eco-Drama." *New Zealand Dispatch*, June 2, 2001.

Underdown, Frank and Janna

The Reverend Frank and Janna Underdown are a white Episcopalian couple who superintend expenditures by the Mission League in *The Poisonwood Bible* (1998). They extend a necessary lifeline to the sojourn of the Reverend Nathan Price and his family in the Congo. The experienced mission couple who pioneered the outpost school and church welcomes the newcomers to Léopoldville and assists in translating English to French. Janna snidely ridicules the family's Georgian drawl, creating an ominous subtext indicating pride and un–Christian disdain for people who are different. The Underdowns hustle the Prices aboard Eeben Axelroot's bush plane for transport to Kilanga, where the new family must fend for themselves. The unceremonious disconnect also suggests a couple who invest little of themselves in the needs of others.

Kingsolver's later image of the Underdowns is ambiguous. Returning to urban ease and better schools for their boys, the couple retreats to a Léopoldville home offering "Persian rugs and silver tea service and chocolate cookies, surrounded by miles of tin shanties and hunger" (p. 232). Leah Price is aware that Janna Underdown slights the native boy scout troop, another suggestion of snobbery in the missionary's behavior. Orleanna Price recalls learning from Janna the staple source of nutrition for Kilangans, whose women grow, pound, dry, and boil manioc tubers into fufu. Orleanna remarks wryly, "It has the nutritional value of a brown paper bag, with the added bonus of trace amounts of cyanide. Yet it fills the stomach" (p. 92). On other occasions, dressed humbly in khaki with home haircuts, the Underdowns hover on the periphery of the story, supplying such limited aid as American news magazines, a slim tether to civilization.

Nathan's lack of rapport with African villagers coincides with the growing Congolese rebellion against colonialism. When the Underdowns return to Kilanga in January 1960 as overseers of the Mission League's finances, they break the news of strikes and riots in Léopoldville and Stanleyville as natives battle the Belgians for independence. As the nation reaches for freedom, Frank reminds the Prices that they willingly embraced risks by accepting an African post without undergoing language training and without an enthusiastic sendoff from headquarters. He sees their posting as a bureaucratic "act of kindness" (p. 164). The special flight the Underdowns arrange on June 28 is a gesture of mercy that goes unacknowledged. Nathan appears to dissolve his relationship with the mission couple and to accept full responsibility for a serious deterioration in his ministry. Without the Underdowns, Orleanna and the Price children have little hope of advice or rescue.

Walker, Garnett

A former agriculture teacher and third generation farmer in his late seventies, in *Prodigal Summer* (2000), Garnett Sheldon Walker, III, is a puzzling blend of kindness and arrogance. He takes strength and courage from his acreage in Zebulon Valley, named for a bible character by his grandfather, the first Garnett Walker. While teaching vo-ag (vocational agriculture), Garnett the Third earned for himself the title of "goat maven" by encouraging 4-H'ers like Little Rickie to raise kids for market (p. 336). In retirement, Garnett's life seems busy and focused as though he needs to occupy a mind easily saddened by memories of his dead wife, alienated grandchildren, and an alcoholic son who embarrassed the family and left town.

In the estimation of reviewer Susan Lumpkin, Garnett is Kingsolver's "most poignantly drawn character" (Lumpkin, p. 1). Eight years after his wife Ellen's death from lung cancer, he misses having a woman to share his bed and iron his shirts and regrets the onset of old age. In memories of married life, he takes pride in having been cared for by a woman. As cataracts dim his vision, he grounds his days in a mountaineer's pragmatism and the familiarity of place, comprised of house, tree lot, barn, grain shed, and root cellar. In tribute to his grandfather, who built the family's fortune on chestnut trees, Garnett longs to re-establish the Walker American chestnut, to which he has dedicated a decade of cross-breeding original stock with the blight-resistant Chinese chestnut. His longing to succeed supplies a glimpse of the inner man, who wants to assure a valuable legacy to the wild before he dies.

Reviewer Lumpkin describes Garnett as "a proud champion of manicured farmscapes managed with chemicals" (*Ibid.*). Because of a reliance on Sevin, 2-4-D, Roundup, and Malathion, he becomes the sworn enemy of his organic apple-growing neighbor Nannie Land Rawley, who shares the frontage along Highway 6. He holds the agrarian tenet that "success without chemicals [is] impossible" (p. 87). As he sinks in Nannie's presence from what he believes to be incipient stroke, he prays, "I obeyed thy fifth commandment. I didn't kill her" (p. 88). To his chagrin, Nannie saves him from a fifteen-pound snapping turtle that numbs his leg, causing the symptoms that Garnett misdiagnoses. His humiliation and resultant animosity conjure up imaginary gossip in Little Brothers' Hardware and force him to depart in confusion without paying for a spray bottle of Malathion. The author uses the incident as a revelation of Garnett's befuddlement from advancing age and increasing exasperation with a disagreeable neighbor.

Kingsolver uses the Walker-Rawley clash as a form of comic relief. In subsequent annoyance with his neighbor, he considers her "worse than mildew" (p. 270). By exaggerating Garnett's complaints about Nannie, the author creates opportunities for hyperbole, e.g., Garnett's remark that "in another day and age they'd have burned [Nannie] for a witch" (p. 258). To his snorts and rejoinders, she patiently explains how nature, if left unsprayed and untampered-with, balances itself. She mows down his arguments with lyricism: "It's glory, to be part of a bigger something. The glory of an evolving world" (p. 277). The reference to evolution incites his religious fundamentalism. He redirects to the bible their long-standing argument, a cyclical trading of viewpoints with no end in sight. The author uses the eventual decrease in their animosity as a model of compromise, one of her favorite themes.

• *Further Reading*

Lumpkin, Susan. "Review: *Prodigal Summer*." *Smithsonian Zoogoer*, March/April 2001, p. l.
Uschuk, J. "Green Light: Barbara Kingsolver's New Novel Fights for Life and Love in the Natural World." *Tucson Weekly*, November 2, 2000.

Walker, Jewel Widener

The Widener sister in *Prodigal Summer* (2000) whom Lusa Landowski at first dismisses as "an empty vessel," Jewel Widener redeems herself as a friend, adviser, and fellow widow (p. 70). After the unforeseen death of her brother Cole, Jewel earns her name by remaining at the Widener homeplace to receive visitors and comfort Lusa. Jewel is a grass widow and single parent deserted three or four years earlier by husband Shel, an alcoholic house painter and handyman who ran off with a waitress from Cracker Barrel. Jewel recognizes need in Lusa and offers sleeping pills. She surprises her sister-in-law by summarizing the post-funeral ache: "You want to just close your eyes on all of it, but at the same time you're thinking there's something you need to see, and you'll miss it" (p. 77). Of the five Widener sisters, she is the only one who has lived the suffering that torments Lusa and the only one to establish a sisterly relationship.

Kingsolver uses Jewel as spokeswoman for belabored farm wives, especially those without husbands. While helping Lusa put up June cherries as preserves and pie filling, Jewel notes that "having a house and a farm's not the same as having money" (p. 117). She describes as sad "pretending that part of my life never happened," a reference to the discomfort among family members and shoppers at Kroger's who avoid the subject of a wayward husband (p. 111). She shares inside information about the family's disapproval of Cole's elopement with an outsider who chose to keep her own patronym. Jewel accounts for the family's response as normal: "We're just regular country people, with country ways" (p. 126). As a joke, she promises Lusa that debt will not consume her: "You are not going to starve, Loretta Lynn," a reference to a country singer who grew up in poverty in a coal-mining community (p. 124). With Jewel's help, Lusa finds new sources of strength and begins to study her predicament from a new perspective.

The reversal of roles in the falling action allows Lusa to repay Jewel for her support. From Little Rickie, Lusa learns that her estimation of Jewel's age is considerably too high, for Jewel was Cole's beloved youngest sister and companion. As she weakens from chemotherapy for cancer, she fears for her children, Crystal and Lowell. Because Lusa enjoys tending them, she proposes adopting them. In considering her last months of life, Jewel offers wisdom acquired from bitter experience: "Don't wait around thinking you've got all the time in the world. Maybe you've just got this one summer" (p. 405).

• *Further Reading*

Eastburn, Kathryn. "On Solid Ground." *Colorado Springs Independent*, December 14, 2000.
James, Rebecca. "Booked Solid." *LETTERS from CAMP Rehobeth*, Vol. 11, No. 6, June 1, 2001.

Walker genealogy

In *Prodigal Summer* (2000), the Walker family tree allies neatly with the Widener family line and explains the connection between Garnett S. Walker, III, and Jewel Widener Walker.

Garnett Sheldon Walker, Sr.
(lumber baron who
built the mountain
cabin in the 1930s)
```
              |
    |-------------------------|
```

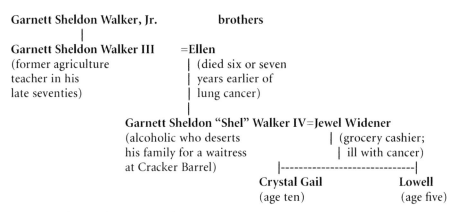

Garnett Sheldon Walker, Jr.   brothers
         |
Garnett Sheldon Walker III   =Ellen
(former agriculture | (died six or seven
teacher in his | years earlier of
late seventies) | lung cancer)
                                  |
         Garnett Sheldon "Shel" Walker IV=Jewel Widener
         (alcoholic who deserts | (grocery cashier;
         his family for a waitress | ill with cancer)
         at Cracker Barrel) |----------------------------|
                                  Crystal Gail   Lowell
                                  (age ten)   (age five)

See also **Widener genealogy**

Widener, Cole

The husband of entomologist Lusa Maluf Landowski, an irritatingly citified wife in *Prodigal Summer* (2000), Cole Widener is a salt-of-the-earth Appalachian farmer. The sole son and heir of Dad Widener, Cole inherited a one-hundred-year-old house and sixty-acre farm located near Egg Fork, the hub of family life. In addition to plowing his land and tending livestock, he played football in high school and bass fiddle for Out of the Blue, a bluegrass band. He met Lusa while he attended a pest management workshop she taught at the University of Kentucky in Lexington. His interest in scientific farming methods indicates an active mind not wholly dependent on tradition.

Kingsolver has only a brief chapter in which to picture Cole and Lusa in the flesh. In their first year of marriage, he displays a combative and a sensitive side. Daily, he holds out against her ridicule of the local newspaper and Appalachian argot, a hurtful insult to his homeland. Shortly, he rewards her with a honeysuckle sprig to make amends for their ongoing arguments about organic farming. By placing an ecology issue in a family setting, Kingsolver illustrates the human side of serious debates about the planet's health.

As the youngest of six siblings and the only boy, Cole is a proud male who resents female badinage. He has a stock breeder's appreciation of his voluptuous wife, to whom he proposed after three days of intense love-making in her Lexington apartment. After a year's courtship and their elopement the previous June, she became mistress of the Widener homeplace. He smarts at her harsh criticisms, then supplies a constructive compromise, the suggestion that she write her own gardening column to "teach us sorry-ass bumpkins" (p. 34). His death while delivering grain part-time to supplement their income leaves her sad and chilled by the bitter words they exchanged only ten days before the wreck.

In retrospect, Lusa keeps Cole alive through visions of his childhood companionship with his sister Jewel and impressions of his spirit, which haunts the house and barn. To Jewel's urging that she stop canning green beans, Lusa replies that the garden vegetables are precious because Cole planted them. Late into summer, she recalls his hatred of honeysuckle, which threatens to cover the barn. She treasures beans as though they were gifts from Cole that continue bearing long after his death. Lusa's need to surround herself with palpable reminders of her husband attest to a satisfying relationship during the early stages of marriage.

• *Further Reading*

Bush, Trudy. "Back to Nature." *Christian Century*, Vol. 117, No. 33, November 22, pp. 1245–1246.

Eberson, Sharon. "Appalachian Romance Has Kingsolver in Top Form." *Pittsburgh Post-Gazette*, January 14, 2001.

Widener genealogy

In *Prodigal Summer* (2000), the Widener family line expresses in a diagram the numerous cultural and familial pressures on Lusa Maluf Landowski, including the two Walker children she intends to adopt.

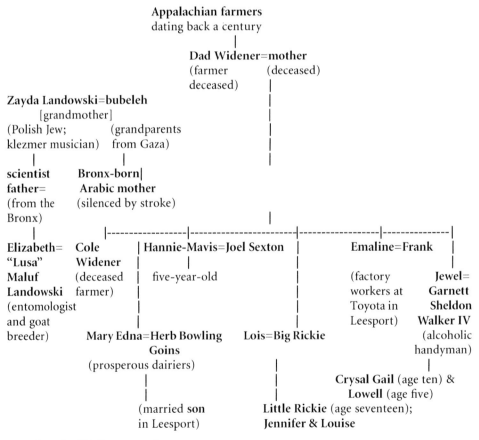

See also **Walker genealogy**

wisdom

For the sake of humor and enlightenment, Kingsolver salts her texts with frequent adages. In *The Bean Trees* (1988), the grocery clerk Lee Sing remarks that "Feeding a girl is like feeding the neighbor's New Year pig," a patriarchal, but pragmatic Chinese truism (p. 31). After a Valentine's Day frost kills Mattie's purple beans, she muses philosophically, "The old has to pass on before the new can come around" (p. 77). Taylor Greer recalls her mother's image that "Even a spotted pig looks black at night" (p. 141). In reference to kids and unsanitary conditions, Taylor cites a rural woman: "You've got to eat a peck of dirt before you die" (p. 183). All four adages emphasize the homespun imagery and agricultural analogies that permeate Kingsolver's fiction.

Much of the author's wisdom derives from a gut-level pragmatism. In the falling action of *The Bean Trees*, as Taylor bids farewell to Estevan, the married Mayan refugee she loves, he tries to smooth out the wrongs and falsehoods that beset their brief friendship. Referring to oppression in Guatemala and to Taylor's falsification of adoption papers, he declares, "In a world as wrong as this one, all we can do is to make things as right as we can" (p. 220). The practicality of the author's views resurges in *Pigs in Heaven* (1993) with such womanly observations as "Sympathizing over the behavior of men is the baking soda of women's friendships, it seems, the thing that makes them bubble and rise" (p. 190). While acclimating to Sugar Hornbuckle's ways in Heaven, Oklahoma, Alice Greer sinks into the serenity of the family swimming hole and thinks about speaking in tongues at evangelical religious services. She concludes that "Anybody can get worked up, if they have the intention. It's *peacefulness* that is hard to come by on purpose" (p. 224). On a global scale, Alice's observation summarizes Kingsolver's views on world conflict.

The disseminators of wisdom in the author's masterwork, *The Poisonwood Bible* (1998), are an unlikely group of advisers. From Nelson, houseboy to the missionary Price family, comes day-to-day advice on which snakes to avoid and how to retain good fortune in a universe a-swarm with evil. Anatole Ngemba, the village teacher, is the idealistic philosopher capable of explaining yin and yang to Leah. After the *kakakaka* (enteritis) epidemic, by pointing out how death to a family's young makes children more precious, he illustrates the mounting value of old people, who have survived the longest. On the night of the army ant invasion, he extends the metaphor of hungry ants to describe starving people: "When they are pushed down long enough they will rise up" (p. 308). He adds that the bite of revolutionaries results from their "trying to fix things in the only way they know," an observation that exonerates natives for the crudeness of their methods (*Ibid.*).

More influential to the Congolese is Brother Fyntan Fowles, the Santa-like missionary who visits the Prices at one of their low points. He indicates that the best way to aid Africans is to appreciate what they are and how they live while reserving pious judgments. In his view, "Everything they do is with one eye to the spirit," a liberal view of the Congolese appreciation of God's grace (p. 246). By sipping palm wine with Chief Tata Ndu and exchanging views on domestic strife, Fowles impacts wife abuse and causes grateful wives to raise altars to Tata Jesus in their kitchens. By opening his ministry to a broad range of views, Fowles achieves more sharing and cooperation among support groups and villages than Nathan with his narrow, pinch-lipped evangelical approach.

Kingsolver's fifth novel *Prodigal Summer* (2000) brims with less lethal adages, such as Hannie-Mavis Sexton's acceptance of her birth name, "You get what you get" and Deanna Wolfe's belief that "Anything you're willing to eat, you ought to be willing to look under its hood first" (pp. 308, 316). During the Fourth of July celebration at the Widener homeplace, Lusa Maluf Landowski takes the time to side with her niece and nephew, Crystal and Lowell, against the criticism of Jewel Walker, their mother. Lusa maintains that "being a little person in a big world with nobody taking you very seriously is tough" (p. 232). A surprising touch of perception comes from Little Rickie, another of Lusa's nephews, who consoles her for Cole's death: "I think it'd be worse losing the person you love than dying yourself" (p. 241). In a rush of feelings that erupts with a noisy fireworks display, Lusa takes comfort in the family celebration by conceding, "We're only what we are" (p. 244). The ability to accept what comes her way is the anchor that enables her to remain as the outsider of the Widener family and to earn a profit from a debt-ridden farm.

In another personal war, Nannie Land Rawley and her neighbor, Garnett S. Walker, III, trade insults and points of view on organic farming. After Nannie strays into a personal attack on Garnett's alienation from his alcoholic son, she takes the opportunity to apologize and comfort the old man. Her reasoning bears a rural sense of logic: "There's always more to a story than a body can see from the fence line" (p. 283). After he accepts her touch of grace, she summarizes their mutual pain, his from a runaway son and hers from the death of her daughter, Rachel Carson Rawley: "What worse grief can there be than to be old without young ones to treasure?" (*Ibid.*). The quiet moment in their long-running battle lapses during their negotiations over the oak that falls from Nannie's land onto Garnett's. She recovers her feistiness and charges, "You are a sanctimonious old fart," a glimmer of humor that the author inserts when the story grows too sad or ponderous (*Ibid.*).

In like fashion, Kingsolver uses wisdom to ease other misgivings. A broadened view of family standoffs enlightens Lusa's bewilderment at life among the clannish Wideners. During a chat with Hannie-Mavis, Lusa observes, "Every family's its own trip to China" (p. 305). Likewise, the promise of a pit-roasted turkey relieves the tedium of cabin food for Deanna Wolfe and Eddie Bondo. While collecting the vegetables and seasonings for their feast, Deanna is pleased to note, "Nothing was more wonderful than waiting for a happiness you could be sure of" (p. 318). When their pleasant idyll gives place to a serious discussion of bounty hunting, Deanna sums up the Forest Service philosophy with a brief warning: "There's no such thing as killing one thing," a scientific precept that takes in the interconnectedness of all nature (p. 325).

See also **Ledger Fourkiller, Brother Fowles, Alice Greer, Mama Bekwa Tataba, women**

• *Further Reading*

"Barbara Kingsolver: Coming Home to a Prodigal Summer." http://www.ivillage.com/ books/intervu/fict/articles.

Krasny, Michael. "Interview: Barbara Kingsolver, Author, Discusses Her New Book." *Talk of the Nation* (NPR), December 13, 1999.

Shulman, Polly. "Wild Lives/Human Fortunes Are Rooted in the Fate of the Chestnut Tree — and Other Flora and Fauna — in the Ecological Romance." *New York Newsday*, October 29, 2000, p. B9.

Wolfe, Deanna

At age forty-seven, wildlife biologist Deanna Wolfe, a native of the Appalachian town of Egg Fork and protagonist of *Prodigal Summer* (2000), is dangerously low on satisfaction. A farm girl who once fished with her dad, she recalls an uninitiated adolescence in which a motherless girl stood outside "that secret church of female knowledge that had never let her in" (p. 387). She was outflanked by her nubile peers and "too far outside the game to learn" (p. 26). In college, she rebuilt self-esteem through a string of affairs with professors, whom she describes collectively as a "daddy complex" (p. 263). She dismisses her former existence as suburbanite and wife of one of her instructors and middle school teacher of math and science in Knoxville. To her, it seemed like "[life] in a brick house, neatly pressed between a husband and neighbors" (p. 5). The author uses the statement as an implication of urban unrest in a woman who prefers the outdoors and solitude.

Kingsolver uses Deanna as a model of the ecological hermit. She admits that she completed a graduate degree in wildlife biology and retreated from civilization out of despair that "people act so hateful to every kind but their own" (p. 175). For twenty-five months in a tiny chestnut log cabin as forest warder of Zebulon Mountain, she tends trails in a hybrid job with both the Forest Service and the National Park Service. She succeeds because she possesses the kind of instinctive love of the wild that links her with Artemis, the Greek goddess of wild animals. To put starch into activism, Kingsolver uses terms like "frank" and "pure concentration" to describe her protagonist, who is an apt guardian of nature.

Enjoying "this diamond solitaire of a life," Wolfe works at her specialty, the twentieth-century migration of coyotes in the wild (p. 55). She tracks a young canid family, Kingsolver's emblematic endangered species, and rejoices in locating the sire, whom she dubs a "magnificent son of a bitch" (p. 62). The den replicates a common strand in the author's fiction — the out-of-place and unacceptable fleeing to less hostile territory. In its initial arrival in the southern Appalachians, the coyote became what renowned zoologist Robert T. Paine labeled a "keystone predator," a species that controls the populations of smaller species (p. 62). Restoration of the coyote is the core of Deanna's effort to support wildlife in the Zebulon area.

While working out the details of the coyote's re-establishment, the protagonist's personal life is a nest of contradictions, beginning with self-possession and veering into ill-advised, but mutually pleasing casual sex with bounty hunger Eddie Bondo. On her first encounter with him, Deanna rebukes him for carrying a rifle on National Forest land, but finds herself blushing on his abrupt departure into rhododendrons, a suggestion of Eden and its gender myths. The as-yet unmated couple meet a second time with roles reversed, Eddie unarmed with his phallic firearm and Deanna carrying a government-issue pistol with the safety on. She admits to herself that she wants him to walk ahead of her so she can observes his body in motion.

The author develops Deanna's complexity through intimate conversations with Eddie. After explaining the intricacies of animal overpopulation and the role of predators, she summarizes the signal rule of ecology: "To kill a natural predator is a sin" (p. 179). She later raises the ante with a command: "*Leave* it ... the *hell* ... *alone*" (p. 323). Without rancor, Bondo observes her hostility toward animal slaughter and reduces her to "three parts pissed off to four parts dignified" (*Ibid.*). Kingsolver dilutes the belligerence in Deanna in a subsequent scene in which she worries that the phoebe nestlings may freeze in the cold of a July blackberry winter. Deanna must later admit her live-and-let-live philosophy took backseat to protecting the baby birds, which she later discovered eaten by a black snake that she allows to eat mice in the attic. The vision of lumps in the snake's body in the glowing circle of her flashlight introduces a shift in her thinking from guarding nature, to protecting human young.

Deanna proves Eddie's claim that she is maternal by weeping for the baby birds. Through introspection, she misidentifies sleeplessness and unease as normal responses to the climacteric and her ability to bear children. She later taunts herself for failing to recognize that pregnancy "had gotten her out of whack" (p. 347). Emotions seize her in the final scene as a fierce storm threatens the cabin. Kingsolver comments on the life-changing events of the summer: "Unaware that she would never again be herself alone — that *solitude* was the faultiest of human presumptions" (p. 434).

See also **Robert T. Paine, motherhood, Adolph Murie**

• *Further Reading*

Eberson, Sharon. "Appalachian Romance Has Kingsolver in Top Form." *Pittsburgh Post-Gazette*, January 14, 2001.
Hollands, Barbara. "Languid Eco-Drama." *New Zealand Dispatch*, June 2, 2001.

Wolfe genealogy

In *Prodigal Summer* (2000), the family tree of biologist Deanna Wolfe illustrates the connected lives of much of the area around Egg Fork.

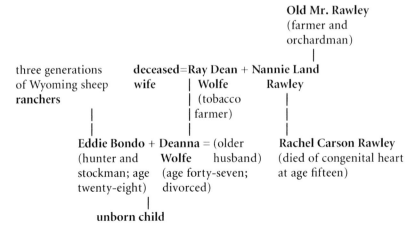

women

In Kingsolver's writings, female strength emerges in women like Sugar Horn-buckle, Alice Greer, Lou Ann Ruiz, Annawake Fourkiller, Mama Tataba and her Kilangan sisters, Deanna Wolfe, Rose-Johnny, and Mattie the tire dealer, all of whom endure and fight for self and community. Examples are as disparate as the innkeeper Mrs. Hoge at the Broken Arrow Motor Lodge in *The Bean Trees* (1988), hard-hatted female mine workers in Kingsolver's documentary *Holding the Line: Women in the Great Arizona Mine Strike of 1983* (1989), a suspected lesbian and her friend Georgeann in the story "Homeland" (1989), the forest ranger in *Prodigal Summer* (2000), and Great Mam in *Homeland and Other Stories* (1989), the Cherokee matriarch who "was like an old pine, whose accumulated years cause one to ponder how long it has stood, not how soon it will fall" (p. 6). Kingsolver rejects a pervasive misperception about women: "A woman without a man — a condition of 'manlessness' — is defined as alone. But a single mother is less alone than the average housewife" (Karbo, p. 9). The author's ability to overturn erroneous stereotypes informs her fiction, enabling her female characters with an inborn courage and feistiness.

The redoubtable female in Kingsolver's writings is capable of bonding with other women to empower the circle and energize its members according to the needs of the moment. They batter themselves and their hopes against age-old double standards that keep females powerless, disenfranchised, and, in some cases, hopeless. Taylor Greer, protagonist in *The Bean Trees*, thinks of women as homey dispensers of food and consolation. When Estevan, a Mayan refugee, reports his wife's near-suicide from an overdose of baby aspirin, Taylor offers him food and a beer and muses, "From my earliest memory, times of crisis seemed to end up with women in the kitchen preparing food for men" (p. 132). She identifies the ritual as "good solid female traditions" (*Ibid.*).

In a choice between the roles of wife and parent, Kingsolver characterizes motherhood as the height of womanly attainment. Most maintain a tight-lipped empathy with their daughters, particularly Alice Greer in *The Bean Trees* (1988), who "always said barefoot and pregnant was not [Taylor's] style" (p. 3). When Taylor faces her first predicament — the abrupt receipt of a homeless, parentless Cherokee child through her car window — she stops at the first motel in which a woman works. The instinct for woman-to-woman empathy is unfailing. The aid of Mrs. Hoge, innkeeper at the Broken Arrow Motor Lodge, suffices to get Taylor and the child through Christmas.

Poet Clive Matson praised the author's hard-shell females for their moral conviction and righteous energy, forces that keep them alive and thriving. Taylor's toughness arises in her response to Lou Ann Ruiz's description of the door to Fanny Heaven with a doorknob at the crotch of a painted female figure, "like a woman is something you shove on and walk right through" (p. 150). Instead of feeling put down, she advises her roommate, "You got to get pissed off" (*Ibid.*). When faced with endangerment to the Mayan couple, Taylor remarks on woman's place in rescue scenarios: "More often than not ... the woman carried the man through the tragedy. The man and the grandma and all the kids" (p. 182). Through Taylor, the author champions the bulwark matriarch, women like John Steinbeck's Ma Joad in *The Grapes of Wrath* (1939) and the rebel Pilar in Ernest Hemingway's *For Whom the Bell Tolls* (1940).

Kingsolver exalts networking among female characters, a method attesting to commonalities in women's lives. Because no single person, no single plan of action, and no formal behavior code or personal philosophy is any matriarchal community's salvation, each member must depend on make-it-up-as-you-go logic and teamwork. Mattie teaches Taylor that small children must have liquids to ward off dehydration in Tucson's desert climate. Taylor shares Turtle with Esperanza to begin the healing process that will carry her Mayan friend through the loss of her little girl Ismene to a political nightmare. Edna Poppy relies on the sound of the attacker and a wide swath with her cane to rescue Turtle. Perhaps the most rewarded by female invincibility is Lou Ann Ruiz, who finds in herself parallels to Taylor's resolve and self-respect.

For *Holding the Line: Women in the Great Arizona Mine Strike of 1983* (1989), the author sifted and weighed the experiences of female citizens of copper-mining communities. Her first inkling of gender bias lay in a perusal of mining folklore that marginalized women as jinxes who allegedly could cause a cave-in just by their presence in the shaft. Their worse evil lay in violating the men-only dictum of "the devil's domain" (p. 2). The women who fought management's devaluation of labor obtained "a new perspective on a power structure in which they were lodged like gravel in a tire" (p. 21). The sturdiest among them encountered racial profiling, false arrest, corporate conspiracy with police, and the tear-gassing of a liquor store. Annie Jones, head of a women's auxiliary in Ajo, modeled female strength against coercion with a feisty motto: "We come back fighting every time they try to slap us down" (p. 64).

Kingsolver's self-assured women draw critical complaint for their smugness, e.g., Sugar Hornbuckle's thought that "A woman knows she can walk away from a pot to tend something else and the pot will go on boiling; if she couldn't, this world would end at once" (p. 185). Within a few paragraphs, the author can't resist describing Cherokee matrons as having "The obstinate practicality [that] pierces and fortifies these families like the steel rods buried in walls of powdery concrete" (p. 187). Less bristly is Alice Greer's generous compliment to Cash Stillwater's self-effacing ways: "Modesty makes women fall in love faster than all the cock-a-doodling in the world" (p. 300).

Pigs in Heaven perpetuates Kingsolver's theme of female solidarity during perplexing and threatening times, as demonstrated by the women at the stomp dance who converse in Cherokee sprinkled with three English terms—permapress, gallbladder, and Crisco—each an answer to a domestic quandary. In an attempt to locate Sugar Marie Boss Hornbuckle, a beloved cousin, Alice Greer comes upon the familiar dead end of searching for a woman who may have remarried and changed her surname. Through Alice, the author speaks an observation on the shift: "Isn't that the dumbest thing, how the wife ends up getting filed under the husband? The husband is not the most reliable thing for your friends to try and keep track of" (p. 182). The witty complaint implies the displacement of women from historical data by the custom of cloaking them under a new family name.

Extolled by critic Henry Aay are Kingsolver's strong set of female figures in

Animal Dreams (1990), a work of ecofiction grounded in cultural anthropology. The author takes particular delight in self-reliant Latinas like Doña Althea and Viola Domingos, who are willing to fight the Black Mountain mining firm for clean water in Grace, Arizona. Kingsolver noted in "Lush Language," a 1993 book review for the *Los Angeles Times*, that Mexicans produced "a culture whose pantheon includes the Virgin Mary, Pancho Villa, and Aztec goddesses" (p. 1). The two-out-of-three logic gives women the lion's share, a source of courage that emboldens and consoles them in difficult times.

In the novel, the author pictures a Latina circle of fighting matriarchs under the unlikely moniker of the Stitch and Bitch Club. As the art dealer Sean Rideheart explains, the women of Grace brought to the lifeless ores of the canyon a unique "economic identity" comprised of "embroidery and peacocks and fruit trees and piñatas and children" (p. 277). While selling feathered piñatas in Tucson's upscale area, they link up with Jessie, a bag lady, who offers her shopping cart as transportation. The first day's sale goes so well that the women up their stock to five hundred piñatas, each accompanied by a broadside explaining the town's endangerment by threatened water rights. When Hallie disappears in Nicaragua, the clubwomen turn their efforts to a letter-writing campaign sending a thousand messages to members of Congress and the media. In both instances, they refuse to be stymied by fear or female political powerlessness. When the Black Mountain Mining company backs down from its leaching operation and its plans to dam the river, the twenty-two activists triumph at the thing they do best — preserving the natural resources of their homeland to nurture both family and nature. Codi Noline ponders how "mountains could be moved," in this case, by having the community declared a national treasure on the historic registry (p. 313).

Womanhood takes on new angles in *The Poisonwood Bible* (1998), in which female roles and dress in the Congo are more stringently one-sidedly gender-based than in the white world. Leah Price views Kilangan girls her own age already married and bearing babies. She recognizes the change from youth by the torpor in their eyes, which "look happy and sad at the same time, but unexcited by anything.... *Married* eyes" (p. 107). She deduces that, while little boys continue climbing trees and playing army, "little girls were running the country," a veiled comment on the value of African women in a land where men value them like dray labor (p. 113).

To five-year-old Ruth May Price, Leah's little sister, the lesson of African womanhood is embodied in Mama Mwanza, a Congolese woman who arouses compassion because she survives a catastrophic roof fire and learns to scoot around using her hands for leverage. In deplorable condition, she still must feed and tend seven or eight children and a demanding father. Laden with a laundry basket on her head, she follows the other women of Kilanga village to the river to attend to the wash. In the direst situations, her ability to organize family labor and delegate authority proves beneficial to the Mwanzas' survival as well as to starving neighbors whom she surreptitiously aids with gifts of food. Ironically, she is more Christ-like in extending kindness than is the Reverend Nathan Price, who comes to the Congo to save heathens like her.

Nathan's wife, Orleanna Price, herself a discounted and devalued wife and mother, pictures Congolese women as the tall-stalked lilies who bear blooms on their heads in the form of "manioc-root bundles the size of crumpled horses" (p. 93). Their gathering, pounding, drying, and boiling of manioc into a tasteless blob called fufu contrasts the "thirty-minute production [of a meal] in the land of General Electric" (p. 93). Their travail parallels Orleanna's thankless chores of keeping the Price family fed, dressed, and safe against the onslaught of everyday ills and dangers, such as the spread of hookworm and *kakakaka* (enteritis) and a fall from a tree that requires setting of a broken arm bone. Her wifeliness seems perpetually aimed at some threat to life and health which arises from life at the jungle's rim.

Because Orleanna hovers on the edge of her husband's good graces, she must watch her tongue above all for the danger of arousing Nathan's ire. As an outlet for anger, wordlessly, she slams plates and pots at dinner. She comes close to rebuking his thinking about human bodies by reminding him that black women "do a hateful lot of work in a day ... like we use *things* at home" (p. 53). To herself, she admits, "I was his instrument, his animal. Nothing more" (p. 89). Surprisingly, Mama Tataba, the housekeeper, stands up to Nathan's bullying and quits her job. The example presages Orleanna's last straw and her departure from Kilanga with two of her girls in tow.

When the idealism of missionary work in Kilanga unravels, Orleanna is the only voice accusing Belgian King Baudouin I of enriching himself on the misery of black Africans. She stands out among the gathering of four white adults as the one thinking resident who foresees chaos after the Belgians leave the Congolese to run their own nation, school, bureaucracies, and military. In contrast to Nathan, who dismisses local people as know-nothings on a par with sheep and chickens, Orleanna rejoices that the Underdowns charter a plane to evacuate the Prices on June 28, 1960. When the plane leaves without her, she takes to her bed. Thirty years later, she "[tries] to wear the marks of the boot on my back as gracefully as the Congo wears hers," the author's subtextual overlay of wifely servitude on colonialism (p. 385).

In contrast to Orleanna, her married daughter Leah Ngemba is Kingsolver's image of woman as sanctuary. Grown deep and compassionate from decades of coping with Mobutu's atrocities, she makes a new nest for her family in Sanza Pombo, Angola. At a cooperative farm, she welcomes women and children fleeing the madness that Zaire has become for its peasants. With the wisdom of a survivor, she lets the silent women acclimate to safety, then listens to "the accounting of places and people they've lost" (p. 523). The stories of transient women's travails vary only in the details. In place of pain, "Mama Ngemba" offers them lessons in sanitation and nutrition, but realizes that life on the run has stripped these refugees of family stability and denied them hope of anything better than brief respites.

In naturalist Deanna Wolfe in *Prodigal Summer*, Kingsolver removes the woman from the nuclear family and resituates her in the natural family. Wisps of commentary about a former marriage ending in divorce indicate that Deanna was unable to adapt to the urban stereotype of wife, in part because she is scholarly and maintains a fast gait rather than a wifely stroll. She summarizes the split as "an older husband facing his own age badly and suddenly critical of a wife past forty" (p. 19). In her estimate, femininity is "a test like some witch trial she was preordained to fail" (p. 14).

Thus "discarded," she withdrew to the mountains, trailing her husband's surname like a male scent mark (p. 21). She wastes no time in brooding and accepts the divorce as one stage of her education in the price of independence.

For those women immersed in the womanly arts, Kingsolver makes her standard obeisance, spoken through widower Garnett S. Walker, III, who admits that "God's world and the better part of daily life were full of mysteries known only to women" (p. 134). Unlike Deanna, Lusa Maluf Landowski, a widowed farm wife, fights her battles in the confines of the Widener kitchen. Alienated by her husband's siblings who think of the appliances and cabinets as their mother's, Lusa believes that a kitchen ghost "stirs up fights," both with Cole and his five sisters (p. 127). During late-summer canning chores, she receives a womanly gift from Cole's youngest sister Jewel, who imparts guidance on how to fathom her four jealous sisters. Searching for an appropriate compliment to Lusa's dedicated gardening and preserving fruits and vegetables, Jewel compares her to Mother Widener, an appropriate choice of paragons of womanhood. Jewel concludes, "You should be real proud of yourself," a suggestion that women must reward themselves for their labors (p. 401).

See also **Emelina Domingos, Viola Domingos, ecofeminism, Alice Greer, Taylor Greer, Lusa Maluf Landowski, Mattie, Mama Mwanza, Codi Noline, Hallie Noline, Nannie Rawley, rescue, Spider Woman, Deanna Wolfe**

- *Further Reading*

Aay, Henry. "Environmental Themes in Ecofiction: *In the Center of the Nation* and *Animal Dreams*." *Journal of Cultural Geography*, Vol. 14, No. 2, Spring/Summer 1994, pp. 65–85.

Cox, Bonnie Jean. "The Need in Us All: A Caring Dynamic Connection with Past." *Lexington Herald-Leader*, September 16, 1990, p. F6.

Cryer, Dan. "Gladdening Stories of Hope and Strength." *New York Newsday*, June 26, 1989, p. 6.

Karbo, Karen. "And Baby Makes Two." *New York Times Book Review*, June 27, 1993, p. 9.

Appendix A:
Chronology of
The Poisonwood Bible

1885	King Leopold II of Belgium creates the Congo Free State.
1891	The Katanga Company begins marketing Congolese copper.
1920	Nathan Price is born.
1920s	Whites in the Congo see the fabled okapi.
1922	Orleanna Wharton is born in Pearl, Mississippi.
1925	Patrice Lumumba is born in Kasai Province in the rural Belgian Congo.
1930	Joseph Désiré Mobutu is born in Lisala, Congo.
1935	Anatole Ngemba is born in the Congo.
1939	Orleanna Wharton marries Nathan Price, a young preacher.

1941
December 7	The Japanese bomb Pearl Harbor.
ca. December 14	Nathan is drafted and sent to the Philippines.

1942
April 9	Nathan hovers in a pig sty to avoid being herded on the Bataan death march. The Japanese force 70,000 American and Philippine prisoners of war from Mariveles over sixty-three miles on foot to Camp O'Donnell. Nathan is shipped home.

1944
August 20	Rachel Price is born.
1945	Orleanna gives birth to twins, Leah and Adah. Adah suffers from congenital hemiplegia.
1951	Miss Leep discovers that the Price twins are gifted.
1953	Dwight D. Eisenhower begins serving two consecutive terms as United States president.

1954	Orleanna gives birth to her fourth child, Ruth May.
1956	The Congolese issue a manifesto calling for independence from colonial rule.
1957	Through government reforms, the Congolese receive partial liberation.
1959	Patrice Lumumba emerges from obscurity as a writer and radical political presence called the barefoot postman.
June	Kilangans welcome the Price family with a goat roast.
next day	Nathan Price plants a garden Southern style.
July 4	The Price family celebrates Easter with a biblical pageant and picnic.
end of July	Monsoon rain destroys Nathan's garden.
August	Nathan considers Methuselah, the grey parrot, a potential heretic and banishes him from the house.
August 20	Rachel celebrates her sixteenth birthday.
end of summer	Nathan dynamites the Kwilu River to provide a fish feast for Kilangans.
December 25	The Price family makes a Christmas tree out of a palm frond. Orleanna gives her daughters needlework materials.
1960 January	The Underdowns visit Kilanga to announce the date of Congolese elections and to warn that the Prices will receive no more money from the Mission League. The death rate for Kilangan children rises from an epidemic of enteritis.
May	The Congo holds elections.
June	Orleanna Price is bedfast with malaria.
June 28	After the Underdowns charter a plane to evacuate the Prices from Kilanga, Nathan refuses to leave.
June 30	Nathan Price travels to Stanleyville and hears by radio that Lumumba supports neutrality and African unity. Lumumba declares the date Independence Day. A civet cat kills Methuselah.
July	Orleanna teaches Rachel to cook.
July 5	The Congolese army rebels.
July 11	Under Moise Tshombe, the Katanga province secedes from the Congo.
August	Chief Ndu offers food and other gifts to the Prices, a gesture of courtship to Rachel. Rachel begins flirting with Eeben Axelroot. Brother Fowles visits Kilanga and brings supplies to the Price family.
August 20	Orleanna gives Rachel earrings and bracelet for her seventeenth birthday.
August 21	Eeben Axelroot confides to Rachel that there is an assassination plot afoot against Lumumba.
days later	Army ants attack Kilanga.
September 10	Mobutu accepts a United Nations bribe of one million dollars in exchange for a U.S.-sanctioned coup.

September 14	General Joseph Mobutu imprisons Premier Lumumba under house arrest and places the army in control of the Congo.
late fall	As drought consumes Kilanga, Kuvudundu uses bones to divine the future. A fire surround results in a squabble over Leah's use of bow and arrow to hunt meat for hungry villagers. Chief Ndu conducts a vote that allows Leah to hunt with the men. Kuvudundu prophesies disaster for the tribe's affront to tradition. Leah kills a male impala.
November 27	Lumumba escapes with housemaids in a station wagon that mires on impassable roads.
December	Lumumba is recaptured.
1961 January 17	A firing squad executes Lumumba in a Katangan prison at Elisabethville. Mobutu seizes control of the Congo. Ruth May dies from the bite of a green mamba. Orleanna, Leah, and Adah slog through rain, mud, and mosquitoes as they flee from Kilanga.
January 18	Rachel arrives in Johannesburg in Eeben Axelroot's plane.
January 20	When the Price women come down with fever, native men make a pallet on which to carry Leah to Bulungu.
February	Orleanna and Adah receive treatment in the infirmary of the Belgian Embassy before flying to the U.S. in a hospital plane.
later	Adah and her mother take up residence in Bethlehem, Georgia in a plywood shack. Leah marries Anatole Ngemba.
1962 summer	Adah recovers from physical handicap and takes science courses at Emory University.
1963	Barbara Kingsolver's family lives in the Congo for two years.
1964	Rachel marries diplomat Daniel Duprée. Leah lives in the Mission Notre Dame de Douleur under the name Soeur Liselin.
1965	Leah gives birth to Pascal.
November 24	Mobutu leads a second coup.
1968	The Price twins reunite in Atlanta, where Adah meets nephew Pascal Ngemba. Leah gives birth to Patrice and enters Emory University to study agronomics.
1971	Mobutu renames the Congo Zaire.
1974	Anatole and Leah live in Kinshasa with their three sons and teach school in a compound for Americans.
October 30	The George Foreman–Muhammad Ali fight takes place at Kinshasa's Stadium.
1975	Anatole rejects an offer to work in the provisional government of Angola.

1978
January   Rachel owns the Equatorial Hotel, which she inherits from her third husband, Remy Fairley.

1981   Leah survives Anatole's imprisonment for treason.

1982   Before Anatole's release, he receives a second job offer from Angola.

1984   For the reunion of the surviving Price sisters, Rachel drives the Ngembas' Land Rover from Senegal to Zaire.

1985
January   Adah tends to her mother's physical and emotional health and reports on Nathan's death from immolation in a field tower.
                 Anatole delivers Nataniel, his fourth son, by the roadside. The couple force-feed the infant for a week until he begins to eat on his own.

1986   The Ngembas live in the Kumvula District, where Anatole reorganizes the secondary school.

ca. **1991**   The Ngembas live in Sanza Pombo, Angola.

1993   Barbara Kingsolver lives in Benin to collect material for *The Poisonwood Bible*.

1997   Mobutu dies of prostate cancer.

1998   Barbara Kingsolver publishes *The Poisonwood Bible*.

Appendix B:
Writing and Research Topics

1. Create a scenario in which Barbara Kingsolver's arrogant Baptist minister, the Reverend Nathan Price, discusses alternative folkways with Mr. Smith, the white newcomer to Nigeria in Chinua Achebe's *Things Fall Apart*, agents from the Bureau of Indian Affairs in Dee Brown's *Bury My Heart at Wounded Knee*, neighborhood children in Sandra Cisneros's *The House on Mango Street*, the *curandera* in the title of Rudolfo Anaya's *Bless Me, Ultima*, Brave Orchid in Maxine Hong Kingston's *The Woman Warrior*, rabbis in Elie Wiesel's *Night*, servile women in Margaret Atwood's *The Handmaid's Tale*, South African teachers and nuns in Mark Mathabane's *Kaffir Boy*, or heiress Clara del Valle in Isabel Allende's *The House of the Spirits*. Discuss issues of family, belief systems, tyranny, patriarchy, colonialism, and/or profiteering.

2. Characterize reactions to desert life in Barbara Kingsolver's *Last Stand: America's Virgin Lands* and either Mary Hunter Austin, James Vance Marshall, Joy Adamson, Antoine de Saint-Exupéry, Suzanne Fisher Staples, or John Steinbeck. Describe their literary sensibilities to nature and compare them with the visual imagery of artists Georgia O'Keeffe and Frida Kahlo and photographer Ansel Adams.

3. Analyze elements of colonialism and bigotry that inform both Barbara Kingsolver's *The Poisonwood Bible* and one of these works: Isabel Allende's *The House of the Spirits*, Robert Montgomery Bird's *Nick of the Woods*, Jane Campion's *The Piano*, Peter Carey's *Oscar and Lucinda*, Joseph Conrad's *Heart of Darkness*, Louise Erdrich's "Fleur," E. M. Forster's *A Passage to India*, George Orwell's "Shooting an Elephant," Ruth Prawer Jhabvala's *Heat and Dust*, Rudyard Kipling's *Kim*, Alan Paton's *Cry the Beloved Country*, Jean Rhys's *Wide Sargasso Sea*, or Sam Watson's *The Kadaitcha Sung*.

4. Explain the value of composing a novel to express racial issues and conflicts caused by outside forces in successive decades of the colonization and control of the Congo. Outline controversies that Barbara Kingsolver's *The Poisonwood Bible* omitted, downplayed, or overlooked, particularly women's place in Congolese society, local violence, child labor, child prostitution and enslavement, inaccessible health care, land and water pollution, and West African religious rights.

5. Outline topics for a book like *The Poisonwood Bible* that would employ political allegory as a means of expressing current issues, for example, American wars in the

Middle East, world struggle against terrorism, emerging epidemics from new diseases or more virulent forms of malaria and other scourges, the place of American industry in the global economy, extermination of child labor and sweat shops, protection of children from draft by mercenaries, and protection of the wild and endangered species.

6. Compare masculine traits in Kingsolver's "Rose-Johnny" (1987), Leah Price Ngemba in *The Poisonwood Bible*, miners' wives in *Holding the Line: Women in the Great Arizona Mine Strike of 1983*, and Deanna Wolfe, Lusa Maluf Landowski, and Crystal Walker in *Prodigal Summer* with descriptions of the outdoorsy or athletic females in Sandra Cisneros's *The House on Mango Street*, Scott O'Dell's *The Island of the Blue Dolphins*, Laura Esquivel's *Like Water for Chocolate*, Suzanne Staples Fisher's *Shabanu: Daughter of the Wind*, Avi's *The True Confessions of Charlotte Doyle*, or Carson McCullers's *The Heart Is a Lonely Hunter* or *The Member of the Wedding*.

7. Summarize the political milieu that caused the flight of Mayan refugees like Estevan and Esperanza in *The Bean Trees*. Compare the historical conflicts of the Contra-Sandinista era in Guatemala to the situations producing the Long Walk, the Trail of Tears, the Underground Railroad, the Great Migration of Southern blacks to industrialized cities in the North, the Okie migration during the Dust Bowl, and the murder of Hallie Noline by Nicaraguan kidnappers in *Animal Dreams*.

8. Identify and explain in *The Bean Trees* and Harriette Arnow's *The Dollmaker* opposing elements resulting from emigration from Appalachia to more prosperous industrialized sections of the United States. Consider examples of neighborliness, urban dangers, economic opportunity, religious bigotry, self-respect, bad fortune, family disruptions, poverty and hunger, sickness, and death.

9. Account for the domination of self-serving mothers in Lillian Hellman's *The Little Foxes*, Amy Tan's *The Joy Luck Club*, Marsha Norman's *'night, Mother*, or Tennessee Williams's *The Glass Menagerie*. Contrast the women who control and manipulate their daughters with the loving generosity and encouragement of mothers such as Clara del Valle in Isabel Allende's *The House of the Spirits*, the title character in Margaret Atwood's *The Handmaid's Tale*, Eliza Birdwell in Jessamyn West's *Except for Me and Thee*, Rose in August Wilson's *Fences*, Orleanna Price in *The Poisonwood Bible*, Emelina Domingos in *Animal Dreams*, or Alice Greer and Taylor Greer in *The Bean Trees* and *Pigs in Heaven*.

10. Contrast Ledger Fourkiller's native prayers in *Pigs in Heaven* with those that the grandson hears from his Kiowa grandmother in N. Scott Momaday's *The Way to Rainy Mountain* and that Black Elk directs at grandfathers in the sky in *Black Elk Speaks*. Explain how intonation, timbre, gesture, and stance express words and concepts that hearers can understand, but can't translate from native languages.

11. Select poems that characterize feelings of detachment in Codi Noline in *Animal Dreams*, Orleanna Price in *The Poisonwood Bible*, Deanna Wolfe in *Prodigal Summer*, and Taylor and Alice Greer in *Pigs in Heaven*, such as Robert Frost's "The Death of the Hired Man." Analyze emotions, ambitions, losses, and frustrations that weigh heavily on love relationships, for example, Codi's concealment of a miscarriage from Loyd Peregrine, Orleanna's disillusion with Nathan and his religious fanaticism, Deanna's decision to keep her pregnancy a secret, Taylor's inability to love Jax Thibodeaux as much as he loves and needs her, and Alice Greer's disillusion with a second marriage and her departure from Harland Elleston, who spends his days watching television.

12. Outline the town of Grace, Arizona, in a schematic drawing. Locate the Baptist Grocery, Hollywood Dress Shop window displaying silver shoes, Doc Homer's house and office, the canyon, courthouse, Jonny's Breakfast, Black Mountain copper mine and brick smokestack, the river, Grace High School,

cemetery, orchards along the river, Horny Toad Saloon, Little Dipper, State Line, Watering Hole, depot alley, exercise salon and Video Rodeo, hospital, railway station, Loyd Peregrina's vine-covered trailer, Doña Althea's restaurant, and the guesthouse at Emelina Domingos's home.

13. Chart similarities between Spider Woman, the Navajo and Pueblo creator of Canyon de Chelly, and other world creation stories, including biblical, Greek, Roman, Buddhist, Quechuan, Sioux, Cherokee, and Babylonian lore. Note the presence of menace or overt violence in stories and the punishments meted out to humans who express pride or who violate the sanctity of the gods.

14. Compare the source of anger and mistrust of whites in Dee Brown's *Bury My Heart at Wounded Knee*, Hal Borland's *When the Legends Die*, Conrad Richter's *The Light in the Forest*, Michael Dorris's *Yellow Raft in Blue Water*, Forrest Carter's *The Education of Little Tree*, or *Black Elk Speaks* to a similar discontent in *Pigs in Heaven*. Outline elements of the native settlement of Oklahoma that Kingsolver alludes to in her presentation of Cherokee reservation life.

15. Compare the ambitions, regrets, and yearnings in Robert Cormier's *I Am the Cheese*, Michael Dorris's *Yellow Raft in Blue Water*, Sharon Creech's *Walk Two Moons*, Tim O'Brien's *The Things They Carried*, John Steinbeck's *Of Mice and Men*, or Jerry Bock's musical drama *Fiddler on the Roof* with the emotions of Adah, Leah, Orleanna, Rachel, and Ruth May Price in *The Poisonwood Bible*. Stress how survivors enjoy freedom, but carry a burden of guilt and regret for the past.

16. Compare scenes of marital discord in Beth Henley's *Crimes of the Heart*, Arthur Miller's *Death of a Salesman*, Lillian Hellman's *The Little Foxes*, Tennessee Williams's *Cat on a Hot Tin Roof*, or August Wilson's *Fences* to the Price sisters' multiple marriages in Kingsolver's *The Poisonwood Bible*. Note insights and epiphanies that increase the un-

derstanding of Rachel Price Fairley and Leah Price Ngemba after their experiences with husbands, loss, and the unpredictability of their fortunes in Africa.

17. Explore similarities between Nannie Land Rawley in *Prodigal Summer* and either Lucy Marsden in Allan Gurganous's *The Oldest Living Confederate Widow Tells All*, Mrs. Ninny Threadgoode in Fannie Flagg's *Fried Green Tomatoes at the Whistlestop Cafe*, Mother Miriam Ruth in Leonore Fleischer's *Agnes of God*, or Mattie Rigsbee in Clyde Edgerton's *Walking across Egypt*. Note in particular attitudes toward nature, sharing, secrecy, dedication, and relatives and other people. Explain how the women provide humor as well as wisdom to the text.

18. Summarize elements of Donna M. Gershten's *Kissing the Virgin's Mouth* that warrant its choice as the first winner of the Bellwether Prize. Note similarities between the author's presentation of hardship and empathy in Teatlan, Mexico, with Kingsolver's depiction of Leah Price Ngemba's life and activism in the Congo in *The Poisonwood Bible*, Hallie Noline's volunteerism in *Animal Dreams*, and Lusa Maluf Landowski's solution to widowhood, alienation, and penury in *Prodigal Summer*.

19. Contrast the struggles of the sisters in Yoko Kawashima Watkins's autobiographical *So Far from the Bamboo Grove*, Anita Diamant's *The Red Tent*, or Suzanne Staples Fisher's *Shabanu: Daughter of the Wind* with Hallie and Codi Noline in *Animal Dreams* or Adah and Leah Price in *The Poisonwood Bible*. Determine how local customs, violence, and unavoidable events impact the lives of these pairs of siblings.

20. Select contrasting scenes and describe their pictorial qualities, for example:

• Adah Price's value as a translator for her missionary family in *The Poisonwood Bible*
• Taylor Greer's visit with Esperanza after the attempted suicide in *The Bean Trees*
• Doc Homer's sadness at the reburial of

Codi's stillborn child in Alice's garden in *Animal Dreams*
- Edna Poppy's attempt to buy citrus fruit at a Mexican market in *The Bean Trees*
- Jewel Widener Walker's collapse with a basket of tomatoes in *Prodigal Summer*
- the arrival of police in *Holding the Line: Women in the Great Arizona Mine Strike of 1983*
- Turtle Greer's recognition of Cash Stillwater as Pop-Pop in *Pigs in Heaven*
- Adah Price's awkward attempt to flee from army ants in *The Poisonwood Bible*
- members of the Stitch and Bitch Club displaying piñatas in Tucson in *Animal Dreams*
- Deanna Wolfe's flashlight beam on four bulges in a black snake in *Prodigal Summer*
- Chief Ndu's courtship of Rachel Price with food and native crafts in *The Poisonwood Bible*
- the Grace, Arizona, high school biology class gathering specimens from the river in *Animal Dreams*
- Ledger Fourkiller's leadership of worship at the stomp dance in *Pigs in Heaven*
- Lou Ann Ruiz's protection of Dwayne Ray at the zoo in *The Bean Trees*
- media interviews with miners' wives in *Holding the Line: Women in the Great Arizona Mine Strike of 1983*
- the Price sisters viewing skeletal remains in the Abomey palace in *The Poisonwood Bible*
- Barbie's robbery of her employer and departure from Nevada with Alice, Turtle, and Taylor Greer in *Pigs in Heaven*.

21. Discuss farming, family, and ecology as themes in *Prodigal Summer* and *Animal Dreams*. Contrast Nannie Land Rawley, Lusa Maluf Landowski, Deanna Wolfe, Hallie Noline, and Codi Noline as stewards of the land.

22. Compare the courtships and sexual relationships in *Animal Dreams*, *The Poisonwood Bible*, and *Pigs in Heaven* to similar male-female matchups in Alice Walker's *The Color Purple*, Virginia Renfro Ellis's *The Wedding Dress*, Isabel Allende's *Daughter of Fortune*, Olive Ann Burns's *Cold Sassy Tree*, or Ernest J. Gaines's *The Autobiography of Miss Jane Pittman*. Contrast obstacles to each couple's happiness.

23. Write an extended definition of *conservatism* using examples from Newt Gingrich's *To Renew America* (1995). Contrast each social, political, and economic tenet with Kingsolver's beliefs as stated in her essays, poems, non-fiction, and novels.

24. Compare the romantic elements of *Prodigal Summer*, *The Bean Trees*, *Pigs in Heaven*, or *Animal Dreams* with those of James Waller's *The Bridges of Madison County*. Note pictorial elements in nature as well as human traits that build the intensity of love relationships.

25. Compare the autobiographical memories of growing up in the Appalachias in Barbara Kingsolver's writings and the descriptions of youth in Homer Hickam's *October Sky*, Eliot Wigginton's Foxfire series, Cynthia Rylant's *Missing May*, or Jesse Stuart's *The Thread That Runs So True*. Discuss how intellectual curiosity uplifts children who attend substandard mountain schools.

26. Improvise a conference of Garnett S. Walker, III, Rachel Price Fairley, Jax Thibodeaux, Lusa Maluf Landowski, Little Rickie, Taylor Greer, Anatole Ngemba, Loyd Peregrina, Mattie, Cash Stillwater, Carlo, striking miners' wives, and Hallie Noline about the nature of human happiness as regards to money. As a model, explain through dialogue why Garnett invests his time in hybridizing a chestnut tree that he will never live to enjoy, why Rachel prefers to date or marry older men, how Hallie invests her agronomic expertise in Nicaragua, how miners' wives support their families, why Loyd Peregrina gives up cockfighting, why Cash Stillwater returns to Heaven, how Little Rickie increases the earning potential of his Uncle Cole Widener's farm, how Taylor survives after Barbie robs her of traveling money, why Jax encourages Taylor to come home, why Mattie divides her time between the tire store and rescuing illegal aliens, and

how Anatole intends to uplift peasant Congolese and his own sons through education.

27. Summarize the resources of strong women in Kingsolver's *Prodigal Summer* and in Kaye Gibbons's *Charms for the Easy Life*. Note the reliance on education and hard work in folk healer and midwife Miss Charlie Kate Birch and her granddaughter Margaret, orchard keeper Nannie Land Rawley, forest ranger Deanna Wolfe, cancer victim Jewel Widener Walker, and farmer and goatherd Lusa Maluf Landowski. Express efforts to pass worthy virtues to the younger generation.

28. List and describe a variety of narrative forms and styles in Barbara Kingsolver's writings, including verse, personal essay, dialogue, anecdote, ecology lecture, satire, genealogy, scripture, fable, quip, adage, eulogy, elegy, lament, epistle, comic relief, pun, palindrome, and debate.

29. Compare the roles of Nannie Land Rawley, Ledger Fourkiller, Mattie, Mama Tataba, Anatole Ngemba, Cash Stillwater, Viola Domingos, Estevan, Alice Greer, Chief Ndu, Patrice Lumumba, Granny Logan, Mama Mwanza, Jewel Widener Walker, Brother Fyntan Fowles, or Uda Dell as advisers and bearers of wisdom with creators of disorder and chaos, particularly Angel Ruiz, Mary Edna Goins, Tata Kuvudundu, Barbie, Doc Homer, Eddie Bondo, Mobutu Sese Seko, Annawake Fourkiller, Eeben Axelroot, and Nathan Price. Explain how Kingsolver uses compromise and nonviolence as strategies to neutralize disruptive situations.

30. Choose two characters from Kingsolver's works to compare in terms of religious beliefs, for example, Ledger Fourkiller's expression of Cherokee animism and Grandma Logan's intense fundamentalism, Tata Kuvudundu's shamanism and Nannie Land Rawley's faith in nature, Brother Fyntan Fowles's humanism and Great Mam's reverence for native customs, and Loyd Peregrina's explanation of Spider Woman and Nathan Price's belief in baptism.

31. Hypothesize the attitudes and roles of characters in Kingsolver's novels who are only mentioned. Include Rachel Price Fairley's aged husband, Harland Elleston, Cissy Ramon, Sue Stillwater, Mother Widener, Celine Fowles, Foster Greer, Patrice Lumumba, Leander Peregrina, Elizabet and Christiane, Alice Noline, Deanna Wolfe's former husband, Ismene, owners of the Black Mountain mining company, Gabriel Fourkiller, Alma Stillwater, Nataniel Ngemba, Terry, Mama Ruiz, Zayda Landowski, Rachel Carson Rawley, and Shel Walker.

32. Characterize the importance of setting to significant scenes, for example, Taylor's relaxation with Estevan on the Lake o' the Cherokees, Loyd and Codi's visit to Kinishba, the three Price sisters' tour of a deserted palace at Abomey, Deanna Wolfe's sighting of a coyote den, the Kilangans' flight from army ants, Garnett Walker's humiliation in Little Brothers' Hardware, the eagle dancer's swoop south during the Christmas Day celebration at Santa Rosalia Pueblo, Mattie's trip to the desert after rain, the goat roast welcoming the Price family to Kilanga, Nannie's words of comfort to Lusa at Cole's wake, Turtle's lesson in bean planting at Mattie's Jesus Is Lord tire store, the rescue of Lucky Buster from the Hoover Dam sluiceway, Anatole Ngemba's part in delivering his fourth child by the roadside, Jack's survival after the other coyote pups are drowned, and Alice's presence at the Cherokee stomp dance in Heaven, Oklahoma.

33. Summarize the native American values of Great Mam in the short story "Homeland." Compare her devotion to ritual or tradition with that of Ledger Fourkiller and Cash Stillwater in *Pigs in Heaven*, Chief Ndu and Tata Kuvudundu in *The Poisonwood Bible*, Eddie Bondo in *Prodigal Summer*, Granny Logan in *The Bean Trees*, and Viola Domingos, Doña Althea, and Loyd Peregrina in *Animal Dreams*.

34. Using characters from Kingsolver's novels, documentary, and stories, describe the female angst that Betty Friedan challenges in *The Feminine Mystique*.

35. Locate examples of racism and lack of charity in James Michener's *Hawaii* or Peter Carey's *Oscar and Lucinda* that correspond to the Reverend Nathan Price's lack of love and understanding for Kilangans in *The Poisonwood Bible* and community outsiders in *Holding the Line: Women in the Great Arizona Mine Strike of 1983*.

36. Describe qualities in the hovering spirit of Ruth May Price in *The Poisonwood Bible* that reflect similar qualities in the child ghost in Toni Morrison's *Beloved*.

37. Account for the images that Barbara Kingsolver chooses for book titles: *The Bean Trees, Homeland, Holding the Line: Women in the Great Arizona Mine Strike of 1983, Animal Dreams, Another America: Otra America, Pigs in Heaven, High Tide in Tucson, The Poisonwood Bible, Prodigal Summer, Small Wonder,* and *Last Stand: America's Virgin Lands*.

38. Locate the strengths of John Steinbeck's Ma Joad, the matriarch of *The Grapes of Wrath*, in Kingsolver's staunch female survivors, including Alice Greer and Mattie in *The Bean Trees*, Alice Greer, Sugar Boss Hornbuckle, and Angie Buster in *Pigs in Heaven*, Doña Althea and Viola Domingos in *Animal Dreams*, wives of strikers in *Holding the Line: Women in the Great Arizona Mine Strike of 1983*, Nannie Land Rawley, Jewel Widener Walker, and Lusa Maluf Landowski in *Prodigal Summer*, and Orleanna Price, Leah Price Ngemba, Mama Tataba, and Mama Mwanza in *The Poisonwood Bible*.

39. List and describe the dramatic importance of realistic elements from *Prodigal Summer, Animal Dreams, Pigs in Heaven, The Poisonwood Bible,* and *The Bean Trees,* including spousal and child abuse, suicide, poaching in a national forest, rescuing a failing farm, fraudulent adoption, false identity, interstate flight, theft, cruel boarding schools, water pollution, kidnap, execution of a public official, bureaucratic corruption, treatment of cancer, hunting by fire surround, false imprisonment, nudity at public ceremonies, guerrilla warfare, the burning death of a missionary, murder by poisonous snake,

and the death of a truck driver in a highway accident.

40. Compare the vision of community in *The Poisonwood Bible, Animal Dreams, Holding the Line: Women in the Great Arizona Mine Strike of 1983*, and *Pigs in Heaven* to that of Dubose Heyward and George Gershwin in *Porgy and Bess*, the first American opera. Include superstitions, faith, grief, shared labors, ritual, fears, love, violence, and trust.

41. Contrast various examples of motherhood from literature. In addition to Taylor Greer and Esperanza in *The Bean Trees*, Leah Price Ngemba, Mama Mwanza, and Orleanna Price in *The Poisonwood Bible*, and Emelina Domingos and Codi Noline in *Animal Dreams*, comment on mothering in Anne Frank's *The Diary of a Young Girl*, Carson McCullers's *The Member of the Wedding*, Conrad Richter's *The Light in the Forest*, Anita Diamant's *The Red Tent*, Toni Morrison's *The Bluest Eye*, Isabel Allende's *The House of the Spirits*, Yoko Kawashima Watkins's *So Far from the Bamboo Grove*, Louisa May Alcott's *Little Women*, Jane Austen's *Pride and Prejudice*, and John Steinbeck's *The Grapes of Wrath*.

42. Create a role for a social worker who will visit Turtle Greer and help her overcome the effects of child abuse in *The Bean Trees*. Suggest activities that will develop trust, particularly sharing toys, making photographs and keeping a scrapbook, playing "just pretend" games, cooking and eating, playing a musical instrument, doing chores, singing with a group, planting a garden, and fingerpainting.

43. Act out an interview with Eleanor Roosevelt, who presided over the establishment of human rights for the United Nations Charter. List her views on the rights of displaced persons, children, the elderly and handicapped, orphans, prisoners of war, and refugees that would apply to Esperanza, Ismene, and Estevan in *The Bean Trees* or to Orleanna and Adah Price, Anatole and Leah Ngemba, Elizabet and Christiane, Patrice

Lumumba, Patrice and Pascal Ngemba, Mama Mwanza, and Nelson in *The Poisonwood Bible*.

44. Analyze the lyrics of Stevie Wonder's "Love's in Need of Love Today." Determine why the song refers to refugees like Esperanza and Estevan in *The Bean Trees*, Cash Stillwater and Sue in *Pigs in Heaven*, Doc Homer and Codi Noline in *Animal Dreams*, Orleanna and Adah Price in *The Poisonwood Bible*, and Crystal and Lowell Walker in *Prodigal Summer*

45. Conduct an interview with Father William, Mattie, Hallie Noline, Carlo, and Terry in *The Bean Trees*. Ask how sanctuary workers meet the needs of dispossessed people, including communication, medicine, food, farm equipment, clothing, translators, false papers, transportation, and places to hide.

46. Discuss Kingsolver's use of disease as character motivation, as with catalepsy and blindness in *The Bean Trees*, Gracela syndrome and Alzheimer's disease in *Animal Dreams*, hemiplegia, muteness, hookworm, kwashiorkor, malaria, and burned legs in *The Poisonwood Bible*, and nystagmus, Down syndrome, and cancer in *Prodigal Summer*.

Bibliography

Primary Sources

"An Address from Barbara Kingsolver — Delivered at the 1993 American Booksellers Convention." http://www.readinggroup guides.com/guides/poisonwood_bible-author.asp

"After a Finger Workout, It's Great Pumping Iron." *Smithsonian,* September 1990, p. 168.

"Ah, Sweet Mystery of ... Well, Not Exactly Love." *Smithsonian,* June 1990, p. 168.

"And Our Flag Was Still There." *San Francisco Chronicle,* September 25, 2001.

Animal Dreams. New York: HarperCollins, 1990.

Another America: Otra America (verse). Seattle: Seal Press, 1992; reissued, 1998.

The Bean Trees. New York: Harper & Row, 1988; reissued, 1998.

"Bereaved Apartments." *Tucson Guide Quarterly,* Spring 1989, p. 11.

Best American Short Stories 2001. (co-editor) Boston: Houghton Mifflin, 2001.

"Between the Covers." *Washington Post,* May 24, 1998, p. 1.

"Cabbages and Kings" in *Women Respond to the Men's Movement: A Feminist Collection.* San Francisco: Pandora, 1992.

"Canary Islands." *Our Own Anthology, New York Times,* November 16, 2003.

"Celebration of Bookselling" (speech). *Booksense,* June 19, 2000, pp. 6–7.

Chism, Olin. "Questions of Right; Author Presents Indians' Answers." *Dallas Morning News,* July 9, 1993, p. 1C.

"Confession of the Reluctant Remainder" in *Mid-Life Confidential: The Rock Bottom Remainders.* New York: Viking Penguin, 1994.

"Creation Stories" in *Getting Over the Color Green: Southwestern American Literature: An Anthology of Contemporary Environmental Literature from the American Southwest.* University of Nevada Press November 1995.

"Deadline" in *A Map of Hope: Women's Writings on Human Rights, An International Literary Anthology.* Rutgers University Press, 1999.

"Desert Blooms." *Natural History,* May 1999, p. 76.

"Desire Under the Palms." *New York Times,* February 6, 1994.

The Essential Agrarian Reader: The Future of Culture, Community and the Land (Foreword). Lexington: University of Kentucky Press, 2003.

"Everybody's Somebody's Baby." *New York Times Magazine,* February 9, 1992, pp. 20, 49.

"Fault Lines." *Frontiers: A Journal of Women Studies,* Vol. 12, No. 3, Winter 1992, pp. 182–189.

"A Fist in the Eye of God." *Mother Earth News,* August 1, 2002.

Florilegia, an Anthology of Art and Literature by Women (contributor) 1987.

"A Forbidden Territory Familiar to All." *New York Times*, March 27, 2000, p. E1.

"Going to Japan" in *Journeys*. Rockville, Md.: Quill & Brush, 1994.

"A Good Farmer." *Nation*, November 3, 2003.

High Tide in Tucson: Essays from Now or Never (essays). New York: HarperCollins, 1995.

"His-and-Hers Politics." *Utne Reader*, January-February 1993, pp. 70–71.

Holding the Line: Women in the Great Arizona Mine Strike of 1983 (documentary). Ithaca, N.Y.: Cornell University Press, 1989; reissued, 1997.

Homeland and Other Stories. New York: HarperCollins, 1989.

"How Poems Happen" in *Utne Reader*, Vol. 88, July/August 1998, pp. 36–37; reprinted in *The Beacon Best of 1999: Creative Writing by Women and Men of All Colors*. Boston: Beacon Press, 1999.

"In the Belly of the Beast" in *Learning to Glow: A Nuclear Reader*. Tucson: University of Arizona Press, April 2000.

"It's My Flag, Too." *San Francisco Chronicle*, January 13, 2002.

I've Always Meant to Tell You: Letters to Our Mothers: An Anthology of Contemporary Women Writers (contributor). New York: Pocket Star, 1997.

"Knowing Our Place" in *Off the Beaten Path: Stories of Place*. Nature Conservancy, 1998.

"Lacewings." *Redbook*, November 2000, p. 109.

Last Stand: America's Virgin Lands. Washington, D.C.: National Geographic Society, 2002.

"Life Is Precious— or It's Not." *Los Angeles Times*, May 2, 1999, p. 5.

"Local Foods That Please the Soul." *New York Times*, November 22, 2001.

"The Lost Language of Love." *Mademoiselle*, May 1989.

"Lush Language." *Los Angeles Times*, May 16, 1993, p. 1.

"Making Peace" in *Intimate Nature: The Bond Between Women and Animals*. New York: Ballantine, 1998.

"A Mean Eye" in *Walking the Twilight: Women Writers of the Southwest*. Flagstaff, Ariz.: Northland, 1997.

"The Memory Place" in *Heart of the Land: Essays on Last Great Places*. New York: Pantheon, 1994.

"Mormon Memories" (book review). *Los Angeles Times*, November 19, 1989, p. 1.

"My Father's Africa." *McCall's*, August 1991, pp. 115–123.

New Stories from the South (contributor). New York: Algonquin, 1988.

"No Glory in Unjust War on the Weak." *Los Angeles Times*, October 14, 2001, p. M1.

Off the Beaten Path: Stories of Place (contributor). New York: North Point Press, 1998.

"Old Chestnuts." *Book*, September 2000, p. 60.

"The Patience of a Saint." *National Geographic*, April 2000, pp. 80–97.

"Personal Perspective; A Pure, High Note of Anguish." *Los Angeles Times*, September 23, 2001, p. M1.

Pigs in Heaven. New York: HarperCollins, 1993.

"Poetic Fiction with a Tex-Mex Tilt." *Los Angeles Times*, April 28, 1991, p. 3.

The Poisonwood Bible. New York: HarperCollins, 1998.

"Precious Little Time." *Redbook,* July 1989, p. 28.

"The Prince Thing." *Woman's Day*, February 18, 1992, pp. 26, 28, 110.

Prodigal Summer. New York: HarperCollins, 2000.

"Quality Time" in *The Single Mother's Companion*. Seattle: Seal Press, 1994.

Rebirth of Power: Overcoming the Effects of Sexual Abuse Through the Experiences of Others (contributor). Racine, Wisc.: Mother Courage Press, 1987.

"Reflections on 'Wartime.'" *Washington Post*, November 23, 2001, p. A43.

"Remember the Moon Survives." *Calyx*, 1986.

"Rose-Johnny." *Virginia Quarterly*, Vol. 63, Winter 1987, pp. 88–109.

"Saying Grace." *Audubon*, January 2002, pp 40–42.

"Secret Animals." *Turnstile*, Vol. 3, No. 2, 1992, pp. 11–22.

"Seeing Scarlet" in *The Best American Science and Nature Writing*. New York: Houghton Mifflin, 2001.

Small Wonder (essays co-authored by Stephen Hopp). New York: HarperCollins, 2002.

"Somebody's Baby." *Plough Reader*, Autumn 2000, pp. 9–14.

"Stone Soup: What Does It Mean to Be a Family, Anyway?" *Tucson Weekly*, September 28-October 4, 1995.

"Untitled" in *Letters to Our Mothers: I've Always Meant to Tell You: An Anthology of Contemporary Women Writers*. New York: Pocket Books, 1997.

"The Way to Nueva Vida." *Sierra*, September/October 2003, pp. 34–37.

"The Way We Are." *Parenting*, March 1995, pp. 74–81.

"What Happens When Justice Turns a Blind Eye." *New York Newsday*, October 25, 1992.

"What Has Changed for All of Us." *Boston Globe*, September 26, 2001, p. A19.

"Where Love Is Nurtured and Confined." *Los Angeles Times*, February 18, 1990, p. 2.

"Where the Map Stopped." *New York Times*, May 17, 1992.

"Why I Am a Danger to the Public." *New Times*, January 4-10, 1986, p. 37.

"Widows at the Wheel." *Los Angeles Times*, October 1, 1989, p. 1.

"A Woman's Unease About the Men's Movement" in *Goodlife: Mastering the Art of Everyday Living*. Minneapolis: Utne Reader Books, 1997.

"Women on the Line" (with Jill Barrett Fein). *Progressive*, March 1984, p. 15.

"Worlds in Collision." *Los Angeles Times*, November 4, 1990, p. 3.

"Writers on Writing." *New York Times*, March 27, 2000, p. 1.

"Your Mother's Eyes." *Calyx*, 1986.

Secondary Sources

Aay, Henry. "Environmental Themes in Ecofiction: *In the Center of the Nation* and *Animal Dreams*." *Journal of Cultural Geography*, Vol. 14, No. 2, Spring/Summer 1994, pp. 65–85.

Abu-Jaber, Diana. "Women's Fiction Tends to Congregate at the Middle of Things." *Oregonian*, July 25, 1999.

Adams, Noah. "Commentary: Time Has Come for Reviewing the Executive Order That Forbids U.S. Government Sponsorship of Political Assassinations." *All Things Considered* (NPR), September 17, 2001.

Anderson, Loraine. "Barbie — More Than Just a Doll." Traverse City, Michigan *Record-Eagle*, March 26, 2000.

Aprile, Dianne. "Kinship with Kingsolver: Author's Characters Long to Belong, Something That Touches Readers." *Louisville Courier-Journal*, July 25, 1993, p. I1.

Arten, Isaac. "Review: *The Poisonwood Bible*." *Midwest Book Review*, December 2001.

Ascher-Walsh, Rebecca. "Kingsolver for a Day." *Entertainment Weekly*, No. 511, November 5, 1999, p. 75.

Atkinson, Barbara. "Nicaragua Hosts Ben Linder Alternative Energy Conference." *Earth Island Journal*, Vol. 5, No. 2, Spring 1990, pp. 22–23.

Aulette, Judy, and Trudy Mills. "Something Old, Something New: Auxiliary Work in the 1983–1986 Copper Strike." *Feminist Studies*, Vol. 14, No. 2, Summer 1988, pp. 251–267.

Bakopoulos, Paul. "Review: *Prodigal Summer*." *Progressive*, Vol. 64, No. 12, December 2000, p. 41.

Banks, Russell. "Distant as a Cherokee Childhood." *New York Times Book Review*, July 11, 1989, p. 16.

"Barbara Kingsolver." http://www.maui.com/~sbdc/writers/kingsolver.html.

"Barbara Kingsolver." http://www.pbs.org/newshour/gercpn/kingsolver.html.

"Barbara Kingsolver." *Journal of the National Writers Union*, Vol. 16 No. 4, Winter 1998-1999, pp. 6–7.

"Barbara Kingsolver." *Salon*, December 16, 1995.

"Barbara Kingsolver: Coming Home to a Prodigal Summer." http://www.ivillage.com/books/intervu/fict/articles.

"Barbara Kingsolver Page." http://www.csc.eku.edu/honors/kingsolver/.

Bargreen, Melinda. "Characters Are Saving Grace of 'Prodigal Summer.'" *Seattle Times*, November 5, 2000.

Barkley, Tona. "KET Reading Program Takes First Place in National Competition." *Commonwealth Communique*, April 2003.

Barnette, Martha. "Back to the Blue Ridge: A Kentucky Writer Rediscovers Her Roots." *Louisville Courier-Journal*, June 24, 2000.

Barrett, Sharon. "Kingsolver's Heart of

Darkness." *Chicago Sun-Times,* October 25, 1998, p. 18.

Bayard, Louis. "Last Stand: America's Virgin Lands." http://nature.org/magazine/books/misc/art9328.html.

Beal, Tom. "Tucson's Wonder." *Arizona Daily Star,* April 19, 2002, p. E1.

Beam, Alex. "Lumumba: Man, Myth, and Movie." *Boston Globe,* October 4, 2001.

Bell, Millicent. "Fiction Chronicle: *The Poisonwood Bible.*" *Partisan Review,* Vol. 66, 1999, pp. 417–430.

"The Bellwether Prize." http://www.bellwetherprize.org/default.htm.

Bertsche, Jim. "The Good and Bad in *The Poisonwood Bible.*" *The Mennonite,* February 6, 2001, p. 15.

"Best Local Authors: Barbara Kingsolver." http://www.desert.net/disk$ebony/tw/www/tw/bot96/nonframed/art4.htmlx.

Bierhorst, John, ed. *The Way of the Earth: Native America and the Environment.* New York: William Morrow, 1994.

Birnie, Sue. "The Poisonwood Bible." *National Catholic Reporter,* Vol. 37, No. 32, 2001, p. 16.

Bisson, Michele. "Adoptive Mom, Phone Home." *Seattle Times,* July 18, 1993.

Blake, Fanny. "Interview." *YOU,* January 5, 2000.

Boateng, Osei. "United Against 'Satan.'" *New African,* No. 400, October 2001.

Bolick, Katie. "As the World Thrums: An Interview with Francine Prose." *Atlantic,* March 11, 1998.

Born, Brad S. "Kingsolver's Gospel for Africa: (Western White Female) Heart of Goodness." *Mennonite Life,* Vol. 56, No. 1, March 2001.

"Briefly Noted: *The Bean Trees.*" *New Yorker,* April 4, 1988, pp. 101–102.

Bromberg, Judith. "A Complex Novel About Faith, Family and Dysfunction." *National Catholic Reporter,* Vol. 35, No. 20, March 19, 1999, p. 13.

Brosi, George. "Barbara Kingsolver." http://www.english.eku.edu/services/kylit/kingslvr.htm, September 30, 1997.

Brussat, Frederic, and Mary Ann Brussat. "Review: 'High Tide in Tucson.'" *Spirituality and Health,* http://www.spiritualityhealth.com/newsh/items/bookreview/item_5961.html.

Bush, Trudy. "Back to Nature." *Christian Century,* Vol. 117, No. 33, November 22, 2000, pp. 1245–1246.

Butler, Jack. "She Hung the Moon and Plugged in All the Stars." *New York Times Book Review,* April 10, 1988, p. 15.

Byfield, Ted, and Virginia Byfield. "The Evil Missionary." *Alberta Report/Newsmagazine,* Vol. 26, No. 7, February 8, 1999, p. 35.

Camp, Jennie A. "Activist Short on Solutions." *Rocky Mountain Times,* May 3, 2002.

Campbell, Kim. "Barbara Kingsolver Gets Uncomfortable." *Christian Science Monitor,* Vol. 90, No. 249, November 19, 1998, p. 20.

Carman, Diane. "Kingsolver Hits Stride in Africa; Missionary's Muddling Creates Cultural Disaster." *Denver Post,* October 18, 1998.

Carpenter, Mackenzie. "Kingsolver's Essays Stumble on U.S. Guilt for Sept. 11." *Pittsburgh Post-Gazette,* April 13, 2002, p. B-7.

Carr, Jo. "Review: *Animal Dreams.*" *Library Journal,* Vol. 120, No. 1, January 1, 1995, p. 158.

Charles, Ron. "A Dark Heart in the Congo." *Christian Science Monitor,* Vol. 90, No. 249, November 19, 1998, p. 20.

_____. "Mothers of Nature Howling at the Moon." *Christian Science Monitor,* Vol. 92, No. 230, October 19, 2000.

"Cheap Thrills." *Tucson Weekly,* November 20, 1997.

Ciccarelli, Sheryl, and Marie Rose Napierkowski. "Presenting Analysis, Context, and Criticism on Commonly Studied Novels." *Novels for Students,* Vol. 5, No. 1, 1999, pp. 27–46.

Cincotti, Joseph. "Intimate Revelations." *New York Times,* September 2, 1990.

Ciolkowski, Laura. "Review: *Small Wonder.*" *New York Times,* May 5, 2002.

Cockburn, Alexander. "The Execution of Ben Linder." *Nation,* Vol. 245, October 17, 1987, pp. 402–403.

Cockrell, Amanda. "Luna Moths, Coyotes, Sugar Skulls: The Fiction of Barbara Kingsolver." *Hollins Critic,* Vol. 38, No 2, April 2001, pp. 1–15.

Cohen, Leslie. "Two Tiers in a Saga of Nature." *Boston Globe,* December 24, 2000.

Conniff, Ruth. "Review: *The Poisonwood Bible*." *Progressive*, December 1998.

Contemporary Southern Writers. Detroit: St. James Press, 1999.

"A Conversation with Barbara Kingsolver." http://www.readinggroupguides.com/guides /animal_dreams-author.asp.

Cooke, Carolyn. "Review: *Animal Dreams.*" *Nation*, Vol. 251, No. 18, November 26, 1990, pp. 653–654.

Cooperman, Bernard D. "Review: *Prodigal Summer.*" *Kliatt*, Vol. 36, No. 3, May 2002, pp. 52–53.

Cox, Bonnie Jean. "The Need in Us All: A Caring Dynamic Connection with Past." *Lexington Herald-Leader*, September 16, 1990, p. F6.

Crosbie, Lynn. "Carnal Lightning in Appalachia." *Toronto Star*, December 10, 2000.

Cryer, Dan. "Gladdening Stories of Hope and Strength." *New York Newsday*, June 26, 1989, p. 6.

_____. "Talking with Barbara Kingsolver/ The Good Book." *New York Newsday*, November 15, 1998, p. B11.

_____. "An Unexpected Miracle and a Conflict of Roots." *New York Newsday*, June 21, 1993, p. 46.

_____. "You Can Go Home Again." *New York Newsday*, August 26, 1990, p. 19.

Cullen, Paul. "What Mobutu Learned from King Léopold." *Irish Times*, August 12, 2000.

Culp, Mary Beth. "Review: *The Poisonwood Bible*." Mobile, Alabama, *Harbinger*, February 2, 1999.

Danley-Kilgo, Reese. "Kingsolver's Latest Scores Hit." *Huntsville Times*, November 26, 2000.

Darling, Juanita. "A Nation Tempered by Poetry." *Los Angeles Times*, July 26, 1999, p. A1.

Davison, Liam. "Writing as Incest." *Australian*, September 28, 2002.

Delorme, Marie-Laure. "Barbara Kingsolver: Un Roman Foisonnant." *L'Humanité*, November 4, 1999.

DeMarr, Mary Jean. *Barbara Kingsolver: A Critical Companion.* Westport, Conn.: Greenwood, 1999.

Doenges, Judy. "The Political Is Personal —

Barbara Kingsolver's Novel Measures Tragedy in the Congo in Terms of Intimate, Individual Costs." *Seattle Times*, October 29, 1998.

Donahue, Deirdre. "Interview." *USA Today*, July 15, 1993, p. F3.

Douthat, Ross. "Kumbaya Watch: Barbara Kingsolver's America." *National Review*, September 26, 2001.

Doyle, R. Erica. "Barbara Kingsolver: The Bellwether Prize." *Ms.*, June/July 2001, p. 89.

DuPlessis, Rachel Blau. *Writing Beyond the Ending: Narrative Strategies of Twentieth-Century Women Writers.* Bloomington: Indiana University Press, 1985.

Duval, Alex. "Shafted: How Phelps Dodge Strips Miners of Their Rights," *Tucson Weekly*, March 19, 1998.

Eastburn, Kathryn. "On Solid Ground." *Colorado Springs Independent*, December 14, 2000.

Eberson, Sharon. "Appalachian Romance Has Kingsolver in Top Form." *Pittsburgh Post-Gazette*, January 14, 2001.

Eckhoff, Sally. "Scents and Sensibility." *Wall Street Journal*, October 20, 2000. p. W10.

Ede, Piers Moore. "Small Wonder." *Earth Island Journal*, Vol. 17, No. 4, Winter 2002-2003, pp. 45–46.

"Editor's Choice." *New York Times*, December 6, 1998, p. 6.

Eisele, Kim. "The Where and Why of Literature: A Conversation with Barbara Kingsolver." *You Are Here*, Vol. 2 No 2, Fall 1999, pp. 10–15.

Eisler, Riane. "The Gaia Tradition and the Partnership Future: An Ecofeminist Manifesto" in *Reweaving the World: The Emergence of Ecofeminism.* San Francisco: Sierra Club, 1990.

Epstein, Robin. "Barbara Kingsolver." *Progressive*, Vol. 60, No. 2, February 1996, pp. 33–37.

Ewert, Jeanne. "Shadows of 'Darkness': The Specter of Joseph Conrad's Classic Tale of Oppression Emerges Throughout Barbara Kingsolver's Latest Novel." *Chicago Tribune*, October 11, 1998, p. 6.

Fahringer, Catherine. "Treat Yourself to *The Poisonwood Bible*." *Freethought Today*, June/July 2001.

Farrell, Michael J. "In Life, Art, Writer

Plumbs Politics of Hope." *National Catholic Reporter*, May 22, 1992, pp. 21, 29–30.

Finkel, Mike. "The Ultimate Survivor." *Audubon*, Vol. 101, No. 3, May-June 1999.

FitzGerald, Karen. "A Major New Talent." *Ms.*, April 1988, p. 28.

Flairty, Steve. "Barbara Kingsolver: Kentucky's 'Polite Firebrand' Author." *Kentucky Monthly*, February 2002.

Fleming, Bruce. "Woolf Cubs: Current Fiction." *Antioch Review*, Vol. 52, No. 4, Fall 1994, p. 549.

Fletcher, Yael Simpson. "History Will One Day Have Its Say: New Perspectives on Colonial and Postcolonial Congo." *Radical History Review*, Vol. 84, 2002, pp. 195–207.

Flexman, Ellen. "Review." *Library Journal*, Vol. 123, No. 14, September 1, 1998, p. 214.

Flynn, Kelly. "The Rural Experience and Definitions." http://www.ruralwomyn.net/.

Freitag, Michael. "Writing to Pay the Rent." *New York Times Book Review*, April 10, 1988, p. 2.

Frucht, Abby. "'Saving' the Heathen Barbara Kingsolver's Missionary Goes into Africa, but He Just Doesn't Get It." *Boston Globe*, October 18, 1998, p. K1.

Fry, Donn. "How to Be Useful and Happy." *Seattle Times*, September 16, 1990.

Gabb, Sally. "Into Africa: A Review of *The Poisonwood Bible*." *Field Notes*, Vol. 11, No. 1, Summer 2001.

Garner, Karen. "Review: *The Poisonwood Bible*." *Muse Newsletter*, September 2000.

Gates, David. "The Voices of Dissent." *Newsweek*, November 19, 2001, pp. 66–67.

Gergen, David. "Interview: Barbara Kingsolver." *U.S. News and World Report*, November 24, 1995.

Gibson, Anne. "Review: *Small Wonder*." *New Zealand Herald*, October 1, 2002.

Gilbert, Matthew. "The Moral Passion of Barbara Kingsolver." *Boston Globe*, June 23, 1993, p. 1.

Giles, Jeff. "Getting Back to Nature." *Newsweek*, Vol. 136, No. 18, October 30, 2000, p. 82.

Glazebrook, Olivia. "Abandoning the Code." *Spectator*, Vol. 37, February 27, 1999.

Go, Kristen. "Tribe Works to Guard Sacred Kinishba Ruins." *Arizona Republic*, July 18, 2003.

Goldstein, Bill. "An Author Chat with Barbara Kingsolver." *New York Times*, October 30, 1998.

Gonzalez, Mike. "Into the Heart of Darkness." *Socialist Review*, No. 261, March 2002.

Gonzalez-Crussi, Frank. *The Day of the Dead and Other Mortal Reflections*. New York: Harcourt-Brace, 1993.

Goodman, Bill. "What If All Kentucky Reads the Same Book?" *Kentucky Educational Television*, May 31, 2001.

Goodman, Ellen. "Books for Many Tastes." *Boston Globe*, July 18, 2000.

Gossett, Polly Paddock. "Review: *Prodigal Summer*." *Charlotte Observer*, November 29, 2000.

Goudie, Jeffrey Ann. "Poisonwood Bible Delivers a Powerful Tale." *Kansas City Star*, November 29, 1998, p. K5.

Grant, Michael. "Interview." *Books & Co.*, KAET-TV, April 4, 2002.

Gray, Paul. "Call of the Eco-Feminist." *Time*, Vol. 136, No. 13, September 24, 1990, p. 87.

_____. "On Familiar Ground." *Time*, Vol. 156, No. 18, October 30, 2000, p. 90.

Green, Subie. "Prodigal Summer." *Dallas Morning News*, November 22, 2000.

_____. "Review: *Prodigal Summer*." *Dallas Morning News*, November 22, 2000.

Greene, Gayle. "Independence Struggle." *Women's Review of Books*, Vol. 16, No. 7, April 1999, pp. 8–9.

Gritton, Vicki. "Kingsolver Gives Characters the Drive to Achieve Success." *Kentucky Kernal*, April 7, 1988, p. 3.

Gussow, Joan. "Calling Across the Fence." *Green Guide*, No. 93, November/December 2002, p. 4.

Hall, Christopher. "Earth Day Award Goes to Blackacre Resource Teacher." *Louisville Courier-Journal*, April 30, 2003.

Hall, Wade. "Barbara Kingsolver." *The Kentucky Encyclopedia*. Lexington: University of Kentucky, 1992.

Higdon, Barbara. "Nathan Responds to God's Call, but Not His Family's." *San Antonio Express-News*, October 18, 1998, p. 4G.

Higgins-Freese, Jonna. "The Kingsolver and I." *Grist*, July 16, 2002.

Hile, Janet L. "Barbara Kingsolver." *Authors & Artists, Gale Group*, Vol. 15, 1995.

Hinkemeyer, Joan. "Characters Tell the Story, Social Consciousness, Lives in Story of Southwest Town." *Rocky Mountain News*, October 14, 1990.

_____. "*High Tide* Washes in Thoughtful Collection of Kingsolver Essays." *Rocky Mountain News*, November 12, 1995.

Hirsch, Marianne. *The Mother/Daughter Plot: Narrative, Psychoanalysis, Feminism.* Bloomington: Indiana University Press, 1989.

Hoback, Jane. "Kingsolver's Holy Grail Mythic in Tone." *Rocky Mountain News*, October 18, 1998, p. 1e.

_____. "Sensual Season." *Rocky Mountain News*, November 12, 2000.

Hoffman, Dillene. "Photographer at Kinishba." *Expedition*, Vol. 37, No. 1, 1995, p. 67.

"Holding the Line." http//www.ilr.cornell.edu/depts/ILRPress/97cat/NewTitles/Holding_the_Line.html.

Hollands, Barbara. "Languid Eco-Drama." *New Zealand Dispatch*, June 2, 2001.

Holt, Patricia. "Review." *San Francisco Chronicle*, March 6, 1988.

"Homegrown Talent." *Tucson Weekly*, November 20, 1997.

Hussein, Aamer. "Daughters of Africa." *Times Literary Supplement*, February 5, 1999, p. 21.

Hymowitz, Kay S. "Why Feminism Is AWOL on Islam." *New York City Journal*, Winter 2003.

"Interview with Barbara Kingsolver." http://www3.baylor.edu:80/Rel_Lit/archives/interviews/kingsolver_intv.html.

"Invent People from Scratch." *ParisVoice*, October 2002.

Jackson, Jason Baird. "The Opposite of Powwow: Ignoring and Incorporating the Intertribal War Dance in the Oklahoma Stomp Dance Community." *Plains Anthropologist*, Vol. 48, No. 187, 2003, pp. 237–253.

Jadrnak, Jackie. "Novel Forges Connections." *Albuquerque Journal*, November 5, 2000.

James, Rebecca. "Booked Solid." *LETTERS from CAMP Rehobeth*, Vol. 11, No. 6, June 1, 2001.

Jamison, Laura, and Christina Cheakalos.

"Pages." *People Weekly*, Vol. 54, No. 18, October 30, 2000, p. 49.

Jefferson, Margo. "There Goes the Neighborhood." *New York Times*, November 25, 2001.

Jennings, Judy V., and Robert Mossman. "A Feast of Books Published Since 1987." *English Journal*, pp. 81, 85.

Jones, Elin. "From the Sublime to the Ridiculous." *Marietta Leader*, November 3, 1999.

Jones, Jenny. "Review: *Prodigal Summer*." *New Zealand Herald*, February 10, 2001.

Jones, Mary Paumier. "Small Wonder." *Library Journal*, Vol. 127, No. 8, p. 101.

Judd, Elizabeth. "Review: *Prodigal Summer*." *Salon*, November 17, 2000.

Kakesako, Gregg K. "'America's Storyteller' James Michener, Dies: Author Came to Love Isles While Writing 'Hawaii.'" *Honolulu Star-Bulletin*, October 17, 1997.

Kakutani, Michiko. "The Poisonwood Bible: A Family a Heart of Darkness." *New York Times*, October 16, 1998, p. 45.

Kanner, Ellen. "Barbara Kingsolver Turns to Her Past to Understand the Present." *Book Page*, 1998.

_____. "The Calm 10 A.M. Writer Meets the 10 P.M. Thunder Vixen of the Keyboards." *Oxford Review*, July 1993.

Karbo, Karen. "And Baby Makes Two." *New York Times Book Review*, June 27, 1993, p. 9.

Karpen, Lynn. "The Role of Poverty." *New York Times Book Review*, June 27, 1993.

Kelley, Klara Bonsack, and Harris Francis. *Navajo Sacred Places.* Bloomington: Indiana University Press, 1994

Kerr, Sarah. "The Novel as Indictment." *New York Times*, October 11, 1998, pp. 52–55.

Keymer, David. "Review." *Library Journal*, August 1990, p. 143.

King, Casey. "Books in Brief: Nonfiction." *New York Times*, October 15, 1995.

Kjos, Tiffany. "Kingsolver Touts National Writers' Union." *Inside Tucson Business*, Vol. 9, No. 49, February 28, 2000, p. 13.

Klinkenborg, Verlyn. "Going Native." *New York Times*, October 18, 1998, p. 7.

Koza, Kimberly. "The Africa of Two Western Women Writers: Barbara Kingsolver and Margaret Laurence." *Critique*, Vol. 44, No. 3, Spring 2003, pp. 284–294.

Krasny, Michael. "Interview: Barbara Kingsolver, Author, Discusses Her New Book." *Talk of the Nation* (NPR), December 13, 1999.

Kreimer, Peggy. "Covington Center Wins State Arts Award." *Kentucky Post*, November 17, 2001.

Kruckewitt, Joan. *The Death of Ben Under: The Story of a North American in Sandinista Nicaragua.* New York: Seven Stories Press, 1999.

Kuhn, Deanna. "Review: *Another America: Otra America.*" *School Library Journal*, August 1992.

Labuik, Karen. "President's Message." *PNLA Quarterly*, Vol. 64, No. 3, Spring 2000, p. 1.

Lane, Tahree. "A Lust for Nature." *Toledo Blade*, November 26, 2000.

Lark, Lolita. "Barbara Kingsolver." *Review of Arts, Literature, Philosophy and the Humanities*, No. 106, Late Fall 2003.

LeBlanc, Pamela. "Kingsolver Reacts to the Pain of Sept. 11 with Small Wonders and Big Messages." *Austin American-Statesman*, April 21, 2002.

Lee, Lisa. "Interview." *Publishers Weekly*, August 31, 1990, pp. 46–47.

LeGuin, Ursula K. "Review." *Washington Post Book World*, September 2, 1990.

Leonard, John. "Kingsolver in the Jungle, Catullus & Wolfe at the Door." *Nation*, Vol. 268, No. 2, January 11-18, 1999, pp. 28–33.

Levin, Simon, and Marty Peale. "Beyond Extinction: Rethinking Biodiversity." *SFI Bulletin*, Winter 1995-1996.

Levin, Will. "People Rise Up." *KBOO Radio*, Portland, Ore., November 2, 2001.

Litovitz, Malca. "Huck Finn, Barbara Kingsolver, and the American Dream." *Queen's Quarterly*, Winter 1998, pp. 3–12.

"Little Big Voice." *Economist*, Vol. 363, No. 8,272, May 11, 2002, p. 79.

Lumpkin, Susan. "Review: *Prodigal Summer.*" *Smithsonian Zoogoer*, March/April 2001, p. 1.

Lyall, Sarah. "Termites Are Interesting but Books Sell Better." *New York Times*, September 1, 1993.

MacDougall, Ruth Doan. "Becoming Mother to a Little Turtle." *New York Newsday*, March 13, 1988, p. 18.

MacEoin, Gary. "Prodigal Summer: A Novel."

National Catholic Reporter, Vol. 38, No. 3, November 9, 2001, p. 19.

Mahin, Bill. "Review." *Chicago Tribune*, June 23, 1989.

"Making a Difference." *Humanities*, January/February 2001.

Malinowitz, Harriet. "Down-Home Dissident." *Women's Review of Books*, Vol. 19, No. 10-11, July 2002, pp. 36–37.

Manuel, Diane. "A Roundup of First Novels About Coming of Age." *Christian Science Monitor*, April 22, 1988, p. 20.

Markels, Julian. "Coda: Imagining History in *The Poisonwood Bible.*" *Monthly Review Press*, September 2003, p. 1.

Marshall, John. "Fast Ride on 'Pigs.'" *Seattle Post-Gazette*, July 26, 1993, p. 1.

Martinez, Pila. "'Chick Book' Author Fills Literary Gap: Kingsolver Focuses on Women, Southwest." *Arizona Republic*, October 18, 1992, p. 12B.

Maslin, Janet. "3 Story Lines United by the Fecundity of Summer." *New York Times*, November 2, 2000.

Maxwell, Gloria. "Review: *Prodigal Summer.*" *Library Journal*, Vol. 126, No. 2, February 1, 2001, p. 144.

McCoy, Ronald. "Spider Woman's Legacy: The Art of Navajo Weaving." *World & I*, September 1990.

McDonald, Maggie. "Words from the Wild." *New Scientist*, Vol. 175, No. 2,350, July 6, 2002, p. 57.

McGee, Celia. "'Bible' Offers Two Good Books in One." *USA Today*, October 22, 1998, p. 6D.

McMahon, Regan. "Barbara Kingsolver: An Army of One." *San Francisco Chronicle*, April 28, 2002.

McMichael, Barbara Lloyd. "Kingsolver 'Giving Blood' through Essays." *Seattle Times*, May 12, 2002.

McPherson, Robert S. *Sacred Land, Sacred View: Navajo Perceptions of the Four Corners.* Salt Lake City, Utah: Signature Books, 1992.

Meadows, Bonnie J. "Serendipity and the Southwest: A Conversation with Barbara Kingsolver." *Bloomsbury Review*, November-December 1990, p. 3.

Milne, Courtney. *Sacred Places in North America: A Journey Into the Medicine*

Wheel. New York: Stewart, Tabori & Chang, 1995.

Modjeska, Drusilla. "Writing as Incest." *The Australian,* September 28, 2002.

Moreno, Sylvia. "Exploring Downtown; D.C. Students on Photo Expedition for National Geographic." *Washington Post,* July 18, 2003, p. B1.

Mossman, Robert. "Review." *Library Journal,* December 1994, p. 85.

Moyers, Bill. "Interview with Barbara Walters." *PBS,* May 24, 2002.

Murie, O. J. *A Field Guide to Animal Tracks.* Boston: Houghton Mifflin, 1954.

Murie, Olaus. *Food Habits of the Coyote in Jackson Hole, Wyoming.* Washington: U.S. Department of Agriculture, 1935.

Murrey, Loretta Martin. "The Loner and the Matriarchal Community in Barbara Kingsolver's *The Bean Trees* and *Pigs in Heaven.*" *Southern Studies,* Vol. 5, No. 1–2, Spring & Summer 1994, pp. 155–164.

Myzska, Jessica. "Barbara Kingsolver: 'Burning a Hole in the Pockets of My Heart.'" *De Pauw Magazine,* Vol. 5, No. 2, Spring 1994, pp. 18–20.

Nack, William. "Muhammad Ali." *Sports Illustrated,* Vol. 81, No. 12, September 19, 1994, p. 48.

Neely, Alan. "The Poisonwood Bible." *International Bulletin of Missionary Research,* Vol. 24, No. 3, July 2000, p. 138.

Negri, Sam, and Jerry Jacka. "Kinishba: The Ruin That Refuses to Go Away." *Arizona Highways,* Vol. 69, No. 2, February 1993, pp. 52–55.

Neill, Michael. "La Pasionaria." *People,* Vol. 40, No. 15, October 11, 1993, pp. 109–110.

Neilson, Melany. *The Persia Cafe.* New York: St. Martin's, 2002.

Newman, Vicky. "Compelling Ties: Landscape, Community, and Sense of Place." *Peabody Journal of Education,* Vol. 70, No. 4, Summer 1995, pp. 105–118.

Nolan, Kate. "Kingsolver: Author for Our Place and Time." *Arizona Republic,* March 30, 2002, p. V3.

Norman, Liane Ellison. "The Poisonwood Bible." *Sojourners,* Vol. 22, March/April 1999, pp. 59–61.

"Noted by the Editors." *Antioch Review,* Vol. 48, No. 4, Fall 1990, p. 546.

Ogle, Connie. "Review: Small Wonder." *Miami Herald,* April 10, 2002.

_____. "A Tapestry of Life, Death in Appalachia." *Miami Herald,* November 5, 2000, p. 5M.

Ognibene, Elaine R. "The Missionary Position: Barbara Kingsolver's *The Poisonwood Bible.*" *College Literature,* Vol. 30, No. 3, Summer 2003, pp. 19–36.

"Orange Prize Hoo-ha." *Irish Times,* May 15, 1999.

Owen, Katie. "Novel of the Week." *New Statesman,* Vol. 129, No. 4,513, November 20, 2000, p. 54.

Paddock, Polly. "Pages Hold Hope for the World." *Charlotte Observer,* April 14, 2002.

Paine, R. T. "Food Web Complexity and Species Diversity." *American Naturalist,* Vol. 100, 1966, pp. 65–75.

_____. "A Note on Trophic Complexity and Species Diversity." *American Naturalist,* Vol. 103, 1969, pp. 91–93.

Parini, Jay, ed. *American Writers: A Collection of Literary Biographies.* Vol. 7. New York: Charles Scribner's Sons, 2001.

Parsell, D. L. "New Photo Book an Homage to Last U.S. Wildlands." *National Geographic News,* October 29, 2002.

Pate, Nancy. "Faith in the Future: Kingsolver Finds Hope in Natural World." *Orlando Sentinel,* April 7, 2002, p. F8.

_____. "Five Distinctive Voices Narrate Kingsolver's Remarkable 'Bible.'" *Tulsa World,* November 1, 1998, p. 4.

_____. "Review: *Prodigal Summer.*" *Orlando Sentinel,* October 25, 2000.

"Patrice Lumumba." http://www.sci.pfu.edu.ru/~asemenov/lumumba/LUMUMBA.HTM.

Pearl, Nancy. "The Moral of the Story: Fiction of Conscience." *Library Journal,* Vol. 126, No. 7, April 15, 2001, p. 164.

Pearlman, Cindy. "A Rumble to Remember." *Chicago Sun-Times,* February 23, 1997, p. 4.

Pearlman, Mickey, ed. *Introduction to American Women Writing Fiction: Memory, Identity, Family, Space.* Lexington: University Press of Kentucky, 1989.

Pence, Amy. "The Embroidery of Imagination." *Tucson Guide Quarterly,* Fall 1992, pp. 122–129, 142.

Perry, Donna. *Backtalk: Women Writers Speak*

Out. New Brunswick, N.J.: Rutgers University Press, 1993.

Pollack-Pelzner, Emma. "Acts Big and Small." *Yale Review of Books*, Vol. 6, No. 3, Summer 2003.

Pritchard, Melissa. "Review." *Chicago Tribune Books*, May 18, 1988.

"Prodigal Summer." *Africa News Service*, November 1, 2001.

Quick, Susan Chamberlin. "Barbara Kingsolver: A Voice of the Southwest — An Annotated Bibliography." *Bulletin of Bibliography*, Vol. 54, 1997, pp. 283–302.

Quinn, Judy. "HarperCollins Gets to Keep Kingsolver." *Publishers Weekly*, Vol. 244, No. 6, February 10, 1997, p. 19.

Randall, Margaret. "Human Comedy." *Women's Review of Books*, May 1988, pp. 1, 3.

Ratner, Rochelle. "Poetry: Barbara Kingsolver." *Library Journal*, February 15, 1992.

Regier, Amy M. "Replacing the Hero with the Reader: Public Story Structure in *The Poisonwood Bible*." *Mennonite Life*, Vol. 56, No. 1, March 2001.

Reichard, Gladys A. *Spider Woman*. Tucson: University of New Mexico Press, 1997.

Reid, Calvin. "SMP Author Copies Kingsolver Text." *Publishers Weekly*, April 30, 2001.

"Review: *Prodigal Summer*." *AudioFile*, June/July 2001.

"Review: *The Poisonwood Bible*." *Publishers Weekly*, Vol. 245, No. 32, August 10, 1998, p. 366.

"Review: *The Poisonwood Bible*." *Timbrel*, September-October 1999.

Reynolds, Janet. "Review: *The Poisonwood Bible*." *Wintertimes*, Winter 1998.

Reynolds, Susan Salter. "Review: *Prodigal Summer*." *Los Angeles Times*, October 22, 2000, p. 1.

Robinson, Judith. "Small Wonder." *Library Journal*, Vol. 127, No. 20, December 1, 2002, pp. 197–198.

Rosen, Judith. "Kingsolver Tour Helps Indies Clean Up." *Publishers Weekly*, Vol. 247, No. 48, November 27, 2000, pp. 26–27.

Rosenfeld, Megan. "Novelist in Hog Heaven; 'Pigs' Brings Home the Bacon While Its Author Writes Her Heart Out." *Washington Post*, July 14, 1993, p. D1.

Roses, Lorraine Elena. "Language and Other Barriers." *Women's Review of Books*, July 1992, p. 42.

Ross, Jean W. "Interview." *Contemporary Authors*. Vol. 134. Detroit: Gale Research, 1992, pp. 284–290.

Rowbotham, Jill. "Naturally Charming." *Australian*, December 2, 2000.

Rozen, Frieda Schoenberg. "Holding the Line." *Library Journal*, November 1, 1989, p. 104.

Rubin, Sylvia. "Africa Kept Its Hold on Kingsolver." *San Francisco Chronicle*, October 30, 1998, p. C1.

Rubinstein, Roberta. "The Mark of Africa." *World & I*, Vol. 14, No. 4, April 1999, p. 254.

Ryan, Maureen. "Barbara Kingsolver's Low-fat Fiction." *Journal of American Culture*, Vol. 18, No. 4, Winter 1995, pp. 77–82.

Salamon, Julia. "Mobilizing a Theater of Protest." *New York Times*, February 6, 2003.

_____. "Telling the Story of Congo's War, amid the Chaos." *New York Times*, September 6, 2001.

Salij, Marta. "Prodigal Summer." *Detroit Free Press*, October 25, 2000.

Saricks, Joyce. "Review: *Prodigal Summer*." *Booklist*, Vol. 98, No. 3, October 1, 2001, p. 343.

Sarnataro, Barbara Russi. "Novel Approach." *Tucson Citizen*, November 19, 1998, p. B-1.

Schuessler, Jennifer. "Men, Women, and Coyotes." *New York Times*, November 5, 2000, p. 38.

Schwarzbaum, Lisa. "Summer Fling." *Entertainment Weekly*, No. 566, October 27, 2000.

"A Science to Her Fiction." *Newsweek*, Vol. 122, No. 2, July 12, 1993, p. 61.

Seaman, Donna. "Barbara Kingsolver Focuses on the Big Picture." *Chicago Tribune*, June 16, 2002.

_____. "Upfront." *Booklist*, Vol. 94, No. 22, August 1989, p. 1922.

See, Lisa. "Review." *Publishers Weekly*, August 31, 1990.

"Setting the Record Straight." *Publishers Weekly*, Vol. 246, No. 38, September 20, 1999, p. 67.

Shapiro, Laura. "A Novel Full of Miracles."

Newsweek, Vol. 122, No. 2, July 12, 1993, p. 61.

Sheppard, R. Z. "Little Big Girl." *Time*, Vol. 142, No. 9, August 30, 1993.

Shilling, James. "Animal Instincts." *London Times*, December 23, 2000, p. 25.

"A Short History of the Murie Family." http://www.muriecenter.org/family.htm.

Shulman, Polly. "Wild Lives/Human Fortunes Are Rooted in the Fate of the Chestnut Tree — and Other Flora and Fauna — in the Ecological Romance." *New York Newsday*, October 29, 2000, p. B9.

Siegel, Lee. "Sweet and Low." *New Republic*, Vol. 220, No. 12, March 22, 1999, pp. 30–37.

Signature: Contemporary Southern Writers (video). New York: Annenburg/CPB, 1997.

Skow, John. "Hearts of Darkness: Matters of Race, Religion and Gender Collide as a Missionary Family Moves to the Congo in 1959." *Time*, Vol. 152, No. 9, November 9, 1998, p. 113.

Smiley, Jane. "In Our Small Town, the Weight of the World." *New York Times Book Review*, September 2, 1990, p. 2.

_____. "In the Fields of the Lord." *Washington Post*, October 11, 1998.

Smith, Lee. "Mountain Music's Moment in the Sun." *Washington Post*, August 12, 2001, p. G1.

Smith, Starr E. "Review: *Prodigal Summer*." *Library Journal*, Vol. 125, No. 17, October 15, 2000, p. 102.

Smith, Wendy. "Talking with Barbara Kingsolver: Reality with a Punch Line." *New York Newsday*, August 8, 1993, p. 34.

Stafford, Tim. "Poisonous Gospel." *Christianity Today*, Vol. 43, No. 1, January 11, 1999, pp. 88–89.

Stegner, Page. "Holding the Line: Women in the Great Arizona Mine Strike of 1983." *New York Times Book Review*, January 7, 1990, p. 31.

Steinberg, Sylvia S. "Prodigal Summer." *Publishers Weekly*, Vol. 247, No. 40, October 2, 2000, p. 57.

Stephenson, Ann. "Author Mixes Art, Politics." *Arizona Republic*, November 14, 1995.

Stevens, Penny. "Kingsolver, Barbara. *High Tide in Tucson*." *School Library Journal*, Vol. 42, No. 2, February 1996, p. 134.

Stobie, Mary. "Kingsolver Sequel Emphasizes Importance of Family Roots." *Rocky Mountain News*, July 4, 1993.

Stolba, Christine. "Feminists Go to War." *Women's Quarterly*, Winter 2002.

Suchy, Angie. "Kingsolver Examines Issue of Governmental Injustice." *Oregon Daily Emerald*, April 25, 1997.

Sullivan, Patrick. "'Poisonwood Bible' Makes a Departure." *Sonoma County Independent*, October 22, 1998.

Sutterfield, Ragan. "Books & Culture's Books of the Week: *From Dust to Dust*." *Christianity Today*, November 3, 2003.

Szekely, Julie. "Rape Victims Speak Out." *Tucson Citizen*, July 16, 1991, p. 1B.

Tamayo, Juan O. "Rethinking Option for Poor." *Miami Herald*, January 21, 1999.

Tanabe, Kunio Francis. "The Book Club." *Washington Post*, September 2, 2001, p. T10.

Tanenbaum, Laura. "Review: *Prodigal Summer*." *Women Writers*, May 2001.

Tekulve, Susan. "Review: *Prodigal Summer*." *Book*, November 2000, p. 69.

Thornton, Bruce S. "Barbara Kingsolver's Intellectual Offenses." *FrontPage Magazine*, March 6, 2003.

Tischler, Barbara L. "Holding the Line: Women in the Great Arizona Mine Strike of 1983." *Labor Studies Journal*, Vol. 17, No. 1, Spring 1992, pp. 82–83.

Trachtman, Paul. "High Tide in Tucson." *Smithsonian*, Vol. 27, No. 3, June 1996, p. 24.

"Two Female Buddies on the Run." *Literary Review*, November 1993.

Uschuk, J. "Green Light: Barbara Kingsolver's New Novel Fights for Life and Love in the Natural World." *Tucson Weekly*, November 2, 2000.

Van Boven, Sarah. "Review." *Newsweek*, Vol. 132, No. 19, November 9, 1998, p. 76.

Vilbig, Pete. "Meet the Author." *Literary Cavalcade*, Vol. 52, No. 1, September 1999, p. 13.

Vivian, Steve. "Literature as Politics." *FrontPage Magazine*, November 12, 2003.

Wanner, Irene. "'Best' Short-story Anthology Lives Up to Its Name." *Seattle Times*, December 2, 2001.

Warner, Sharon Oard. "Getting in Touch

with Reality." *Dallas Morning News*, October 22, 1995.

Warren, Colleen Kelly. "Family Tragedy Plays Out in Congo." *St. Louis Post-Dispatch*, October 18, 1998, p. C5.

_____. "Literature, Biology Fuse in Kingsolver's Novel About Life." *St. Louis Post-Dispatch*, October 15, 2000, p. F10.

Warren, Tim. "Write-On Rock — Best-Selling Authors Put Their Talents to Another Sort of Creativity: Music." *Baltimore Sun*, May 27, 1993.

"We Won't Deny Our Consciences: Prominent Americans Have Issued This Statement on the War on Terror." *Guardian Unlimited*, June 14, 2002.

Weaver, Teresa K. "Stranger Than Fiction: Writers Turn Rockers — Musical Talent Optional." *Atlanta Journal-Constitution*, May 18, 2003, p. M1.

Weeks, Jerome. "Where Historians, Authors Part." *Dallas Morning News*, June 17, 2001.

Weinberg-Hill, Lynne. "Dream Writer." *Tucson Lifestyle*, November 1990, pp. 55–56.

Wertheimer, Linda. "Interview: Barbara Kingsolver Discusses Her Latest Novel, 'Prodigal Summer.'" *All Things Considered* (NPR), October 23, 2000.

"Where the Wild Things Are." *Economist*, December 16, 2000, p. 8.

Whitelaw, Kevin. "A Killing in Congo." *U.S. News and World Report*, July 24, 2000.

Wilder, Katherine. *Walking the Twilight: Women Writers of the Southwest*. Flagstaff, Ariz.: Northland, 1994.

Willis, Meredith Sue. "Barbara Kingsolver, Moving On." *Appalachian Journal*, Vol. 22, No. 1, 1994, pp. 78–86.

Woodrell, Daniel. "Ah, Wilderness." *Washington Post*, November 19, 2000, p. X6.

Wootten, Susan. "In a State of Hopefulness." *Sojourner*, May-June 1996.

World Authors 1985–1990. New York: H. W. Wilson, 1995.

York, Byron. "At War, Follow the Money." *National Review*, February 24, 2003.

Index

bureaucracy 10, 44, 50, 54–55, 95–96, 119, 125, 136, 194
Bush, George H. W. 27, 28, 136
Bush, George W. 107
Buster, Angie 113, 188
Buster, Lucky 79, 89, 113, 176
Bwanga 100

Canary Islands 19, 136
cancer 106, 111, 141, 150, 167, 185, 194, 196
Canyon de Chelly 67, 102, 142, 169, 173, 183–184
Cardenal, Ernesto 9, 56–57
Cardenal, Rita 138
Carlo 55–56, 109, 113, 134, 136, 143
Carson, Rachel 170
Cartes, Rebeca 44
catharsis 113
Catholicism 10, 37, 56, 83, 112, 172
Central America 39, 65, 78, 79, 92, 103, 108, 136, 173, 176, 192; see also Costa Rica; El Salvador; Guatemala; Nicaragua
cereus, night-blooming 125
Cherokee 22, 40, 50, 54, 57–59, 60, 61–62, 67, 79, 80–81, 85, 86–89, 90–91, 95, 98, 102, 112, 113, 120–121, 126, 141, 143–144, 150, 172, 176, 184–185, 190–191, 203
chestnut trees 111, 127–128, 166, 195
child abuse 59–61, 65, 78, 86, 88, 95–96, 102, 121, 180, 191, 193
childbirth 7, 68, 76, 99, 110, 112, 113, 121, 122–123, 156, 170, 178–179, 184
Chile 15, 125
Christiane 77
Christian Marxism 9, 56–57
Christianity 72, 83–84, 100, 114, 124, 130, 131, 145–147, 151–165, 172, 173–174; see also baptism; Baptists; biblical allusions; Catholicism; missionaries
CIA 72, 92, 146
clear-cutting see logging
Clinton, Bill 26
Clinton, Hillary Rodham 26
cockfighting 121, 142–143, 187
Cold War 8–9, 18–19, 56, 71
colonialism 9, 13, 19, 21, 23, 34, 36, 37, 47, 57, 66, 72, 75, 92, 99, 118, 122, 132, 144–145, 146, 147, 150, 155, 160, 162, 164, 173, 194, 206, 209, 210
communism 12, 71, 115, 118, 132, 164
community 17, 45, 61–63, 91,

109, 133–134, 143–144, 184–185, 187, 192, 203, 204
compromise 46, 53, 60, 63–64, 81, 172, 175, 195
"Confessions of a Reluctant Rock Goddess" (1995)
Congo 9, 18–19, 21, 23, 35–37, 45, 47, 52, 55, 62, 64–65, 68, 70–72, 77, 79, 83–84, 92–93, 96, 97, 99–101, 104, 109, 111, 114–116, 118–119, 122, 124, 127, 130, 131, 132–133, 144–147, 151–152, 171, 178, 180–181, 187, 193–194, 199, 205, 209–212
Conrad, Joseph 145
conservation 14, 107–108, 120, 127; see also pollution
Contras 43, 77, 102, 108, 137, 176
cooperation 64–65, 66, 73, 74, 75, 152, 199–200
Corn Dance 173
Cornell University Press 23
Corregidor 174
Costa Rica 25
coyotes 53–54, 63, 69, 93, 106, 123–124, 126, 127, 128, 150, 166, 167, 169, 176, 178, 187, 193, 201
Crete 41, 55
crime 19, 65–66, 78, 117; see also child abuse; Mobutu Sese Seko; rape; refugees
Cuban Missile Crisis 8, 56

Daniel 105, 130, 153
Dawes Rolls of 1902–1905 86, 95
"Deadline" (1992) 19, 44
"The Death of the Hired Man" (1914) 76
DePauw University 12, 22
desert 14, 15, 66–67, 108, 120, 125
discontent 67–69; see also Price, Rachel
disease 35, 99, 101, 122, 127–128, 149, 153, 166, 174, 188, 195
distemper 140
divorce 20, 50, 62, 79, 85, 178–179, 190, 206; see also Greer, Alice; Ruiz, Lou Ann
Dr. Jekyll and Mr. Hyde (1886) 153
Domingos, Emelina 69, 121, 135, 190
Domingos, J. T. 52, 69–70, 142
Domingos, Mason 121, 177
Domingos, Viola 38, 69–70, 97, 187, 188, 205
doppelgänger 136, 176
Down syndrome 169, 175

drilling, oil 107
Dulles, Allen 146

ecofeminism 70–71, 148
ecofiction 24, 204–205
ecology 18, 25, 26–27, 28, 34, 41–42, 104, 106, 107–108, 123, 126, 150,166–167, 197, 201–202; see also nature; pollution
Eisenhower, Dwight D. 71–72, 92, 115, 118, 146, 147, 209
elections 37, 48, 141, 145–146, 158, 210; see also voting
"Elections, Nicaragua, 1984" (1992) 48
Elévée 60–61
Elisabet, Aunt 77
Elleston, Harland 85, 185, 190
El Salvador 15, 18, 33, 117, 175–176
Emory University 80, 96, 133, 149, 154, 211
enteritis 35, 122, 124, 132, 149, 174, 199, 206, 210
Environmental Protection Agency 33–34, 70, 149
Episcopalianism 35–36, 193–194
Epley maneuver 170
"Escape" (1992) 19
Esperanza 50, 51, 54–55, 59, 72–73, 79, 87, 92, 109, 112, 117, 120, 122, 140, 151, 180, 186–187, 192, 203, 204
Estevan 39, 42, 50, 54–55, 59, 64, 72, 73, 74, 75, 79, 87, 92, 109, 112, 117, 120, 125, 140, 151, 180, 186–187, 192, 199, 203
ethnicity 39, 64, 81, 95, 100–101, 113, 121, 126, 143, 161, 185
ethnocentrism 39
"Everybody's Somebody's Baby" (1992) 19, 61
exclusion 10, 74, 201

fable 73, 75, 113–114, 153
"Faith in a Seed" (1854) 12
family 15, 58, 61, 75–78, 80, 84–89, 94, 99, 109, 114, 120–123, 133–134, 138, 139, 140–142, 150–165, 167–168, 185, 192, 193, 197–198, 203–207
"Family Secrets" (1992) 15
Fein, Jill Barrett 17, 93–95
female genital mutilation 61, 113
feminism 12, 36, 78–79; see also ecofeminism
flight 39, 44, 54–55, 64, 71, 74, 75, 76, 78, 79–80, 87, 92, 96, 97, 108, 112, 185, 187–188, 201
"For Richard After All" (1992) 110
"For Sacco and Vanzetti" (1992) 44